Running Wild

David Darcey

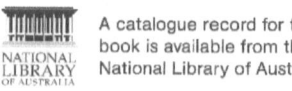

A catalogue record for this
book is available from the
National Library of Australia

Copyright © 2021 David Darcey
All rights reserved.
ISBN-13: 978-1-922727-08-4

Linellen Press
265 Boomerang Road
Oldbury, Western Australia
www.linellenpress.com.au

Disclaimer

This story is told as David Darcey lived it.

Please be aware that there are sexual references, political incorrectness and coarse language contained within, and some content may offend. But the story is told as it was back then.

Contents

	Orphans of Aussie	vi
	Prologue	1
Part 1	My Orphanage Years	7
Part 2	My Adoptive Family	49
Part 3	Bindoon Boys Town	77
Part 4	Back Home with the Darceys	91
Part 5	My Working Life	101
Part 6	Vietnam	155
Part 7	Life Goes On	193
Part 8	Work and Family	391
Part 9	Finding Mum	443
	What Happened Next	452
	About the Author	459

Orphans of Aussie

We left our home shores like numbered horses,
and travelled southward on chartered courses,
there were no bands when we first landed,
but given numbers like horses branded.

Put in small groups in numbered places,
then pulled apart from my childhood faces,
we left by trucks for far off places,
amidst a group of strange new races.

The heat was strong and full of bite,
but we stood our course and stood the fright,
they drove through bush that never stopped,
and arrived in darkness at a faraway spot.

We thanked our God for our arrival,
and still thank Him for his deprival,
families torn, our childhood had
to send us southward to this hot burnt land.

We were battered and booted until we were rooted,
with no one to tell of this Holy Hell,
with bodies torn, cut and bruised,
we were silent children of abuse.

RUNNING WILD

We were sent to Bindoon, Clontarf and Castledare,
our homes of which we had to bear,
we were greeted by Brothers all dressed in black,
but soon to fear the feel of that black leather strap.

Then up at dawn to work till dark,
our little bodies sore, cut and marked,
we worked in teams to make work light
yet all the time were in fear and fright.

The crying at night never stopped,
for it was really hard at the faraway spot,
for things we did never seemed quite right,
but it was the beatings that left us crying with fright.

There were no sums, reading or writing,
but labours to the land was our only enlightening,
we were greeted with smiles and open arms
as we were sent off to places as labourers to farms.

We were battered and booted until we were rooted,
with no one to tell of this Holy Hell,
with bodies torn, cut and bruised,
we were silent children of abuse.

D. A. Darcey 1989

Prologue

3rd October 1987

I shall never forget that evening. I had arrived back from Sydney, where I'd been for the Welcome Home Parade of Vietnam Veterans. Mum Darcey and I sat down and discussed the possibility of obtaining my file from the Catholic Migration Centre and perhaps making contact with my Welsh family.

I had often felt torn between my loyalties towards my adoptive family and the longing to find my natural mother. My adoptive family had supported me through good times and bad and had showered me with a family love I had never known. How to put this longing to find *my* family to my adoptive parents was something I could never come to terms with.

My mind would constantly drift back to Wales and those early but clouded memories of someone waving me goodbye, which always gave me hope that I had some family there.

I was overjoyed when Mum brought up this offer of help. I can only conclude that her feelings must have been emotionally high as she too had recently had the opportunity of meeting her long lost relatives. My brother Tommy explained to me that it was a highly emotionally charged event, and he was certainly proud to have been a part of it.

With this on my mind, my thoughts drifted back to Sydney, and the Welcome Home Parade, which was belated by some twenty years. I had stayed with a friend of the family, Nora. After knowing her for so many years, it was only now that she had poured out her emotions to me regarding her child, whom she had adopted out at birth.

It saddened me to think that when a young, single woman

got pregnant, her parents would push her to be rid of the embarrassment, irrespective of the long term mental anguish of the mother who wanted to know and see the child.

We had discussed this subject for a good few hours, and it was then that I decided to tell Mum of my longing to find my natural mother. Nora agreed and said not to delay the search for my family any longer.

I had for many years during my married life found it difficult to openly impart my inner thoughts and feelings about finding family, but especially could not speak of the abuse and cruelties of an orphan's life. I felt it better to leave these things unsaid as my wife had always looked upon me for strength and support. Following my conversation with Mum and her showing her eagerness in helping to trace family, I slowly began to also be open to the wife of my longing to find family.

Lita had been brought up in a sheltered environment and was subjected to rigid rules but was never without the care and love of her family. I explained to her some of my inner emotions regarding her families association with each other and that I had never really had these deep feelings of family connections. This often made me feel the odd one out. This seemed the right time to investigate the whereabouts of my family.

I explained to Lita that Mum was really seeking my permission to make inquiries regarding the information held in my file, which Mum knew was being withheld at the Catholic Child Migration Centre (CCMC) in Perth. This lifted a big barrier for me, which I had felt confronted with for so many years. I was overjoyed at Mum wanting to take this course of action and naturally had no objection to her doing so.

Five months after this discussion with Mum, I received a phone call at work.

"Son, this is Mum. I just thought I'd let you know that I have located your file, but they won't release it to me. You are the only person who can pick it up at the Catholic Child Migration Centre anytime tomorrow."

Armed with this information, I notified Lita and told her I was heading to Perth the same day to collect it. I left my office like a bat out of hell, with no explanation to my superiors except throwing my arms up in the air and informing them that I would see them tomorrow – a matter of urgency had arisen.

Travelling to Perth seemed to take forever, with all the thoughts running through my mind about what secrets of my past would be exposed. Arriving at the Catholic Child Migration Centre, I explained what I had come for. Without any barriers, I was given my file to read but was informed that I shouldn't get upset at information regarding myself as it was collective thoughts and opinions of me as a child.

I quickly browsed through some of the first pages but was unable to retain any information as my mind was too full of mixed emotions. The main thing I could think of was to get the file to Mum, so we could go through it together.

The Catholic Child Migration Centre informed me that other relevant information about me could be picked up from the Child Welfare Department in Perth, so I headed straight there.

Upon arriving, I was amazed at the compassion shown by the personnel of this department and their unwavering efforts to obtain 90% of the information in a matter of an hour. The Government of Western Australia had just passed an Act through Parliament stating that all information held at the Welfare Department regarding 'orphans' should be released. I was not aware of this. The passing of this Act also helped in obtaining further information from the Catholic Child Migration Centre. Not long before that, I had read in the press about a man who had broken into the CCMC to obtain his file. I believe this case brought to the Government's attention the desperation of the orphan migrants to know about their past.

Once this information was handed to me, my heart became full when I flicked through the file and noticed the first page was a letter dated 1956 from Mum requesting the department to allow her to care for me over the weekends. It saddened me to think that it had taken some thirty-odd years to eventually see documents relating to my past whilst under the care of the Welfare Department.

Satisfied that I had sufficient information to begin the search for my family, I thanked all those concerned with an emotional goodbye. They wished me success, followed by the offer of more assistance and counselling if needed.

I travelled across to Mum and Dad's house, some six miles in the inner suburbs of Perth, and arrived unexpected but, as always, was warmly welcomed. I didn't have to explain the purpose of my visit, as one look at my face said it all. I handed the file to Mum as I told her the day's events. Then Mum, Dad and I began to read the contents.

We sat around the table with open minds.

On the first page, we were confronted with a shipping document with my original name in heavy print: **Winston Franklyn Derek Lyne.** We looked at this with amusement, and I had to confess I was truly grateful for my name change! We had known my given name for some time, and it was often said that with a name like that, it would not be difficult to jolt memories back in Wales.

My mind started to drift back to those early days of my childhood and my recall of a woman sitting in a green field crying and, though I was only seven years old at the time, that memory has never faded. I had put my arms around her, and she had offered me a bar of teddy bear chocolate. I don't know the time-lapse between that and my next recollection of being waved goodbye through a train window. There were two people, one most definitely a woman, and the other a mist of confusion. Although I had no tears in my eyes, I could clearly see the woman was filled with sadness. I had no idea where this train journey was taking the other children and me, but, being so young, there was certainly no fear in my mind.

I have, for many years, recalled these precious memories, especially when depressed or moody. I have never told anyone about them; I guess I felt keeping them to myself was my only escape from my depressive moods. I certainly found them quite comforting in my childhood and early teenage years.

The reason for my being placed in an orphanage was never known to me. My records showed that I was admitted on the 20th April 1946, into Nazareth House, Swansea, Wales, aged eight months, the reason stated being: 'This child's mother was unable to look after him as she had to go out to work daily.'

I remained at Nazareth House until 20th August, 1952, aged seven years and one day.

Part One

My Orphanage Years

My Story

My mind started to drift back to those early days of my childhood. I recall a woman sitting in a green field crying, and although I was only six years old at the time, that memory has never faded. I had put my arms around her and she had offered me a bar of teddy bear chocolate. I don't have or know the time-lapse between that and my next recollection of being waved goodbye through a train window. There were two people, one most definitely a woman and the other a mist of confusion. Although I had no tears in my eyes, I could clearly see the woman was filled with sadness. I had no idea where this train was taking the other children and me, but being so young, there was certainly no fear in my mind.

Another memory was being fed, washed, and then placed back in the cot; I was then placed at Nazareth House in Swansea, where I have some very unpleasant memories that still haven't faded. Though at times the thoughts I have for many years recalled, these precious memories, especially when depressed or moody, I have never told anyone about. I guess I felt safe by keeping them to myself, and I was not going to share them with anyone – yet they were my only escape from my depressive moods. I certainly found them quite comforting in my early childhood and early teens; I just knew they could not be shared as everything I had been given was taken from me.

I never knew the reason for my being placed in an orphanage. My records showed that I was admitted on the 20th April 1946 into Nazareth House, Cardiff at eight months old, the reason stated being 'This child's mother was unable to look after him as she had to go out to work daily'.

RESULT OF ANY INTELLIGENCE TESTS, IF AVAILABLE:
Test __Nil__ Age __—__ Score __—__ I.Q. __—__
DATE OF FIRST ADMISSION TO AN INSTITUTION ? __20TH APRIL 1946__
NAMES OF INSTITUTIONS TO WHICH ADMITTED AND DATES ?
__NAZARETH HOUSE, BISHOPSTON, SWANSEA, GLAM. 20TH APRIL 1946.__

REASONS FOR ADMISSION ? __THIS CHILDS MOTHER WAS UNABLE TO LOOK AFTER HIM AS SHE HAD TO GO OUT TO WORK DAILY__

FAMILY BACKGROUND. (Significant facts, including any history of mental disorders)

ATTITUDE TO SUPERIORS : __NORMAL__
    To Teachers: __NORMAL__
    To fellow pupils : __NORMAL__
    How regarded by fellow pupils? (e.g., rejected, accepted, leads) __ACCEPTED__
ANY BED WETTING ? __NO__ Chronic __NO__ Periodic __NO__
Remarks
DOES CHILD STAMMER OR STUTTER? __NO__
Remarks
ANY FITS OR FAINTS ? __NO__
ANY OTHER NERVOUS SYMPTOMS ? (e.g., tics, facial grimaces, twitches, night terrors)
__NO__

SIGNATURE __S.M. Jerome__
POSITION __MOTHER SUPERIOR__ Date __13TH JUNE 1952__
ADDRESS __NAZARETH HOUSE, BISHOPSTON, SWANSEA, GLAM.__

TO BE FILLED IN BY OVERSEAS REPRESENTATIVE.
Abovementioned child interviewed on __25/4/52__
Remarks __average__
    Medical and baptismal certificates attached.
SIGNATURE __William Nic[?]__
POSITION _____ Date __8/8/52__

When completed this form should be sent to:—
    Federal Catholic Immigration Committee, 150 Elizabeth Street, Sydney.

Taken into care

I was left at Nazareth House Cardiff until three or four years old. I have no memories of my stay in Cardiff at this time but understand I would not have had any contact from a mother to child. But more to the point, of returns to the better, I have moved forward and believe that is the way for now.

So I guess this is the best place to start my orphan childhood to my passage to adult – and parenthood and the odyssey for the moulding of myself and life. I was to leave Nazareth House on 20th August 1952.

Federal Catholic Immigration Committee
(By appointment of the Hierarchy of Australia)

Application for Transfer to Australia
(To be filled in by Superior of Institution).

NAME __WINSTON FRANKLYN DEREK LYNE__ Institution __NAZARETH HOUSE, BISHOPSTON, SWANSEA, GLAM.__

DATE OF BIRTH __19TH AUGUST 1945__ Place of Birth __CARDIFF, WALES__

FATHER'S NAME _____ Religion __ROMAN CATHOLIC__

Address _____

MOTHER'S MAIDEN NAME __JOYCE LYNE__ Religion __ROMAN CATHOLIC__

Address __29, REDHOUSE ROAD, ELY, CARDIFF, WALES__

OTHER CHILDREN—

Name	Address	Age	Religion

DATE AND PLACE OF MARRIAGE OF PARENTS _____

DATE AND PLACE OF BAPTISM __17TH APRIL 1946 ST. JOSEPH'S CHURCH, CARDIFF__
(Certificate necessary)

DATE AND PLACE OF CONFIRMATION _____

Confession ? __NO__ Holy Communion ? __NO__

HAS CHILD BEEN IMMUNISED ? (a) Whooping Cough __NO__ (b) Diphtheria __YES__

HAS CHILD HAD CHEST X-RAYED ? __NO__ Result _____

ANY SIGHT DEFECTS ? __NO__ Hearing ? __NO__

ANY SERIOUS ILLNESSES ?
(e.g. Rheumatic Fever, Meningitis, Poliomyelitis, Diabetes) __NO__

ANY SERIOUS ACCIDENTS ? __NO__

ANY PHYSICAL DEFORMITIES ? __NO__

CLASS IN SCHOOL ? __INFANTS 2__ Average age of class ? __6+__

NUMBER IN CLASS ? __37__ Position in class ? __28__

WILL CHILD BE CAPABLE OF SECONDARY EDUCATION ? _____

TO WHAT STANDARD DO YOU CONSIDER ? _____
(e.g. First Year, Matriculation)

ANY SCHOLASTIC WEAKNESSES ? _____

REASONS ? _____

SUGGESTED REMEDIES ? _____

Immigration permit

20th August 1952

It was a cold morning when we were placed in lines and given a small case to look after. I well remember the Nuns running around and putting tags on our coats and cases and did not know what the fuss was about. Then a tall man started to tell us about the long journey we were going on. This started to bring great joy to the boys I was standing with. I didn't quite know what he meant and what the fuss was about until we were placed on the bus. I remember how cold it was – all the windows were frosted over, yet at times I could see buildings that were broken but had no idea why. Then we stopped near an old building with no roof, and we were all told to leave the bus. As we started to walk, I noticed these strange smells and loud hissing sounds as we filed onto a platform, which I now know was Swansea Railway Station.

We were put on the train. I had a window seat, and when I started to clean the frost from the window, I noticed this lady and man waving to me, but the man was a mist of confusion. We pulled out of the station with a big jolt and a loud whistle. It wasn't long before I could see green grass and lots of black hills with smoke coming from them, and lots of small buildings joined up in rows, and people with big coats on. Then the hills were so tall all us kids were peering up out the windows just to see how far into the sky they reached.

Not long after that, I must have fallen asleep as the next memory was of this man pulling me up and telling me we were getting off at the next station. As I pulled myself up to the window, I noticed bigger buildings that were broken. Rubble lay all around the place. Then the train came to a stop and everyone on board got off.

We were put into groups and had a rope tied around us, then we were moved up to a large platform and, from this spot, we could see a large ship with two big funnels with lots of smoke coming from them.

It seemed we were in this place all day, and I remember how we were all hungry and how cold we were. Some of the other groups were crying and started screaming out, then we were told to move up this big plank and hold onto the rope rail. At this time, I heard a woman calling out to us to 'keep moving, keep moving'. When we reached the top, we were taken down inside the ship and placed eight to a cabin, two of us to a bunk. I got the top one as I remember looking out the round window and clearly seeing the tops of the waves. Then we could go up to the deck and see all the people waving and hear the loud music playing. Then this loud horn that seemed to never stop blurted out, and I noticed the ship was now moving away from the Southampton Docks.

Looking out to where all the people were waving, I remember trying to find that lady from the train station who had waved goodbye to me. Even though I didn't know who she was, I felt a strong yearning to see her again.

The ship was now moving faster, and it wasn't long before we were sent down to the cabin. The next time we were let out was for meals in a big hall full of people. There was lots and lots of food and some things I had never seen before, but I will never forget the smells! They have always remained with me, and at times, even now as a man, they bring back this event in my life.

We were being looked after by a lady, who I think was about thirty years old. She kept us together at all times, making sure we were not running around like some of the other kids. When meals were over, we were allowed to walk around the decks with her at our side. It was very cold and damp, but I didn't mind as the cabin was hot. After the walk, she sent us back to the cabin and made sure we were settled for the night. Then she locked the door.

Manifest names

The Orama

In the morning, we were taken to the large shower room, stripped off and showered, then given clean clothes. Our wet beds and clothes were sent to the laundry while we went for the morning meal. After this, we were allowed up on deck but remained in a small area with many other kids I didn't know.

This is how we spent most of our days if it was fine, but not long after it became very hot. One morning we were on deck when many people were shouting out to someone alongside the ship. I looked over the side and noticed a small boat, and the people on the ship had ropes with things being pulled up. These people were strange and had strange hats (turbans) and were yelling out in a language totally unknown to me. I now understand that we had come via the Suez Canal.

During the hot days, we were on deck and given a good hosing down. This was usually followed by games. In the one game I remember, most had to crawl under a rope net just to get to the other side! The rope net was very heavy, and I found it painfully difficult. This memory stays with me, as it was the first time I had felt pain to this degree. I had a nail stuck in my kneecap, and the added weight of the rope net on top of me brought further tears to my eyes. I was then given another good hosing for being a wimp! I still carry that scar today.

I was sent to my cabin for reasons unknown to me, and it seemed quite sometime before I was allowed back on deck. During the time in my cabin, I somehow managed to open this round window, and without any fear, stuck my head out, only to be kissed in the face by the ocean. I was thrown back with such a tremendous force that I lay winded on the floor. When I finally got to my feet, the cabin had water in it up to my ankles. I didn't know what to do, so just sat there and watched the waves roll in! Thinking back, the water must have got into the passage area because the burst door open and a woman came in and closed the window.

Then she gave me what I recall to be my first belting. It was more than likely well-deserved as this woman was responsible for the rest of the boys in our cabin and me. And the fact that I threw her brush and comb out the window to watch what would happen to them in the ocean didn't help matters either. In my mind, I thought they would come back into the cabin with the water.

When I did go back on deck, we would run around amongst the other passengers, and during these times, I would suck on sugar cubes taken from our breakfast table. One time on deck, these very dark men, each wearing a fez, were trying to talk to me. I became wary but learnt their intentions were honourable, as they were really offering me a drink of this black substance from a bottle – which tasted vile – in exchange for my sugar cubes. Each time I was encouraged to have a mouthful, they would begin to laugh and get quite excited as I began to cough and splutter this black substance out. I now know this as camp coffee.

I can't recall anything else of my four weeks voyage to Australia. We arrived at Fremantle docks on a very hot day and stood around in the sun for hours. Then we were divided into groups and placed on the back of an open truck, my destination again unknown. I, and about thirty other boys aged between six and twelve, eventually arrived at Castledare Orphanage, Wilson, West Australia – the date: 19th September 1952.

My early memories of Castledare were always mixed with happy times followed by a lot of sadness. Even though we had nothing, adventure and childhood antics were never far away. Our daily routine was to be woken up around 6am by one of the Brothers. All our wet beds were stripped and placed in piles. We were then marched into the shower in big groups and, after drying ourselves, were issued with shorts, a tee-shirt and sandals.

Then it was back to our bed, which we made up and stood

by for the Brother to inspect. The dormitory I was in had some thirty-eight beds with very little room to walk between. Once this task was finished, it was down to the mess hall for breakfast, where hot milk and bread was the meal for the morning.

From time to time, we were all given little jobs to do, sometimes washing the pots and pans or cleaning the tables and sweeping the floor, after which we played in this big paddock where we stayed until called in. Sometimes we were taken up to the loft of the main building and would paint and cut out little toys, but most times, it was generally playing.

Castledare Dormitory

I recall my first swimming lesson at Castledare: the Brother took us down to the river in groups of about five. Not having any fear and being too young to understand fear, the brother coaxed me into the water and taught me how to dog-paddle. He then said once I had learnt how to dog-paddle and could swim well, he'd take me to the other side of the river, my first adventure.

After a week or so, he satisfied himself that I'd be okay. I had to put my arms around his neck and lay on his back, then he swam to the other side of the river where he left me with some other boys. He wouldn't come and get us and told us to dog-paddle back, which we all did together. After doing this, we were allowed to go to the river for a swim each Saturday afternoon; this now became part of our playground activities. But as boys, we became more adventurous and started to wander further afield, always exploring the outside boundaries, where we were told not to go.

Some time had passed when a couple of boys and I went for a swim up the river and found an old boatshed with a rowing boat inside. We decided to take it and have some fun. After getting it out of the shed, I started to push it up the river while the other boys were in it. It was a good thing we could swim because within five minutes, it began to sink, and, not knowing what to do, we just casually swam back to our playground. Although we felt we'd done something wrong, our main fear was whether we'd been missed from the playground. I don't know to this day what happened about the boat, but I guess the owner retrieved it, as we never went back that way again.

Sometime in 1953

Some nights I would be lying in bed and some of the boys would be crying – I don't know what for, but I know these boys were older than me. Only a few weeks later, they were sent away to another far-off orphanage. We would never see these boys again, though now I am sure they would have been sent to Clontarf Boys Home, as that was the usual progression from Castledare.

During one of these nights, the boys were talking about running away. This sounded like another real good adventure so I asked if I could go along with them. The next afternoon, seven of us walked down to the river and followed it along the bank. This was my first experience in hearing and seeing the Australian wildlife and the memories of those boys with larger than life stories. It now seems like yesterday – the imaginations. We arrived at a large opening in the bush where the ground was like a saltpan because an aircraft had crashed there. This only drove my enthusiasm and my adventurous mind to travel further afield and, as we crossed this swampy area, I noticed my legs were covered with worm-like things, only to find out they were leaches. Apart from being severely bitten by mosquitoes, it must have been around three o'clock in the afternoon as I could still feel the hot summer wind on my face. Yet, still with no fear, we walked out of the swamp into a high-grassed area, not knowing or caring where we were nor the danger in the grass, of which I was totally unaware. It just amazed me as I remember as I approached it, a severe hissing noise would come very close to me, and when I walked away, it stopped. We did this several times and could not understand why the grass hissed at us.

I did not know what events lay ahead that late afternoon, but when we finally walked out of the bush, we came across a huge road with lots of cars and trucks going up and down. We all stood there in total amazement, saying that we had found a new world. Our imaginations were running rampant. Then the street lights came on and, as we were becoming hungry, we decided to walk along this big road. I don't know how long or how far we walked, but I now know this road was Albany Highway, and the area we were in was Cannington.

After some time, we saw an old house with a veranda around the front. We all marched in as if we owned the place and yelled out to see if anyone was there. Once we had satisfied ourselves that no one was in, one of the boys found the kitchen and, looking around at the table, saw a big cake sitting on a plate. Without any hesitation or thoughts of wrongdoing, we demolished it then began to settle in. Then, to our total shock and surprise, this very old lady appeared at the door. With a couple of loud screams from one of the boys, this followed a terrifying screech that I will never forget as the boy started yelling out: "There's a witch at the door!!"

I didn't know what a witch was but understood all was not well; I bolted for the door, running in hot pursuit behind the others. I don't know how far we ran, but I do know it was very late. I also knew we should go back to the orphanage. Then suddenly, a car pulled up, and two big men in uniforms came over to talk to us. They asked me what my name was, and I can recall saying the name everyone else calls me.

"Lynny," I told them.

They then said, "We are Police officers, and a lot of people are looking for you lot in the swamp."

They then bundled us all in the car and drove off to the police station. Once inside, we were given hot drinks and asked a lot of questions about our day's adventures. We all talked at once. Though they could see we were covered in crap and well bitten with sunburn and one of the boys had lost a sandal, we were asked to listen to this box that had a voice coming out of it. No matter how much I looked over and under it, I just could not see a man hiding in it. This was the first time we had all heard a radio talking. The conversation was about us orphanage kids and relayed the news that we were all well, apart from minor scrapes.

Then the Brother came in and gave us a long look, more with relief, that we were okay. So, we were back in the orphanage and given a hot shower and a bloody good talking to. We were asked who the leader was, and no one said a thing as we were all the leaders. Well, that put things off – like swimming and playing – as from that day we started to do more work around the buildings, like gardening and sweeping the grounds, washing windows, helping out in the kitchen and laundry work.

Working in the garden

And just to remind us of our adventure, we had to have cold showers each night and after work. Sometimes I felt very hungry, and it seemed that I just couldn't get enough to eat.

Once, on my day for cleaning the dining room the Brothers ate in, I noticed this red glue type of stuff in a tin. So, as one has to, I fingered a little out and tasted it. Well, this tasted like nothing I'd ever had before, so I decided to hide this tin outside the kitchen and placed it in the tree branch for later that night.

It was some time before I climbed out of bed and, as I did, two of the other boys asked me where I was going. They wanted to come with me, so very quietly, we headed for the back of the kitchen. I got this red stuff in the tin and, at the same time, told the boys, "This is really great stuff."

But before I could finger a bit out, one of the boys grabbed the tin from me and fingered this big amount out and into his mouth then he gave the tin back to me. That's when I felt something crawling over my hands. At the same time, this boy started to scream at the top of his voice and started coughing, spitting, and yelling out loud. I then became aware that the tin was full of ants. He had them in his neck, biting, and I could do nothing but hit the track. I just reached the end of the kitchen when the other boy and I were caught red-handed. The other boy was taken to hospital, and I was given a bloody good hiding that left me blue and sore for quite a while.

Well, the only good thing that came from that humorous night was that I never had to work around the kitchen or the mess hall. I was given harder work, helping with some building work, and also on the farm side, like feeding the chicken and pigs. Also, we had a horse for a playmate, and it became my job to look after it.

Castledare House

One day we were placed into small groups and asked to read this book, and were then sent onto the next to do some sums. The next group was to write a few lines the Brother was reading.

After this, we were marched into these classrooms – this was the start of our education. It was well above anything I understood or had heard of. How hard it was, being left to do things like basic sums, of which nothing was explained to us. I had to learn that we were the dumb bums and unable to read, write and do sums. I found this separation from our play-mates was now a changed style of playing – like those that have it and the likes of us not given the chance to have it. This was soon the way things became.

I and the dumb bums would be like labourers around the orphanage while the smart ones were given minor work around the classrooms and the like. It was the start of 'them and us'.

On Saturday, I had to collect the eggs from the chicken farm and, recalling my days on kitchen duties and what you can do with eggs, I decided to keep two in my pocket to take to the playground. After delivering the eggs to the kitchen, I took two big handfuls of flour that I also put in my pocket. Then I picked an empty tin out of the rubbish bin and bolted straight to the playground, only to find one of the eggs had burst in my pocket. With no self-dignity, I pulled off my pants and emptied the broken egg into the tin, shell and all. Then I added the flour. I picked up a stick and stirred it up into a gooey mess. I can remember the boys were watching me and once I satisfied myself it was all mixed up, we all started to eat it. It then became obvious that my first experience at cooking was not appreciated by boys – the looks on their faces gave that away.

Most Sundays, we were showered with walnuts as a special treat, and we would eat them until they came out of our ears. Soon after, we would become very sick and tired of them, although now I have the odd one. On other occasions, we were given broken and crumbly biscuits, which we all enjoyed as we could eat them until we were full.

On some Sunday mornings after church, we were put into

small groups of three or four. Brothers would walk us through the bush to the next orphanage, called Clontarf.

The walk was a lot of fun for all of us as we walked from Castledare up to the hill, and from there, we could see this big river. We would follow the river while still in the bush until we arrived at an old house where we were all given water from a well. Then we started off again and shortly after leaving the house we arrived in a plantation of pine trees. We found the needles were very hard under our feet as we only had sandals on. This we all found very exhausting as the walk took about two hours, and in the heat of the day. When we arrived at Clontarf, we were given dinner with all these other kids who were a lot bigger than we were. After dinner, we were put into small groups, and one of the big boys from Clontarf would look after us for the rest of the day.

Clontarf House

One big boy that looked after me was John Mullin, and the reason I remember was because John showed me around Clontarf, and it was my first time to see pigs, cows, bulls; he showed me the work he had to do each day before school started, also on Saturdays and Sundays.

I can well remember these trips being very tiring, and we would sometimes get back to Castledare when it was dark. As it was all bush between the orphanages, it was at times hard going for us. Though I had no fear of the bush, the Brothers drove us on real hard, pushing us to the limits until we arrived home.

It was about this time that things around me changed. The boys seemed to have no time for play or just didn't want to. Even though we had our small jobs to do, it just seemed different.

Then one day this particular Brother started to call me David! I remember him saying that I was a Welsh boy, and should be called after my patron Saint – though I didn't understand what he meant by 'Welsh boy'. This Brother seemed gentle and different from the rest as he would show me things and explain some schoolwork stuff, and I always looked forward to doing things with him and learn the things he taught me. I am sure his name was Brother Moore. I now knew that things were going to be different for me.

During holiday breaks, we were all dressed up in nice clothing and taken into Perth for viewing. Some of the boys protested, but I was always eager to go as I'd always felt that little trip away and seeing all sorts of new things was an exciting adventure in itself. We were all placed onto the back of this truck and taken to Victoria Avenue, Perth, where we had to stand in single file. Although I didn't know what this was about at first, after several times I became very sad as people walked up and down looking at us. They would then talk to the Brother and walk away with one of the boys. As for me, along with some other boys, we were taken back to the orphanage.

We didn't understand this, but I and the others felt quite sad. Our playmates had been taken away, and we had nothing much to do over the holidays except some work cleaning or pulling weeds from the gardens.

Then on the next holiday break, we were once again taken into Perth for a viewing.

As luck would have it, I was picked out. A man and lady took me away to their orchard farm. I had never seen or been to an orchard before, but this place was near the Gosnells hills. When we arrived, two boys came down to meet me. They were much older than me; bigger too. We were soon asked to go with the man – their father, I think – and before long, I was eating apricots they had pulled from the tree, my first taste of an apricot. Wow!! I stuffed myself full and suffered for it about two hours later with the trots. The next day I was asked to help pick apricots. I didn't mind helping with that, but later in the afternoon, the two boys started to tease me and wanted to fight me. I'd not heard the type of words they were saying to me but felt as though it was about me and not what I was doing. Then, without notice, this boy started throwing rotten apricots at me. I looked over to see him coming at me; he started to rub apricots in my hair. I pulled away, but he wouldn't let go, then I let my anger out. With all my strength, I started on him like a wild cat, and picked up anything I could find to hit him with. When he fell backwards, I jumped down and swung a left blow then a right blow to his head. Then I noticed his brother coming towards me and, as he drew closer, I grabbed a handful of mud and let him have it before I ran like a bat out of hell.

I didn't know that he was only going to stop the fighting, but their father and mother put me in the car and drove me to Castledare and handed me over to Brother Moore. I could hear them talking about me but couldn't understand what they were saying. When they left, Brother Moore asked me, and I told him that the boys had started it, that all they wanted was me to pick their apricots. And then the fighting started. No more was said about this event.

When they finally left, I was taken away and given a shower and a change of clothing. I felt a lot happier back at the orphanage. So, if that was what was going on out on a weekend holiday, I surely wouldn't enjoy the next one. I also now understood why some of the boys protested at going.

I now became warier of other people after that holiday, although I never had a single playmate. We boys just seemed to get on great as a group, but over time I could feel this change in moods. Some of the boys became very wild in their ways, and the aggression and anger would come out during these times. We would be playing to the point that I could no longer be a part of it. I think back now that this attitude may have grown from the segregation between those going to school and the likes of me working. It was even more noticeable after our dormitories were divided into two groups. The boys who went to the classrooms were put into one, and those doing all the manual work were put into another. I can only conclude this was so we did not disturb them, as we would be up early doing our work.

This segregation always brings back memories of our sexual awareness. Although I was only eight years old, the other boys and I talked about our bodies and that we were all different. Some of the stories I heard were totally outside my thinking at this age of my life. But I do remember things from Wales that was not, as they were talking about when I was living with the nuns – and yet I would go into the shower in the nude from the dormitory as I have always done.

It must have been 7.30 pm this night as I lay in bed in my cubical. On many nights I could hear some of the boys crying. I could not understand this, as I had nothing to cry about and was not in any pain. But at times I was very sad, but that was gone by the next day as I went about my work.

Then one night about 'lights out', I could hear a Brother talking to one of the boys outside my cubical and noticed he had his hand under the sheets rubbing his tummy. I didn't know what the matter was, but I thought he was sick or something as I only remember the nuns holding me and keeping me warm but not any bonding. When the Brother left him, I asked him, "What's wrong?"

He came into my cubical; sat on my bed, and I asked again, "Are you the Brother's pet?"

"No," he replied. Then he put his hand on my 'willy' and began to rub it. He sat up, saying, "This is what the Brother does to me!"

I didn't know quite what was meant from these actions as I could feel no sexual feelings other than his cold hand on my body. When I protested that his hand was cold, he said, "That is what I say to the Brother." Then he said, "Open your legs and I'll make you feel good, like the Brother does to me."

I didn't protest as I didn't understand fully. I liked this boy and had always got on pretty well with him when we worked together. Yet I didn't know anything like this happened. As I quite recall, I was always to lie on my back with my arms across my chest – to stop the devil taking over our minds with thoughts of the flesh. This is what was always drummed into me in Wales, UK.

He would come into my cubical every night and tell me what the Brother had done. Then this night, he was rubbing real hard until it was standing up, then he pulled back my foreskin and that hurt. I started protesting loudly at him to leave me alone. When he didn't, I pulled my feet back and pushed him in the chest. He ran back to his bed and never came back to my cubical.

Looking back at this boy, he was obviously the victim of sexual abuse. He was always given the best jobs and special treatment and treats. As for me, I was never approached or fondled by any of the Brothers during my time at Castledare, though I was becoming more and more wary of them and would keep out of their way. But there was also something else on my mind.

There were other flashbacks that at times woke me at night. Although they had happened in Swansea in the Gower, they seem very real to me now. On most occasions, I would wake up gasping for air, and feel a heavy load on my face. But I was in the dark, and as I sat up there was nothing on top of me, yet it took me some time before I fell back to sleep. I do not know what it was but I have never felt right when these memories flood back, mostly without any warning.

Not long after, I started work and some schoolwork with another boy about a year older than me. He was very quiet and didn't say much, but one night he wanted to stay in my cubical to talk – he explained about the Brother. I told him about the other boy, and he said that it was okay and sometimes he got good things for being good to them. When I asked him what he had to do, he said:

"Just lay back and close your eyes and let me show you."
When I felt his hand pulling my pants down, I opened my eyes and asked what was happening. Once again, I was told not to worry and to close my eyes. If I did, this boy would put my willy in his mouth. And that is when I jumped up as I thought he was going to bite it off. Not giving him a second chance, I punched him hard and pushed him off my bed. By now, I was really yelling out for him to stop it. Then one of the Brothers came over to find out what was the problem. To avoid getting a belting, I said that I'd had a night fright and was afraid. He put his arms around me, but I pulled away, telling him to leave me alone. He told me to get back into bed and to stop all the fuss, but I found it very hard to sleep and decided now to sleep under the bed. It remained like that for a very long time.

Things were much different now as the boys never did much swimming or playing games together and at times I would sit under a tree binding dandelions into ringlocks. Then one of the brothers asked me if I would like to sing songs.

Not quite sure about it, I just said yes, jumping up to follow him away as I really felt down and needed something to do. This could be the thing I needed.

Brother Moore led about five of us into the big hall and started with one at a time to sing various notes. After about twenty minutes, he told us that he would get things together, and left the hall, leaving us again, so I went back to the playground and sat down under a tree.

I always kept to myself, and when asked to do things, I never protested. On one occasion, the toilet block in the middle of the playground was blocked and one of the workmen living at the orphanage called me over. I recall the horrible smell coming from this hole. He asked me to put my arm up this pipe to feel if there was anything up there. I didn't protest but just carried out his instructions as we should obey him.

The next day I became sick, and it was only when one of the sisters had found out what I had done, they suddenly realised I had been in contact with raw sewage. I don't know what illness I had, but I do know I was very sick.

Sometime in 1954

After my sickness, I settled into a normal routine. We became very much attached to our animals – we had cats, dogs, and horses – Brother Moore, who had named me David, and now the Brother who called me Derek (Brother Doal) – I am using this so not to offend – we were now very much alone with a new Brother, Brother Doughty. This Brother could touch the clouds, and I really liked him as he always bent down to talk to us. No matter how small the group, he was right there for us, always talking and laughing at our stupid ways but still having control of our situation. Now we all felt like we had a Brother.

We had cats, dogs and horses

I remember the day Brother Moore decided to build an aviary for his birds, and I think for us as well! I still remember a truck loaded with sand and bricks had collapsed into a cesspit, causing a great commotion. We all gathered around, our hearts full of laughter, watching this truck slowly disappearing, but more so in the way the Brothers panicked. They finally got the truck out and thus, the construction started. We ended up with a round aviary with lots of birds and chickens. It will always remain with me how wonderful these days were, and it still brings great joy to watch life unfold with much pleasure as a child with nothing but sitting watching all these things, the birds like willy wagtails, magpies, storks, and one crow, and then the bent beaks. The latter I would avoid but would never be afraid to feed them and or clean the cage out. I will hold this time as a loving memory of those days, never to forget.

Around this time, I found a kitten and decided to take it to a house down the road. This was totally forbidden to do, but the kitten jumped out of my arms and ran up a big, big tree in our playground – it's still standing today, laughing at me. However, this kitten was up the tree and I just had to get it down, so I started to climb up. Though it was night, I was not afraid to try and get the kitten down. Before long, I felt I couldn't go much further up as the bark was wet and slippery. Too late though, I slipped off and fell, hitting all that was beneath me. That is all I remember until sometime in the morning when I awoke from my fall. I felt broken and sore, cold and wet, but still had to get back into the dormitory before I was discovered missing. It took all my strength to get there, and I just fell down in my cubical on the bed, not under it. Not long after that I was being yelled at to get up and dressed or "Are you going without breakfast!"

I just didn't have the strength to go and eat. I think I must have broken some bones as I could not move crap and laugh, and breathing was very painful. Nevertheless, I still got on with my duties, but I shall never forget or forgive that cat/kitten, and see this again as life without much, but yourself and what you break of it!!

The night after my fall, I went to bed early, and not long after one of the Brothers came into my cubical and sat on my bed. I pretended to be asleep. Then he asked me about the previous night and said I didn't look well. I did not move a muscle or flinch an eyelid but, as he sat there softly talking to me, he started to stroke my brow, ran his fingers across my forehead, not waking me at all. Then he left me, assuming I was asleep.

This was my first experience of feeling that one of the Brothers cared about me as the things he said were all soft, kind words, about us boys and our way of life, and that we were chosen by God and that he was there as God's helper and shouldn't be afraid of anything because if he couldn't help us, then we should ask God ourselves to help us. I have thought of his words often.

Each night we would go to Benediction, where we would say the rosary. I could never understand why we were kneeling and standing to the statue of a man on a cross. Even though I had been in the Catholic organisation since the age of eight months and now I was eight years old, it had never been explained to me what these ceremonies were about. I recall attending them and doing the same thing over and over again. The word 'God' was quite often spoken but the fact that I couldn't see him made these events more confusing and mysterious.

I have never asked God for help because I guess I didn't know what to ask him for. I must have been content within myself, as I have always had everything done for me apart from the work I had to do. So later, I thought I could be cheeky enough to ask him to do my work for me and allow me to get along with my adventurous ways.

At first, I asked him to collect the eggs in the morning then could he light the boiler and for that I would do my rosary twice that night. But as I thought, I went down to the chicken pen to find he had not been and so I collected the eggs, then off to the boiler room, and just as well … he hadn't been there either. So now I couldn't trust him to do anything for me and had lost interest in asking because I now knew he wasn't listening to me. I learnt very quickly that to make things happen, I would have to do it myself, and that was how it has been.

Sometime late 1954

We were subjected to all religious ceremonies. I can recall two separate occasions: the first was going into the Christian Brothers College on the corner of St Georges Terrace and

Victoria Avenue in Perth, where we went into church. There was a strange ceremony held where us boys were marched past this box and told to kiss the forehead of the person laying in it. On the second occasion, we were put onto the back of a truck like cattle and taken on one of the longest rides I'd been on since arriving at Castladare.

Our destination was Bindoon Boys Town. We sang songs most of the way, especially *It's a Long Way to Tipperary*. During this trip, the truck's sides would move to and fro when the driver turned corners. Although we were packed in like sardines, we would be jammed in tightly against the sides. I remember one boy getting his big toe jammed underneath the side gate and could not get it out. No matter how loud this boy screamed, the truck never stopped, and it was only released when the weight of our bodies was thrown against that side of the truck to which his toe was stuck. He was in a lot of pain, and I remember seeing the bones of his big toe.

When we finally arrived at our destination, we were very hungry, thirsty, and exhausted. We didn't have any cover over us, and me being fair-skinned with no protection, I became blistered on my shoulders and face, and my lips were bleeding. In fact, we were all sun and wind burnt; my mouth was very dry and swollen, as we had been in the back of that truck for about three hours without stopping.

Bindoon Boys Town is some eighty miles north of Perth, and though we were up very early for breakfast, we left around nine in the morning to arrive at midday. We were given a big lunch with lots of fruit, and milk, which was nice and cold, but the food was fantastic, and I believe we acted like a bunch of pigs. Not only that, we hid food on any part of our bodies just in case, and for the trip home.

Then we, and all the big boys at that orphanage, were lined up and marched down to the front of a big building where there were lots and lots of other people. After some time, we had to walk up to this box and kiss the forehead of the person inside, who I now know was Brother Keaney, the founder of Bindoon Boys Town. After this ceremony was over, we were taken to a large bedroom and shower room as we were staying the night. It was a great delight to all of us.

During that afternoon, the big boys showed me and some of the boys from Clontarf around this big farm with lots of cows, bulls, pigs and chickens, and a hay stack where we had lots of fun and games. Then it was back to the main building for showers and meals, followed by evening prayers and Benediction before bedtime.

But all was not quiet as I could hear screaming and crying from the other dormitories and it seemed to take some time before all was quiet.

The next morning after breakfast, we were bundled back into the truck and taken back to Castledare. By the time we arrived, we were all sore and red and full of bruises on our buttocks and legs as most of us fell asleep and just laid on the floor of the truck as it bounced its way back the eighty miles to Castledare. I arrived again with blisters and windburn all over my legs and face, arms and head and ears.

During the summer months and on Saturdays, we would go and pick up cow manure from the paddocks. Sometimes the cow pads were soft, but we had no fear even though we knew where they came from. We would bag as much as we could then two of us would drag the bags back to Castledare for the boys doing the gardens around the main buildings. We would break the manure down while the other boys forked and dug it into the ground that was so hard and heavy with clay, some of the boys would have to jump up and down to drive the fork as deep as they could. One of the boys who had hold of the fork slammed it down real hard and it went right through his foot and into the ground. He gave out an almighty scream as he couldn't move his foot. One of the Brothers got him free and carried him to the medical bay. We could still hear his excruciating screams. They eventually took him to the hospital, but that didn't stop the rest of us from working in the garden. I always enjoyed doing it because I liked to see the flowers grow as I would pick the petunias very softly, put them to my mouth and suck the nectar out. I would always have to be careful not to get caught doing this as I was often warned not to pull the flowers up.

Then out of the blue, Brother Moore came up to us and said that he wanted to start with our singing lessons. I'd forgotten all about this but understand now that he'd wanted a piano and it had arrived that day from Clontarf for us. So we finished the garden and washed up for evening meals then went down to the main hall for music lessons.

We arrived at the hall very excited and looking forward to being accepted into the concert. Then Brother Moore came in and gave us all a mouthful of honey. He then, with another Brother, sat at the piano and started to play a note and we were asked to reach the high point of the note. And so we were picked into small groups after each stage until he'd achieved what he was after. That is what he wanted. After all this time, he was happy as ever. Then we were informed that he wanted to hear us singing in the showers, at play and before bedtime. He placed us into various groups according to our voice range, and once he found that, we had to sing at that scale and pitch at all times. And so, we would walk around singing at the top of our voices until we tired, only to start again. I can't remember a day go by that someone around the place wasn't singing out loud, and no one seemed to mind Brother Moore standing in front of us.

After about two weeks, we were called back to the hall and put in various orders, and, although some of us couldn't read, we had to learn the lines as Brother Moore would not let that stand in his way. For the rest of that month, we practised our lines until he was satisfied that we were giving him the best he would get from us. Then he explained that he would enter us in a concert with other schools.

During this time, I would be singing two particular songs, which I remember, but I have no idea or know who taught them to me.

A little white rabbit came hopping along
hopping hopping hopping along
He saw a big man with a very big gun,
and said that he'll shoot that little fat bun
But the rabbit said no sir that will be no fun,
as he's hopping hopping hopping along.

Sweet Sicily, why don't you answer me?
I'm so lonely in this country,
Got no mother, no father here,
no brother—sister to give me cheer,
Sweet Sicily why don't you answer me?
I'm so lonely in this country.

Then we were given some nice clothes to put on in the afternoon as we were going to Perth for a singing competition between schools. Come that evening, we were taken into a big hall with lots of people, and once settled down, we started to sing the best we could. We sang, and everybody clapped and clapped for us. Then we had to stand outside until the competition was over to find out who the winners were. Not long after that Clontarf was declared the winner. So we left for Castledare, not unhappy as we were told that is what you will achieve, and to try harder to get to the top, then we would sing for our own orphanage and the people that lived around us. From that time, things became less and less as Brother Moore was moved, some of the bigger boys went to Clontarf, and we moved up the little ladder in our school.

In South Wales at this time, 23rd July 1955, my natural mother married Mr Oliver Pearcey at St Luke's Church, Cardiff and had been living at 36 Alexander Road, Canton, Cardiff for the past three years.

During our singing competition in Perth, the public was informed that, with the coming holidays, the Brothers would be grateful for them having one of our boys stay with them over the holidays.

Before the long weekend, we were taken to Perth for viewing and all the events of my previous holidays came back to me. I could feel how unhappy the other boys were, and this was no different. I guess this must have shown, as the Brothers asked us to cheer up. Although these words of encouragement were being passed onto us, I could hear one boy saying he just didn't want to go with anyone. As for me, I kept still and remained quiet.

Standing there, being looked over by anyone that passed by made me feel quite nervous and red in the face. I was at a point of poking my tongue out just so I wouldn't be taken away. Although there were many advantages for the orphanage and perhaps the overall system, I do believe this method of selection was so mentally cruel and very obviously distressing to us all, the boys who had never been out on holidays were themselves becoming disturbed as to what events might lay ahead for them. Back in the orphanage, most of the boys talked about the bad things done to them, but in fairness to most of the boys, there were some good things mentioned as well, and this was more noticed when they would bring lots and lots of goodies back with them and shared them around with the other boys who'd been left behind. Then, as God would have it, this lady came up and started to speak to me.

"Hello ... and what is your name?" She was dressed in an overcoat and had a little boy with her. She looked very pretty.

I must have still had my strong Welsh accent because they would smile at some of the things I would say. Even though I was very shy, I said: "David. That's my name."

Then she asked me if I would like to come with her. I didn't feel any threat as she spoke to me in such a kind, soft way. Then she held her hand out for me to go with her, and after a short discussion with the Brother, I was taken away from that terrible viewing line. After a short trip on the bus, we arrived at 157 Kooyong Road, Rivervale.

I was shown a room with two beds in it, and I can well remember how warm it was. This was much better than the big cold dormitories, yet even this small room didn't give cause for concern. Three children lived in the house – Tommy was with her when I was picked out, and the other two children were Maureen and Barbara. I was asked what I would like to do.

"Play in the paddock?"

"No, we don't have a paddock, just a small yard, and whatever you do, you must always stay inside the fence. Now go outside and play." So we all went out the back.

I can't remember what we played or talked about, but I do remember having a real nice weekend there, and I didn't feel upset at the thought of going back to the orphanage. But I felt I'd done something wrong as I noticed the lady crying, and I didn't like to ask.

Back at the orphanage, life just drifted on with little to no interest of anything around. My schooling was very hard as I'd never had the basics to start with. It was assumed that I had some basics, but this was never so. So at ten or eleven years of age, I was unable to read one word, add 2+2, or write my name. I did, at this time of my life, think this was the best it was ever going to be, yet I was to look forward to all my tomorrows and what adventures would unfold for me.

Christmas Holidays 1955

Although I never understood what Christmas was about, to me it was what the word 'Holidays' was all about. I was informed by Brother Doyle that Mr and Mrs Darcey wanted me over for the Christmas holidays – he said I must have behaved very well to be asked to stay with them for Christmas. Sometime later, I was picked up from Castledare by Mr Darcey and, after a short trip, I was once again with them. Tommy and I became good playmates. Maureen and Barbara, I think, just watched us, always playing cowboys and Indians around the house.

On some occasions, Mr Darcey would take us to his place of work in Belmont. He had a big shed full of broken-down cars and old trucks and spent his day pulling bits off and putting them back. I couldn't understand all of this, but Tom could. I had never seen a person doing these things, but Tom explained that his dad was a mechanic and his job was repairing cars and trucks. But when he was finished work, his arms and face were covered in black oil all over, and at times I thought that was his way of having fun and games for the day.

Tom and I found a lot cleaner things to do, like exploring the old wrecks around the paddock. We let our imaginations and our childhood adventures take over the day, always trying and pretending to drive. Tommy seemed more advanced than me; he could blow some real good raspberries as he changed the wrecked cars' gears. And when we had enough of that, we would chase the cows around the big paddock. There was about six or seven of them, and Tom was not sure about this at times as he felt he may end up in trouble. Well, that was not far away as one day some boys came over into Dad's paddock. When Tom and I noticed them, Tom tried to tell Dad, but he was asleep under the car, and all he did was grunt. That's when Tom said they shouldn't be there so I started to chase them away – I realised then they were throwing stones at us, so we bolted for cover in one of the wrecks and hid.

After a short time, I crawled out to look around and came across one boy by himself. I called Tom over, then asked this boy what he was doing there. He said he just wanted to play in the wrecks.

So I said to him, 'Before you can do that, you have to join our gang, and before you can join our gang, you have to wash yourself in cow dung."

This boy was about Tom's age, then Tom went looking for a real sloppy cow pad and it was not long before he found one. He called me over to look and see if it was fresh enough and told the boy to start washing himself in the dung. At first, he just stood in the middle of it. When he started to refuse, I started to throw stones at him and told him that we had all day. Then he started crying out, and began to wash the dung all up his legs and arms and chest. We then told him to bugger off and not come back. And all this while Dad was asleep under the car.

Then, without much warning, Dad was up and about getting things sorted for the next day. At the same time, he asked, "Did you have a good time here?"

Well, we answered with a big "Yes."

Then he said we could come with him the next day, and looking back across the paddock, I could see the boy walking bandy-legged, which made Tom and I laugh all the way home.

When Dad, Tom, and I next arrived at his place of work, within minutes, this woman was screaming at him about putting cow crap all over her boy – poor Dad had no idea of the events of the previous day. It was only during her screaming and Dad trying to calm her down that he realised we'd done something to the boy. We told him that they were in the paddock and we caught the boy and made him wash the cow dung over his legs and arms and told him not to come back. I could see Dad trying not to laugh about it while the woman was still stressed out. And that was when Dad told her he would sort it out, so we spent the next couple of days at the house.

Two days later, we were back at Dad's place of work and this time we had to remain within sight of Dad. After lunch, we went back playing around the wrecks when I heard a loud bang. I looked over to where it came from and noticed a small truck on its side. Dad quickly ran over, with Tom and myself behind him. When we reached there, we found a man lying on the ground with lots of blood pouring out of his head. When I saw this, I became very shaken and upset as he was screaming out in pain. I had not seen an accident before this, and this, being my first, has remained with me. But that night, I just couldn't sleep and when I finally did, I woke up with it still on my mind.

I do remember Dad talking about it over the next few days, and this would bring back memories of this man screaming. As I was only ten years old, I seemed to find a little bit of fear in me after all the things I'd done. This seemed to have upset me the most.

Friday 16th December 1955

Tommy and I, as usual, played cowboys and Indians around the house. The family down the road had two boys around our age and we all became good playmates. I was always on the verge of mischief.

When Dad arrived home with news of a serious accident

involving a bus which he thought was from Clontarf Boys Home and there was a lot of boys in hospital with bad injuries, I didn't fully understand his words. But he told Mum that he would go over to see the bus. He and Tom went, but I didn't want to go. The memories of the last accident were still quite vivid, and, at times, I could hear that man screaming out in pain.

I learnt upon their return that the bus had its side ripped out, and there was indeed a lot of boys injured. I was never to hear what happened exactly, but I learnt one boy was killed and others had arms and legs cut off. Upon hearing this, I became very upset within myself – I was never told who was killed and who was hurt.

I did find out later that, if the Darcey family hadn't taken me for the Christmas holiday, I would have been on that bus as the Brothers would often take the remaining boys out for the day to some picnic spot. So I felt quite lucky in that respect.

Many years passed before I learned that the Brother who had driven the bus was blameless, leaving the young truck driver to carry the guilt for many years. Just recently, the truck driver was cleared of reckless driving, and I felt quite sorry for him. He must have carried that guilt of so many injuries to the boys. However, I felt more hostile to think that this person was made a scapegoat for the protection of the Roman Catholic Brothers of Clontarf.

My very first joy of Christmas was to wake up with lots of presents at the end of my bed. I can recall all the excitement on the night before Father Christmas was coming, although I could never ever remember it while in the orphanage. It was Maureen's, Barbara's and Tommy's excitement that put a whole new meaning to it. The preparation of the days leading to this special day still has powerful memories that I shall never forget.

My first Christmas: waking up with the whole house full of laughter and fun when we opened our presents and the thrill and happiness of it all. My first treasured thing was a train set which I played with for hours and hours, then we went out to lots of picnics spots, and it always felt really happy even though at times I was getting teased about the way I spoke, and the freckles on my face and the colour of my hair.

After the holidays I went back to Castledare. Mum tried to persuade me not to take my train set with me, but it was the only toy I can ever remember having – I just would not leave it behind.

I can well remember my next few weeks at the orphanage were of a sad nature. Most of my playmates seemed to have changed; we did less with each other, and very little was said of our holiday adventures. Then my train set was pinched, and my whole world seemed to fall apart. It just seemed as though everyone had lost interest in each other. But now, as a man, I believe our emotions were confused simply by the change of our environment and no sense of belonging. This business of push and pull between a home and the orphanage life was tearing apart my childhood playmates and making us all withdraw within ourselves. There were no more hostilities at this point of my internment than before and the crying at night seemed to last longer, thus, in turn, this emotional disturbance would upset the other boys, including myself. This disturbing period had possibly made me a little bitter as I felt I had nothing and no one.

I would often hear the boys reading out loud from the classrooms so one day I asked this boy to show me what he was doing. After he showed me this book and the writing inside, he asked me if I could read a particular word and I couldn't understand it. Then he read some words to me, but I still couldn't understand it or the writing – none of it made any sense to me, and I thought that was the way things were. But I was soon to learn that this was not so. I felt left out for reasons unknown to me, but I also felt betrayed by those responsible for my education and learning. I was not very happy, knowing these Brothers had plenty of time to show and teach me but during my whole time there, not once was I asked or arrangements made for nighttime reading, nor for sums.

24th February 1956

The Darcey family had requested permission to care for me and this was subsequently approved, and I was taken to their home. My records show that I arrived at Mrs Darcey's with four pairs of summer pyjamas pants, no coat, two singlets, two underpants, one good blazer, one white shirt, one pair of grey drawers, one old shirt, one pair of shoes, one pair of sandals, one pair of socks and one suitcase. There was no pullover or cardigan included in this outfit, but the request was made for these items from the orphanage.

Upon arriving at the Darcey's home, I seemed to become unhappy within myself, though I was constantly reminded by Mrs Darcey that I would be staying with them for some time. Even so, my thoughts kept drifting back to all my friends at the orphanage, then to come here and be repeatedly teased by the neighbourhood kids and looked upon as an oddity. I didn't want to go out and play but rather stayed in the house or my bedroom and constantly cried alone, and all the time Mrs Darcey came in and sat down with me. Talking and wiping away my tears and cuddling me must have improved my moods as I began to do things in their backyard only, and tried to stay away from the other kids in the neighbourhood – all this just so I would not be teased. I never went through this type of ordeal, and we never put the other boys through it in the orphanage.

Maureen and Barbara were going to St Augustine's Convent in Rivervale, so I was sent there too. During the following weeks, it became clear that I couldn't read or write or do arithmetic, which I had kept secret. But it was soon uncovered. I had always felt different because I just couldn't do these things, and I guess that made feel really unhappy inside because my secret of illiteracy would be uncovered at this school.

Tommy and me in school uniform

After day school, Mother Superior gave me special attention, showing me and explaining the pronunciation of each word. I would try and try but just couldn't get it. Then Mrs Darcey, at night after tea, would read some lines from the newspaper, and from this, I began to memorise a word until I could write it down and say it. Then, over time, I was able to, in a very small way, write the word down where it should be placed within a sentence, but I still found it quite hard as most of the words were very difficult to say. But I kept trying and trying as I wanted to know just as much as the other kids. But sometime later, I started to keep it to myself so the other neighbourhood kids wouldn't use it against me.

After about two months, I could read simple words and found a great hunger for more. But my mind drifted back to the orphanage and the fact that they just didn't take any interest in my schooling. To this day, I still direct deep anger at them, starting from Wales to Castledare – my major hurt was, they must have known but chose to keep me out of the school. And it wasn't only me. As previously mentioned, my mob was bigger than those who could read and write. So just what was their problem? Just maybe some of us managed to find loving and caring people who stayed with and kept on and on until I was able, within a short time, to write short words.

It was also at this time that the Darcey family held a conference regarding my acceptance to live with them as a brother and, from what I understand, I was accepted with open arms. I was then confronted by Mr and Mrs Darcey asking if I could call them Mum and Dad, just like the other children.

I said, "Yes, please!" but was a little confused about it at first. However, a few words explaining the reason brought a whole new meaning to family bonds, and from that day, I was given the care, shelter, sharing and love from my new Australian family. I now had two sisters and one brother, though I was still a little confused as my Brothers and Sisters were old people and stayed in the orphanage. Yet there seemed something different about my new ones as they never told me what to do and never ordered me about, so it wasn't long before we would wash up and wipe up the plates and pots then clean the table and sweep the floor all without anyone being told what to do. Over the next few months, I settled into the Darcey's way of life, going to school each day and attending every Sunday mass at St Augustine's Church. Life just seemed full of joy for me.

Part Two

My Adoptive Family

6th August 1956

In Wales at this time, my half-sister was born and named Linda Joan Pearcey. She lived at 36 Alexander Road, Canton, Cardiff.

19th August 1956

One morning I was woken up with everyone saying "Happy Birthday" to me. I can never remember this happening before, and was told that this was the day I was born. I was now eleven years old, today! I was given lots of cuddles and kisses, then Mum made a picnic lunch while Dad loaded the car then we went off into the bush. When we arrived at the picnic spot, Mum and Dad gave me a small parcel and told me it was my present from all the family. On opening it, I found a pocket knife. I just couldn't believe what I had, as this was a major thing to have in the orphanage and you would be king of the heap. Now I had one

The first thing I asked Dad was, "Is this really mine ... to keep?"

"Yes," he said with a big smile. He must have thought he had given me a gold bar. I couldn't keep my eyes off it for the whole day. Then Mum and Dad brought this big cake from the car, complete with lit candles, while they sang "Happy birthday to you ..."

At first, I couldn't understand what the fuss was all about as I'd never had a birthday party before. Then Mum explained that this was my first birthday with them and they wanted me to remember it. I always have. Then we all sat around on rocks eating the meat they'd cooked. I was then given a piece of my birthday cake.

We left this spot and visited three other picnic areas, and once again, the cake was lit and happy birthday was sung. But the most striking thing on my mind was, if I was given something, I would have to always give something back for it, and something like a pocket knife would be taken off me at the end of the day. So I asked Dad again, "Is this really mine to keep?" And when he said "Yes," again, that lifted all the weight off my mind and made this day truly special to me. I really had a fantastic time on this, my first family birthday party.

August 20 1956

My first school reports read rather sadly, but one remark on this report was, "this child has improved in appearance since Mrs Darcey has taken him and also a marvellous improvement in conduct and manners!"

I guess it was after the school holidays that I was starting to become mischievous and adventurous. I can recall we were all walking to school together with the family dog Poodles, who would sometimes follow us. On one of these occasions, Maureen and Barbara had left early with a friend. They came running down the road saying the dogcatcher had got Poodles. I had no idea what they meant by this, but I could see they were both extremely upset. I asked Maureen to show me where he was and, when we arrived at school, I understood what she meant. There, sitting on the side of the road, was a utility with a metal cage on the back. It was full of dogs.

Without any second thought or hesitation, I snuck up to the back of the ute so the driver couldn't see me and slowly undid the latch. I opened the cage gate then ran away about twenty yards. All of us started calling "Poodles! Poodles!"

Then all the dogs, including Poodles, flew out of the cage like bats out of hell. I remember how sad he looked when he was sitting in that cage, but when he heard us calling him, he burst out of that cage, not even stopping to thank me. He just bolted for home where we learned that he went under the house and remained there for the rest of the day. But, during the time I let the dogs loose, the driver was out of the ute and yelling words I had never heard before. He was really cranky and more than a little mad with it. As we arrived at school, I was considered the hero, and I guess this must've changed some of my thinking as I became more boisterous and mischievous.

During the next few months, I found myself going further afield exploring my neighbourhood. We always found new things to do, and our time was mostly spent playing bushrangers or cowboys and Indians. Some weekends, Dad's sister would come and visit. On one of these occasions, her son, Barry, came to play with us. Barry, or Butch as he was called, and I just seemed to have something in common. One day, Butch and I were sitting on the back steps at the rear of Mum's house when he started to tell me words I had never heard. I thought he was trying to teach me something new, as in some cases, Mum would explain to me what things were and expand on the word I had never heard. So Butch was doing the same as Mum. However, this day the word he was teaching me was "Fuck." Then he told me to say 'fuck'. So, without any hesitation, I did, but of course, still speaking in a Welsh accent. It must have sounded funny to him as he burst out laughing. Then he asked me to say it again. So I said, "fuck."

Butch said, "Not like that! I mean, fuck! Fuckety-fuck!" So I said started to say, "Fuck, fuck, fuckety-fuck," and after satisfying myself, we both started to sing it out loud and clear. As I now knew how to sing, it wasn't long before I was at my top notes, and also Butch, singing "Fuck, fuck, fuckety-fuck – fuck, fuck, fuckety-fuck."

Then I looked up to see Mum standing there and me with a big smile that must have looked like the full moon, still singing,

"Fuck, fuck, fuckety-fuck – fuck, fuck, fuckety-fuck."

Well, I soon learnt that this was not a nice word as Mum reached into the wash trough and grabbed a cake of soap and jammed it into my mouth, and scraped it on my teeth, leaving this foul-tasting stuff for me to swallow.

December 1956

My next school report stated, "David's always punctual for school. This child has been made a real brother by the Darcey children and is very happy." However, they also made a comment that I was retarded!!

On this Christmas holidays, we all went to Wandering, where Dad used to live as a boy. His mother was still living there. Also, Dad's sister came up to stay with all of us. We arrived at this very old mud-brick house with a veranda all around it. This was my first time meeting Grandma and Jock, who just sat around all day.

In the afternoon, Butch and I went off to get the wood in for Jock, and we had to stack it up as he wanted. Then we started to explore our surroundings but was told to remain close to the house. It wasn't long before we found this tree with a dog tied to a chain. Butch started to tease it, and it was getting angry with him. Then the dog was trying to get at me so I picked up a stick to keep it away from me. Butch ran back to the house and told everyone that I was belting the dog about. Dad came down and gave me a good talking to and, no matter what I said, he wouldn't believe me. I just couldn't understand Butch telling them this as I never touched the dog even though Butch was still getting it upset. I soon learned that Butch was a mother's boy and could do nothing wrong, and he really believed that he hadn't done a thing wrong to the dog.

So I had to remain on the veranda, and no one talked to me, which made me depressed. And all this time I could hear Butch laughing and felt he was laughing at me. The next day, we began playing games – cowboys and Indians – around the big paddocks, and come lunchtime, we were told to remain around the house. We played hide and seek, and it just seemed to me that I was caught first simply because of the colour of my hair, being red/ginger. I stopped playing because the teasing had started, so I just sat back on the veranda where I could not feel any hurt.

Not long after that, I was told to chop some more wood and stack it in the wood heap. I started to protest about this, as it didn't seem right, so I went around to the back of the house to where these huge populous trees were, and I climbed to the top. I stayed there in hiding so as not to be told to chop the wood by Butch's Mum. Some time had passed before I was missed, and from my treetop lookout, I could hear and see that everyone was now becoming concerned for me and were looking all over the place. Then I could hear them talking out loud: "Why has he done this?" and when it was told that I was asked to chop the wood and stack it, Dad went wild at his sister. By now, I could see Mum getting upset and worried over what had happened to me. From this point though, I just couldn't bring myself to come down as I feared I would get a good belting.

I knew that if I just kept up the tree, I could see for miles around. Some went down to the creek; others went down to where we cut the wood, and all this because of me. By now, they were in a state, standing on the back veranda talking. Then, just as I poked my bloody red hair out from the tree, Aunty Pat, Butch's mother, noticed and yelled out, "There he is! The little bugger's up the tree!"

Dad tried to get me out, but I would not budge as I had the tremendous feeling I was in deep trouble. Then with kind words from Dad and Mum, I finally climbed to the ground, stiff and sore. Then I got a clip around the ear from Aunty Pat and a good whacking from Dad. But it was Mum who wiped away my tears and showered me with kisses and cuddles. She was always there to explain the things I should not do, and if I was smacked, she would then show me a special love and affection, which I've never forgotten.

After that, things seemed to be settled down for the rest of the holidays. Dad's mother's house had no rooms in it but was divided up into cubicles with curtains. Some nights Mum would ask me to sing some songs before we all went to bed. The one song I would sing when the tilly lamps were off, and everything was in darkness was Bless This House, O Lord We Pray, after which the lanterns were relit. But I noticed a scene of quietness, and it was only when the lights were lit that I noticed Mum with tears in her eyes.

The next day we were off to mass at the nearby mission. This is where I first sighted Aboriginals. They were working on a farm, just like Bindoon Boys Town.

We all woke up to the noise of "Merry Christmas! Merry Christmas!" and just like last time, all the presents were at the end of our beds. Tommy and I got a toy gun while Butch got a toy pistol. So for the rest of the holidays played cowboys and Indians. Then, in the late afternoon, Dad took us out to show us how to set a rabbit trap. We would pick them up the next morning. But this would soon all come to an end as one morning Dad started packing up the car. We all left for Rivervale as we were now getting ready for school.

Early 1957

Things seemed a little different at school for me. I became

friends with another boy, John Lennox, and it just appeared we were always getting into trouble of some sort – in the playground or lunch break when playing football the nuns had provided us. However, one day the football was quite flat, so John and I decided to take it to the garage and put some air in it during our lunch break. The man at the garage showed me what to do, and during the course of me putting the air into this football – along with that, I didn't understand physics – I blew the ball up into a million bits, sending bits and pieces all over the place. I couldn't believe it! One second it was in my hands; the next second, it was gone. *Shit! That was magic!* Then I started feeling bits of crap falling around and over me. Lennox was bolting back to school, and I just stood still, trying to work out what had happened. The man from the garage came over laughing at me and picking the bits up to take back to the school. I just didn't know what to say so I nodded to him, took the bits of the football from him and started to walk back to the schoolyard.

When I arrived, the class was already inside and, as I tried to sneak in, John Lennox came to the door and told me I was in big trouble and had better run away, so I grabbed a bike and, without any hesitation, headed off down the hill from the school only to find that it was a fixed wheel with no brakes. But it was now too late because I must have been doing thirty miles an hour. As I reached the bottom of the hill, I ran straight into this bloody tea-tree hedge that sent me flying through the air. I landed in a very undignified heap, only to notice the bike falling on top of me. I lay there winded, cut and frightened, but feeling *'Wow! What a ride!'* But, looking back at the bike, the wheel was bent and I knew my troubles had gone to a second level.

I decided to do a runner. With as much pain as I was in, I headed for a special place – Tomato Lake – where I could hide on the small island in the middle. And so I spent the rest of the day there. When it was discovered what I had done, Mum's neighbour suggested they look in Tomato Lake. Well, I remember when they arrived, all standing on the bank of the lake encouraging me to come back. But I would not budge. They kept assuring me that nothing was wrong, and it was only when I saw John Lennox there that I decided to swim back.

May 1957

My school reports read that 'David is receiving special attention daily, he speaks intelligently but script work is below average'. Although I was still branded a Retard, however, the reports stated 'he is progressing slowly'.

Also, on the 12th of May 1957, we were all informed that we had a new sister – Wendy Maree Darcey. I was not sure what was meant by this, but all the neighbourhood people came to see Dad, and a few days later, Mum brought my little sister home. This was the first time I had seen a baby, and I found it quite frightening at first, but soon got over it.

I was now twelve years old, and my school report reads that 'in the playground, David is quite a bully!'

I didn't understand where that would have come from, as I never, to my thinking, was a bully. But I would rather think this was to have me moved to a special school.

September 18 1957

I left St Augustan's Convent and was sent to a special school at Carlisle as the Child Welfare Department's reports read: 'David has had a lot of difficulty at school. This has made him cheeky at home and he has started a little petty thieving.'

To attend the Carlisle school, I had to travel by bus. This

was the first time I had seen money and could never understand fully why these bits of copper were so important to have a ride on a bus when previously I'd been taken everywhere without having to give anything. I very quickly learnt that these coins could be used to get anything, and I remember seeing some of them at home. Without any regard to whom they belonged, I used these coins to buy some lollies for myself and John Lennox. When I got back home, Mum became very angry with me and asked if I'd taken some money. I said 'no,' and yet it must've been obvious as the remnants of a chocolate bar was covering my mouth. That was all the evidence she needed. I just couldn't understand the problem as I'd never been told how to get them and where you got them from. But after I was given a long talking to on the things you had to do to be given money and where it came from, I understood. But I didn't understand the word 'stealing' because in the orphanage, we just took what was around for us to have, and if you wanted something, you would offer something that was just as good. But that was now going to change.

One night, John Lennox and I were playing down at the local playground. I had Maureen's bike, which she had been given for her birthday in May. At times she would let me ride it. Then John and I headed to the local fish shop. It must have been around eight o'clock when we got there. He told me to go inside and help him pinch some sweets and a bottle of coke. As I never had done this sort of thing before, I really didn't know what I was supposed to do but, like the cheeky boy I was, I walked into the shop, and John asked the man for something out the back. Then he told me to jump the counter and grab the coke bottle while he put some sweets in his pocket. I was too slow, however, and, still not sure about this pinching caper, I was halfway back over the counter when the shopkeeper started yelling at me. John grabbed the coke out of my hand and bolted for the door with me right on his heels. I only just made it, but the one thing I forgot was Maureen's bike. I looked around to see the shopkeeper take it inside and I became quite distressed. John told me to keep quiet, and I just couldn't, so I went home minus the bike. Later that night, John jumped the back fence to the shop and took the bike out of the yard. Boy, I was relieved to see it and told him I wouldn't be doing that again. He never even gave me a sweet, though we did laugh about it.

Deep inside, I was very frightened, yet I got on well with John. He always got himself into trouble, and sometimes I was with him.

It just seemed we couldn't get enough adventure as Tommy and I on Saturday went down to the rubbish tip near the Rivervale cement works, and while playing there, found this old rowing boat, which brought back some good memories of my days in the orphanage. We decided to use it to get over to Heirisson Island, about 200 yards away.

I found a piece of timber to use as a paddle and we both set off. About halfway across, Tommy started to scream that the boat was sinking and he couldn't swim. Then I, too, noticed water coming into the boat. I started to paddle like mad, then jumped into the water and, grabbing the back of the boat, pushed while I was swimming until we got to the mud bank. Tommy would not get out there, so I had to push harder till we found soily ground. He was really pleased to be back onshore again while I was covered in crap from head to toe, and he was just laughing at me.

On other Saturdays, us kids would go to the local swimming hole down at the Swan River about a mile away. Sometimes other kids were there and we all joined in the fun. But on this day, one of the boys brought a horse down, and I was asked if I'd like to ride him. Of course, I said yes! Just as I got on, the boy gave it a big slap and the bloody thing went into a wild gallop down the sandy slopes towards the river. I never had a chance to grab the strap but hung on around its neck. What a ride! This thing was a nutter, and I was hanging on for grim death when it suddenly stopped dead, sending me flying through the air. It seemed to take ages before I hit the ground. By hell, I just missed these tree roots and stumps, but it was an experience I shall never forget.

I really looked forward to the weekends as we had plenty to do and fun to have, and our playground was non-stop full of adventure. Nothing seemed to worry Mum or Dad about our day out as long as we behaved ourselves, which we always did.

On some Saturdays, we would go to Aunty Pat and Uncle Don's and play games with Butch, but most times, I would find myself singing and belting a rubbish bin lid with a stick, and all the other kids would join in behind me banging on tins. This was great fun for all of us, even for the adults.

At times Butch would come and stay with us, and it would appear that no matter where trouble was, I was not far away. One weekend Butch decided to give our next-door neighbour a surprise. He got a couple of large barker's nests [dog crap] and wrapped them up in a sheet of paper, then told me to knock on the rear door. After I did this, he placed the barker's nests on the front door mat and set fire to it, then rang the bell. We bolted for cover but not before seeing the owner open the door and slam his foot wildly onto the burning surprise parcel, leaving hot dog crap over his slippers and yelling at the dark, knowing who it was. This was done to another neighbour the following night.

But then came Guy Fawkes night! We placed ten four-penny crackers in his mailbox with all the wicks joined together. Butch lit them and we bolted for cover, turning just in time to hear this horrendous bang and see the mailbox flying through the air and landing in his own yard, bringing him out in one hell of a rage.

We all well remember the day they left our neighbourhood. We kids were out the front with little flags left over from the

Queen's visit and gave them a great cheery send-off. Apart from that, we kids got on really well with all our neighbours, but this chapter was now coming to a close.

January 1 1958

On the first of January 1958, the Child Welfare Department report read that my behaviour was good at home and that I was good at doing manual work.

Perhaps they should have made a visit to the orphanage to find out why!

During the past three months, my father had enlisted in the Royal Australian Air Force and was posted to Pearce, Western Australia. On April 10th, we left Kooyong Road Rivervale to live in Chittering Road, East Bullsbrook. I transferred school to Midland Junction, some sixteen miles away, while Maureen, Barbara and Tommy went to East Bullsbrook. Tommy later though went to the Catholic College in Midland.

Our new home had no electric lights, and the toilet was down the backyard. In the summer, the house was very hot, and in the winter very cold. Lots of planes flew over the house, which was quite exciting, and my playground was as far as we could see. Our new neighbours were also our landlord. They had four children – two boys, Max and Jeff, and two girls, Lorraine and Jennifer Broad – who became good friends to the family.

Max and I were about the same age and would quite often play together. He went to a Catholic School, and I went to the State School at Midland, but we travelled on the same bus each day. It wasn't long before we started to play up, as boys always do – there just seemed to be this little devil inside me trying to fight its way out – and I was always ready to let him go, but the bugger would always find its way back. So my mischievous adventures started again.

I can remember one older boy, a lot bigger than me, on the bus. He always wore a straw hat and went to Guilford Grammar School. Max would get off the bus before me as he was going to De La Salle College, and I would get off at Midland High School. Then, during our return trip home, Max and I would become quite boisterous. On one occasion, I jumped over a seat right on top of the straw hat, completely breaking it. When this boy stood up, I could feel his mood was not happy, so I grabbed the stop cord of the bus and bolted for the door. Once off the bus, I ran to the back and grabbed hold of the pram hooks and stayed there hanging on for my life. When I put my head up, Max saw me and quietly opened the rear door to let me in. I sat down on the floor until we got to Bullsbrook.

I was now thirteen years old and settling down in the country way of life, enjoying each weekend and having some fantastic times playing in the paddocks at the back of the house.

November 6th 1958

Child Welfare Department report:
Mr and Mrs Darcey are desirous of adoptng David, and so, on this date, the search for my natural mother began. The last known address some six years previous was 29 Redhouse Road, Ely, Cardiff.

On the 12th of November 1958, Child Welfare Department received an answer back from London. Their comments were 'that their representative in Cardiff was unable to trace a Miss Joyce Lyne to obtain adoption consent.

On the 15th of September 1958, the Catholic Migration Welfare Department received another letter from the Reverend

Father F M Poyner, who claimed he was unable to trace Joyce Lyne but was making further efforts.

It was at this point of looking through my file and childhood reports within, and looking closely at the dates of the above letters and placing them in chronological order, that the 6th of November report to the Child Welfare Department; then by some miracle unknown in 1958, the second letter dated 12th November was unable to trace Joyce Lyne. Then again, another letter on the 15th of November from F M Poyner. I know we are working with the Catholics one miracle, but what was the Child Welfare Department's good fortune in having a returned letter from Wales, taking into consideration the time to search through local records, task someone to go to the known address and follow it through. I can only conclude that the Catholics should take some miracle-making lessons from the Child Welfare Department. I can't accept that in 1958 to pass through each department of an office a request to send a letter to Wales with its request, and have an answer returned within six days and that includes the handling of one day each way in Perth, or how the Reverend F M Poyner's miracle returned within nine days, just maybe I am not facing quite EAST when asking for such miracles.

Christmas 1958 found me quite alone, although not at first, as I remember us kids exploring and creating our own adventures and enjoying each other's company very much, and nothing to be a threat to us.

December 12th 1958

Child Welfare Department School report reads that my health and behaviour was good. However, school ability was still poor, particularly reading and getting restless at school.

I can recall the restlessness I felt and remember sometimes not even turning up for school. I would instead arrive at Midland Junction and walk around aimlessly. On some occasions, I would go to the train station and watch the trains coming and going. Each time I did this, my mind drifted back to Wales, remembering this woman holding me and crying then waving to me through the window of a train. The sadness filled me up to the point of crying as I just couldn't understand what I had done to have been sent down to Australia. Though at times I didn't know who this lady was, at times I thought she was my mother.

These flashbacks were now coming into my mind each time I went to the trains. Then at times, I would walk along the tracks to see where they were going, only to be confronted with a tunnel and not having the courage to go in; I would then return. On other days, I would follow the tracks to what I now know is Perth but, on these occasions, I was chased away by the men working on the tracks. I don't know how many times I had not gone to school, and I don't know the reason why, apart from just wanting to remember that woman giving me a cuddle then waving to me through the train window.

Maureen was now twelve years old and didn't overly enjoy the frivolities us boys would get up to, but we always got along, and we liked her company. I am sure she was quite happy in mine, and on some occasions we all would walk over the hills and through the bush to her friend's farm. These particular friends were school pals from East Bullsbrook School, and this is when I met Sander Taylor for the first time.

After a little while, we would start walking back home. Maureen was abound with intelligence, which I didn't have, but I would have given anything to be able to read and write like she could. I looked up to her – a lot – but I don't know if she knew my weakness and, if she didn't or did, she really never showed it or treated me with any difference as I always listened to her. No matter what was said, she was never wrong to me, and I became a little jealous of her concerning my weakness. Yet, she was never unfriendly to me and, on some occasions, would defend me.

Barbara was now eleven years old and somewhat shy. She would never join in our games as we became too rough, apart from hopscotch which all of us quite often played. The same as for Maureen, Barbara meant the same to me. But I must confess that both Tom and I would start teasing her, and at times made her life a misery. She was soon over it, only to find the next day we would start again. 'Snarzy', which derives itself from 'the snares of the devil', would fire her temper up and provide Tom and me with unlimited entertainment. After all this though, we still got along like real mates and protected each other when needed.

The Darcey kids

Tommy, now nine years old, was a great companion, always prepared to do anything silly irrespective of the danger. Like Maureen and Barbara, Tom meant the same to me but always looked to me for support and encouragement when a situation called for it.

January 1959

Our weekends were always full of fun. During the summer, all us kids would head off to the paddocks over the back fence. Just to the west was a creek. During the winter, we'd build a dam for our summer swim, and now we were to enjoy a good couple of weeks playing and keeping cool until the water was gone. When that happened, we'd be off to start something else, even though it was now back to school for us all.

My first few months at school were quite restless for me, but my weekends were full of different adventures. Max, Jeff, Tom and I would have some fantastic times together. One of our most dangerous escapades was when we made a flying fox. Max got this large coil of wire and tied it to the base of a tree, then we rolled it out and slid a foot-long pipe down the wire. Then I, with my tree climbing skills, went up about thirty feet as the wire was some sixty feet long. After I securely tied the wire, Max, with all his might, threw the pipe up the wire for me to get hold of. Once this was done, I grabbed hold of it tight and let myself go from the tree without thinking of safety. I was flying like bats out of hell and feeling how hot the pipe was getting but was soon on the ground. What a ride! Without any time lost, I was back up the tree for a second go, followed by Max, then Tom. Jeff was next but was to wear the full brunt of the exercise as the wire snapped when he was halfway down. He landed on his back. As we ran up to see how he was, I noticed Max getting upset, and Tom thought he was dead. I also became worried when he began to gasp for air. He could not stand for a few minutes and, when we realised he was only winded, we began to laugh. Poor Jeff could not see the funny side of it and went home. We didn't see him for the next two weeks. We never did make another flying fox.

It was mainly on the bus that Max and I would start to play jokes on some of the passengers, but, more to the point, Max and I were becoming quite mischievous. I had just finished eating an apple and tied it onto a length of string. Then I crawled up and tied it onto a girl's dress where it hung down the side of the seat. I knew what I was doing was wrong, but we knew where this girl got off and took advantage for a laugh. When she started walking down the aisle, she felt this thing following her and, within a split second knew it was us two – it was written all over our faces. She grabbed the string and swung it around, dislodging the core and sending it into the front windscreen close to the driver.

This brought the second problem into the equation. Max and I looked at each other, and as nothing was said, we both bolted for the back door. The next day we were banned from the bus, so we thumbed our way to and from school. That was top fun!

The school I was going to in Midland had taken us out for nature studies and a walk around some bushland nearby to explain to us about the animals' life in our natural environment. I had really taken a deep interest in this and hungered to learn more. On one occasion, we were asked to bring a pet or animal to school, and just as my luck would have it, that weekend Barbara was walking Wendy, now two years old, on the seat of her bike, when Max and I heard this almighty scream from Barbara. She was frozen at the one spot on the road yelling out at me: "There's a snake … there's a snake!" so I grabbed the axe and ran to where this snake was. To my surprise, it was about five feet long and, with one good blow, separated its head from its body. I thought this too good to be true – it was absolutely fantastic!

Max found a shoebox, and I punched a hole in the lid and tied the head of the snake to it, and curled the rest of the snake inside the box. On Monday morning, I arrived at school, and when the time came to show our pets, the teacher, in turn, asked each kid what they had brought. As she gently emptied each box or bottle, she would expand on topics of her knowledge about them.

When it came to my shoebox, she looked at me and said, "And what do you have here, David?"

My smile was so wide I couldn't come out with the words.

As she gently opened the box, she saw the contents and gave out a piercing scream, and dropped the box and its contents to the floor. Then she bolted for the door, which in turn brought other teachers to her aid. As I was the only one laughing, and not realising the severity of the shock it must have given her, I was marched off to the principal's office and given six of the best and told to remove the snake from the classroom. This other boy – who sometimes got into trouble with me – and I walked away from the school to throw the dead snake into the bush, but in doing so, found ourselves outside Coles in the centre of Midland Junction. I thought it would be a good laugh if I just dropped the snake on the floor there.

Once the task was done, I bolted for the exit, and stood outside on the footpath. I could hear the screaming start. Then women with their kids all tried to squeeze through the doorway at the same time. I found this event more humorous than scaring the pants off my teacher! Men running around with brooms started to belt the already dead snake. Boy, I laughed so much tears started pouring out of my eyes.

About this time, Mum thought it would be good for me to join the local boy scouts, and I was introduced to our local air scout leader and accepted. I was shown lots of new things and really enjoyed the activities and the work involved, and had many pleasurable experiences. On one summer camp, we went to the Chittering Valley. We put up our tents, collected firewood and made the camp safe. That evening we were each given a spring-loaded rabbit trap. Although I knew how to use them, I had never set one by myself. I remember Dad showing me firstly to bang the stake into the ground, which I did. Then I placed my foot on the pedal to expand the jaws, only to find I was not heavy enough to expand the jaws fully so I decided to put my finger in the centre of the trap to push the trip plate into position but my lack of weight, and my wobbling knees, resulted in my thumb being caught in the jaws. I stayed there, bent over, yelling out to the other boys for help. But it took them some time before they could release me, leaving me with an extremely swollen thumb and in excruciating pain. I went to bed that night complaining about how sore it was, but my pain fell on deaf ears.

The next morning, the scout master decided to take me to the doctor at the RAAF base, about ten miles away. After a short time, I was informed that all was fine so we headed back to camp, stopping to pick two dozen eggs up from the local shop. But on our return trip, I found it difficult to hold onto the eggs and stay on the scooter. On arriving at the campsite, where the gravel was very loose, he started yelling to me to bend left. I still didn't know my left from my right, and bent the wrong way, which caused him to panic and the scooter to slip on the gravel, throwing us to the ground. When we stood up and the dust settled, although we were shaken and unhurt, we were covered in two dozen eggs and red dust. He never took me for another scooter ride, and I never asked why.

16th June 1959

Dad informed us that we had another brother, named Peter Wayne Darcey. He arrived home later that week amidst all the excitement from the neighbours.

School Holidays Mid-1959

On these holidays, Aunty Pat and Uncle Don came up to stay for the weekend with their family, and during this time, Butch and I really started to become mischievous.

Our other neighbour was the Capons – he was about fifty years old, his mother about seventy years old. Without any reason at all, this man started accusing Butch and me of stealing his tomatoes. We hadn't and came to realise that he was just a nasty person. So, later on that night, we watched him go down to the dunny in his backyard. Butch suggested we lock the old bugger in there, and without a second thought, I was over the fence, slipped the latch across and bolted back over the fence. It took about five minutes before all hell broke loose and, as the rest of the family were at the front of the house and couldn't hear him screaming out for help and his mother couldn't hear as she was 90% deaf, the more he yelled and screamed the louder both Butch and I laughed. We don't quite know how he got out that night because the one thing Butch and I were not going to do was go over to let him out.

A few nights later, Butch and I jumped the fence and took one of his big pumpkins and raced it to the back of our dunny, where we cut a Halloween face into it. Once this task was finished, we lay in wait for the old girl to go to the dunny. It was now reasonably dark when we heard her walking to the back and, though we were both laughing at what we were doing, we scaled the fence with our pumpkin head and put a lit candle inside. We left it on the footpath. When she came out of the dunny, she must've seen it quite clearly as she started to scream out for her son. The funny thing was, she could see it, but he couldn't, and running up the path, stumbled over the pumpkin head, went arse-over-tit and crashed into all his tomatoes. Without any hesitation or thought for his mother, he jumped the fence in hot pursuit of both Butch and me and chased us around our yard. Aunty Pat came to the rescue.

Picking up a bucket of water, she raced up to him and threw it all over him, saying, "That should cool you off, you old bugger!"

The both of us denied stirring him up.

Some days later, Max had introduced me to how to make 'gings' – handheld catapults. Even though Dad had shown us how to use them, he had explained the dangers involved. Max, Butch, Tom and I would wander through the bush selecting various targets to shoot at. We were all confident and understood how far these small boondies (stones)] could travel.

One day we took ourselves to a high grassed area in front of the Capon's house, laid on our backs and, with our collected ammunition, fired them onto the tin roof of his house. Listening to the noise, we laughed when our target was reached. We could hear old Capon screaming and yelling at us, but we felt quite safe in the high grass. We kept up our attack on his roof for some time, although we couldn't see or hear him towards the end. It was only when we stood up, ready to leave, that we realised he was just about on top of us. Butch and I saw him and bolted from the scene, only to look around and see Max getting kicked up the arse, which sent him flying. Old Mr Capon complained to Mum bitterly about our nuisance attacks on his house. Butch went back home with Aunty Pat the following day, and Max, Jeff, Tom and I went looking for another adventure.

Even though we had no money, we managed to repair a pushbike. This bike, with no tyres, gave us a lot of joy. We would walk it up to the top of Bullsbrook Hill, and one of us would ride it down, not knowing how or where we were going to stop it. On one occasion, I came belting down the hill and, unable to stop the bike, turned off the road into a soft sandy patch. My shin came in contact with a rusty piece of corrugated metal sticking out of the ground, severely cutting my leg to the bone. I lay there in excruciating pain with blood pouring from my leg. I had the courage to put up with the pain, but no courage to confront Mum with my injury. This was because of all the trouble we had caused in the previous week or so, and I was sure I would get no sympathy from her. However, that evening she became suspicious of my wound and was not very happy with me concealing it. I still carry that scar today as a reminder of that ride.

June 27 1958

My Child Welfare Departments School Report reads: "David has been stealing again, money and cigarettes both from home and neighbour. Was given a good hiding after last episode and no evidence of stealing since. David denied guilt until found with positive proof."

Our next-door neighbour, Mr Broad, had lots of interests. He was the local East Bullsbrook School bus driver, and his hobby was showing motion pictures each Saturday night. I remember lying in bed with Tom, looking through the opened louvres watching the pictures when he started yelling at us for watching without paying our ten pence. We both got angry with him, so after the pictures were over, I snuck over there and pinched a hot bottle of soft drink. When I finally got the bottle opened, and after my first swig, he appeared at the door. I was completely cornered with him blocking the exit. No words were said, but he grabbed me by the arm and proceeded to kick me up the arse for what seemed to be several hundred times. He just wouldn't stop until he knew I was hurt, which I was. Black and blue, I crawled off back to bed only to be confronted by him the next morning telling Mum and Dad what I had done. Over the next few weeks, I tried to stay out of his way but it became more difficult because this man was our landlord, and one thing was for sure, this man had never liked me. The final straw came when I was sitting in the yard with his son, Jeff, playing with his toys, when, for no reason, he started kicking me in the back, then the buttocks. I tried to get up but he would kick me down and no matter which way I moved, he kept kicking. As I got on all fours, he continued to kick me up the arse. I was like a dog trying to run away, but he kept his attack going until I managed to get into our yard. I could never understand why he treated me so differently. Then he stopped Max and Jeff from having any association with me whatsoever and made me resentful towards him.

At the end of the holidays, I was sent to Governor Stirling Senior High School, Midland Junction. At this school, I was teased and harassed, making my school life hell. I just couldn't fit in anywhere. No one talked to me apart from some of my classroom students, but overall little was done for me to join in the activities the others were involved in. Nevertheless, some parts of schooling I really enjoyed, like woodwork and metalwork, but mostly I frequently ran away from school. Most times, I felt an oddity and unable to fit in; I was quite often teased and humiliated due to my school work being behind – though I had come a long way and understood the reasons for being there was for my development in school work.

During the next school holidays, Maureen and Barbara were sent to Aunty Pat's, and Mr Broad asked if Tommy could go with Max and Jeff to his farm at Moora. I was not invited, and I didn't ask why.

In the following weeks, I became quite lonely and depressed, although Mum quite often kept me occupied by getting firewood from the bush and then raking the honky-nuts from the backyard. I was always given various tasks to do and never complained, but it just seemed, on this occasion, I was not happy doing any of the work and would find myself sitting in our backyard in an old bus wreck that belonged to Mr Broad. While sitting there alone, my mind would constantly drift back to my early childhood thoughts of that woman who gave me Teddy Bear chocolates, and I would find myself crying for her and wanting to be back in the orphanage again.

Most times, I felt this might be the only way this woman would be able to find me. This made me very moody and unhappy and uncaring about the work I had to do or what anyone had to say to me. I don't know how long I was in these moods, but I had lost interest in everything around me. I had nothing, yet I wanted for nothing but this one thought of this woman who was on my mind. I never told anyone about my thoughts and my deep feelings because I just might lose what little I had.

I was told some time back that I was from Britain, and I understood it was far away but could not understand what I was doing here. I would sit in this bus on many occasions and withdraw into myself, thinking of this woman.

When my sisters arrived back from holidays, I took little interest in them and like-wise when Tommy, Max and Jeff arrived. We all seemed different and didn't mix much over the next few months. Then, on the next school holidays, Tommy was asked to go to the farm again, and mother said no as she understood what his game was. It didn't bother me about Tommy going, only the manner in which it was being done and why.

While in the bus wreck, drifting from thought to thought, Mum was so pleased for Tommy and mentioned that Mr Broad might take me on the next holidays. I never answered as I already knew he wouldn't.

July 29th 1959

The Child Welfare Department had written a letter to the Catholic Migrant Centre asking whether they'd had any information on the whereabouts of a Miss Joyce Lyne as the Darceys were awaiting adoption consent.

I became deeply depressed and again more withdrawn, not taking notice and causing a lot of disruption within the Darcey household. I remember Dad coming into the bathroom to give me a belting for something I'd said, though when he started to give me the second whack, I fought back. When I pushed him into the asbestos wall, breaking the sheet, he stopped his attack on me. I ran out to the backyard into the pitch black of the evening.

It must've been seen by now that I was becoming disruptive, and it was then, on July 15th 1959, I was sent to Bindoon Boys Town for two weeks' holiday.

On arrival, I was shown around with Mum and Dad. When they left, I went with the other boys to the olive grove, where we spent many hours picking olives. I now felt equal with everyone and what we did. Over this holiday break, we would play football without any boots, and most of us had severe foot and toe injuries. I never enjoyed football – I just didn't see what the big deal was about, and I am still of the same views today. Yet I could never recall any hostilities between us, and I also felt we all had something in common.

Part Three

Bindoon Boys Town

September 1st 1959

The Child Welfare Department received a letter from the London office advising that Father Poyner, who was in charge of the Catholic Rescue Society in Cardiff, had not been successful in tracing the whereabouts of Miss Joyce Lyne. He had enquired from every possible source, and they could not think of any other line of enquiry that might lead to results.

A letter from the Catholic Child Welfare Council, London to the Catholic Migrant Centre, Perth, stated that the Reverend Canon Flood had written to the Reverend Father Poyner to trace Miss Joyce Lyne, but to no avail. However, he was making further efforts and will let you know of any further developments.

My records and corresponding dates have once again shown an overlapping of information. What sort of conspiracy was hidden here? I could only conclude again that the Child Welfare Department CRYSTAL BALL was working overtime, as the miracle of knowing the answer before the question was asked was amazing! What was the advantage to them for keeping me locked into the system? What was the divine truth? After all, my natural mother had signed papers to relieve her of any responsibility and further contact with me, then why was the system that was set up to place us into a secure home environment, to give us the best our childhood could offer, holding me back and preventing my foster parents from adopting me, as they had so long ago requested from the Department of Child Welfare.

I wasn't given a good kick start with my education from the Welsh and Australian System; now it still appeared I was an asset like the rest of us were brought here for the financial benefit of the Catholics – until we became a financial liability, then we ended up being kicked out of the orphanage with little or no skills, and unable to read or write. The very basic start to life had been denied me and possibly a lot more.

I returned to Mum and Dad after the holidays, but arrangements were made for me to return to Bindoon. Upon arriving, I was informed that I would be staying with them for some time and given schooling and farm duties.

My first job on arriving was milking the cows, and the time I had to start was 4.30 am each day. I had no clock or sense of time, so one of the other boys would wake me. I was very happy to do this and felt proud to have been asked as it showed that I had something none of the other kids at those schools I went to could do. Now I felt some point of belonging and was appreciated for those things I could do.

I found my way to the milking shed, as in the early morning I could just see this light and hear the power plant working. Even though the track down was rough and littered with loose stones like marbles, I wasn't going to be late even though it was about half a mile from the main buildings. Once there, I moved all the cows into their milking cages and started placing feed to help relax them. Then I would wash the teats and placed on the sucker heads and continued this until all was completed, releasing each group to the paddocks after each stage. Then with a 10-gallon milk container placed on a steel-wheeled trolley, I headed back up the track pulling the trolley behind me. This was really hard work as I had to keep an eye on the milk container as it would start to move all over the place due to the stones, making this trip up the hill more difficult. When I finally got to the kitchen, I sat back to get my wind, only to notice it was just after 6 am and I had to be cleaned up and in line for breakfast by 6.30 am. I would just make the end of the line.

Our standard breakfast was hot milk and bread, sometimes orange or apple juice and hot tea. Then after breakfast, we were off to morning mass which finished at 7.15 am. Then it was back to the dormitories to make beds and clean and sweep our area and, by 7.45, we were in the school rooms. This was how things were going to be, or at least that's what I thought until the next day.

Just like yesterday, I was woken up and headed towards the milking shed and carried on my duties like the previous day. Pulling the trolley up the hill, I left it in the kitchen. Then I cleaned up for breakfast and was confronted by Brother Doyle. He grabbed me by the ear, pulling as hard as he could and said that I'd been drinking the milk. He also said it had happened the previous day. All the while, he had hold of my ear and was dragging me towards his room [office]. Then he laid into me with this black leather strap. He was twice my size, and I felt every blow he levelled at me, not stopping for a moment. I became so weak I just couldn't find any strength to defend myself. And he kept on going, sending one blow after another without slowing down, his belt slashing into my body. I just lay there while he continued, not even trying to protect myself. Then, without any reason, he stopped and told me to get ready for school.

I tried to turn over on the floor to get up from all fours but fell on my side. I was bleeding from various places, and the floor had my blood on it, making it more difficult for me. But slowly, I got to my feet, quite shaken and in pain, and limped back to the dormitories and tried to clean myself up. Some of the other boys were there but stayed out of my way.

Though I was cut about and thoroughly sore, I made my way to the classroom where he was also my teacher, and sat there looking at him. In all the years I had spent at Castledare, he was now teaching me how to do the things he should have taught me years before. In my mind, he wasn't any good to me, then I mentally questioned the reason for the belting … what was it for?! I hadn't done a thing to bring it on – I never drank any milk; in fact, it had never dawned on me to do such a thing.

For the rest of the day, I just looked at him with a growing anger towards him.

The next day, as sore as I was, I went down to the milk shed and started my work, and for the first time, one of the boys started talking to me.

"Doyle give it to you?"

"Yes."

"He said you were drinking the milk?"

"Yes."

"You know you're going to get it again today because that is what he does ... so you'd better get a big belly of milk as you're going to get a belting for it anyway."

After finishing milking, these boys came in and took a big mug of milk and filled the container up with water, and I just stood there laughing.

"Remember, you're going to get it anyway," one of the boys said.

I started pulling the trolley up the hill towards the kitchen, and like yesterday, left to clean up for breakfast. As expected, he was waiting for me at the mess hall door, and this time I was not frightened of him, but more so let him think so. Pulling on my ear, he dragged me back to his room and started laying into me just like the previous day. The pain was twice as bad due to one beating on top of the other. This time my bleeding was all about the place, and the level of treatment no different as I was left to clean up and again go to the classroom. I was unable to sit still in one place for long.

Although I remained on milking duties for another week, I never received any more beltings, but each day the other boys at the shed and I would drink the milk and eat raw eggs, followed by large portions of molasses.

After that, I was put on boiler duties, and during the nights,

I would lay awake, too frightened to sleep as I had to be up at 4.30 am, and there was no one to wake me for this duty. During these nights, I could hear crying coming from other beds within my dormitory. On most occasions, the boy next to me started to cry also and around the same time each night, this would bring the Brother in, and he would start belting the bed with his strap and telling the boys to shut up. Not long after he was gone, it would start again but more a whimpering, then silence at last. Then the birds would start to sing, which was my time to get up, and not long after, the boy next to my bed was up as well, as he was doing something in the laundry. I noticed that everything he did was at double-time: he would walk real fast and moved around picking up sheets and whatever else needed washing. He would run down the stairs and be filling two buckets at a time. The boy was a mess for reasons unknown to me. I just stuck to my thing and that way I was to blame for my ways.

My mind was always blank, except for the task at hand and my next day's duties. I could still recall from my Castledare days and asking God for a helping hand – well, forget that now as what we were all facing was the reality of our future. This was the last stop for our moulding, and what turned out was looked over. Then, if no cracks appeared, it could be kept while the rest was forgotten about.

I was now starting to wet my bed again, sometimes twice a night, as I was too frightened to go to the toilet. The boy in the bed next to mine had the task of packing up into bundles all the wet sheets and take them to the laundry where the nuns would wash them once the water was hot – and that could only happen when I was up to light the boiler. So this was the way it was with our duties, changing from job to job throughout the months.

The boy who slept in the bed next to me was very good at sums, and we started talking about why I just couldn't understand them, so over a period of time we would, in the mornings, go to the boiler room as it was quite warm and the nuns didn't mind as they really kept to themselves. The only time I ever remember seeing them was at mass, which was twice a day, though I later saw them in the kitchen. Anyway, this boy started to show me the very basic sum, and over time, I was able to understand and work through all the little sums he left as a note in the boiler room. Each morning I would go and try and do them, and in turn, he left the answers for me.

Then one day, without warning, we had an exam. Brother Doyle was the teacher. Without any trouble, I filled in the questions and sat back as he came up to me and looked at the completed paper. He gave me a closed fist to the face that sent stars and flashing blue and red lights through my head as I fell backwards to the floor. He yelled out that I was cheating.

I didn't know what I had done as he started dragging me up to the front of the class. I could see this boy who'd helped me nearly in tears. When I looked at him, I swung my head from side to side to let him know that I had at least got them right. This Brother couldn't do for me what this boy had done in half the time. But I was beginning to get upset over all these beltings, and for what? I just couldn't understand. *Why? Why? Why?!*

This boy and I were close friends now, and I kept learning from him over the next few months. Even today, as a man, I still recall him, and I don't even know his name. Like most of us, I have no childhood names from all the years I have been with the orphanage. I can only recall two, but I well remember this boy as each morning we both went to the boiler room and he taught me algebra. I knew he was the right person to show me how to do these sums, as in the classroom, he would always have the right answer. Just because the Brother had no time for me, and others like me, I wasn't going to be left behind, and for some reason, I was not going to let this Brother win. By hell, the more he belted me, the stronger I became towards it, for I was working like a man and treated like a child.

Sometimes I would look at things in my past and find nothing but childish fun, and growing as a child should be about stuffing up — it is part of it, and if I didn't, I would have been sent to the Nut-house to find out why?

And so I was now looking forward to everything I couldn't do and enjoying everything I wouldn't do!

On most Saturdays, us boys were sent out to the paddocks to help clear the land of trees and place them into wind-rows for summer burning. As small as we all were, though, we could work hard, and this would be my turning point while staying there because I was now developing and could feel my body changing. We were given axes and spent the full day chopping branches off while others would remove them to the heap. We changed around in the afternoon, and I would be pushing these large logs along with other boys only to have them swing back, throwing me to the ground. I constantly feared being trapped under these huge tree trunks and would always fight back with inner strength until our day was done. That was around sunset when we arrived back at Boys Town! After the evening meal, we would have to go to evening Benediction.

Sundays were about prayer, and I just couldn't get any interest in it — wasn't it the Roman Catholics that nailed their boss to a cross? — so I was not going to join up for that mob. Especially when what he did wasn't much different to our situation, being kicked and belted at will to give them control over the likes of God's children. What a joke this was! And my mind is still the same, even though mother would love me to go to church with her … I just couldn't come to terms with it.

On some weekends, Mum and Dad would come and take me home to their place. I was always welcomed and had a good time, but it was on one of these weekends that I tried to sneak a packet of cigarettes back to the orphanage, only to be found out.

For my troubles, I was once again given the most common sort of punishment, and that was to do the twelve commandments. This was the major sort of punishment that was given out as the Brothers could watch you from their shaded verandas while we would kneel at each station on the gravel track to complete one decker of the rosary until we completed the full twelve stations. By this time, you felt every stone from start to finish, and I still have the scars to prove and remind me, and at times wonder if that in itself was to keep me on the straight and narrow road!

Bindoon Boys Town was situated some eighty miles north of Perth on the Great Northern Highway, the last three miles or so a gravel road that winds to a very pretty valley. The road descends, and to your right stands the stations of the cross. Every boy that has been through there will well remember, in my thinking, no boy would have done the full stations during his time under the tender care of the Christian Brothers. If for some reason you didn't have the pleasure, then you must have just passed through on the same day, as had happened on my first visit, which was Brother Keaney's funeral – a special day.

I was now accustomed to any sort of punishment as it was dealt out for every small thing. For example, I failed to kick a goal due to having no boots and fearing cutting my feet as I had before, so I copped it for the non-performance at football. I was punished swiftly but wouldn't complain as I always felt the belt no matter what. But, my feet were okay, and that to me was more important than a sore arse or strap welts.

I was now fourteen years old and with a deep resentment of being at Bindoon Boys Town. The beatings and punishment were never far away, and it seemed we all lived with that constant threat on our minds. On several occasions, some other boys and I discussed running away. When the agreement was made to leave after dark and for us to go to Mum and Dad's, on each occasion, we would sneak out of the orphanage and follow the dirt road to the Great Northern Highway, only to find ourselves returning because we were too cold and wet as our clothing was shorts, sandals and a tee-shirt.

On some Saturday nights, if there was no rain and on returning from spending a full day rolling tree trunks into heaps, we were informed that a movie would be shown after tea and evening mass. We would scramble up a flight of stairs to the rooftop of our dormitory.

On one occasion, just as I reached the top stairs, this big Brother grabbed me by the ear and literally dragged me out of the queue. I was pushed aside with a group of other boys. When everyone was seated, we were placed in the second last row with our backs to the screen, while the Brothers sat in the last row looking at us and the picture screen. This sort of punishment was quite often given out and, for reasons I could never understand, as I was becoming older, I could feel the mental cruelty associated with it. On this particular night, when everybody was laughing, I turned my head slightly to see why. A closed fist slammed into my left ear and cheek, sending me and the chair I was sitting on flying backwards, leaving me dazed and confused. A half a minute must have passed when I heard him telling me to get up.

With the full strength of my temper, greater than I had ever known, I picked up the chair by the seat with both hands and slammed it down all my strength over the Brother's head and shoulder. Then I slammed the legs of the chair into his face.

At that time, I could feel blood running down my face from my ear and head and started tasting blood in my mouth. The other brothers tried to stop me, but I ran straight to the front of the two-storey building and, without fear, slid down the drainpipe. There was no noise from the boys that I can remember, only the overriding voices of the Brothers. I ran and ran as I'd had enough of this treatment, both mental and physical. I kept heading towards the bush and feeling hopelessly lost. When there was no sound of anyone following, I sat down and fell asleep. The next thing I remember was the sun on my face.

When I stood up I couldn't hear a thing as my ear was full of dried blood and my cheek was swollen. I started to walk into the sun and sometime later could see the buildings of Boys Town in the distance. I didn't know what to do or what would happen to me, but I knew I could hide in the cowshed, and I remained hidden there for the rest of the day in the haystack where I could eat raw eggs and molasses.

After some time, I felt I should go and talk to the sisters as my first experience at Castledare with the nuns never seemed hostile or unfriendly. I made my way over to them as their buildings were some two hundred yards from the main buildings. Upon arriving, I was given a wash around my hair and ear. I told them I was too frightened to go back, so they took me to the priest where I again told my story. As I stood there, I began to tremble and then wet myself. I told him I didn't want to be hit anymore as I always do my work. He took me over the Brothers' rooms, and they began to talk about me, but I couldn't hear what about. After that, I was given twice as much to do, but the beltings were less over this time.

Each Saturday during the summer months, we would be given the job of polishing all the terrazzo floors in the main building entrance. This work was very hard and very slow as each section first had to be rubbed with tin oxide, then followed with tin oxide, and each stage would bring the surface to a shine. The work took time but I would get satisfaction as we were most of the time left alone. Then one Saturday, this Brother had started to make an appearance and start becoming abusive towards one of the boys. This particular boy could not speak much English, and I later learned he was from Malta. I could never understand why this Brother was always nasty; he must have known we had a pitiful existence as it was. His pleasure was to boot us up the backside while we were on all fours scrubbing the floor. When he left, we would do our work at twice the pace just to get it over with.

On this particular occasion, while working at this pace, the Malta boy slipped and fell to the next level. I heard the thud, but he didn't speak to us as he couldn't understand much other than when shown what he needed to. I thought he was going to pick up more water, or something work-related when I heard a lot of commotion. We were asked to leave our work area and go to the playground.

A couple of days later, we learnt he'd died from his fall.

Soon after, I was relieved of terrazzo floor cleaning and sent to pig-feeding duties. I don't remember any schooling after my chair-throwing exercise but was given more work around the farming side of the orphanage. During this time, I'd seen more types of green vegetables than ever before, and on all occasions that we spent working at the piggery, chicken coop and the milk shed, we would devour them.

The boiler we used to cook the pig's-swill was emptied each day. I would crawl inside and lay loaves of bread out over the bottom, then place beans on top of the bread, then wheat grain, apples, tomatoes and then more bread. The lid was then tightly closed and water was poured in. We would then light this huge pressure cooker and leave it for some hours. We spent the rest of our time cleaning the pig pens and the milking shed and the outside surrounds of the barn. Once the cooking was finished, we would help ourselves to the tucker, not caring whether the pigs had enough but just thinking of ourselves. This was soon to stop for me as the last time I went to open the cooker, I got a steam burn to my chest, legs and crutch, as I hadn't let all the pressure out of the cooker. The other boys told me to put some molasses on my crutch and legs as the skin had really red welts and small blisters.

That evening, like all other evenings, shower times was in large groups, and always with our heads bowed so not to look at any other person within the shower room. This, we were always told, was to deny the devil ways, and I just couldn't understand fully what was meant by this even though I had been at the orphanage most of my life. On this occasion, I was told to wait outside in the cold, completely in the nude, and when all the others were finished, this big Brother set himself upon me with his black belt, saying I should not masturbate. I never understood what he was talking about but just stood there as he continued to lay his belt over me. Then he stopped and told me to dress and go to Father and confess my sin.

Crying and hurt as the belting was again over my scolding burn, how could I confess to something I hadn't any idea what it was about? I was told by the priest that we should not conceive to the devil's wishes but was never asked how I had these red welts over my chest and crutch. Then again, if I had told him, I still would have been given the same treatment as handed out to me now.

So, over the next few weeks, my work varied from cow milking to pig feeding. I had become even more withdrawn and disinterested in all around me – it just seemed now that I really wanted to get out of this place. I was most aware of the Brothers and always tried to avoid them by making myself look busy at doing nothing. I always tried to have a broom or spade nearby to grab just so I wouldn't be asked to do other work, as by now I understood that if I was doing something, they would think another Brother had told me to do it. I kept this situation going for as long as I could get away with it.

I felt we were an embarrassment as we were all put out of sight when visitors came to Bindoon over the weekends to look around. I also can never recall bonding with any boy, not even knowing a name, and as a sixty-year-old man, I can't remember a single one of them. And I should think it would be the same for the rest of the boys that have passed through its gates. I always felt alone, which only made me bitter, like the rest of the boys. I remember trying to get a smile or a sound from them. But nothing. I really do not think it was me, but the way we were handled and worked, and most of all, being robbed of our childhood. I could only thank them for getting me ready for hardworking labour as they failed to provide me with anything academically.

I was to leave Bindoon Boys Town and was sent to Perth for an ability test, the results of which were forwarded to Mum and Dad Darcey. It read that the only skill I was good at was glass blowing! When I was told this, I was totally dumbfounded as to how they reached this conclusion. I always felt I had a greater expectation of myself, even though I couldn't read very well and do sums, I knew how much I wanted to be able to. And I would often wonder if this was the same for the other boys as none of us ever talked about it. Thinking back, I believe there were more boys doing manual labour than were in the classrooms.

June 25th 1960

This was the day I left Bindoon Boys Town for good and returned to the shelter of the Darcey family. It took me a little time to settle that day as I was still quite frightened of adults, and knowing Mr Broad was next door didn't make things any easy for me.

Part Four

Back Home with the Darceys

June 26th 1960

In Wales, at this time, my half-brother, Philip John Pearcey, was born and was living at 36 Alexander Road, Canton, Cardiff.

I always remember how it was at home during those winter months. We would all sit around the kitchen fire to keep warm by the stove. Mum would sometimes play the accordion, and we would sing along. On other occasions, Mum would read the paper to me and explain what the words were, and once again, I slowly started to read again. Dad explained how to do sums, and I found no threat in this way of learning. Any chance spare time I had, I would read the newspaper and do the sums Dad had left me before going to work.

So this was going to be my basic education, and my working life had already been set for me, with great thanks. To all the Brothers, I can only say thanks for nothing but the mental scars and mental cruelty.

Over the following weeks, we boys started to build a treehouse in the bush, where we could hide while having a smoke. Then we would head off to the creek to build our dams for the summer swimming. At times we would go fishing for yabbies, using nets we made from hessian and wire, though we never caught many. We did, however, have lots of fun and gained much pleasure from it.

I was now fifteen years old and working very hard at whatever was offered to me by Mum and Dad around the house. It wasn't long after that we drove up to Chittering Valley and helped pick oranges for various farmers. Although the pay was crap, we had a lot of fun.

Some weekends, Butch and his friend Sid would arrive to stay. On these occasions, Dad took us out shooting kangaroos and rabbits, which were cooked up the next day into a curry, which Dad always loved to make. We all enjoyed it though it would make the sweat pour out of our faces.

On some Saturday nights, there was a dance held in East Bullsbrook. It seemed everyone in Chittering was there, and when, at times, a new dance started, like the stomp, the whole building became one big dust bowl. Mr Picket would try to prevent this dance by stopping the music, but we just kept stomping and slamming our feet to the floor. The faster they played, the harder we slammed our feet until Mr Picket got so mad at us that he stopped the dance before the building collapsed. When things were still settling down, Sid, Butch and I placed some stink bombs under the seats, and this was the humorous part of the night as everyone started to blame each other for the bad smells. Mr Picket would fly around trying to open the windows, only to find we had also removed the long pole used to unlatch them. We had lots of fun at these dances but more so as both Sid and Butch started to notice girls.

Butch and Sid were now working, Butch as an apprentice sheet metal worker and Sid … I wasn't sure what he was doing. As for me, I was leaving school in July one month before my birthday and was taken on at a local farm called Darling Downs about three miles south of East Bullsbrook. It was owned by two brothers with small families. My wage for six days work was £3 per week. For this, I only had to pick up rocks and put them into big heaps, all by hand, over this large paddock. These piles are still visible from the Great Northern Highway just past the Walyunga National Park road entrance. Although the work required much walking as I had no wheelbarrow, I just kept at it. The farmer would come out every three or so hours to see how I was going and give me food and water.

I asked him, "When do I finish my day's work?"

He looked at me and stretched out his arm to the west.

"When the sun hits the horizon."

"What time do I start?"

Again he said, pointing to the east, "When the sun hits the horizon."

So after my short break, I continued this work and he would bring food and water to me. I was never under stress to work harder as the ground was very soft as it had not long being ploughed. Over the full week, in rain and all, I arrived and worked as he wanted, then left at sunset. Come Saturday, he handed me £3, which I hadn't seen the likes of before.

"Look after it," he said, "and be back Monday to do the same job. You should be completed by the weekend."

These farmers were very kind and without rage; they treated me like a man and didn't talk down to me, and I enjoyed my work while it lasted with them.

On some occasions, I would be asked to help out rounding sheep for dipping, and other times, help repair fencing. This type of work was offered by some of the other farmers up the valley, but nothing lasted for more than two weeks.

Other weekends, we would all drive to Leederville, just outside Perth, to see Uncle Don and Aunty Pat. They had a very big house and looked after elderly people. During Uncle Don's spare time, he built a boat in his shed, which I used to look at each time I went there. He was very good with his hands as before this project he had made plaster models of various things. Now they lived in this big house with some twelve rooms and looked after these old people. At the back of the house was a sign he had put up. It read: 'Dunrooting-home-for-old-ladies', which would bring a smile to anyone's face that visited him.

Butch was now in a gymnastic club and would often show us what he had learnt. It was there we got up to more mischief, as his cousin John Stocker would also be there. The three of us would set off down to the local football match, and any time the ball went out of bounds, Butch or John would grab it and bolt from the area, causing the boundary umpire to give chase down the road until they were caught, or dropped the ball before he got there.

January 15th 1961

I started my apprenticeship as a painter with a Mr Riddahoff for £5 for five and half days' work. I was really looking forward to this as I gained a lot of satisfaction from painting. I was to work at the RAAF base painting the hangars inside and outside. After two weeks I hadn't received my wages, so I asked him for them. This carried on for a month, so I asked my Dad to talk to him. After this, I was given small amounts he had in his pocket, even though I was the first one on the job and always the last to leave. And I worked all day on Saturdays. And once again, I complained to Dad that I wasn't getting my wages, so Dad contacted the apprentice board to complain on my behalf. The whole time I had worked for him, I never received a full week's wage, so I stopped working Saturdays and arrived at work without any interest in flogging my guts out for him. Instead, I spent time with Mum and Dad as they would go down to see Uncle Don and Aunty Pat.

On one occasion, Butch showed me the things he was making at work. One thing I shall never forget was a gymnastic see-saw. I recall him saying, "Come on, Dave ... aver go!" and he explained what I had to do. I started to jump and let all my weight fall hard onto the plank while Butch stood on the other end, the effect shooting him upward. After a few times, we were getting pretty good, and it provided us with a lot of entertainment ... until we wanted to gain a much bigger thrill.

To get more height, I decided to climb onto the roof of the

shed some ten feet high and, without any fear, jumped down onto the plank, catapulting Butch skyward into a somersault. Upon his return to his end of the upraised plank, I began to laugh as I was only half prepared. When his whole weight slammed down onto the plank, I was catapulted skywards, still totally unprepared. Although I'd taken the impact of him hitting the plank, my position didn't allow me to complete a full somersault, sending me down hands first. I came in contact with the upraised plank, spraining both my wrists and hitting my jaw. The sudden pain became overpowering, and when I stood up, both my hands were just dangling.

Dad came out of the house to see what the commotion was and, after calling us a silly pair of buggers, marched me off down to the doctors. From there, I was taken to Perth Hospital. The last thing I heard from Butch was: "There won't be any wanking for you for a while, Dave."

While the nurse was putting the plaster on both my wrists, I began to complain severely: "What am I going to do? These are my prime wanking years!"

Again Butch said, "There'll be no wanking for you for a while, Dave," and the nurse began to laugh with us. I left Perth Hospital, and we arrived back at Uncle Don's then headed back to Bullsbrook.

The next morning Dad had already gone to work; Maureen and Barbara were ready for school when I realised I'd better let my boss know that I wouldn't be at work for a while. So, grabbing my bike, I started to pedal my way over to the Base with both wrists in plaster. To rest my arms, I decided to slip the handlebars inside the cast. I was belting along fast when I found that I couldn't control the bloody bike – it had started to have a mind of its own. As I left the main road to take the track we all used, I realised it was out of control, and I ended up kissing this 'black boy' tree headfirst. It sent me and the bloody bike to the ground hard, and I lay there winded and somewhat sore around the neck.

I have no idea how long I had been there, but my old mate Max found me and asked me what I was up to.

I just said, "I feel like a dingo's donger, mate."

After picking me up, we walked off to the RAAF. Dad was informed that I was being sent to Perth Hospital with a dislocated shoulder. I understand he became cranky with me. But he'd cooled down by the time he picked me up that afternoon.

The same nurse that had looked after me the previous day looked after me this time. When she asked me what had happened, I looked at her and said, "Just a case of over-wanking, bush style."

April 2nd 1961

After all my bones were healed, I was given another job as a painter in South Perth. I was to board with an old family friend of the Darcey's in Rivervale, a Mrs Ryan. My wages were £5 17 shillings and 4 pence for five and half day's work. Paying £3 for board, £1/1 shilling for bus fares, left me with 16 shillings and 4 pence for the local dance at Bullsbrook and my travel back to Mrs Ryan. While staying at Mrs Ryan's, my old friend John Lennox came to see me.

He also came to Bullsbrook for the dancing, which was always good fun over the weekends.

Although John was bigger than me, we had things in common and always found something to talk about. He kept me interested in them as well – his family came from Scotland some years before. He could remember things from his old hometown that I had since forgotten, though I still remember the time we shared together. Then the subject came up about running away again as some time back he had said the same thing.

I asked him, "Where would we run to?"

"Kalgoorlie," he said.

To this day, I have no idea why but I left with John for Kalgoorlie, without any reason for going nor without knowing what to expect when we got there. I didn't know how far or how long this would be as I never asked him. So off we both went down the road, me with around twelve shillings in my pocket. Before long, we were picked up and dropped off at Midland, then after a short walk, we had another lift to Northam. Even though it was about three or four in the afternoon, it was not long before we were travelling again, only to be dropped off at Baandee where we stayed in the football ground change rooms. Though cold and hungry, at least we were dry.

The following day we found an old Gladstone bag, and I found a big overcoat that kept me warm as we headed off again towards the main highway. Not long after reaching the highway, a car with three people inside stopped and asked where we were going. John told them. They were about John's age but quite rough-looking. Not that that was a worry, but the drinking was. I had never had anything to do with it even at home, nor at the dancing at Bullsbrook. On occasion, the boys would have a bottle to share around, but I was never interested in it. Mum and Dad had talked about booze and the trouble it caused. Yet these men had one laugh after another as the bottle was handed around. Then one of them said, "Don't knock it until you try it," so with that, I took my first swig. I didn't enjoy it as much as John.

Before long, we reached Southern Cross, and these blokes were off, laughing into the distance.

John looked at me and said he was getting some food, so I gave him the money I had. At this point, I noticed a policeman and recalled my last running away from Castaldare. He walked towards me and asked me where I was going.

I replied, "Kalgoorlie."

"What is your name?" he asked.

"David Lyne," I said.

"And who is that you are with?"

"John Lennox."

Right then, John came out of the shop and, noticing the policeman, turned and bolted. A very large hand clamped down on my shoulder as the policeman said, "Better you come along with me, son." And off I went with him.

It wasn't long before John and I were together again, but this time in a cell.

June 11th 1961

Southern Cross is 370 kilometres east of Perth. Although we arrived late in the morning, it was still quite cold, and we'd little to nothing to eat or drink. And now we were taken down to the Police station for reasons I had no idea of.

At the interview, we were asked about the coat I wore, and the pliers John had – I still couldn't understand what we'd done as these items had been lying on the ground outside the football change room and just didn't seem to belong to anyone. But that was not the case. We were both charged with stealing and sent back to the lock-up. The policeman's wife brought in the biggest meal I had ever seen and started to talk to us about the trouble it was going to cause our parents.

I thought hard and long about her words, and I really knew I'd done the wrong thing running away and now being locked up for stealing.

The next morning after going to court, we were driven back

to Perth and put in the lock-up for boys at Mt Lawley. What a place! The other boys there didn't give a damn about anything or anyone and were totally of control, yelling and screaming at the warders. When told to keep quiet, the swearing and screaming got louder and louder.

I was not very happy about being there as this was something I had never experienced, not even at the worst events of my orphanage life. This was the big, bad house. I was to spend nearly two weeks there.

Then Mum and Dad took me home, and I shall never forgive myself for the trouble I put them through.

Part Five

My Working Life

September 29th 1961

Of course, I lost my job and any further chance of painting, so once more I was given odd jobs around the local farms; I painted a house for an old friend, then went off picking oranges for anyone who needed a labourer for the day. Then a chance came up for me to work at Katanning, 360 kilometres from Perth. I had to travel there by train but didn't know who was to pick me up. All I knew was I was going out to a farm for fencing work.

Upon arriving at the station, I sat down to wait for the person to pick me up and tried hard to stay awake, as I didn't want to look bad and lazy. At about dawn, after waiting some two hours, a man came up and gruffly asked my name. I answered him as I rose to introduce myself.

He just said, "Follow me."

I arrived at his ute, in which sat a lady. He placed my case in the back and told me to get in the front with the lady. I was very cold and had grown numb sitting at the station for so long but, once inside the ute, I started to warm up again.

When we arrived at this house, which was just out of town, he said, "Grab your gear," and pointed to a shed. "That's your hut for sleeping in."

I went over and opened the door only to find a dirt floor and a bed without a mattress. Though the sun was still rising, I could just see the inside of my sleeping quarters. Then I heard him yelling for me to help feed the pigs, so I grabbed the two buckets of swill and started walking down about twenty-five yards from my hut to the pigpen. The trough sat next to the wire fence, and as I bent over the wire, I was given this almighty shock that threw me to the ground, the swill spilling over me. I regained my feet, not knowing what had happened, but did the very same thing again, only now this man was laughing at me. Then he started to yell and scream at me for spilling the pig food. I soon realised I'd received an electric shock from the wire fence around the pigpen, and I wasn't too happy about it. But I kept my cool.

After that event, we travelled towards Tambellup and it was difficult to stay awake. My head kept falling against the lady's shoulder, only to have her nudge me off. We travelled for about sixty miles into the heart of the Wheatbelt and arrived at a campsite that had one caravan, a large tent to one side and a smaller tent just out from a water tank. As I climbed out of the ute, he said, "That's your tent for sleeping, and don't waste the water. Wash once a week." As he was talking to me, the lady – I am not sure if they were married – drove away in the ute.

I was taken out to the fence line on the tractor, where another man got on. We were to cut fence posts for the rest of the day, and boy, this was hard work, and it was non-stop. Bob, the other man, swore quietly to himself as by now it was late afternoon and I was thirsty and tired and had had nothing to eat since leaving Mum's house the day before. But I wasn't going to give up so I kept going the best I could. Bob gave me a hand as needed. We worked like this until we couldn't see a thing in front of us, then the boss started to pack up, and so did we, and we headed back to camp on the back of the tractor.

Once there, the lady gave me a meal, but it wasn't enough for me, so I asked for a second helping. The boss started jumping up and down, yelling at me. In turn, my face grew red as I hadn't seen a grown man act like that before – I never did have a second helping. Then, when I went to wash my face and hands, I copped it again from him, even though I had just had a dump and needed to wash up after it.

As we only had Tilley lamps for light, both Bob and I headed for bed. Bob wasn't happy with things and turned off the lamp to avoid bringing all the bugs in. I told him that this was no way to live, and, as he had also spent a lot of time around the bush fencing, he agreed. Nevertheless, as tired as I was, I fell asleep while he was still talking.

Then, without any warning, I was kicked on the foot. "Come on now, get up! It's work time."

It was just starting to get light and, within a minute, both Bob and I were outside while he was pulling overalls over his pyjamas. We both looked at each other with amusement and tried not to laugh at him. Then he climbed on the tractor, signalled us to climb aboard as he started it up and headed off to the jam timber country. When we arrived, he dropped us off and said, "I'll be back later," and he left us there, unfed, and with no water.

By now, Bob had become quite displeased with our situation and said he was going to leave; said this was no way for me to be treated either. For the first time, I knew he was right and that my situation wasn't going to improve. But where would I go without water or food? This was quite frightening and I asked Bob which way he would go. His reply: "Walk to the fence line – follow that until you see the gravel track, then walk into the sunset."

That morning the boss returned and gave us each a sandwich and a cup of tea, and even though Bob wasn't going to stay, he worked through the day. That evening while I slept, he left in the dark of night. As for me, I was awoken with a boot to the foot.

While getting ready for the day's event, the lady came over to the water tank and handed me my breakfast with a cup of tea. I never said anything about Bob, but I knew they had expected it as nothing was said to me. That morning the lady had a small girl around seven years old with her. She must have brought her up the previous day.

I was told that I was digging holes for the posts that day and spent from sunrise to sunset digging until my hands were full of blisters. I was sunburnt from head to toe and had only two drinks of water for the full day's work, and my mouth and throat were drying out, making it very hard to swallow. I asked him for water when we got back to camp and was offered a cup full.

After tea, I just went to bed and fell asleep. The next morning, I was given a boot to the foot. I could hardly move with all the sunburn I'd had from the previous day, and when I did get on my feet, my mouth was split with sunburns and bleeding. Then, without any words said, I got on the back of the tractor and we headed off to the fence line.

When he left and was out of sight, I could see a windmill so I headed down to it from my position. The water was covered in green slime, and I just pushed it aside and put my whole head straight into it; rested for a moment, then plunged my head in again, taking as much water as I could. Eventually, I returned to the fence line to dig more holes with little strength and blistered hands.

Then the boss returned to the fence with the lady and this little girl. They began drilling holes through the posts while the little girl was driving the tractor. By then, I had completed digging, and he was putting the posts in the ground and packing the dirt around them. When he'd completed, he and the little girl headed back to the camp, leaving the lady and me to carry on working.

About two hours later – 3.30pm – he came back and started to unroll the barbed wire and tied it to the main strainer post while the little girl drove the tractor down the fence line. At the same time, he wanted the lady and me to tie it to the head of each post. All this was carried out with him yelling out to me and the lady while the little girl was still trying to do what he wanted. Then all hell broke loose. The little girl couldn't slow the tractor down, which put stress on the barbed wire. By now there was some 100 feet rolled out. Then it snapped! It just cracked and at super speed re-rolled itself. I well remembered my time at

Bindoon when this had happened and it was everyone for themselves so I bolted in the opposite direction with the lady right on my heels.

About a minute passed.

When we stopped to look back, he was climbing onto the tractor and bringing it to a stop. Then he ducked under it with the little girl. The lady was pretty shaken up over it, and so was I. Then, as if nothing had happened, he was back yelling at us. This was crap! This man was dangerous! Nevertheless, I kept on working. We finished the barbed wire then started on the main strands, working into such darkness I had to count the holes down the post to pass the wire through.

It must have been around eight o'clock when we finished. I was so tired I could barely hang onto the tractor on our way back to camp and went straight to bed, deciding that I had to leave – my clothes were a mess, and I was covered in crap from head to toe after the fourth days' work.

When I was again woken up, I just got onto the tractor and we arrived at the fence line. The wire was all over the place as I passed it through the wrong holes. Well, this fired him up and he started calling me all the names I already knew and some others I hadn't yet heard. That was the last straw – I decided to leave him – so, when he dropped me down the fence line to start digging and drove out of sight, I started walking while it was still cool. Following Bob's advice, I came across the gravel track and was now well on the way.

After some time, I noticed a house further down the track and decided to make for it, but as I reached it, the boss drove up in the ute and started yelling at me again. Then another man came over and told him to leave me alone. This other man was quite big, so the boss got back into his ute saying that if I ever went near his house, he would get the police onto me. That was not what I wanted, and I felt shaken and tired, sore and sunburnt.

The big man came over to me. "Are you okay?" he asked.

I nodded.

He put his hand out and said, "My name's Barry Pollard. What's yours?"

"David," I said.

We started to talk about my boss when Barry said that another chap had come through three days ago. I told him that was probably Bob and that he had left, just like me, and now the police would get involved as I hadn't been paid and all my clothes were in his shed at Katanning. Barry told me not to worry and offered to take me to Katanning and talk to the Police. When we arrived, I first noticed these big feet and remembered them from before. When the policeman looked at me, he said, "Have we met before?"

I said, "Yes," and told him when. Then Barry started telling him why I was there. By the way I looked and the state of my clothes, he could see that I'd had a pretty rough time in the hands of the 'Dutchman'.

But I do remember Mum saying to me, 'if you ever need help, go to the local Priest'. I told the Policeman this and he understood and said, "Let's get your case," and with that, we set off. I could never understand how the policeman knew where the boss's house was, until later.

We arrived there just as the boss was going to feed his pigs, and I was in the right place at the right time. Where we had stopped was right near the switch for the electric wire. I turned it on just as he was bending over the fence and he was thrown to the ground. I started to laugh, and the more he grabbed the wire, the more I laughed at him.

"What's so funny, and what have you done?" the policeman asked.

"I turned the electric fence on like he did to me," I said.

"Well, that's all right," the policeman said, "but you'd better turn it off now."

I did. Then the boss was informed he was being charged with holding personal belongings and failing to pay wages to me. I was told to pick up my stuff, and we left him standing while the policeman drove me to see the priest. I was allowed to stay with him until other arrangements were made.

October 25th 1961

About two weeks later, Barry Pollard came to see how I was getting on and, as I was doing gardening and painting around the church. The Father was giving me a meal each day. Then Barry Pollard asked me to work for him at £10 per six days a week, and I said yes. I was now getting enough money to stay in lodgings at the local hotel, but I had to find my own meals. It wasn't long before I was well settled and, with the Policeman giving me guidance, it was an even greater advantage as I was quite young for a boy looking after himself, even for those days – from paying for food to washing my own clothes and keeping my own area tidy. I would still go to the presbytery on some occasions to do the garden. Then the priest contacted Mum and told her of my situation, and the following weekend they came to see me. I was more upset at saying goodbye as I was happy with my new boss, Barry, and I was getting to know other people within the township.

Barry and I got along really well. He had a wife and two young girls, and a son around four years old. It just seemed we had something in common. During our working day, he asked me about myself and, just as I started to tell him about the orphanage life, he said he couldn't believe it – he too had been at all those orphanages: Castledare and Clontarf, and ending up at Bindoon. That is where Barry learnt his trade, and it just seemed right for him to teach me as I was already quite good at some building trades. But I knew this was the way I would have to go as, like Barry, the Brothers never taught us how to read or gave us the basics of doing sums. In fact, everything was about doing the project rather than having the understanding of what we were doing and how it was to be finished. It seemed as if all they wanted was labour for themselves to build their buildings as, without giving us any other knowledge but to work within their guidelines, they must have needed to have this control over us. Though I really did think at times there was some good about it as we were bloody good workers, and that was an asset to us when we got in the mainstream of our working life. It was wonderful for Barry and me as we had this in common, as well as our good sense of humour.

Barry was always straight with me and never belittled me. We were also a good working team as he would show me new skills, and each day became more interesting. On top of that, having £10 when we finished on Saturday afternoon was even better. All our work, I understood, was to be around the Katanning Wheatbelt, and we often travelled, which meant an early morning, which I never complained about.

I remember on some mornings how bitter and cold it was. We arrived one morning at this new site in Cranbrook only to find all the bricks were frozen over. My first job was to light a fire under a 44-gallon drum then pour the hot water over the bricks. I also used the drum for mixing while Barry was laying. My other project was to dig two holes for septic tanks, and it wasn't long before I had my shirt off as this work was hard and the ground unforgiving with each blow of the pick. I also had to keep both mortar and bricks ahead for Barry.

Working at this pace, time went quickly over the week and I now looked forward to Sunday for a rest and a sleep in. On our way back, Barry mentioned that he had another bricklayer starting mid-next week, not that I had a problem dealing with that as I knew my work would be twice as much unless I stopped digging the holes.

On Tuesday morning, we arrived at the site and it was again quite cold and bitter. I quickly got about my work, and it wasn't long before we were both laying bricks. After a quick cuppa – which Barry always brought for me – I was at it again non-stop.

This kept up for the rest of the day, and we left the site in the dark, not like the previous night. We would arrive at Katanning at dusk. So it wasn't long before I was in bed and again up with the birds and waiting for Barry. When we arrived on-site, the other bricklayer was just standing around, so I just got to work, moving fast to keep warm as once again it was bitter and ice lay over the bricks. While waiting for the hot water, this chap – a foreigner – started to yell at me to give him the bricks. I told him it wouldn't be long now but he just kept asking for the bricks and just wouldn't stop yelling at me.

So I said, "Get them yourself!"

He then started saying, "You're a lazy boy, and a cheeky one."

"Get lost!" I told him and walked away.

He threw some mortar at me then shouted, "Giv a me the bricks ... giv a me the bricks!"

That fired me up. "Do you want the bricks, prick? Then fucken hav'um!" And with that, I began throwing bricks at him and didn't stop until Barry started yelling at me to stop. He told the other chap to get his own bricks up then. Without anything else said, he packed up his tools and left. Boy, Barry wasn't too pleased with me, saying that he needed to have him as this work was getting behind. I turned towards him, saying, "Why don't you teach me to lay the internal walls?" and from that time I was soon learning to lay bricks. We shared the mixing and loading of the bricks to the scaffolding.

I did find it hard at first, but with Barry on my back, I soon learnt each stage of the overall task and was beginning to enjoy it so much that the time of leaving the site didn't matter.

I remained with Barry until he couldn't get any more work due to a downturn in the industry. Then, on the last week of working and cleaning up, Barry just came out with it.

"You know, David, I too was at Bindoon."

I couldn't believe this at first until he started to tell me about his time there, and the only thing he got from them was this bricklaying lark, and a lot of beatings. Then I told him about my time there, and it just seemed that we were getting upset at looking at where we had got to in our life; the various stories he started telling rang a bell, and the flashbacks of those beatings that we received came back.

Mid October 1961

I went back to the umbrella of the Darcey home for about three weeks, then a job at a farm came up at a small town called Bencubbin, about 300 kilometres east of Perth. This time the farmer came down to pick me up from home and, during the long drive back, I got to know my new boss and what he expected from me. Upon arriving at dusk, I was shown my sleeping quarters, which was a little caravan that was very clean and fresh with a proper bed and small gas stove, all for my use. I couldn't be happier with it compared to my last experience.

Then his wife came over and introduced herself and her children, and explained about the times I was expected to be clean and tidy and at the table. I was to do my own washing and the farmer's wife provided clean sheets each week. So now the ground rules were set. After tea that night, I went for a long walk around the farm as it was quite warm, and I really didn't feel tired. Then I was off to bed sometime later.

The next morning, after a big breakfast, the farmer and I set off towards his shed. I was shown how to change plough disks, then shown how to drive a tractor, and all about the harvester [A L] – it was very old. I soon began to understand how it all worked, and it was almost harvesting time. We were both getting all the machinery ready, and I felt a little excited about it by the very way the farmer was looking each day and watching the weather. Then, without warning, I was told to 'get up – it's time for harvesting,' and off we both went.

Even though it was early and warm, it wasn't long before I was driving all this machinery while he drove back and forth towing other trailers with lots of bags on. Then he would stop me and look in the bin to see how much was there, then wave me on, only to stop and empty all the grain into these bags on the next trip around the paddock. This work of taking the grain from the harvester bin and bagging it then trying to lift it onto this trailer was too much for me to handle as three bushels was three times me, so he had to do all the lifting himself. Then I was given a big breakfast again, and was off harvesting until sunset.

After cleaning and washing myself, I arrived at the farmer's house for tea, and after some small talk, I really needed to get to bed as I knew the next day wasn't going to be any easier. This kept up for the full week. Just before dinner one night, I was asked to replace the cutting blades on the harvester, so the next day I climbed underneath the harvester and started to remove the blades and replace them. I was about halfway through this task when I noticed out the corner of my eye a snake sitting up ready to strike at my feet, which were swinging with the motion of undoing the very tight nuts. The snake was following my foot movement and didn't allow me a second thought … I swiftly pulled myself further under the harvester, scrambled until I was out from under it, all the time keeping my eye on its movements. At the same time, the farmer arrived, and I started to yell about the snake. In the split second I had taken my eye off it, it had disappeared, and we both went through the rubbish to find it, but to no avail. So he remained with me until I completed the job.

We never saw that snake again over the next few weeks but the farmer knew it was still around and kept a watchful eye out as he had young children and their work was to feed his three pigs and one big pig, which was his pride and joy.

At the end of my week's work, I received £6 for six days work.

I was enjoying what I was doing, and though we were nearly finishing harvesting, I was being well looked after and never felt any threat from them, though at times, they would yell at the kids for getting over-excited.

Then, just as it started, it was over. The harvester was cleaned down and stored, along with all the other equipment, and I was given this project to fence a large paddock into two. He took me out and showed me the area requiring fencing and all the wire and metal star posts. I looked over the length of the fence he wanted and realised I would be there for about a month. With that, he drove off, leaving me with all the equipment for the job without saying anything else to me.

I started to look over all the material lying in this big heap and knew the task ahead was going to be quite hard, but I never knew just how hard, as, come sunset, I wasn't picked up by the farmer. So I began to walk back to the house. I was quite dry and somewhat burnt but knew that would be sorted once at the house. I walked about one and a half miles to the house only to find no one around and no lights were on, so I made my way to the caravan. There was a note on the door and, as I couldn't read, I couldn't understand what it said. But I knew the feeling that something wasn't quite as it should be. I lit my tilly lamp and noticed a box with some food in it, and started to take my fill of it. Then I went for a short walk before bed, a little confused as to what was expected of me.

The following morning, I looked around for the farmer but no one was around so, getting the food box and a water container, I headed off to the fence line and started to pace out the ground for the posts, and set to work. I remained doing that without pushing myself and stayed there for the whole day, heading home again just before sunset. Again nobody was around, and there was no food for my meals. I took the note from my pocket and tried to understand its contents but I was unable to. I was now very confused as to what was going on. I started to become quite tired after my long day's work and was soon asleep.

The next morning, I was up with the birds and very hungry so decided to get a couple chook eggs and soon downed them. Then I got a handful of wheat and mashed it to powder then blowing the husk away began to chew on it until all was gone then once again, I headed for the fence line, not really feeling up to carrying out my duties.

About an hour after arriving, I heard someone calling and, looking towards the neighbour's boundary, I saw a person calling and walked over to them. It was a boy a little older than me.

With a big smile, he said, "G'day. I am John."

I held my hand out and said, "David."

He seemed quiet for a moment, then started asking me about the job. "And was your boss at home and just up and left without saying a thing?"

I raised an eyebrow and handed him the note that had been left.

He read it then said: "What an arse he is! He's gone to Perth for the week and wants you to keep working on the fence and also feed and water the pigs."

I just looked at him. "He didn't leave any food for me, and I was eating wheat and eggs."

John wasn't too pleased about that. "Come along with me, and Mum will give you a feed."

I didn't need another invite and jumped his fence and walked back across his farm until I could see the house. I soon met the rest of the family while having this big breakfast, and all the time John kept calling my boss an arse. I now learnt that this was what he'd been doing to other boys, and I was told I should leave him. Then John showed his mother the note; she became a little disturbed about it and told John to go back with me and get my stuff out.

With that, we both got onto his tractor and headed back to the boundary fence then walked the rest of the way. It was around mid-morning when we reached the farm sheds and he asked me if I had fed the pigs, and I told him no.

When we went to the pen, the big pig was dead, blue in colour and cold and stiff. I said to John, "I couldn't understand the note!"

"Don't worry," he said. "This might teach him a lesson."

I gathered my things from the caravan and headed back with John. I really did feel bad about the pigs, but it just didn't enter my mind, even though I just couldn't understand the note left for me.

On arriving back at John's, he told his father what the arse had done to me, and about the pig, and as John explained to his father the pig was a blue colour, he just said, "Snakebite."

I was pleased that I hadn't starved the pig to death, but felt guilty for just leaving and said to John that I should go back, and thanked him for the breakfast. Then he dropped me at the fence line, and I started to bang the star post in until around 4.30 pm at which time I was getting tired and still had to lug my belongings back to the caravan.

Arriving at the farm, I stayed in the caravan for the night, just lying there asking myself if I should have stayed with John. I must have eventually fallen asleep as I could now hear the birds singing for me to get up. I knew I couldn't stay any longer and decided to leave, and with that, found some binda-twine and tied my belongings together. At about eight in the morning, I walked, not to the back boundary of John's, but across country towards the main road.

About an hour later, I heard a car coming up the fire break of the property I'd just left. It was the farmer and he was going off his head at me, and also saying he was reporting me to the police for stealing his binda-twine. On top of this, he bounded the fence and gave me a slapping across the head, sending me flying backwards onto my back. I dropped my bundle and grabbed a mallee root and stood up ready to let him have it, but he backed off and left, leaving me well shaken up. I then decided to walk the boundary across to John's.

I arrived at his house and called out, only to find his mother was there. We never said much to each other, and I think she knew what he had done to me. She made me a big sandwich and I began to relax yet still did not know what I should do. Around 5pm when John arrived back, I was told that a job was available fifteen miles east of Koorda. The man's name was Mr Schulze and he had two boys that went to boarding school. So next day I was driven to Mr Schulze's farm and was soon shown my bedroom. It was a tin shed about 50 yards from the main house but it had a fireplace, a concrete floor, and a good solid bed and mattress. Upon getting the fire lit and putting my belongings away, I started to get settled and just like the last job I was told to be clean and tidy for all meals, and I was.

I was now full and ready for bed and looking forward to my warm fire to sleep by.

Upon getting up the next day, I felt really good about this job. Mr Bill Schulze was quite a tall man in his thirties, and didn't seem to get over-excited about any situation. I felt at ease while we worked on various machinery in readiness for the coming wet weather or 'early rain'. I had half of Saturday off for the same money as the previous farmer. Then he said that he wanted to build a sheep dip run so I told him I'd been taught bricklaying and he got started on it the following day, digging out the trench with his machinery. I got busy mixing the concrete for the base and I could see by his expression he was very happy with me.

The next morning, I was up and mixing mortar for bricklaying, and I was well at it before breakfast which I didn't waste much time with as I just had to complete as much laying as possible over that day. We both worked for the next two days and it was finished, apart from putting water and chemicals in it. That happened about three days later, then we rounded up all his sheep and passed them through dip. By nightfall, all was completed and he was ever so pleased with me.

Come Saturday, Bill came to my hut and introduced me to his two sons and mentioned that I was to start learning how to drive as I would be required to drive his machinery over to his farm. He also said, "I have an old Sunbeam car over there, and Dave, if you can get the thing going, you and my boys can use it as you like."

His two sons were fourteen and twelve and we became good mates. Each holiday we were always doing something around the farm. Bill was pleased with all the work I would do without any supervision and it wasn't long after starting with him that arrangements were made for a driving test at the Koorda Police station. When the time came, the police officer asked me some questions and must have been satisfied with my answers for I then had to take him for a drive. He explained what was required of me then told me to drive down this gravel road at the correct speed. Without any warning, he slammed his hand onto the dashboard and started yelling, "Stop!"

Without any hesitation, I slammed the brakes on hard and, as instructed by Bill, kept the ute dead straight.

The police officer looked at me and said, "Well done. Now take me back to the station." On the way back, he told me, "No drinking beer when you're driving, and no racing around town. Apart from that, you have your agriculture driving licence ... you are only permitted to drive in the country and not the city."

I felt great! This was the very first test that I had ever sat and passed. When I had finished at the police station, I headed back to the farm, and from there, I was to drive all the farming equipment to and from both farms, as it was now coming into the wet weather. I just knew it would be non-stop when we started but over the next few weekends, I would get the Sunbeam and drive over to John's house. I was asked if I would like to join the rifle club and the new tennis club that had just started, and I did just that.

Over the following weekends, John, Bill and I went over to the rifle range and Bill said I could use one of his rifles. I paid 1 shilling for the club shoot winner, 5 shillings to join the club, and gave Bill 2 shillings for my bullets. We all, in turn, fired one shot into our targets, and this was repeated for an hour. While I was using Bill's rifle, the sights fell off, and bringing it to his attention, he asked me if I should have another shot. But the others didn't like that idea, and I much felt the same way. Upon the scores being announced, I was deemed the winner outright, with 8 bulls eyes and 4 inners. Bill's mouth dropped open, and he said, "He did that and the bloody sight was loose ..."

I also couldn't believe it. So this was going to be on every second weekend, and the tennis was on every second weekend. This was great. Though I couldn't play tennis very well – my wrists were quite weak from my see-saw days! – but I still had a go.

The following second Saturday I was told that we were all going to build a proper toilet as no one wanted to empty the old one. When Bill and I arrived, there were others digging and talking, while others were just standing and talking. I thought, *where have I seen this before?* As I climbed out of Bill's ute, I was handed a shovel to start digging and so the rest of the morning was over, with the old dunny being changed to a flush type.

The next meeting, when the septic tanks still had to be installed, only three of us arrived and, as Bill wasn't feeling very well and went home about an hour later, I was on my own. When John arrived, he knew I wasn't too pleased about it, and suggested using some gelignite.

"That's the easiest way," he said.

"What's gelignite?" I asked.

He replied, "Hang on, mate, I'll be back in half an hour with some."

I kept digging with this playing on my mind when he returned with the gelignite.

"How much do you think we need?" he asked.

"I haven't any idea," I replied. "How much would you use?"

"Well, sometimes Dad puts half a stick in the hole for a strainer post, and you know how deep that has to be." So we summed it up that the hole that was needed was fifteen times bigger than that.

So we started to drill this hole into the hard clay. Once we had drilled three of them, John showed me how to set them until we had five sticks in each hole with the detonators and fuses now joined.

"What do we do now?" I asked.

John just looked at me. "See that log on the horizon?"

"Yes."

"Well, when I light this, we run like hell and hide behind it."

And with that, we both bolted for cover.

About thirty seconds later, there was this almighty *BANG* and we both felt the earth move around us. Then a big cloud of red dust came down all over us. We started to laugh at the way the red dust came down and covered us. When the dust had settled, not one sound could be heard – no blowflies, no birds. Nothing! Then we noticed that something wasn't quite right. The hole was now the size of the grand canyon.

"Shit! What have we done! This is a bloody, really big hole …"

Then we noticed the dunny was missing; we couldn't find it anywhere. We looked at each, trying figure out what went wrong but, rather that trying figure it through, we grabbed the tools and left via all the outback paddocks, laughing all the way, and I, no matter what, would never admit to that. We arrived at John's house and cleaned up while his mother was cooking their tea, then around sunset, John drove me home to Bill's farm.

When I arrived at the house for tea, I noticed Bill wasn't looking too well. On the Monday, he was sent to Perth for medical attention. I looked after the farm while he was away, with John coming over each night for a laugh. Though the question went around town, and we, in turn, were asked about it, my answer to the gigantic hole was 'I haven't any idea as I left just after the others when John picked me up.'

And so, on the following weekends, we arrived to finish off, helping out with the club and a new dunny. And the mystery of who blew the dunny away was never found out.

John and I had a lot of fun around Koorda and Bencubbin, and at times went to Wyalkatchem as he had friends from his school days he would meet up with. We had some great afternoons and, just when everything seemed okay, I arrived back at Bill Schulze's farm and was informed by his wife that Mr

Schulze was quite ill. It was caused by the sheep, and I understood later that the wool and the oil affected him badly. He was putting the farm up for sale and was moving to Perth. I was to leave by the end of the week and was offered a job in Koorda working at tyre-changing and farm machinery maintenance. My lodging was at the local Train Station master's house, arranged by my new employer.

I quite enjoyed working with this company as I was trusted with changing tyres on tractors, trucks and harvesters. Then I started going out to the farms to help grease up all the new equipment. As my luck would have it, the station master was moved and I had to find other lodgings. Over the next few weeks, I was never settled and the only place I found was also with their son, and we just couldn't get along. I then decided to leave and return home, much to everyone's disappointment who knew me. My wage was less than Mr Schulze's and the hours were only eight, for five days. I did like my job, and the people, but my wages couldn't support me and I ended up back home in Bullsbrook.

Mid February 1963

I arrived home and found nothing had changed. I couldn't find work so I spent my time hanging around the house. Sometimes the local shopkeeper would get me to clean up his yard and help out with fuel drums as he was the local agent for the farmers. Mr and Mrs Bindi would have me down at least once a week to help out and became good friends to Mum and Dad. At the time, I would just go down and find something to do around his yard. Then one day, I was sitting on my bike leaning against a lamp post eating an orange when, without any warning, I was on the ground and looking up to see Mr Capone's car just about on top of me. At the same time, he was getting out of his car, yelling at me, accusing me of stealing the orange from Mrs Burnett's yard as she was away and her house was next door to Mr Bindi's. He was yelling so loud that Mum came down to see what was going on.

When she could see what was going on, she was soon down with Peter under her arm and the broom in the other, telling him to leave me alone. As he jumped back, his straw hat fell off, and I just couldn't help myself. I jumped on it and wiped my feet over it. Killed it. And all this time Mum was yelling at him for knocking me off my bike. He was informed that *she* had given me the orange and he had no right to pick on me.

He quickly got into his car and drove off. Apart from my bike, I was okay.

The following weekend Max was walking to Bindi's shop when Mr Capone jumped him and gave him a good arse-kicking. Max told his Dad and he was soon down to see him as they lived two doors up from him. When he got there, he called for him to come out. Then he asked him to step outside his gate, and when he did, Mr Broad slapped him across the face. Capone told him not to hit him so Mr Broad grabbed his shirt and gave him another hit that sent him to the ground. While Capone was on the ground, Mr Broad told him to get up but he wouldn't move so Mr Broad sat down on top of his guts and started to slap him around the face until he'd had his fill. Then he warned him to leave us alone. From that day, we never again had any trouble from him.

I was now getting some work up the Chittering valley picking oranges or making the boxes for them. On other occasions, I would help out at Mr Taylor's farm, either chaff cutting and hay carting, and sometimes working as a rouse-about at shearing time. Other times I would do contract orange picking and, along with Tom and Jeff, would spend some weekend just picking oranges. We made around 15 shillings each. I also got a job plastering water tanks.

I was that year in and out of work. Then a labourer's job was available at the RAAF Pearce. I was over there like a flash the next morning and got the job labouring for a building firm.

Being back at home was becoming normal again as Max and I now played around with model aeroplanes. After quite a few failures, I decided to mount the motors onto a board with wheels. This gave us a lot of fun at the local schoolyard as there was no control. Once started, we just let it go and it could end up in the grass area of the schoolyard or smash into the buildings. We tried to use a long strand of wire passing through a big staple under the board but that wasn't as much fun so we did away with that idea. Just as our luck would have it, Wenny, the school cleaner, appeared. We all loved Wenny as she lived in the area with her mother and always gave us a laugh. Nevertheless, Max and I decided to start our motor up and let it go just as she was emptying the bins. It would frighten the pants off her. Which it did, and she made a dash for the nearest door, hearing us laughing guts up over it. Each time she appeared, we let her have it.

Then we decided to split up. As Max let it go, I would be up the other end to get it and send it back. By now, though, old mate Wenny was getting upset with us – but that was okay, she was our mate – and so she came out of the classroom. But this time she had a bass broom.

By the time I noticed her with it, I had already let the contraption go and watched as Wenny stood her ground with the broom at the ready. She gave it a good clobbering as it was passing and killed it with one good swift blow. All we heard was her loud laughter, which would put a kookaburra to shame. Apart from all that, we got along great with our Wenny.

December 1963

Butch and Sid were now driving and had a car each. They came up to Bullsbrook each weekend for the dancing and weekend fun. Max was courting Barbara. Maureen was well into her nursing career at Fremantle Hospital while Tom was playing with his friend Ray Maf'a. As for me, I was now known as Choo-Choo Bar because I would always have one in my mouth and I would never share them with anybody.

We were all making new friends now and each weekend our house was full of people. Sometimes we would eat in three shifts, and the only way Mum and Dad could afford to feed the hungry mob was to give them 'roo meat. Most of them never knew what they were eating as Dad was a great cook and his curries were the best. Maybe that is why we had such a big mob over the weekends. I look back over those days when we had no phones, no electric power, just the joy of people turning up and always having great fun. I never heard Mum or Dad say no to anyone.

Wendy was going to Bullsbrook and Peter was four years old when Dad's father came to live with us. On each Pension Thursday he would go to the local pub – the Chequers Hotel at Bullsbrook East – and walk back after he swallowed five or six five-penny darkies. He'd prop himself against the fireplace mantle and keep us amused listening to his poems until we went to bed. Then on Saturday nights, we were off to the local dance for more fun though it became noticeable beer was now coming into our lives. I only remember taking a small swig and threw it out of my mouth as I didn't like it at all … yet. Occasionally I had wine, and that wasn't at all as bitter, but over the years, that soon changed.

The Darcey family

Mid January 1964

Mum and Dad moved out of the rented house and into a RAAF married quarters just down Chittering Road, close to the shops. I was now looking for work on the Base in the carpenters' workshop at the Department of Works, which carried out all maintenance work on the Base. I was No. 1 in line that morning and was accepted as I was local and of the right age. This was to become the second changing point in my life.

I remember getting to work a half an hour early, overly keen to get started. The foreman arrived to open the main gates to the works compound, and not long after, all the others arrived. I was told to report to a chap named Ken, who required help. Once I located him, we went down to the main aircraft hangars, and I saw for the first time the Vampire jets up close. I had only seen them in the air flying around and around as this was a training base for pilots in the RAAF.

On this job, we were to take out all the cracked glass from the roof lights and replace it with new ones. And so began a good working relationship between Ken and I. Though the work was dangerous and the scaffolding not subject to today's standards, we had over the month removed and replaced one half of the total roof. As Ken was required to start some other project, I was asked to help out the plumbers, then the tilers. This pattern was to assess my work ability and trade influence as to where it started and where it stopped, for the next person. For example, I would dig the hole and the plumber laid the pipe in it. Then I would fill it back up. And that is the way I had to have my thinking, as any labourer didn't like anyone doing his work, etc etc.

I gained a lot from doing that and helping each tradesman for the next two months. I was then asked to report to the sewerage farm as Mr Healy was going on leave, and the only person available was me. Although I knew Mr Healy and his daughter, who attended the Saturday night dances, I wasn't looking forward to the coming events. But my foreman needed someone local, and that was me, though he mentioned that it was only for a month. I went down to speak to Mr Healy about my duties and what trouble I might encounter, and before long I began to get the idea of it. I just didn't like it at all and, no matter what I did, I was to remain there until he returned.

Even when I didn't arrive for work no one knew I was missing, and I thought I would work that to my advantage – but it didn't work. The bloody job was enough to make you sick with these big brownies looking at me as if I was the owner, and I can remember Mr Healy saying to me, "Don't let it get you down, Dave. Just treat them like your pets."

The last thing he said was, "I know everyone on the Base by their TURD name." So after one month was up, I was more than happy to be finished with it and get back to the carpenters' workshop. From that day on, the foreman made sure I was allocated to it and the carpenters on the field and doing what I was to get great satisfaction from.

During my time working on the Base, I came to know quite a few of the personnel working in the various sections, and this gave me a good understanding of how the Base was run. These boys/men would soon be around our house to go shooting and sometimes camping at the Taylor's farm, then back to work Monday morning.

These were fantastic times as I had nothing and didn't want for anything. Mum and Dad were always there and all our friends would call in to see us every weekend. I could never recall any memories of my past and early childhood years in Wales coming back to me.

There were other occasions: we three – Tom, Jeff and I – would go up the valley and plaster water tanks. Jeff would mix and Tom would pull the bucket up and tip it into the tank. On one special occasion, a Mr King asked me to cement his tank and arrangements were made. Jeff was to meet his future wife, Lynne, here. These projects were short-lived though, due to the lack of profit.

During my time working at Pearce RAAF Base, I used to have access to any building on and around the Base. It wasn't long before I was replacing windows at the Officers' Mess and kitchen.

Here I met Gwen Klane, a steward there. We would go to badminton every Tuesday evening then back to the WRAAF guest room for coffee and light bites. Even though she was four years older than me, we got on great, and the more we saw each other, the longer we spent together. I had no transport to go anywhere, so most of our time was spent around the Base. Then one day, I asked Dad if he would lend us the car for Friday evening. After a little protest from him, both Mum and I gave an assurance that all would be okay as I was only going to the Base then up Bullsbrook Hill with the rest of her friends where we sat around the fires and some drank beer. Most just sat around talking.

Her friends were great and I never heard anyone talking about another person other than in a good way. We both looked forward to these Friday evenings and I was never late home with Dad's car. After a short time, he was fine with me using it.

Then one day Gwen brought a Mini Minor, and from then on we went everywhere, even down to Busselton where her Mum, Dad, and brother lived. This was around 230 kilometres from Perth. Her brother and I would go shooting with one of his mates and be back for tea. Then we were back down the road as she had to be on Base by 10.30 pm Sunday.

Then one week she went on leave, and that was the last time I saw her – it left a big hole in my evenings, apart from feeling hurt over it.

Butch was now riding a motorbike and would always let the district know of his arrival as the bike had no or very little exhaust on it. Still, that was Butch and his style. On the Saturday nights, he would give the boys a laugh by doing hand-stands on the handlebars, then race off down the road at high speed just to keep the local traffic patrolman on his toes. On one occasion, the patrolman was laying in wait for him. As Butch flew past, the patrolman rammed his throttle fully open then dropped the clutch, but the bike just raised itself off the ground and threw the patrolman to the gravel, still holding the handlebars. He was dragged around by the bike, which gave us onlookers the biggest laugh for the night. Butch stayed away from Bullsbrook for the next two weeks.

Maureen now had a boyfriend – John – and he too had a motor bike. Dad and Mum were always concerned about it as the number of accidents was quite high. John, however, was not at all like Butch acting stupid with his bike and wouldn't jeopardise the safety of his passenger.

John worked at Bunnings in Leederville and lived with his brother, Con, who was studying accountancy. Maureen saw a lot of John but I only saw him when he came to see Mum and Dad.

Max was now into a butcher's apprenticeship at Midland, and Barbara was also working in Midland for Singer Sewing Machines, so it wasn't long before they were going out together. At this time, we were all doing our 'thing', sharing the same boyhood interests but having nothing in common as we grew older. Max left his Dad's farm, and Jeff took over the place. I never did get to look over it.

It was now that the papers were reporting the outbreak of war in South Vietnam and the Australian Government was looking to send troops to the region to support the South Vietnamese. Therefore a ballot conscription for 19-year-old boys would take place.

June 1964

Dad came home one evening and told me about a car his friend was selling at the Base for £30 – it would be ideal for me to run around in. We went over that night to look it over. It was a 1932 Chevy, converted to a shooting ute, and I fell in love with it! Its age didn't bother me as all I could think of was having that independence with my own set of wheels. After settling the account, we were on our way, and that weekend we were off to the bombing range to see how it would go. It never missed a beat.

We would, over the next few months, go shooting each weekend with friends and get back around 2.30 am, cold, hungry and tired.

On other occasions during the summer months, Tom and I would go out to the bush and load up firewood. One day we found two women lying on a rug, completely nude. We didn't know if they were sunbaking or what, but we were both surprised and they just up and ran for the cover of the bush. We just kept picking up firewood and left for home and told Mum of the events that had taken place. We were advised not to go back to that area again, but boys being boys, we went back only to be disappointed.

Our family and the Taylor's became very close friends and we never seemed far from going shooting late on some afternoons. We would walk around the property, Dad and old Bill good cobbers joking around with each other as if nothing worried them. Should a 'roo appear, a few shots would be fired and it really didn't matter if you missed because there were more around the next bend. Bill's land was very hilly with lots of rocky outcrops that overlooked the Avon valley down to the river and at times it was hard work walking around them.

I remember one trip walking around with Bill, Dad, and Bill's son Eric. It was cold and the wind was bitter as we walked around looking for 'roos, the ground was loose gravel mixed with clover. To top it off, I was walking behind the shooters with both hands jammed into the pockets of my tight jeans. I wasn't quite quick enough to remove them when I slipped on the clover and gravel and fell face-first to the ground and the sheep crap. I tried to get my hands out before the others noticed but I couldn't. As I was trying to roll over on my back, I could feel myself slipping down the hill. It was only when Eric helped me to my feet that I could get my hands out of my pockets. Well, that provided them with unlimited entertainment at my expense and was often spoken about.

I would often go up to Taylor's property during these times as the Trans-rail was being built through the Avon valley at the time. Bill didn't mind as I would always ask first then would drive over to the lookout. On one occasion, my old ute's handbrake wasn't the best so I parked nose-first into a small tree about 200mm, then wandered down the hill and sat on a rock that looked over the whole valley. Below I could see the work being done for the rail, the workers at it hammer and tongs while their voices could be heard from where I was sitting. About an hour later, I left to drive back and, upon starting the old ute, it wouldn't go backwards as the wheels were slipping and bogging down. I climbed out and tried to jack it up, but that didn't work. On each occasion, the front bumper was getting more damaged. I tried everything to no avail, so I started to walk back to Bill's house for help.

When I got there, he looked at me. "Stuck, Dave?"

"Yes," I said.

"What's the problem?" he asked.

"I need to chop a small tree down as I leant the ute against it and I can't back it off as the ground's too loose."

With that, Bill grabbed the axe and said, "Drop it in on your way back."

I didn't say anything as I understood him and so started to walk back to the ute. Once there, I looked at various ways to sort out what would happen then started to chop the tree so it would fall uphill. I already had it started, and within five or six blows, it started to fall with the weight of the ute against it. Then, without any sound, the tree was down. I threw the axe in the back, jumped in the driver's seat and gave it all I could as the bloody tree was now stuck underneath the ute. My situation was even worse. But I now decided to reverse it downhill and take my chance to drive around the slope of the hill. It was a bit spooky but I got there.

When I arrived at Bill's house, he came over, smiling widely. "Learn anything from that lot?" he asked.

"Yes," I said as I handed back his axe. "Bill, I won't be doing that again."

I used to go up to my lookout point and sit on my 'thinking rock' and there were occasions when once again my mind went back to Wales and those people who waved at me. I also had flashbacks of Swansea and would wake up trying to breathe, screaming out as I walked down the very long, dimly lit passage. These thoughts would never go away, and I would sometimes drift back to Bindoon and the loving care I received. Yet I couldn't have wished for a better family and friends that were around me.

Now that Gwen had gone out of my life, I felt I was not wanted. I would love to have had someone to be with me and share these thoughts, someone who wouldn't belittle me or treat me as an oddity, as the local girls sometimes would. But the only place to find a girlfriend was at the local dance, and I knew it would not happen there. I would leave my thinking rock and feel I had unloaded my issues, but instead, my feelings were deeper, and while I felt better, sometimes I felt sorry for myself rather than trying to forget it.

Dad once again wanted to go shooting and arrangements were made with an old mate of Dad's, an ex-RAAF fireman who had brought property outside Gingin about fifty miles away. So Dad, Tom and I loaded up the ute and food supplies and headed out for his mate's farm. It wasn't long after and nearly dark before we were out on the plains. As usual, he would kick the back of my seat once to stop and twice to move on, and like this, we moved through the plains for about an hour. And spotted nothing. So we stopped and had a bite to eat then set off again.

As Tommy was small, he stood beside Dad through the shooting hole controlling the spotlight while I kept an eye open for better ground to travel over as it was very rough country. The last thing we needed was a blow-out. Although the opening in the roof was padded, Dad still complained about my driving and at times got quite pissed off with me. I tried to explain that this country was rough and full of gidgees and at times hard to see, then he started to kick the back of my seat harder – one to stop, two to go – but this time when he kicked, I wasn't sure what he wanted, so I stopped, then moved again.

"What the fuck are you doing?" he yelled.

"Make your mind up, Dad. One to stop. Two to go, then yelling again. "Just drive!"

"Okay?" I said.

Then again came a hard kick to the seat, so I stopped. "What do you *want*?" I asked, turning my head around. The next kick got me straight in the face. "FUCKYA!!" I yelled. Then I jammed the ute into fast mode, not giving a damn about the battering they were having as I drove over the roughest bit of ground. I could hear him yelling to stop and when I finally did, it was to wipe the blood running down my face.

Tom and Dad were bruised, and I said to Dad, "Shove it! I'm going home," and nothing was said the whole trip back. We never went back to Gingin again but stayed shooting around the Taylor's property.

While working on the Base, I met Ashley Crow, a steward at the Officer's Mess. We were always together, swimming, playing badminton, sometimes squash. We would often go to the WRAAF guest room for coffee and talk to his workmates, and on some occasions, they would join us down at the swimming pool. Other nights we would go to the open-air pictures on the Base. I felt good in Ashley's company and more so, I was becoming more confident in myself. He would often ask the girls out for sing-a-long on Bullsbrook Hill and I would meet them there.

Sometimes we would go to Burns Beach for the day. I did find that the older girls were much easier to get along with and good all-around company.

October 1964

Sometimes, Ashley and I would go to his friend's quarters to hear him playing his guitar, and after listening to him, I began to wonder if I could learn to play. So I asked him where I should go and what type of guitar he thought would be best for me. He offered me his old one for a trial, and if it was any good, I could buy it from him. I found a music teacher in Midland, and each Wednesday I would have a half-hour lesson and gained a lot of personal satisfaction from it. I was learning something new and could apply it to my singing, but the cost and travel there was getting too much, and my social life was being taken over by music lessons.

As I was going to my last lesson, Ashley arrived and wanted to go to Perth after it was over. I wasn't feeling like it but went anyway. When we arrived in Perth, the dance had been cancelled so we started to walk around Perth. That's when we noticed two girls walking around. Ashley stopped and started talking to them; he introduced us, and, while the girls were a bit shy at first, that soon changed when we found our common ground —the dance that was cancelled.

Then one of the girls said, "My name is Ann, and this is my friend Lita. We were waiting for the bus."

Ashley asked if they wanted to go for coffee with us and we all went off. During our coffee time, Ashley told them we were in the Air Force, and I was about to tell Lita that I only worked on the Base when Ashley overrode me. I noticed Lita was getting concerned about the time so we walked them back to the bus stop and continued to talk. When I asked Lita for her phone number, she said that Ann had given it to Ashley. Then her bus arrived and I gave her hand a light kiss, saying I would like to see her again. She just smiled as she got onto the bus and was gone, but not forgotten.

Ashley and I also started for home and all we could talk about were Ann and Lita.

I mentioned to Dad that I would like to buy another car as the old Chevy was not good enough when it was raining, so over the weekend, I was off to the car yards around Midland but found nothing I could afford.

Maureen was sometimes home on Thursday and I asked her if she would like to go to Perth for a Chinese meal. What a fantastic night it was. I liked Maureen's company – she was always the perfect woman, and I believed she understood me best. I told her about Lita and that I was hoping to see her within the week.

The trip home in the old ute was cold and windy and, on arriving home, Mum and Dad were still up waiting for us. We told them what a good night it was and that it was the best opportunity for us to exercise our manners in public.

Friday evening, I arrived home to find a car salesman waiting for me with a Holden sedan. He was rather pushy even though the car was very nice. Upon Dad looking it over, I said it was fine, paid my deposit, and he took my old Chevy. Now, my first real car! I was king of the road when driving it. I raced over to show it to Ashley and that evening we drove to Armadale to meet the girls.

After introducing myself to Lita's Mum and Dad, we were off to the drive-in movies about seven miles towards Perth. During the movies, Ashley and Ann were grunting and growling in the back, and at first I thought the seats must have been uncomfortable to sit on. At half-time, we both went for a wee and to get some nibbles and drinks, and I asked if the back seat was okay as they both sounded as if it wasn't. Then it just hit me – he was having it off with Ann – then Ashley just smiled as he walked off back to the car. I made straight for Lita's house, wanting to make a good impression as I really wanted to see her again. But that big lie Ashley had told was hanging over my head, and I was playing along with it.

Our main conversation on the way home was about me not having a go with Lita, and I told Ashley that I had more respect for her than that. I just had this wonderful feeling when I was with her and it was my intention to see her again.

Christmas 1964

I had three weeks holidays for Christmas and decided to go to the South-West via Albany and return via Mandurah. I asked Tom and Jeff to come along for the trip and it was organised for the following weekend. Soon it was time to leave. This was going to be my first chance to see Western Australia. While I had been to Katanning before, this trip was going to be much better.

We arrived in Katanning only to find all the people I knew had gone, so we stayed in my old hotel, played pool in the lounge, then went off to bed without any events. The next morning, we paid our bill and set off for Albany, about two hours away. After looking at all the sites, we headed towards Denmark and booked into this old hotel, then it was off down to the beach.

As it was a nice warm night, we sat there talking to other travellers – I think they were the new thing: Hippies – as they looked like it was more than a bottle of beer that was being passed around. We hadn't been exposed to it before, so we up and left after a short while. We were up early the next day and, with breakfast over, headed off for the Valley of the Giants, stopping at various spots along the way. Then from Walpole, we headed towards Northcliffe, stopping at Pemberton for the night. The next morning, we arrived in Manjimup and had a bite to eat and looked around Fonty's Pool, leaving for the long drive back home, but not before detouring to Armadale to see Lita. I introduced my brother Tom and friend Jeff to her. Then we headed back home to Bullsbrook and a long rest as we were all incredibly tired.

January 1965

I returned to work and back to the carpenters' shop and was starting to make steps for the timber huts and replacing windows, and the odd door as required when I was asked to help set out a building and give a hand to dig out the footings. I would arrive at work only to find that someone had filled my Wellington boots with water and I just couldn't find out who was doing it. I never complained about it; I would just tip it out and slip them on. After a month of this, it stopped.

During my lunch break, I would phone Lita at her place of work and this was a pleasure I always looked forward to. Each Wednesday, I would drive the long distance to Armadale to be with her, and during these times, I got to know her family. How close they were with each other.

I got along great with Lita's dad, Mr Horton. He was retired and enjoyed his surroundings as he had just retired from the position of Gardener at the Armadale High School, that job coming to him just after he was made redundant from the Byford Munition Dump. He now spent all his time doing his own garden.

Lita's mother was all right, at first, but soon became too nosy for my liking. The one thing she wanted to know about was my orphanage life, where I came from and where I stayed. I found this quite overpowering, and I soon noted that she was the major player and the backbone of the family. I understood the one thing that was not tolerated was beer and drunks, and I had no worries about that lot. Yet, I was always questioned as to the last time I had a drink. Little did she know that I much preferred wine, which we had at home, and I found this got right up her nose. I wondered how Mr Horton managed to keep his sanity intact – he provided me with the required experience to look up to. Apart from that, Lita and I would drive to Rockingham then in the evening go to the drive-in movies.

Vietnam was the main topic of conversation during these times and the main thing concerning most people was being selected by way of ballot vote. This seemed a little unfair, but the Government made it quite clear that all boys reaching nineteen years of age having birthdays between selected months must register their names. As I was still eighteen years old, I put a lot of thought into it as I felt I would much prefer to join the service of my choice rather than be conscripted.

During the following weekend, I went and spoke to the recruiting officer for the RAAF and asked what I would be most suitable for. I was to return around May and sit an exam, and from that, I would be told what mustering I would be sent into.

That night at the table, I told Mum and Dad what I was doing and that I'd decided to join the RAAF. They were really happy for me at the thought of making a positive decision for my future. BUT again that ugly question raised its head of 'Who am I?' I told them I was joining up under the name David Anthony Darcey.

Mum said she had written to the Child Welfare Department requesting Adoption consent. As I was no longer a ward of the state – in fact, I had nothing further to do with them – how could I be adopted into the family? As yet, she had not received a reply. I told them I wasn't worried about using the name as I had only been known as belonging to them and that I really didn't like my old name anyway – it didn't bother me one little bit. And really, I had enough to think about with the coming exam. If I failed that, I would try the navy because I wasn't going into the army. I felt I had already been well-regimented as, after the past eighteen years, starting at nine months old and finishing at sixteen years old, I think they would be dealing with a smart arse, and the recall of my first encounters hit me like a ton of bricks. Apart from that, I was doing something for me, rather than being told once again what to do.

June 1965

Around this time, I informed Lita that I was joining the RAAF and that I should know within the week if I'd been accepted. If I was, then I would be sent to South Australia for recruit training for three months. From there, I had no idea where I would be sent. Also about this time, I brought Lita up to meet my family. She stayed the weekend with us and, although she was a little shy at first, she mixed in well with the family. Barbara spent a lot of time with her as they seemed to find some common ground. That Saturday afternoon, Maureen and John arrived on John's motorbike, and I remember asking them to be on their best behaviour, even to the point of washing up the dinner plates. Apart from that, they really liked her as she was a real nice girl with absolutely no bad habits.

On this weekend, I took her up to my hilltop lookout on the Taylor's property and told her that this was my special place. Here I could clearly think and, as far as the eye could see on a clear day, my mind could as well. I started to tell her that, when I was much younger, I would get these flashbacks of events in England; I would see myself fighting for air like heavy things were on top of me. Then nothing, and when I woke up, I would be covered in sweat and gasping. Then a lady and a misty figure with her was waving to me while I was on a train. I could see her crying, but I had no idea who they were. And so, any time I felt upset or down, I would find myself sitting here looking at the clear open space of the valley below. I just couldn't understand why I was sent to Australia. After some time, I would feel better as this was a happy place and I could rest my troubles here without talking about them. Lita was the only one I had told this to, as she was very special to me and treated me differently from the local girls. That respect went a long way in my thinking. I also told her that it was here I had made my mind up to find a very special girl, and that girl was her. And I had thanked my God at church when we first met for answering me. There was no way I was going to upset this very special person.

We left my hilltop lookout and headed back home, where we spent a fantastic time for the remainder of the week.

The following week I received my letter from the RAAF recruiting office in Perth. I had passed my exam and was to report for my medical within two weeks. I was over the moon with it and couldn't wait to tell Mum and Dad, and also my employer, The Department of Works.

I then had to go and see Lita and break the news to her. Although she was happy for me, I felt she wasn't sure about the outcome of the next few weeks, and I tried to give her as much information as was available to me. There was a possibility that things could change due to medical conditions and fitness.

So that is how I left it for the next two weeks.

I arrived for my medical and was asked about family medical history and what problems they'd had. I explained that I was sent to Australia as a child orphan. I had no idea of my family history because I never knew them. As far as I understood, they were killed during World War II.

He started to give me a complete going over ... stand up, bend down with hands on the floor, twist left and right, jump on one foot then the other, bend backwards as far as possible. All this I did and he seemed happy enough. Then blood was taken, and urine, and I was told to wait with all the others in the passage. About half an hour later, I was informed I was fit enough to enlist. I was to report to the front counter for my intake date, which was to be … 25 July 1965.

I decided to remain with the Department of Works until two days before my enlistment date, and, once again, my Wellington boots were being filled with water. But I was getting a little wild about it now, as this time of the year was very cold, the work was muddy and wet so filling my boots up was getting up my nose. I would still light up the fire for morning tea and try to keep an eye out as to who the culprit was, but to no avail, though I did have an idea. Then the men chipped in for a small gift on my last day with them, wishing me a better future and such. Then my foreman began to speak for the others and asked the question as to why I didn't complain to him about water in my boots.

I just looked at him and said: "The day it stopped was the day I would stop pissing in the teapot."

Well, if that didn't fire a couple of the blokes up, as I suspected it would. It brought the rest of the mob to laughter but these other two were going to rip my head off.

My foreman said, "You'd better bolt for it, Dave."

And with that, I was gone.

When asked about it later, I said, "It will give them something to think about." And I never said I did, and I never said I didn't. And after all that, I left without getting my gift from them.

July 25th 1965

After saying goodbye to my family, I went down to Perth Recruiting Centre and was sworn into the RAAF for six years' service. Later that afternoon, I was taken to Perth train station and boarded the train for Adelaide, South Australia. I had no idea what lay ahead for me though I understood this journey would last for two days non-stop, some 2,725 kilometres away, so I had plenty of time on my hands to be alone with my thoughts. The one thing I was feeling was homesick, or maybe it was fear of going into the unknown. Whichever, it was a strange but mixed feeling that I just couldn't explain away.

During mealtime on the train, the other boys were getting to know each other, me included. We would play cards, or some of them would drink beer, but inside I was too much missing Lita. I decided to try and write her a letter which was going to be a big challenge for me as it was my first love letter to her. I tried to explain that I wasn't very good at writing and spelling, but I was still going to try my best. So my first letter was in my best hand and in print as I just couldn't do running writing. I went over and over it before being satisfied I had done my best. My letter was about the train trip and the country I was going through at that time, about how dry the country was without a green tree in sight and the view was endless from horizon to horizon. I never saw any wildlife 'apart from the other boys getting drunk' and how red the ground was covered with spatters of saltbush and some rocky outcrops. This was a big country and I just felt I wanted to go and explore it all. Though feeling homesick at the start of my journey, I began to look forward to the coming days ahead and what to expect when I arrived at Edinburgh RAAF Recruit Training Base. I had no fear as to what I would be involved in as I was well equipped with my orphanage 'Regimented life' so wasn't overly concerned about what was expected of me or the challenges ahead – more so, the newness of it, and having the same common ground for each and every one of us, without separating 'those who could' and 'those who could not' as was so common in the orphanage.

We finally arrived in Adelaide and were met by Corporal McNaulty, our drill instructor – our tormentor for the next three months. He yelled at us on the rail station to 'Get in line! By the left, quick march!"

That was our 'Welcome' and the sound we would hear over the next three months.

Edinburgh was twenty-odd kilometres north of Adelaide, and my first impression was of how cold it looked and the amount of barbwire everywhere. It looked like a death camp out of the movies. Once inside, we were shown our quarters and told where the mess hall was, and the hours for meals and so on. I stored my belongings in my room and received my bedding; I made it up for the night then headed off for the mess hall about half a mile away. Upon arriving there, I understood what was meant by getting there first as, when the doors opened, we had twenty minutes to get the meal and consume it and be out of the mess hall before the doors were closed. I learnt very quickly as this was normal to me. So that evening, I got all my things stored away and got to bed around 8.30pm, but it took some time before I was asleep due to all the others running around and carrying on. I knew rest was a major factor and a top priority every night.

I was up nice and early the next morning and tidied my room for the coming events, then slipped on the clothes I arrived in. At 5.45am, I headed towards the mess hall and arrived with some two hundred other recruits coming from all directions. When the doors flew open, the sight of 200 people heading in different directions, grabbing the type of meal they wanted, then finding a table to eat it at and getting out as soon as possible, I hadn't seen anything like it in my life. They bogged into their breakfast like wild dogs or pigs at the feeding trough. Not a word was said but the sound of cutlery against crockery was all that could be heard. Within minutes, it was all silent as if nothing had taken place there. So this was to be breakfast time over the following months.

Arriving back at my billet, I started to notice a lot more other recruits around as, like myself, we didn't have our uniforms or our dress of the day, which was overalls and boots, so I just waited around my billet until Corporal McNaulty arrived. We were then divided into groups which brought back my early childhood memories when I first arrived in Australia some thirteen years earlier. In our groups of twenty-five, we were shown how to make a bedroll then marched off for uniform fitment and the like. Upon getting that sorted out, it was back to our barracks where we were shown the remainder of open kit inspection, which included every morning without fail our room was to be free from dust and our bedroll completed as required. Apart from that, we were shown how to spit-polish our boots and shoes. From there, it was down to the Armoury to receive our rifles and learn how to maintain and clean them. Apart from that, it was all drill, drill and more drill. This was how we continued each day with some minor change, like classroom work and gas attacks, and I could see how slowly it was happening that we were all becoming as one.

Mid August 1965

I received a letter from Mum: it was the best news I was to ever get. After eleven years, it was now official – I was now a member of the Darcey Family. The Adoption papers were signed, sealed and delivered on the 13th August 1965, one day before Mum's birthday. Her letter read:

> *Although you are my eldest, you are my last child. Welcome to our family, son. The time waiting and all the pain between, along with the end result, was well and*

truly worth it.

I just couldn't believe it at first. I was so excited with no one to tell, so for the rest of the day, I kept it to myself.

I had a restless night. I just kept reading the letter over and over just to make sure I didn't think it was now all over. The next morning, I said to one of the other recruits, "I had a letter from home with good news," and handed it over for him to read. His eyes just opened wide, then after reading it put his hand around my neck.

"Fantastic news, Dave. Bet you're over the moon about it."

Even though I said, "Yes," I knew now that I wasn't mistaken about the letter and its contents. Morgan – I use his last name as I had forgotten his first name – and I became good pals throughout recruit training – we seemed to always be together. We were up and running to the mess hall for breakfast then a fast walk back; we never put our spit-polished boots on until just before 'stand-to' time; we would also do each other's brass polishing as at times the Brasso wouldn't be available or someone would have removed it – like-wise with the rifle cleaning gear. Sharing each other's workload remained with us throughout our full recruit training, even to sharing the push-ups when things were not quite right.

Wednesday was our main run of eight kilometres around the perimeter of the Base, at times with rifles and backpacks. Doing this, and drill, along with swimming, then up and down ropes, just seemed like child's play. On one occasion on our Wednesday run, about a month before our marching out parade, I was in the back row, the last runner within our flight (group) when I started to run sideways. As I reached the canteen, I disappeared into the phone box where I rang for a taxi to pick me up just outside the main gate out of sight. Within minutes it arrived. I jumped in the back, telling him to drop me off just before the entrance at the rear of the Base. With that, I paid up and got into the ditch alongside the road and waited for the flight to come along, where I jumped out and joined them for the last fifty metres. This I was doing each week and, so far, I hadn't been sprung! Then Morgan decided to join me so we both did it the following week.

The last week we all had our gym whites on, and without thinking, we both got the taxi around the Base and waited. Hearing the mob coming down, we waited until it was safe to join our flight and, as we jumped into line, we just looked at each other. *Shit! We'd been had!* Our corporal, McNaulty, just looked at the pair of us. We were still white while the rest of the flight was covered in mud and crap – he'd taken them through the swamp knowing that I was up to no good but didn't have it quite worked out until this day. So we both just stopped, looked at him and said, "You win, Corporal. What's the deal offered?"

"Fifty push-ups right now!" he said, and while all the flight were looking on, we both gave him fifty without a problem, and that was that.

I received a letter from Maureen letting me know that her boyfriend John had joined the RAAF and was arriving at Edinburgh within the week. I caught up with him when he arrived and asked how the family was and what mustering he expected to go into. It was hard work talking to him as his thoughts seemed elsewhere. I saw him only on the odd occasion, due to our different movements as I was about to pass out during this time, and we were able to freely move about and see some of the sights.

The one place on everyone's lips was the famous Barossa Valley, some forty kilometres north of the Base. For this trip, we hired a car between four of us and, upon arriving, locked the car, booked into a Bed and Breakfast then hit all the wine spots in town. What a bloody drunken mess! I'd never felt so sick in my life, but the more I drank, the more I wanted. I don't remember having a meal, only what came out of a bottle, falling asleep only to wake up to start all over again. I felt completely rooted, drunk and tired, and every part of me hurt in some way or another. A long time passed before I was to try anything that smelt of alcohol again.

After the last eleven weeks, our hard training was becoming much less a burden, and at times a real pleasure. I believe this was because I was very much regimented in my ways due to my time spent in the orphanage. I did, however, notice some of the recruits were unable to accept the discipline, which in turn reflected upon us being handed additional duties. I would get bloody mad about this, and no matter what we tried to do for them, it didn't bother them, and they remained at the training camp until the D.I changed their attitude towards their training and discipline.

October 29th 1965

On my final week of training I was informed that I was going to RAAF Base Pearce, posted to AFTS [Advanced Flying Training School] as a general hand. Although I had other options, I felt this mustering would give me the choice to look and see how I felt about other musterings as there were some ninety-two different types of trades to consider as career options.

So, upon leaving Edinburgh, very much different than when I'd first arrived – and how much I had enjoyed my three months there – I was now going back to my home state, which was fantastic. When I arrived, Lita, Mum and Dad were at the station. We held each other for a long time and all walked off with me being the proudest man to have been so lucky with what God had given me.

I reported to Base the next day as my orders required and, upon getting my room sorted out, I reported to my new section commander at AFTS and was shown my duties and section. As this was the hangar that some two years previous I had helped to change the glass in the skylights, I already knew the area pretty well. I was assigned to Sgt Evershed [Bluey], Dad's next-door neighbour and friend, so it wasn't long before I was well settled. This section was called Rectification – minor fitting and repairs to the aircraft as required. I remained working with Bluey and two other personnel, who were changed about every two weeks, but I remained within that section. I then decided to apply for the enrolment for airframe fitters at Wagga-Wagga, but was refused as my mustering was classified as Critical.

I was taken back a little over this as I was led to believe that I could, at any time, apply for advancement as the service didn't hold anyone back from further and continuation of training within their career. But this was not quite right in my case as, when I mentioned the news to Bluey, he said I could apply again in six months as by then, I should have gained much more experience working there.

I settled into the service way of life without any difficulty and felt quite proud to be in uniform. Having the opportunity to go into the service of my choice was an additional feather in my hat. Conscription was still the main topic of conversation, and the Vietnam conflict was still making headlines. So it was inevitable that most young men of my age would not have the same opportunity of being in the service of their choice.

I tried to read between the lines on the war in Vietnam and the Government's decision to form an alliance to support the American's provision of aid to South Vietnam. Although most of us young men had only experienced war through tabloid presentations, where our ignorance was expressed in a bravado attitude, I can recall the chaps I associated with yelling out and busting their guts to get up there for some action. While we were youthful in mind, we were certainly spirited on as more and more information was presented to us. But the reality of war came to me one evening on night duty when a Hercules Transport aircraft landed at Pearce with two aluminium caskets. I was informed they contained the bodies of two army soldiers killed in action. The aircraft required repairs to bullet holes in the fuselage.

In Wales at this time, February 12th 1966, my half-sister was born and named Carol Elizabeth Pearcey, living at 36 Alexander Road, Canton, Cardiff South, Wales.

I was still at times having flashbacks of my early years in Wales and that same person standing waving with a misty person next to her and there wouldn't be any reason for this to happen. But, as they came into my mind, within minutes, they were gone. I stressed over it as I had supposed they would stop at some point, but why come back for no given reason. I never said anything to anyone, except Lita, about these flashbacks.

I would often visit Mum and Dad during the week, but most of my time was spent with Lita. I would stay the weekend at her home and got along with her family really well. Lita's sister, Janice, worked at the Perth Chest X-ray Clinic and lived at home. Lita worked for Universal Guarantee as a typist clerk.

During the off-pay week, most of us were broke and what little cash we had would be put into petrol when we would head down to wineries at Upper Swan and Middle Swan. We would go into all the wineries on our left, having a little nip of samples, then just before Midland, we'd turn around and do the right-hand wineries back towards Base. I really enjoyed these nights and got to know almost every single man from AFTS over this short period.

One night in the middle of the off-pay week, we arrived back somewhat pissed. It was one of the WRAAF'S 21st Birthday the following day so we decided to wrap the whole building in dunny paper. I happened upon forty rolls, with which we carried out our dirty deed, then on a big notice board wrote: HAPPY 21ST BRENDA. Then we were off to our own barracks only to be woken up by the SP snapping at the bit wanting to know the person who destroyed public property – and they wanted an answer. But we hadn't heard a thing all night and couldn't help with their inquiries. We all stuck to our story, but they just knew we had a part in it, so we had to do an emu-bob around the other sleeping quarters. We never tried that stunt again for fear of being charged and confined to barracks – it would be like losing an arm to us.

June 1966

On the 14th of June, a notification to all sections read as follows:

> *Volunteers from ground staff are required for training as aircrew for the newly formed 9 Squadron based at Canberra ACT.*

My section commander asked me if I had read the sign on the notice board.

I replied, "Yes, sir."

He then explained the ongoing advantages and mentioned it would lead to active service in South Vietnam. Then he praised me for being a self-motivated worker and informed me that, should I decide to apply, he would make sure I was given the highest possible recommendation to give me every chance of being selected.

After a few days of soul-searching and trying to keep an open mind on active service, and that returning from active duty would provide me with a war service home, *and* greater career prospects, *and* the opportunity to travel overseas, all played a major part in my mind. After dwelling on all this, I spoke to Dad and told him my intentions. He just stood there quite shaken. I hadn't realised the effect my decision would have on him.

I went back to my section commander with a "Yes."

Two weeks later, and without warning, I was informed I would fly to Canberra that night, leaving no time to let my family or Lita know of my whereabouts nor when I was coming home. The only money I had was $1.50, not that I was worried about it, but it would have helped if I'd been pre-warned. But, that's the way things are done. I was now headstrong to go for it no matter what. I headed straight for the airport, parked the car and tried to let Tommy know that it was parked there with the keys on top of the front tyre, and hoping he got the message. Within minutes I was in the air.

I arrived in Canberra late that evening as I had to change flights and had some stuffing about, leaving me no time for a late meal at the mess hall. I was shown my billet for the next couple of days as I understood it and, speaking to the duty driver, asked where I could get a meal from the Base. He drove me back to the guardhouse and I soon had a meal that was supplied for them – they usually had some left as my luck would have it.

Mid July 1966

My interview time was 11am, but before this, I was placed in a room with 30 to 40 other personnel from various other Bases. At my interview, I was asked questions about death and would it bother me handling dead bodies. Then I was subjected to combat clips of South Vietnam. I just looked at them with a constructive outlook, not showing any emotion to the contents, such as the dead lying around and bits of bodies being bagged up and much more. From here, I was sent to speak to a psychiatrist and explained my reason for applying for aircrew, and my general attitude regarding the South Vietnam war/conflict. This was followed by a little idle chatter about myself. Then I was ushered off to see a medical officer.

I noticed that, from the initial 30 to 40 men, it was now down to 10 to 15. I had no idea what was happening with each person – we were just being moved from room to room, and now I was to have a medical examination. I think this doctor was from the Army Base as his attitude was quite direct: "Stand here! Jump up and down! Touch the floor with your hands! Hands out! Grip my hand!" Then he tested my eyesight and asked about my alcohol drinking. I gave him my answer: "Some wine during off pay week."

"Drink plenty of water?"

"Yes."

Then I was moved down the passage with a couple of others. We all just sat with our thoughts and after half an hour I was called in and seated, then asked a few more questions about myself. He mentioned that I had been given a very strong recommendation from my section commander, and that the CO would let me know within the week. And that was that. I was told to return to Pearce.

So I found my way back to movements and was told that I was returning by train. I requested to go back by air as I was rushed here at a moment's notice, but that fell on deaf ears. I wasn't going to listen to what he wanted and made my way back to the Commanding Officer and put my case forward. Without anything being said, he phoned up the transport air movements and ordered a ticket for Perth for me. Well, I threw him a big salute and headed for Movements, and upon my arrival, was given a big mouthful and was informed I was insubordinate. I then explained again that my situation wasn't suitable for rail and, typical of an arsehole, I waited for an hour. When I finally got my ticket, he placed me on the late flight to Perth, but at least I had a meal on board and arrived home with my $1.50c. My car was still in the same place with the keys on the front tyre.

The next day was Saturday. I went to see Lita and that afternoon drove over to where Mum and Dad were visiting Uncle Bill. On arriving, I explained where I'd been and the reason for going – they couldn't believe it. I could see Dad was very proud of this move I'd made, and I also felt very proud of my parents – in all that had happened, they hadn't stood in my way. I believe this was the very basic reason for my positive thinking and allowing me to make my own decision as to my future. The direction I was heading, and the doors that could open, was my next challenge. With all the past events of those horrible years, from all the beatings and mental anguish, and my physical development, had case hardened me as I didn't feel the pain anymore. Even so, the memory is very long and unforgiving towards my tormentors as I felt strongly now my life was going to change the way I thought, and the very nature of what I had let myself in for would be realised within the next twelve months.

David's Flight Book

Part Six

Vietnam

Mid August 1966

I was informed by my section commander that out of some 300 personnel, I and five others had been selected for aircrew with the newly founded 9 Squadron and I was to be posted to Canberra, ACT. My orders were to get my kit packed as I was going over by train, and without much fuss, I was gone the same day. I wasn't sure what lay ahead, but I knew it was going to be much better than what I left behind.

The train trip over seemed much more interesting as some parts of the land outside the window were covered with flowers, making the Nullarbor Plain dance with colour from yellows to purple and green carpets surrounded by the typical orange of the Nullarbor. As the sun hit the horizon, it began to fill the whole plains with a purple hue that could be seen until sunset. I knew one day I would explore this vast country as it was now a fact of my life that this was home no matter how often my mind drifted back to those misty figures of my past and how and where they fitted into my life. Right now, this was the way forward.

I remembered my first train trip just over twelve months earlier, though it seemed just like yesterday. I could almost touch it, it was that close to me. With this momentum of the unfolding events that laid ahead for me was never far removed, and yet I was looking forward to all my tomorrows with my future and my beloved family.

I arrived at Port Pirie, South Australia, to change trains, then I was off to Adelaide. There I had to change trains for Melbourne and, on arriving there, I had to change again for Canberra. I arrived at dawn, cold and hungry as this train didn't have a buffet car, which I hadn't been aware of and had therefore boarded without any food.

But when I did arrive at the Canberra station, I couldn't believe the state of it – this was our nation's capital! *What a sight!*

I thought. Then I could hear someone calling me: it was the duty driver, there to pick me up and take me to the Base. I went straight to the mess hall for my breakfast, then reported in at 'stand-too' hours at headquarters, then given directions to the air flight operations and training officer. I was to meet five other members who had just arrived from other parts of Australia.

I introduced myself and met everyone, then sat back to let the events of the next five days unfold.

Our training officer arrived and explained what our role would be as we were the final selection for air gunners within 9 Squadron. Over the next five days, we were introduced to helicopters and our role as air gunners, so from there, we went down to stores to be fitted out with our flying gear. Stupidly, some stores personnel supplied us with WWII rag-bone domes, only to have the OPs officer send us back for the more up-to-date helmet as we needed to be able to speak with each other.

After all that, we all climbed into a chopper and were shown the various bits of equipment and escape items. Then we were sent out to the waiting chopper for our first flight and instruction in how we were to conduct ourselves when a simulation engine failure occurred. Although we never knew when the pilot was going to conduct this movement, we were all ready for any of the simulated conditions levelled at us over the five days, including when winching from various heights and training with body litters and body bags.

A lot of training was put into each day. At times I felt everything was moving very fast, but I wasn't overly worried. When we stood down, we just seemed to finish our evening meal and head for the billets and bed to think over our day, when, without any warning, we were woken up and told we were wanted down at the flight hangar.

"Get your flying gear on and report there ASAP!"

Where had I had this before?

So being well adapted to any condition, I was soon dressed and running down to the flight office. And who should be there but our Commanding Officer explaining the coming operation we were needed for. And with that, we were night flying over Canberra, ready to winch troops up from Lake Burley Griffon.

I had no idea of time: we simply had to complete our mission and get back to Base, as if it had never happened. That was what was expected of us. Other than that, it was taking the time to rest during quiet times – as, without any notice, we were off to any location – and knowing that all our equipment was ready 24 hours a day. We all had to be the same, and at most, we would sleep in our flying gear due to the cold conditions and flying without notice. Even the pilots were treated the same until we became one, working and thinking together.

I was now twenty-one years old, having had my birthday at home with Mum and Dad just before I left West Australia. Though it was generally a big deal, I wasn't worried as my birthdays were just fine with Mum and Dad, and now that I was in Canberra, it just seemed my life was still spinning at a super-fast pace, and I was hanging on for the full ride. While lying there, resting before the next hat trick, I felt butterflies in my guts, as this was the second time I had achieved something on my own. I was a little nervous as to what lay ahead of me as the thought of now going to Vietnam had now become real, and I was pondering thoughts of death and perhaps not returning to Australia. This brought further concern as to whether I would ever see my family. Then the flashbacks from Wales would enter my mind and I would start to wonder if there was anyone there who should know where I was going. I could feel the hair on the back of my neck stand up but there was nothing I could do but hang on for the ride.

I didn't mind going to Vietnam. That in itself didn't overly concern me as I never considered myself a coward. I did have a discussion with my section commander at Pearce prior to leaving for Canberra as I was confused over Vietnam and what the real issues were. Though some were for good reasons, others seemed like double standards. I had no idea or understanding of politics in Australia nor the deeper reasons outside of the newspapers. We were informed that we were part of the peace-keeping force for the interest of our aid; we were being sent there to help the South Vietnamese retain their independence as a nation, yet it appeared to me that no one I spoke to could give me a clear answer. I knew the boy in me wasn't fully matured for politics, and the war being quite young could be some of the reasons I couldn't fully understand, yet apart from that, it was real – I was going there no matter how much we all thought about it.

We were giving each other encouragement and our fellow serviceman wishing they were in my boots inspired me, but no matter what was said, I still felt apprehensive – not at the thought of going but more at the thought of what to expect, as this was my main unanswered question.

We continued our training in Canberra and learnt more about each other due to our close working conditions. Soon we became bonded, working as one, soon to be comrades in arms and we understood each other.

As our training continued, in the last three days we started to open up with each other – Tom Farr, Allen Bloxum, David Spaulding, and Fred Monahan – we all got along pretty well as, like myself, we took to the task and were ready for any surprise moves and the typical simulated engine failure. This was the feeling of dropping down at 2,000 feet a minute, and it felt like my bum hole had jumped into my mouth. Then, when he pulled out of the dive, my mouth was in my bum hole – it was quite a feeling [not tasty]. Then we were exposed to the skills the Viet Cong used on booby traps, then more films on Vietnam, followed by more lessons around the choppers and equipment.

On our final day, we all went back to our home base and were given our orders that, on 28 September 1966, we would all meet at Mascot Airport, bound for Singapore. We were instructed to wear civilian clothes for reasons of security.

At Mascot, it was discovered that I didn't have a passport to leave the country. I didn't know servicemen required passports. This then became a problem for me to pass through Immigration and to stay in Singapore overnight. So the transport officer made a couple of phones calls which eventually allowed me to board the UTA 747 bound for Singapore.

When I got settled in, Fred asked me what the stuff-about was, so I explained to him en-route. I thought I was in the shit as I joined the RAAF under a false name as I couldn't supply them with a birth certificate or any other authentic document proving I was an Australian citizen. He looked at me curiously and we must have both been thinking the same thing: what situation would occur on arrival in Singapore.

This was my first time out of Australia and, after fourteen years since I arrived, I was off to war, and I really did feel that I had only just arrived in Australia.

So it's now time to let the fun begin.

On arriving in Singapore I was greeted by a representative from the British Consulate. After a five-minute discussion and my ears burning, I was going to be detained until providing further proof of my identity. I was driven to a large hotel and booked into a really nice room on the 6th floor and was informed not to leave the room as I didn't have a passport. I was then asked my background history, and so I began to explain.

I told him my name was Winston Franklyn Derek Lyne, and I was shipped out to Australia from Wales UK in 1952 as a War Orphan. I was adopted into the Darcey Family on the 13 August of this year. I had no proof or documentation relating to my origins and, in fact, I was still not sure that I was born on the 19th of August 1945. However, I had been using the family name Darcey for some eleven years. After our discussion, I was reminded to remain in my room. I would be picked up in the morning. I was then asked to sign some documents and he left. I thought about my actions and became quite excited as to where I was born and lived.

I walked over to the window and opened the curtains; looked out over Singapore. I just couldn't stay in my room for another minute and after some time on the phone found out where the others were. I made contact with Fred to come around and pick me up at the Intercontinental Hotel, and before long we were all off to see the sights – I just wasn't going to miss out on this opportunity. Now being with my mates would have a far greater impact to remember. I could only think of the fun we all would have drinking the spirit of the tiger till floating back to our hotels and bed.

I was woken up about eight in the morning by the representative from the British Consulate who handed me my passport. I opened it and noticed the photo of me taken at Mascot. I also noticed where I was born – South Glamorgan, Wales, Cardiff, UK. He then told me that I could now leave my room, and I just couldn't help but laugh. He must have thought I was a nutter, not knowing that I hadn't stayed in my room while the others ran the streets of Singapore. *Well, this fella wasn't going to be left out.*

When we'd met up, Fred had mentioned that I'd probably get information relating to where I was born, and he was right.

While I was packing up my gear, I recalled my first taste of the exotic Asian life; it was something I shall never forget, from their culture to their warm, friendly, and easy-going attitude. I learnt later that fair-headed men such as I were treated like Gods. I still felt a little inebriated as I packed, then it was off to the ground floor where the rest of the boys were waiting. Not too long after, we arrived at Singapore Airport for the final leg to Saigon, about one and half hours away, where I was once again pulled aside. It was explained that I was a British subject, which could be embarrassing, and I was ordered to surrender my passport to my Commander Office upon arriving at Vung Tau, where I would be given another briefing about my situation. Then I was allowed to board my flight for Saigon, thinking what a stuff about that lot was, and it wasn't over yet.

I soon settled next to Fred. Dave was in the seat across the aisle while Tom Farr and Allen Bloxum were two seats down from us. Twenty minutes into our flight, Tom started arguing with Allen. I couldn't hear about what. Dave yelled at Tom to stop it but to no avail. Then they were having a good ding-dong with fisticuffs and really going for it when Dave raced down to stop them. He grabbed Allen and told him to come down with us.

It came out that Tom was having a bad time of going to Vietnam, and Allen was trying to tell him we were all feeling the same and that he should pull himself out of it. But the fighting broke out. While this was being discussed between the four of us, a Muslim Asian lady lit a paraffin stove in the middle of the aisle to do some cooking, which caused a further commotion when Fred scrambled down the aisle and slammed his foot over the small fire, not once or twice, but six or seven times, completely crushing the stove into the carpet. While Fred was entertaining himself, Dave gave the Asian woman a piece of well-established Australian abuse: "You fuck-wit. You dopey, slanty-eyed fuck-wit!"

As for me, I just sat there busting my guts laughing at the sight of Fred and Dave. By the time the steward arrived, most of the fun was over, and the Asian lady was down scraping up what was left of her stove out of the carpet. This was the best onboard entertainment I ever remember having and have never forgotten.

After all that, we sat back and took in the view as we flew across the land to Saigon.

I can remember how lush and green it was when we got below the clouds; it looked so friendly at that height. Then below was Saigon, known as the Paris of the Orient. I could see for miles all the paddy fields, the rivers and small creeks that looked like spider webs across the lush green carpet, a patchwork of light and dark green fields. Then came the sudden jolt of the undercarriage as we touched down in SAIGON. *Well, this is it for twelve months.*

Not long after arriving, we were bundled into one of our choppers and flew low across the paddy fields to Vung Tau, our major base for operations from 9 Squadron and home for the duration.

We went straight into Ops and were given a quick briefing. My name was called out and I handed my passport in. Our role here was explained, which was to deploy the SAS long-range patrols throughout Phuc Tuy Province, fifteen miles due north of the Base. We were then taken down to stores and issued with flying suits, gloves and a bone dome. Then it was over to armoury, where we were issued with a 9mm revolver and ammo. We were shown around the Base, and my first impressions of Vung Tau were: *what a hot, dusty, open place.* The air stunk of burnt kerosene and melting tar, the buildings were all over the place with little or no organisation to the layout. Our quarters were open-sided timber huts, and the showers were some seventy yards away with the dunny between two minefields. *Well, we never expected the Hilton!*

We grabbed a bed that wasn't being used and the best place for sleeping as we all wanted to get that sorted out now. After that, we were taken into town as our mess hall was located at the Officers' quarters. I remember the stink – the foul smell was just like Fred's farts, but there was no escape from it as we drove into town about two miles away. We arrived just in time for evening meals and they were pretty good and there was plenty of it. It was up to us to decide what we wanted to do for the rest of the evening.

Tom was still quiet and headed back to camp while the rest of us decided to walk home and look over the sights of Vung Tau as this was going to be our playground for the next twelve months. It was hard to believe that just up the road was our enemy, the Viet Cong, and the North Vietnam Army, and here we were unarmed in the middle of a strange place looking over the sights. The walk back to Base was slow as we had nowhere to go but bed. We stopped at a street bar to try the local brew and I knew they wouldn't be getting much out of me as it tasted crap, like drain water, 33, or "Bam I bam". Soon enough, we got back to base and started to settle in.

During the night, we were woken up with loud explosions in the distance and were informed the next morning that the B52 bombers were bombing twenty miles away. I had felt the concussions here – what would it have been like at the bomb site?

The next morning we were picked up and taken to the mess hall, but this time we were dressed in our flying gear and armed with pistols. This was to remain our dress of the day for the full duration of our tour. Breakfast was just as pleasing as the evening meal with plenty of fresh fruit, which I would stuff in my pockets just in case. We were then driven to the Base for the day's briefing and introduced to all the flying crew that had arrived about July '66. Then we were given our flight details and assigned to a chopper crew. From there, the fun started.

We were broken into five chopper crews and numbered from 1 to 5. One and Two were based at an army camp at Nui Dat, eighteen miles north of Vung Tau and code-named Kanga.

Three was used to transfer personnel to and from Base to camp and Four was used for mail runs. Five was on standby, but on your day off you could do what you liked but you had to remain on the Base. The waiting game started. We found ourselves playing cards and a board game called 'Sorry', along with cribbage; it seemed to make our days on standby go quicker. Over this period, we would go out to the coast for target practice, throwing boxes into the sea to shoot up, or down to the Rifle Range for pistol practice. We generally did our target practice on Kango 4 and 5 during the afternoon. This was then rotated every five days until the 6-gunner arrived, then the roster changed every six days. This depended on everyone being fit for work at all times as there was no one to replace us should one go off sick, and no one ever let the others down. I never went off sick and never had a day off outside of the weekly roster.

October 18th 1966

On a resupply mission to 5th Battalion, a chopper flown by Flight Lieutenant Dohle and Flight Lieutenant Middleton crashed. Also on board were two engineers. Tom Farr was thrown out attached to his floor strap. Gordon Buttress was also thrown out but was okay. Flight Lieutenant Dohle found his way out. Flight Lieutenant Middleton had to be dragged out after Buttress ripped out part of the front to free his foot and dragged Flight Lieutenant Middleton to safety. He received the George Cross for Gallantry. Tom Farr, although his wounds healed, wasn't himself.

October 22nd 1966

We were on standby Kango 1 and received a message from our Ops Officer that a SAS Patrol had come in contact with Viet Cong. They required our air support and we were to engage as soon as we sighted them. While this was going on, we were already up and flying to their location, and my pilot told crewman Brian Taylor and me to keep an eye open for the SAS as they were throwing blue smoke. It wasn't long before we could see their position and the sampan with three or four Viet Cong shooting at us. We went into a dive and Brian shot off about two hundred rounds. While he was reloading, I unloaded onto the target and then it was Brian's turn again. We repeated this attack until the firing from the sampan was silent ... And the rest becomes history as a credit to the RAAF. We then returned to Nui Dat and re-armed our chopper with 1,200 rounds each, then settled down to finish our game of cards.

I was not confused or ignorant as to what we had just done. Brian and I didn't act with bravado – we simply went out and completed our task and returned. My adrenalin was pumping, however, and I think it would be for all in the same situation. Brian looked over me and said:

"I wonder how we went. I felt this cold feeling coming over me as I tried to picture what sort of a mess we left behind."

The next day we were debriefed on the action, and it was confirmed that our action was credited with three kills, and the weapons used by the Viet Cong were 50mm machine guns mounted onto the sampan. The SAS patrol that was on the ground came over to talk to Brian and me about this particular bunch of Viet Cong: for the past two months, they had been going into the small fishing villages and shooting the locals that wouldn't provide for them, then before leaving they butchered the village chief in front of his wife. Then they butchered her.

This was to keep a strong hand over the village, and this satisfied Brian and me that our actions were well justified, and that was the purpose of us being there ... to help these defenceless South Vietnamese from the Viet Cong.

Dave Champion, Brian Taylor, David Darcey
Vung Tau, Vietnam 1966

We were now settling into a normal routine, even though we were at times on standby. Most nights we could do our own thing before curfew at 2100 hrs, if we had gone to town. During the day, we remained at our billets, keeping our area clean from sand, which was always blowing through the openings along the side of our hut. Then we would write letters home to family. All our letters were opened by our intelligence officer before being posted just in case we had mentioned things of a sensitive nature, so I was only to mention how I was getting along and general news around the camp and things we got up to. At most, I would remain in camp and on many occasions, I would be on Kanga 5. My mate Allen would also be there either on his day off, or mine, while he was on Kango 5.

Dave Champion, Brian Taylor, Dave Darcey

When we were stood down, we would go to our Base wet mess, called the *Ettamogah Hotel,* for a couple tinnies. The hotel, which opened at 1500 hrs, was just a tent with pallets for flooring and was our general social gathering point for 9 Squadron personnel. One night, Allen and I arrived at the hotel and as Allen walked up to the makeshift bar – a big box on its side – his foot slipped down between the pallet and the bar. As Allen started to stand up, the barman, who was always shitty over something, gave him a closed fist to the head, sending Allen back to the floor. I was a couple of feet behind Allen and went forward to help him up. As I stood up, my foot went between the pallet and the bar and the next thing, the barman clobbered me on the head, which sent me falling down over Allen. As I was trying to remove my bloody foot, Allen managed to start standing, and, just as he got to his feet, he had another fist to the head. As he was coming down, I was on my way up and, just as my head reached the bar, another closed fist slammed into my head and down I went alongside Allen again. We both looked at each other. Without a word, we freed our foot and, well pissed off, jointly stood up fast and, in unison, delivered a king hit to his face, which sent him flying back into the back canvas of the tent. Allen, well and truly riled, raced to where he had fallen. We looked at each other, both undid our fly and pissed over him until he came around. As that happened, we sank our boots into him then went to the bar, grabbed a six-pack and left the hotel, with him grumbling at us. We both then settled back in our huts, feeling a little sore but happy.

On the 18th of December, 1966, our CO was posted to the Department of Air, and Wing Commander R.S Royston was appointed our new Commanding Officer. He was to take a big interest in our operations with the Task Force and the SAS patrols, and our workload was becoming more demanding, our days quite long and tiring. This was to bring about two days a month off, which was spent either sleeping or just resting, but we never let anyone down – no matter what our situation was we were there.

I recall a day when my Commanding Officer came down and asked me to get my gear as we had a hot extraction. With that, I got myself ready, and on the way to Base, he explained that the Viet Cong were about to ambush some ARVN and civilians at the Long Hai Peninsula. We'd been asked to get them out.

With our chopper fully armed, we were flying within ten minutes of picking me up. About fifteen minutes later, we found the location but no landing site. We both didn't want to winch them up due to the time it would take and the danger of exposing ourselves. Then we noticed red smoke and headed towards it and we could just see them through the bamboo thicket. Wing Commander Royston looked at me, saying he was going down and with that, I nodded. He descended, using the chopper like a big bloody lawnmower. Then I noticed the ARVN cutting their way to us while chips of bamboo flew everywhere.

I was close enough to grab hold of this little person by the arm and pulled her into the chopper, only to find her other arm was gone apart from a short stump. Then I dragged another one in, then two walking wounded. Gunshots were heard but I kept pulling them aboard, looking at the same time towards my pilot. I gave him a signal for one minute, and with that, the last two were hot-footing over to us. As I reached down, pulling them in, I nodded to my pilot and mouthed 'Go, Go, Go', as my intercom lead was too short while I was standing on the skids. As the last two clambered aboard, I could feel the chopper running rough as guts; looked over to the casualties and realised we had some nine people on board, not counting CO Royston and myself. It didn't take long before we were well clear of the area and flying about twenty feet over the jungle. We both could feel the condition of our chopper and the vibrations, followed by the shaking, so the pilot reduced the airspeed until it settled.

We arrived at the Korean field hospital as it was their job to look after the locals, then we departed for Base. The pilot was now feeling the vibrations through the collective control but kept going. We gained height as he explained we might have to ditch. As he reached two thousand feet, he lowered the airspeed and we glided back towards Base some three miles away. Once safely on the ground, we could see the extent of the damage.

Upon completion of our task, I headed back to my billet as if nothing had happened.

The following day we were informed that the platoon was almost overrun at the point of our landing, and so taking the calculated risk of suffering rotor damage had saved them from certain death. This was two days before Christmas 1966.

January 1967

When we were on standby, we always had a pack of cards or our crib board. Then my pilot, Flight Lieutenant Max Hayes, taught me how to play chess. This opened a whole new world for me. Although Max and I were crewed together many times he had never asked me before and I was quite pleased as I had noticed he would play chess with his own rank. But now we would spend a lot of waiting time playing chess, and when he won, which was all the time, he would explain the moves then the attacks. So for the next few months, I was playing and learning chess while at Nui Dat.

On another occasion we were returning to Base. He always smoked a pipe and somehow his pipe flew out the door window, still smoking.

"Shit," he said, "I'm not letting any noggy bastard have that!" He pulled out his revolver and, plunging the chopper into a dive, took potshots at it while flying. He kept up his attack on the pipe till we reached tree-level, then yelled, "Have the bastard then!"

I was to later learn it was his Christmas present. From then on, if we went bush to pick up troops, he would ask them, "Hey, mate ... seen a noggy with a falcon pipe? If you do it's mine, okay."

Overall, we were very busy with our SAS patrols and the

supplying of the task force, also dust-off's which was almost Kanga 1 or 2. During the next three months, we were put under greater pressure as the two battalions were going bush. Our days would start at first light and finish well into dusk. Just when we were about to leave the Base, a dust-off was needed and no one complained. Without any hesitation, the pilot signed the logbook and we boarded the chopper, rearmed, and within minutes we were flying.

At night it was always a bit tricky as we were never sure what the landing zone would be, if any. Our main concern was to pick up the wounded and have them in medical care, all in fifteen minutes of the call. We became very experienced in providing our troops with this service as it kept their morale and respect for us up, just as we respected them.

At times while on 'stand to' duties, I would experience these flashbacks of those two figures waving to me. There would be no reason for the recall of this; it just seemed that I had them and couldn't figure out why, so I started to refer to them as my 'telegrams'. Why I should call them that, I haven't any idea. Apart from thinking of my own family in Australia, keeping super alert at all times was very draining and demanding, and at times sleeping with one eye open, as I was going home, and that was never off my mind.

March 1967

The whole of 9 Squadron was now deployed in resupplying the army and our time on standby duties amounted to zero. The army was setting up an outpost known as Horseshoe on the rim of an extinct volcano five miles east of Nui Dat. Their project was to construct a minefield 300 yards wide to make it more difficult for the Viet Cong to collect their tax from the villagers, this tax being food or medical supplies. But the minefields caused a lot of casualties for the troops, as during the laying of the mines we would fly them out from Nui Dat and, on landing near the minefield, would give them the 'all clear' and out they would go. On several occasions, we would drop them off and minutes later, we were called back as dust-off as someone had stood on a mine.

These were the worst type of injuries, which we couldn't cope with due to the volume of damage and blood loss. We had them in the chopper within minutes of the injury and had them in medical care within fifteen minutes, but the extent was very overbearing as at times the morphine wasn't effective and we crewman would have to hold them down and keep their wounds covered. On some occasions, all went fine but on others the digger just wouldn't keep himself down.

On one occasion, the rotor's wind wash blew the sheet off his lower limbs, exposing the extent of his injuries and causing us to take far more strength to hold him. In trying to do this, I was slapped in the face with the upper leg bone and we could see that we had no option but to apply force to hold him down. A minute later, he went into shock. I remained holding his lower body down and recovered him while Brian held his head to give him comfort. We tried our best but could see that he wouldn't make it. When we arrived at the Base hospital, the staff were ready for him as the pilot had informed them of our situation. The overall time it took from Horseshoe was twelve minutes.

After returning to Nui Dat, we received a message that, due to the amount of blood loss and shock, they just couldn't save him. These were ongoing events, not only at Horseshoe as the Viet Cong would go into the minefield and dig them out to move them around, and the next of our troops would trip one or two. I think we all went through quite an ordeal during these few weeks.

Brian Taylor, Dave Champion, David Darcey

On standby: David is second from left

April 1967

The action was now beginning to take effect as we were doing twice the amount of flying. The days were again long, hot and tiring as it never let up week after week. When not supplying, we were out picking SAS patrols up at sunset or taking them out. These operations were very tricky as one chopper would remain overhead about 1,500 feet high while our chopper was guided to the landing zone, sometimes below treetop level as the lower we flew, the less the sound was heard until it was on top of you.

At times we were called back to drag them out as contact was made when it should not have happened – they were only doing reconnaissance missions, and we never knew what to expect.

Time to relax

On the 12 April, approval was given for me to go on Rest & Recreation for ten days. My chosen destination was Bangkok, Thailand. I had $2,000 in my pay book, the minimum required for R & R and, with only one week of flying duties left, I would be gone. I was so looking forward to the rest and break after all the events I'd just been through.

I was up early that morning and so was Fred as he was going to Hong Kong. We joined up with some of our army troops and, of course, the Yanks, then we were flown to Saigon to catch our flight to our various R & R destinations. Although we had twelve days off, we spent one day travelling to and from our destinations, which I understood some personnel would get shitty about. As for me, I was just grateful for any time so this was fine by me. In just over an hour, we were landing in Bangkok, Thailand.

On arriving, we were briefed about our conduct and to keep in mind that we were guests in this country and a representative of our own country. Then we were off to find a good hotel. From this moment, I was on my own, although a couple of Australian Army blokes were also keen to look about, so we hailed ourselves into a cab for the nearest hotel. Once I arrived and took a look inside, I realised it was very expensive-looking, and very clean, which was what I was after. The Army guys also joined in, so I paid $300.00 upfront and headed to my room. But I wasn't happy with it so I asked for a bigger and better suite and was taken to the top floor with a front view of the city of Bangkok – for the same money. Service, however, was by tips, and the drinks were double priced, but I didn't give a damn. I was here to please me, and please me I was going to do.

I started unpacking my gear, thinking about what I would like to do – the one thing that was definitely out was an organised tour. Then I thought about having a few beers with the Army guys when the phone rang.

"You likee girlee, tome?"

"No, mate. I am too tired," I replied.

"You no likee girlee! You likee boy, tomee?"

Then I told him, "Get knotted, you dopey slope," and hung the phone up.

As I was sorting out my clothes, the bloody phone started again but I let it ring out, as I took one look at the shower and was ready to enjoy the longest vertical bath my body could handle. I was just about to get in when there was a knock on the door.

"Shit! Who is it?"

"Service, sir," answered a woman.

"I never asked for any," I replied.

"But, sir, you needee service."

Just then the bloody phone rang again. "What the fuck's going on here!" I yelled and grabbed the phone, only to hear this bloody slope saying, "You wan'na girlee now, tomee," and now the bloody door knock again. By now the room was filling up with steam from the still running shower. I slammed the phone down, yelling into it, "Fuck off, shit head," then a little pissed off flung the door open. Then I stood there for a split second with *What a gorgeous looking girl* going through my mind. Then in this soft Thai voice came the words, "Likee me to stay help'a you, sir?"

I could only answer her with "Oh fucken K."

I was about to close the door when the Army guys walked past saying, "The bastards just won't leave you alone."

So now, with that Thai introduction over, I explained to her I was engaged and I pulled Lita's photo out to show her but she didn't want to understand but kept saying, "Me stay, me stay. Show you good time in Bangkok. You likee see Bangkok. Me show you."

"Okay then," I replied and started to enter the already steamed up shower when she said, "No, no, me clean you! and before I could do much about it, she was washing me down and again saying, "Me number 1 girl. I likee stay wit'a you!"

"Look, I am okay," I said.

It was then that I could see she was getting upset with me and asked her to stay and show me Bangkok, and at long last I could enjoy my bloody shower. She was fine with me then.

At first, we found it hard to communicate but with the aid of the hotel brochures, things became a lot clearer; then while I was dressing, she rang up this restaurant and made a booking. We got a taxi and she did the rest. The taxi drove us just out of the city, where we were given a fantastic entry. I was to sit on the floor in front of a small table and all the staff were dressed in their traditional costumes. My escort sat behind me, and five small dishes were placed in front of me, some with rice and some type of vegetable other things I wasn't sure about, so I asked my escort what they were.

She said, "You waitee see," and at that point this dish with a type of mud crab was placed in front of me, with chop sticks. I looked at them and started to figure out what I was supposed to do when my escort leant over to show me, but instead I asked her to sit near me by tapping the floor, so she did. From there, I was able to follow her instructions with hand signs and asked the waiter to bring my escort some food. She backed off but I told her, "No, no, you stay." I really had one of the best meals I could ever remember, even though I didn't know what the hell I was eating. And then the Thai dancers came on and with the background of the sunset, it was totally something I have never forgotten.

When it was over, I paid up and we caught a taxi to something else she wanted to show me. Arriving at this shop full of silk, it was just too much to take in but the one thing I did learn was how to tell real silk from fake. So after buying something small, we caught the same taxi back to the hotel and stayed in the bar with other Australian Army guys. My Thai escort paid the taxi as I understood that she wanted to take me out further afield tomorrow, but for now we men just wanted to talk about the future and nothing was mentioned about Vietnam.

After some time with them, I started to get tired and headed for bed with my escort and a few grounds rules were set as I pointed to a lounge that folded down to a bed and that was it.

The next morning, I was woken by her standing over me holding a drink. I sat up in bed when some breakfast, continental style but small Thai dishes, was offered, then she encouraged me to get up as she had organised something for the day. While getting dressed, she took some clothes out of the cupboard and put them into a bag. I didn't know what she was up to and never asked as she seemed more turned in than I was.

Dave on R & R

We went down and hailed a taxi and I got one of the tour maps from my bag and enquired where we were off to. She pointed to a village about fifty miles down south towards Cambodia so I sat back and looked out at some of the prettiest country I have seen as we drove through rice paddy fields. We arrived at our destination, a small village near Chon Buri. Here we visited more silk works, followed by a Thai lunch, a type of fish paste – not very nice – but I downed it. After buying some gifts, we headed towards the coast and this was something totally unexpected, a small sandy cove with palms trees and grass huts around. It wasn't long before we were both enjoying this beautiful little beach, then the taxi driver brought some other Thai food and drinks. The rest of the day I spent lying about and swimming. I was asked to get ready for the next event. In the late afternoon, we headed back towards Bangkok then about an hour later the taxi driver drove down towards the coast and stopped outside a really traditional restaurant with large carvings around the entrance. We were greeted at the entrance and once again seated on the floor, but this time I asked the taxi drive to join us and, though a little shy at first until my escort spoke to him, he settled in. Once again, I couldn't believe the effort and workmanship put into this building, and it became very clear that these people were very strongly bound to their culture. Our meal was like the previous night, followed by the dancing and a few drinks of the local brew. We stayed until midnight and got back to my hotel then paid the taxi for the full day with a good tip so we could keep him for the next day.

I was sound asleep within one minute of my head hitting my pillow, and it seemed minutes later I was once again woken up with Thai tea and asked to get up and get dressed. During all this, she showed me the brochure pointing to a pile of sampans, then I noticed the words 'floating market' and nodded yes. We went down to the ground floor and our taxi was there waiting for us. A short drive later, we arrived at a very busy market, the likes of which I had never seen before. People walked from sampan to sampan buying vegetables and nuts and a huge variety of other exotic food totally unknown to me. I was asked to buy something and decided on what I knew – peanuts and cashew nuts – so I walked from sampan to sampan and did the trading, trying to keep my balance. Walking back was quite tricky but I made it, and after spending quite some time walking around looking at the place and the hearing people yelling out and dealing from shore to the sampans – what a shambles it seemed, yet everyone got their trading done – we moved on to our next place of interest but stayed in the taxi. I was driven around Bangkok to look at the temples and the King's Palace; then a quiet late afternoon drink with the Army guys at the hotel and it appeared they were having a great deal of girl trouble, but I was fine. Then the subject came up that we had one day left and how quickly it had gone.

While sitting there talking, I came to the conclusion that if I hadn't taken up the use of this Thai girl, my R & R would most definitely not have been the same, and I decided then to take her to the silk shop so she could buy herself a dress. I rose and raced out and got her and the taxi to drive across town to the silk shop and put my money on the counter and a dress, pointing to her to have it. She was shy at first but I was quite determined and made it quite clear to her. Thankfully, the shopkeeper could speak English enough to tell her and that was that, so with two dresses we headed back to the hotel. I said goodbye to them both and went to get my gear packed up for tomorrow. I lay on my bed thinking about my time spent here and this Thai girl's friendship was well worth it and much cheaper than a paid, upfront tour, yet I had seen everything the others had and possibly much more.

I loved the people and their kind and warm welcome given to me but now it was finished as tomorrow I would once again be back in Vietnam.

"Bloody hell," was the only thing that came to mind when I landed at Saigon. If God wanted to give the world a penicillin jab, this place would be his choice as it's one big festering pus-pit, a stinking hole that could be smelt 1,000 feet above ground.

After returning from R & R, this was a big let-down, and yet it just seemed that I became a little bitter about returning here as I now knew what I was doing. But that was the way things were, and in between this hard fact, I was also having these telegrams again – I was becoming more aware of the fact that I wanted to find her again, and in the days before any mission, this seemed to bring home the need to make sure I would be going home.

May 1967

I didn't go to town much as the workload was quite long and so, at best, we stayed on Base and our entertainment was at the *Ettamogah Hotel* [Australian bush pub] and it was here that my drinking really started. I was drunk almost every night, not giving a damn whether I was sober for flying duties the following day, but I always turned up washed and shaved but light-headed.

On my return from R & R, our rosters were changed to each week and at times I was saddled with a Corporal Williams. We became good mates while on the ground, but as soon as we went flying, he began to argue and become irritable. At times I wanted to clobber the bastard. It just seemed he was a nervous flyer. My main concern was, if we got into a hot spot, how would he react, so I confronted my Commanding Officer about it: his answer was for me to ignore it. Yet while we were drinking, Corporal Williams was a different bloke, and almost a pleasure to be with, but when we were called up for gunnery support, he remained quite subdued. In fact, he seemed a lot more level-headed than I'd previously given him credit for.

My old mate Fred Monahan was now getting bloody angry with his situation as he'd been in Vietnam seven months and hadn't fired a shot in anger. So he came to me and said, "Dave, how about changing duties with me as it always appears trouble finds you."

"Well, if that's what you want, Fred, that's fine by me!"

So the next day, Fred was Kanga 1 Nui Dat, and I was Kanga 3 Vung Tau, and was crewed up with my old mates Buttress and Flight Lieutenant Dave Champion and a new pilot Flight Lieutenant Shepherd. We were out on a typical mail run to Nui Dat when a message came from a fixed-wing spotter that he'd found some Viet Cong at yesterday's leaflet drop zone. With this, the pilot was instructed to go to the area and detain them until the American bombers arrived.

Upon one fly-past of the location, we came back with all guns blazing away and kept this up until the bombers arrived to pound the area, then we headed off towards Nui Dat where Fred was kicking the shit out of a rubber tree and yelling at the top of his voice, "What the fuck am I doing here?!"

I started to laugh and said, "Don't worry, Fred. You've still got four months left, mate."

June 1967

I was now crewed up with a new member to our Squadron L A C Henson, and it was my duty to show the new members the drill. On this occasion, though, it was short-lived as an SAS patrol were in a spot of trouble and required a hot extraction. When we reached their location and found their smoke, there wasn't a clear landing zone so winching was the only way to get them out. During this operation, we were fired upon by the Viet Cong, so I left Henson to the winching while I opened up with the M60. After five rounds though the bloody thing jammed up. I sorted it out then fired, and it jammed up again. By now, one of the SAS patrols noticed my problem and handed me his weapon while he removed every fifth round on the belt.

During this time, the second SAS member noticed the situation unfolding and handed me his weapon while the two of them sorted the problem out as the third SAS member being winched was wounded. Henson kept his cool, and so did the pilots.

I was out of ammo and decided to reload the belt while the SAS members gave Henson a hand to pull their mate aboard. Then I got started, short bursts and talking to my pilot to pivot to port. With that, I could deliver my load direct to the Viet Cong location. Just as the last SAS member was on the winch, but hanging about forty feet below, we left just as the yanks arrived with rockets.

Upon landing at Nui Dat, I tried to find out what happened with our ammo as this needed to be sorted out. It appeared that all the tracers were stuffed but how the hell they were mixed up with the resupply? I left for my Section Commander to find out as none of us were going out until he got to the bottom of it. It would appear that the ammo was placed in the wrong container, and the container was then sent to Nui Dat by mistake. So from that day on, we resupplied our own ammo.

Aircrewman/Gunner David Darcey

July 1967

Henson and I worked well together and remained crewed up. On this occasion, and after a big overnight battle at An Loc about twenty miles north of Nui Dat, the next morning we were to resupply the AVON with empty jerry cans. As we were flying at about 200 feet over the main highway, we noticed this ox cart with three noggies with a machine gun firing at us.

I told the pilot, "Incoming! Break Starboard! 50mm I think."

Just then the bullets slammed into the chopper. They whizzed past me and into the jerry cans. Bits of plastic flew around, yet our army passenger hadn't noticed a thing … until the second lot was coming and I pushed him over onto the console panel. We were hit again, sending jerry cans out past Henson. I asked for permission to open fire but was refused. Then the last hit resounded under my feet and, at the angle we were flying, I didn't have any chance of firing back.

Henson looked over at me. "I'm hit," he said, and I noticed blood coming from his upper thigh and grabbed the first aid kit. I applied a temporary bandage, at the same time asking for permission to open fire, my finger ready should another volley come our way as I could still see them. But the pilot flew back to Nui Dat as our chopper was pretty crook.

Henson was now feeling the pain, which I could do nothing about, but when we landed, I fell out of the chopper as I had been hit by flying metal fragments. I was starting to tremble inside, saying to myself, 'Thank God I am down."

Bleeding from my elbows, I went to see Henson and gave the medics a hand to get him clear of the chopper blades, still trembling and thinking: *Stuff this for a joke. Them bloody noggy bastards know how to get you sober!*

August 1967

My crew replacement was a Corporal O'Rouck, a Base defence guard – they were now being trained up as gunners – so my job was to explain the workings. But again, before long we were involved in hot extractions while under fire, and being called out for dust offs. Although he kept to himself, we never struck up a friendship, but worked okay together and our rest periods were spent apart.

One of my rest days with Allen and Dave, I was lying on my back when this bloody old bloke outside our hut began firing rounds through the hut. I looked over to see where it was coming from when Allen yelled at him to put the weapon down. But more rounds were fired into our sleeping quarters, and this time I hit the deck flat, along with Allen, while Dave, who this old bugger hadn't seen, ran around the hut. Allen and I were now trapped as the old bugger had entered the hut. Then Dave burst through the door, sending the old bugger to the floor. Dave hog-tied him as the old bugger just wasn't quite quick enough for him. At the same time, Allen and I scrambled up but, in no mood for a chat, Allen walked over to him and, as Dave wrenched the weapon away and unloaded it, Allen's boot found its mark, just as the SP's arrived. The poor bastard had gone troppo.

Just as we had felt safe, we were now under threat from our own Base personnel.

September 1967

Our CO, Wing Commander Royston, was being replaced by Wing Commander Reed, and I was informed, along with Allen, Dave and Tom, that our flying duties were to finish at the end of August as this was a tradition for all combat aircrew. So when that week arrived we sat around the boozer talking about home and the long leave owing to us.

ROYAL AUSTRALIAN AIR FORCE

S E C R E T

Form P/P. 138
(Revised September, 1950)

AIRCREW RECORD OF OPERATIONAL TOUR

(Do not attempt to fill in return without reading instructions inside front cover.)

Member's Number... **A57288** ...Rank... **LAC** ...

Name... **DARCEY D.A.** ...

Category... **GHAND** ...

Part 1 – RECORD of OPERATIONAL TOUR with No. **2** SQN, in... **SOUTH VIETNAM** ...{ AREA / GROUP

Date Tour Commenced... **27th September 1966** ...By posting to No... **BASPEA** ...Squadron

Date Tour Finished... **12th September 1967** ...By posting from No... **2** ...Squadron to...

Part 2 – DETAILS of FLYING on TOUR between ABOVE DATES

	Whilst on posted strength of No. ...**2**...Squadron	Whilst on posted strength of No. ......Squadron
(a) Number of operational sorties (i) Strikes and attacks performed " " (ii) Other ops " "	**4,770** **691**	
(b) Number of operational hours (i) Day " " flown " " " (ii) Night " "	**11 Hrs 45 M**	
(c) Number of other hours flown " " " " "	**5hrs 30 Min.**	
(d) Approximate date of first operational sortie "	**28th September 1966**	
(e) Approximate date of last operational sortie " "	**2 SEP 67**	
(f) Approximate period, if any, non-effective between (d) and (e) due to minor casualties, sickness, or leave beyond the area " " " " " "	**N/A**	

Signature of Member... *Darcey* ...LAC.

(g) Logbook assessment at Squadron ......

(h) Commanding officer's recommendation as to the subsequent duty for which the member is considered suitable......

......**PITTED**...... **WG CDR**
Officer Commanding

This space for use by R.A.A.F. Hqrs. only.

Flight hours

On the 29th August, we were notified that I was posted to Base Pearce, Fred to Canberra, Dave and Tom to Ambley. We all just sat back and reflected on the last twelve months, from the things we'd done and the way we felt about them. I felt really proud of my active service and combat duties, and the new friends I'd made for life. This place had brought us together and changed us into what we now were. While the time had gone quick – yet was at times a real drag – I felt strong inside, and that boy in me when I first got here was no more. This bloody place had changed us from ignorant young boys to solid, self-minded men. We had given every ounce of ourselves to fully support the South Vietnamese to the point of supreme sacrifice. But little did I know that my own war was just about to start.

I completed filling my flying logbook with a grand total of seven hundred and eight hours and fifteen minutes – 708.15 – with a grand total of four thousand seven hundred and seventy-four operational sorties – 4,774.

Upon arriving at Mascot, I said goodbye to my mates and headed for my flight to Perth. When I arrived, I was welcomed home by Lita and her parents, Aunty Pat and Tommy.

We left the airport and headed for Aunty Pat's house while Lita's parents went home to Armadale. We arrived at Aunty Pat's in Toorak Road, Rivervale, to a small welcome home party for me. It was great to see Tom, and my old car looked great – he was over the moon to have used it – then I took Lita aside, but I just couldn't come up with a conversation; I was stuck for words. I also didn't feel that good as I had lost weight while in Vietnam, but there seemed to be something missing. I felt I was in a time warp, with things around moving too fast, yet I was stationary. My mind was in a state of quandary, unable to put things clearly and trying to make a decision even as I was talking to Lita.

I felt like this until the words "Go home," came from Lita so I thanked Aunty Pat and left for Armadale, feeling strange after twelve months of not driving my car. It wasn't long after settling into bed that I realised my eyes wouldn't close: my mind was still in Vietnam but my body was here. Something was missing.

When I did drift off, I woke in a lather of sweat. During my time staying at Lita's, I would wake up with memories of the war. I could see myself with my hands and my foot missing, unable to run, unable to shoot, only to be crawling on my elbows and knees trying to escape from the Viet Cong. These memories haunted me night after night, and with all this, I was having these telegrams, these misty figure flashbacks and they were together with me crawling around the jungle, unable to fight back. I couldn't even put an end to it all as I had no hands to hold my pistol. I remember only too well these horrid nights waking up trembling inside and started to think about talking to my Base doctor about my problem. So the next day I told Lita that I was going to stay on the Base, to find out why I was having these flashbacks.

As much I wanted to be with her, I really felt it better to be at the Base and this was realised one day soon after my return. While out with Lita's brother, my situation became quite serious. We were returning from Perth where he'd been shopping but he wanted to stop and pick up something in Victoria Park. After parking the car, I just couldn't cross the bloody road. When I finally did, my adrenalin was way over the top, as if I had just crossed a bloody minefield. I could see everything around me moving so fast that my mind could not take it all in. Cars appeared way over the speed limit, and people just rushed around in a rip-tearing hurry, and the loud noise of the traffic didn't help as it grated in my ears. There just wasn't any escape from it all.

I looked at George and said, "I don't feel good about this, mate. I'm having some anxious feelings, and everything is moving too fast. I gotta get out of this place." And with that, he led me to a chemist. The chemist wouldn't give me anything so we headed for home as it would be better and safer for me in that environment.

So, after another crap night, I left early the next morning as I wanted to be on the medical parade first thing.

During the next few weeks, I remained at the Base, and went to see Lita over the weekend. This also gave me the chance to see my old mates and each night we would all get into the wet mess for a quiet chat and a few laughs. Questions were asked about my time in Vietnam and how bad it was getting and how the government was sending more troops. When the questions were of a political nature, I couldn't give them an answer as we hadn't received a great deal of information about our situation while there. I did mention, though, that it was getting worse each day as our flying time doubled in the last six months compared to the first six months. It was difficult for me to explain the things I was going through, and I never mentioned the things I had done and the fact I was speaking to the Base medical officer about it and he was going to talk to another colleague and get back to me.

We often had a beer after our evening meal and shared small talk about the day's events. As always, this old corporal played the piano out of tune and was always half-drunk before we arrived. On one particular night, he became somewhat annoyed with us over our joking and laughing and walked up to the bar, bought another beer, downed half of it then went to the dunny. When he returned, he yelled at us for drinking his beer. As we hadn't, we all looked over and someone told him to behave himself, so he sat back at the piano, again playing out of tune and about ten minutes later went to the bar for another beer. Just like before, he drank half then got his prick out and put it in his own beer glass and said to us all, "That will stop you pinching my beer." Then he went to the dunny. I just walked over, picked up his glass and, getting my donk out, dunked it in his beer and then passed the glass around for rest to dunk their donks in. Then we replaced the glass back on the counter just as he was returning. He walked up to his glass, looked at us and said, "I knew that would stop you pinching it, you bastards." And with that, he downed the lot and left the boozer, leaving us busting our guts with laughter. The news went around the base like wildfire that we weren't to be trusted if you left your beer on the bar.

Part Seven

Life Goes On

December 1967

Mum and Dad, Wendy and Peter were back from Darwin and living at Nollamara. It was great to see them all, though Mum could see the change in me, which she often said. Tommy was well into his apprenticeship, while Barbara had now joined the RAAF and was posted to AFTS HQ Pearce as a clerk. She was now courting Robby Rhoades, also with AFTS, working on engine maintenance. Maureen now lived in Balga and was still nursing, and John was posted to AFTS Pearce, also working on engine maintenance. So we were now all together again after one year apart.

Now we were making plans for my wedding, but deep down, I wasn't overjoyed about the coming event. I asked Tommy to be my best man, as well as a friend from work. I managed to get a flat in Highgate so Lita could still work and I would travel across to Nollamara and get the RAAF bus with Dad to Pearce.

I received a letter from Fred Monahan, who explained that he'd met a girl from WA and would I consider doing an exchange posting between ourselves to enable him to see more of her with the view of marriage? With all the events placed in front of me at this time I had to say no, and also the thought of going to 5 Squadron would put me in line for another tour in Vietnam, which I didn't want after getting married.

December 16th 1967

Lita and I were married at Saint Frances Xavier's Church in Armadale. Lita looked absolutely beautiful. She was very pretty to start with, but in her wedding dress she was a stunner and I was really proud to have her as my wife. As for myself, I didn't feel that well during the whole ceremonial night. I had made no plans to go on a honeymoon as it was too close to Christmas so we spent our time in our flat, as no one knew where it was.

January 1968

It was becoming quite clear that I was developing an attitude problem with my work and workmates. I had just lost interest. I knew my problem was related to my Vietnam experience, and this was coming very much to the head. I was on night shift, driving to Pearce Air Base, my mind blank of thoughts when these lights started flying into me. They looked like tracer bullets and, no matter which direction I went from left to right, I just couldn't avoid them. Then I realised I was in the storm drain alongside the road and brought the car to a skidding halt and jumped out only to notice that I was driving through a swarm of moths. It took me some time before I drove out of the drain and headed to Pearce some eight miles away, keeping my speed down to twenty kilometres until I arrived at the Base.

The following day, I went and spoke to the Base Medical Officer. I tried not to tell him too much for fear of being classed a nut case. He then asked me to bring my wife up to see him for a chat, so the next day I explained to Lita and we both left for Base Pearce Medical Section. After discussing my condition, it was suggested I should voluntarily place myself at Heathcote Hospital. I gave this no real thought and, without any questions as to why I just nodded my approval and the next day admitted myself. Upon doing so, I learnt that I was experiencing battle fatigue and that I should talk my problems through with the medical staff.

That evening, I learnt that another service member from Pearce was also staying over for a couple of weeks and the next morning I introduced myself to Stan. We seemed to have some common ground, although I wasn't sure why he was there. He explained that he wanted out of the RAAF and this was his ticket. As for me, I just wanted my crap to go away.

Though we seemed to have hit it off with our common ground, he did seem a little more distanced from his surroundings. Then he explained some of the rules to me and I understood why he didn't give a hoot as he could leave the hospital anytime he felt like it. I couldn't understand his reasoning and never questioned why until two days later when he asked me to join him for beer around 3pm. I knew then what his caper was. So we would wander off to the Raffles Hotel, Canning Bridge, for a couple middies and arrive back just in time for evening meals. This was to remain our plot for the full two weeks stay at Heathcote.

Though we were quite different in a lot of ways, he would ask me what my reason was for being at Heathcote Hospital and I explained that I was having these flashing lights like tracers coming towards me while driving and some bad dreams. He said I was over-reacting and needed another source of energy outlet. He was into collecting antique China dolls. I thought this quite funny at first and didn't give it much thought until I returned to Pearce Air Base, and doing my day-to-day duties and driving back each afternoon to Highgate to be with Lita. During this time, my Intelligence Officer from Vietnam had put in a request for me to be posted to 25 Squadron, located at the University of Western Australia, for three to four months. I jumped at this opportunity, much to the displeasure of my Section Commander as I was to start the Monday of the following week. This was also good news for Lita as we would have more time together.

So, come Monday, I was there at 'stand to' hours ready to go.

My Officer commanding 25 Squadron explained my duties:

we were to have one late night midweek when I would drive him to the Swan Brewery to collect 18 gallons of beer and return to 25 Squadron. I would take care of the wet mess duties as, at 3.30, we would have the young students wanting information about joining the RAAF and the carrier opportunities along with their various Uni qualifications. The price I was to charge for a middy was 10 cents.

My first weeks with 25 Squadron was pretty uneventful. I did a variety of work from mail-runs to generally keeping myself occupied around the office duties for the Wednesday evening entry aptitude exam. After they were completed, I was then the barman. This was when they would become very unsettled as to their points score and pass marks. Even though all the exams were multi-choice and the answers could be, and were, known five minutes after they were finished their prescribed time, these were very trying times for them. As for ourselves, we just knew who had passed and who had failed. But the biggest factor was how they were in themselves when drinking 10 cent middies and how their attitudes changed, as we from 25 Squadron were in the wet mess with them. It became obvious when some standards were forgotten, as events that were not fitting for Officer material within the Flying Training School was also part of this exam evening, so without anyone knowing, observation was to play a small amount but could help those students with low scores. We would finish the night when the last man had fallen down drunk and I locked up and headed for home around midnight.

I always hated Thursdays as I would still feel drunk the next morning, but after breakfast, for which I thanked my wife as she always got up with me, I caught the bus to the University. On one occasion, when I arrived and opened up the wet mess, I found three bodies lying on the floor. *Shit, I don't quite remember leaving anyone here.* I started to tap their foot to move them, but this became a hopeless task so I poured a half jug of beer and tipped it over them. Finally, they came around and, upon getting to their feet, began to pour the flat beer into glasses while I continued to clean up the previous night's drinking session. When I asked them how they got in, I was told that I locked up while they were in the dunny.

"That's crap," I said, "as I checked them and no one was in them." I told them that I wasn't going to let it rest, so I continued to ask them, but got the same reply.

"Look, mate," I said, "the dunnies are not that big."

Then they all said that they were.

Then it hit me, and I asked them to show me the dunny, and with that, I found I was going into the Ladies along the passage. I had never checked it as we had no women working at 25 Squadron. So from my position, I explained it was my fault and, as there just wasn't a way out and all the lights were master keyed, we all went back to the wet mess and I poured out four middies while they got the darts out. We all started playing while having a middy, while I cleaned up the bar and swept the area until my shot at the darts. Right at that time, my commander officer walked in and looked straight at me.

"Darc, in my office, on the mat now!" So I put my hat on and did the quick march in and stood to attention.

"Sir!"

"L A C, what the hell do you think you're doing?"

"Well … I … aaah," I was about to say when he broke into my dribbling lips.

"The next time I find you playing darts, drinking beer, and sweeping the floor, you're on a charge!"

"Well … I … aaah," I tried to explain again, when again he said, "There is not enough work here to be doing three things together, so please … play darts, then have a beer, and after all that … clean up the bar."

"Well ... I ... aaah," I started to say –

"We need you here for the next six weeks, so only one thing at a time!"

So my work situation became quite organised and gave me time to wander the grounds of UWA. I started asking various students the type of studies they were doing. Some knew me from 25 Squadron from when sitting for their entry exam, and I was to gain quite a lot of information. Though my ability to learn was quite high, I mentioned my situation to my commanding officer and he recommended that I should approach the Base education section to get further advice and a course plan while I was still working at UWA. He also said he could help me once I had found a subject of interest. I should mention at this time that my Commanding Officer was totally aware of my battle fatigue, along with my active duties, and that he wanted me away from Pearce Barracks Section. Now I was able to redirect my thoughts into so many ideas that it was overwhelming and somewhat confusing. It was suggested that I should find a subject that no family member had or was doing as this would allow only me, along with the Education section, to give me the correct guidance, and so I felt that my life was being lifted to a higher dimension.

Upon completion of my duties with 25 Squadron UWA, I returned to Base Pearce Barracks Section, where I was given my duties to grade a section of land west of the swimming pool for a new building. I got the machinery ready and headed for the location.

This project was to take me two days, but upon investigating the overall area and having no plans of what lay hidden underground, I decided to request a detailed map for drainage and cables. I brought this problem to the attention of my section commander and, in turn, explained that I had been with the Department of Works prior to my enlistment and had knowledge of the main sewerage drain at that location. They were not very deep, which I had found out when the sewage-farm overflowed during the winter period. The method used to determine this was a green dye placed into each toilet block, which had indicated all was running fine. However, I then, over the next six months, placed the dye into one storm drain each day until a result discovered that the maintenance hangar next to the building site had stormwater from the roof connected into the main sewerage line. I was concerned due to the depth of the main sewerage and the amount of overburden to be levelled. The detailed drainage drawings would provide this information, and after explaining all this, I learnt that the Department of Works was being closed down and all documented detail drawings were under the arm of the education section and that I should talk to them regarding the matter.

I must have had my "Huie" [bush god] looking after me because when I arrived and requested the information needed, drawings I had seen some five years earlier, I asked about the course work I was also interested in while they were looking for these drawings. The education officer came over and gave me a list of ideas, which was a shortlist taken from a list of my whole family's employment history, all totally different to the best of my knowledge. Well, my heart jumped with joy, and I was a little nervous to say the least, as this wasn't expected but great news.

So, we were now getting involved checking over the contours and the survey benchmarks and I requested a copy of the area in question and headed back to Barracks section. After discussing my findings, he agreed that all looked good in regards to the sewerage pipe and its depth, and no other services were noted. Therefore I returned to the site.

When I started levelling and piling, I uncovered a large cable about 50mm in diameter and, upon checking the drawings, found it wasn't marked there. I had uncovered it for some three metres.

Well, I thought, *this could amount to a tidy sum for Christmas.* Then I backed the grader up and hooked the cable on and gunned the grader about one metre with full stress applied. The cable snapped, sending sparks flying everywhere. *Oh, shit. Looks like it's active*, I thought, still moving. When I stopped, I took one look at it and decided to very carefully poke the snapped ends into the trench and grade more over-burden, then I looked over the area to make sure that nothing was noticeable apart from levelling the site. I departed to Barracks section to stand down then left for home.

As I was driving towards the main gate, I noticed a great deal of activity around HQ.

Well, let the fun begin, went through my mind though I knew what type of crap was going to be flung at me the next morning, but drove home without any great concern about it.

When I arrived home, I sat down with Lita and explained the events that had happened that day and that I well may have caused some serious trouble and that if I was late or didn't arrive home the next day to just give the guard-house a ring – I just might be locked up. Then I mentioned that I would not admit to whatever their issue might be, but I must confess that I really didn't get much sleep that night.

I arrived at Barracks section to be met by two SP (Service Police) and the Base adjutant and was driven off to HQ. On the way, I calmly mentioned what a nice day it was going to be and that it was great to get outside for a change and that it beats working indoors. I said, "I don't mind the dust so much, but the rain and mud isn't much fun … By the way, what is the nature of me being involved with you, if I may ask?"

"Airman, you have brought a lot of trouble upon yourself," I was told, "and we require a lot of answers from you.

"Sure," I replied. "Whatever I can help you with, no

problem.

When we arrived at HQ, I was escorted between the two SP and marched straight into the Officer in Command of Base Pearce. I knew then that the shit had hit the fan. He looked at me and asked about the nature of my work the previous day.

"Yes, sir …" and went through all the details along with my discussion with my section commander regarding sewerage drains and, of course, my previous employment with the Department of Works. I continued to waffle on until I was asked to stop. Then I shoved my shoulders back as if I hadn't given the right answer.

He looked at me and said, "Did you know that twelve men were out till 4pm looking for the breakage to the Base communication, and that the base was totally without any outside national contacts, and you are responsible?"

"How could I be responsible, and for what? And when could I have done this, sir?"

He looked at me again and said, "The main communication link between ourselves and the other outpost is via the cable you ripped out during the course of levelling the site. We believe that your intentions were to remove it for its value. Am I right, airman?"

My reply was sharp. "I am sorry if this is your view of me as I am still trying to figure out what and how I could have done these things. I only started the project about 11am or thereabouts ,and the only problem was the sewer drain. As far as aerials go, there wasn't any around apart from pre-war years so I am sorry if, unknowingly, I may have caused this problem to you. Should I have known about it, I would have made sure that my section was informed ASAP. So, in this case, sir, I just really don't know what I have done. If there is anything I can do to help, I stand here for your command, as I understand."

Then he looked at me again. "Airman, back to your

section!"

So I stood to attention and marched out. The two SP drove me back to my section but on the way said, "You were lucky, Dave ... must have been a loud bang and sparks. Didn't you hear them?"

I looked over and said to them, "I am half deaf, and I drive forward. What I leave behind is level ground."

Upon arriving at Barracks Section, he looked at me and said, "We're keeping an eye on you from now on, LAC Darcey," and with that, I went straight into my Section Commander's office and asked for a meeting. It was requested. He had heard about the cable; in fact, just about all the personnel on the Base knew about it. He asked me how it all went and I answered his questions.

"Sir, did you have any idea about the problem?"

"No, sir."

"This may hang over your head for some time as the SP may now be looking for anything you might be doing and try to connect some problem over it as they can't be trusted ... so I have been thinking about sending you up to Exmouth for maintenance. Or I could make arrangements for a posting to Darwin as that was your first choice, so for now to keep you out of sight, I want you to remain in the carpenters' workshop."

So I was now back with the boys and making small lounge room furniture for myself and, of course, other people that wanted minor bits made. During this time, a new member just out of basic training was also placed within our section – Andy Anderson, a typical Northern Territory cowboy. We got along like long-lost mates. Andy had taken over my work while I was with 25 Squadron and he soon wasn't too happy with the work conditions, but his complaints fell on deaf ears and he was under threat of being charged if he did not complete his duties.

So, over the next few months, Andy and I began to talk

about his various adventures while in the Territory. His wife was a school teacher for Aboriginal kids while he worked on various stations. We had a lot in common as we were also now living near each other, which gave us more time for talking.

Then one subject he began to bring up was gemstones and how the Aboriginals would find them and sell them off to the white man – sometimes small gold nuggets. By now my ears were well-tuned in, and I asked him about the method the Aboriginals used to dig them up.

He then replied, "Ever seen an Aboriginal working?"

"No," I replied.

"Well, Dave, they find them loose on the surface."

"Well, mate, I would have thought they would be quite deep and hard to find."

"No way, Dave! It's like this, mate …you can find out what stones are found in any place if you ask a geologist or buy Gem books with all types of precious stones."

This was like one big light turned on. I just couldn't find the switch to turn it off, or more to the point, I just didn't want to as, written on the list of suitable interest from the Education Section at Pearce was Geology/Gemstones. So I was now directing my thoughts towards taking a deeper plunge into this subject and getting back to Andy to ask more about how the aboriginals know what to look for.

"Well," he explained, "the aboriginal goes on walkabout and finds these stones within their tribal land and the white fella isn't allowed there unless he is given permission by one of the tribal elders …"

"How about yourself, Andy?"

"Well, with the wife looking after the piccaninnies at the mission, they never worried about me. Also, I buy some stones and ask where Jacky found them, and sometimes he tells me and other times he won't. Then I figured it this way, that if Jacky tells me, then he found them on other tribal land and when he didn't, he's found them on his tribal land. And that's when I buy them so I can tell by type and colour of the soil and I know the area pretty bloody good. After all, I was born and raised there. I just wander off looking for cattle when, in fact, I am looking for the gemstones, so you see, I don't worry too much about finding them as they find them for me then I go look for them myself."

So I was now getting very excited about the next day as Andy was bringing some gems to show me. I was also going to speak to the Education Officer and ask him to direct me down these roads as I believed I could well bury my head deep into it. And perhaps, as Stan mentioned, that I should focus my thoughts and energy to brighten up my grey matter and this seemed to excite me beyond my expectations. I just couldn't wait for the next day to get started.

With all this, Lita was taking an interest with me, and I felt my feet were standing solid to the floor. With this whole new world of gemstones now bouncing around my head with no ending, it relaxed me into a deep sleep once I climbed to bed.

The following morning, I arrived at my section and requested to report to the Education Officer from my section commander and was granted one hour, which I thanked him for. Upon arriving at the Education Section, I explained that I was very interested in Gemstones, Geology, and Geomorphology and could he advise me what my first move should be. He then said that the books were not available from the Base library and wrote the name of some books for me to get from my local library. He said to read them and get back to him for more information on the study plan and fieldwork. I thanked him and headed back to Barracks Section and talked to my Section Commander about the Gemology and my interest to study them and learning about three types of stone structures. He looked at me with a large grin.

"Good for you, Dave. This could be the making of you and I really hope it all works out," he said.

Andy arrived that morning and, during our morning tea break, got his bag and opened it. When he exposed the opal to the daylight, the whole thing burst into fire, with flashing green to red to blue. I had never seen anything like it. No matter which direction it was held, the colour just kept bouncing around.

"Bloody hell, Andy, so this is opal!"

"Yes," he said, "and it's worth thousands of dollars." Then he placed it back in its bag and got another bag out. When he opened it, the whole stone burst in colour from a very dark blue to flashing light blue and some velvet blue/black, and again the light went through it at any angle it was held up at.

"Where do they come from?"

All he did was mumble to me, and I knew what he meant as it was from his tribal land and the place was secret, like a sacred site. But knowing Andy, I felt, given time, he would gain trust in me to mention the place, and I would respect him for that. So the rest of our workday was filled with the chatter of gemstones and far-out places that Andy had been to.

Then Friday morning I was asked to report to the Education officer so I hot-footed it there to be told that I could buy the books on a request form via the Base Education Section. The ones of the greatest value were written on the Request form already and he told me I was to pay for them when I picked them up. So I took the form from him and thanked him for his help as I felt that he was going out on a limb with this. I was gone in a flash as we stood down at 1500 hrs each Friday. Within the hour, I was in the Lands and Mines Department on St George Terrace Perth, still in my uniform. I walked to the counter and handed the man the request form and, upon looking over it, he reached under the counter and said '$25.00 please', as he dropped three volumes of Dr Edwards S Simpson *Minerals of*

Western Australia on the counter. Looking at them, I just knew that my Education Officer had a hand in getting these books for me. I handed over the cash, received the payment slip and left to pick up Lita from work on Adelaide Terrace.

While waiting for her, I started to look over these books and found them too hard to put down. While deep into various pages, I almost forgot about Lita as she stood tapping on the window. On the drive back to her Dad's and Mum's home in Armadale, I just couldn't shut up and when we arrived, I began to explain the weekly events to Lita's Dad.

I noticed his eyes brighten while talking about gemstones and opals around the size of a 50c piece, the black ones around a 10c piece, but I wasn't told where they'd come from apart from the southern part of the Northern Territory. Then I started on about the books that my Education Officer arranged for my future studies about gemstones. After looking through the books, I found a far greater amount of information on all minerals and precious metals. So our weekend was full-forward with it as Lita's Dad, much to my surprise, also had a great deal of interest to find gold just up past Kalgoorlie. He brought out some small samples given to him by an old family friend, Mr Doug Cable, a large property holder with a goldmine at a disused town [long gone] named Kanowna. Although he had never been up there, he was very much desirous to go as his old friend Doug had asked him on many occasions but he couldn't find the time. That's when I asked about contacting him to ask if we four could go up. As he felt the urge to go, he gave Doug a call that evening and it was sorted out for two weeks from then. I told Lita's Dad that I would drive up in our vehicle, which was fine with Lita's Dad (Tom).

Both Tom and I started flicking through the three books by Dr Simpson and reading was at times hard, but over the following weeks, it became quite clear and easy to follow, once we had plenty of maps of the area. I still had access to this section on the Base and would take the 1: 250,000 Army survey map of the Kalgoorlie area.

I just couldn't wait for my Leave to come around, as over the previous weeks, Tom and I got everything in order for the women and gathered enough gear for five days at the mine-site and two nights at the Cable home in Boulder, just east of Kalgoorlie. Although we didn't have any agenda in general, this trip was about getting information about the types of rocks and formation of origin, as by now I was aware of the three main categories in order of events. I felt Doug was going to complete the jigsaw that, at times, was not clear to Tom and me, so that week was about information gathering.

The trip to Kalgoorlie took me through Southern Cross, which brought back memories of the time I had run away from home. This brought on those memories of the misty figures standing there waving at me. This memory stayed with me until we reached Coolgardie. I have no idea why I was getting these telegrams now, but it appeared to me that it was a part of my life and something I just couldn't yet understand. I just couldn't forget, and the unanswered question as to who they were, after such a long time since Vietnam, Bindoon and Clontarf, would try to find me in soul but not in body. I was twenty-four years old, and seventeen years living in Australia did make me think that they knew where I was, and that was fine to them. But for me, there was never a closure to so many unanswered questions as to why I was sent here.

We arrived at Doug Cable's home around midday and, as a typical bushman, were there with two most important things: a big smile and an open hand. This was the biggest compliment between old friends. Tom and Doug had a lot in common, and it just seemed fitting that, after all these years, Tom's reward had come to fruition. Just being there was a great reward in itself.

Within minutes, we were driving towards Kanaowna and his mining shack, which would be home for the four of us for five days.

I remember arriving at the shack and Doug waving goodbye as we unloaded the gear from the car. Tom and I gathered the firewood while Lita and her mother made up beds on the floor in the two rooms as it was now becoming sunset. Lita's mother, in my view, was an excellent cook., and we sat around the stove after enjoying the meal and chatted for the remainder of the evening. Then the ladies went to bed while Tom and I sat on the small veranda looking across the vast open plain that was endless in the twilight. The stars seemed to bounce off the horizon like jewels, which made the nights seem endless and gave me this warm feeling that this was home, yet to be explored. I looked into twilight before saying goodnight to Tom then went off to bed.

We were woken the next morning with a bloody donkey braying on the veranda, making such a noise that I had to tell it to bugger off, but he only went a short distance then started again. This time Lita's Mother went out shouting at it and it must have brought the fear of hell to it as it bolted like a bat out of hell. As she was stepping back up onto the veranda, she let out a loud scream of pain.

Going over to her with Tom and Lita, we noticed blood running down her foot. I looked at Tom dumbfounded, and he did the same to me, then we looked closer at the wound but were still lost as to what had caused it. I hopped off the veranda and started to look closer when I noticed a feral tomcat. It wasn't too happy and I was lucky as it took a swipe at me but missed. I could see Tom looking at me and at my sudden jump back and, at the same time, told them to stay on the veranda.

I raced to my car and got out my bayonet [Vietnam war reminder] then covered myself well and, without any fear, flung myself straight under the shack and cornered it at the stone firebase. It was even less happy to see me and flung itself my way. Just in time, I swung my right hand with full force. The bayonet passed through its neck and pinned it to the floor bearer. I backed out, leaving it hanging and trying to free itself. Once out on my feet, I noticed Tom was a little upset but working with Lita to dress the wound. After giving it a close look, I felt that we could handle this situation for twenty-four hours.

So this was a fantastic start to the day!

An hour later, Doug arrived to show us his mine and gold workings. Lita's mother wasn't going to be left behind so Tom gave her a shoulder while Doug told Lita about his working for gold.

"Lita, have you ever seen gold in its natural form?"

"No," she said.

"Well, this will be a day you will never forget. When we reach the mine opening, we just walked into this vast opening with stone piers left for roof supports and small holes around what was used to extract the gold-bearing ore."

We all stopped as he called his foreman over and, after some finger-pointing and discussion taking place, Doug asked us to walk outside as he was going to blow a section of the roof out as he knew how rich in gold it was.

Five minutes later, this almighty bang was followed by a dust cloud pluming out of the entrance. Some ten minutes later, the dust had settled and we all went back to inspect this small amount of rubble. With us now was his foreman, who also had a bucket of water that Doug threw over the rubble. To our amazement, flicking yellow was evident.

"Lita," Doug said, "if you can lift that stone covered with gold, it's yours."

Shit! That's what went through my mind as Lita walked up to it and, without much effort, raised it to her waist and then placed it back. Then she looked over to Doug and, being quite polite, said, "Mr Cable, I can't take this – it's your livelihood."

Well, her father and mother were gob-smacked. As for me, I couldn't believe my ears. At the same time, Doug bent down and handed Tom a good-sized piece of gold and some small samples.

Again he asked Lita, and again she said no. So after showing us around his mine-site, we went back to our shack for morning tea and some bush bum-nuts [scones]. Doug then noticed the map I was reading as he mentioned that he would show us around Lake Lapage to show us the quartz crystals in the centre of the lake. He asked me if he could have one of the maps as it was the first time his family homestead and telephone lines were mentioned – all the maps he had didn't show the details like these ones. I mentioned that they were military maps, so I didn't have a problem with that though I asked if I could hold them until we left and he could take the lot as I had unlimited access to them. I could see he was very grateful but I felt that I was getting more than I had expected. This was the best opportunity I would ever have and one that I had, over the past two months, been looking forward to. If that meant giving the maps away, then so be it.

Then, coming to a sudden stop, he climbed out of his car and waved for us to join him. We followed him through the saltbush and came across what looked like a rubbish heap with a low make-shift fence. In the centre was a steel lid about 450mm diameter, and Doug started to tell us about it.

"This is the grave of Andy, and his donkey, Pandy, who was murdered in late 1800 by his friend and partner. It is mentioned by his friend that he had an argument over gold and food, lost his temper and shot him dead. He tried to cover the body with used food tins but the next morning Pandy was standing over the dead body honking his lungs out, so he shot the donkey and made much more of an effort to conceal the bodies. But they were soon discovered and he was found and taken to Kalgoorlie and hung after a short trial."

As we listened to Doug, we noticed the bleached bones of the donkey and part of Andy's foot under the now well-rusted metal cans and the sign to remind us of Andy and Pandy:

HERE LAYS ANDY AND HIS DONKEY PANDY
MURDERED BY HIS FRIEND 1800.

I thought about how wild this country is, as the heat along with the flies and the arid, barren areas these early miners must have had to put up with. I would be on my guard at all times if I was to protect myself and my found-gold. In most cases, your partner and trusted friend was someone of good character and totally without distrust, who would be the last person to shoot you. Seems that was the way of things at the time.

We left Andy's grave and headed off across the salt plain for a short distance as the ground was getting soft. It was only a short walk and we understood why Doug had brought us here – these crystals were huge. Some were purple, while most were milky white, as thick as a man's arm and about 900mm long. They jutted out of the lake bed in an area of some five metres in diameter. He put their time and age to about two million years then pointed out that his family had known this spot for three generations.

He asked us not to disturb them as it was a sacred aboriginal site and was part of the Dreamtime serpent *warragal* where he came out of the soil when he came down from the sky and made this lake. [Sometimes lightning would hit the ground, and it's why the Aboriginals say that he comes out of the ground and his head can be a spring or waterhole-lake.]

After looking at them, totally dumbfounded at the size of them, I remember looking back and noticing how the sun danced across the salt plain like a beacon of flashings lights.

It was getting late as we all drove back to Kanowna and Doug waved us goodbye as we drove the last five miles to the shack, arriving about an hour before dark, which meant Tom and I had to get our fingers out to get the fires going and store enough mallee roots for the night. Then Tom and I sat on the veranda going over the day's events.

Though we were all tired, I noticed how sharp his eyes were. We were now talking about the next day when we would drive up to Ora Banda. Tom and I checked Lita's mother's leg wound and redressed it and was glad it was well on the mend.

During the evening, it began to rain, bringing a strong smell of the soil into the shack. This mingled with the soft smell of burning mallee roots, and during all this, my mind kept flashing back over the day's events and wondering what tomorrow would bring.

Tom and I were up the early next morning and very anxious to get started but, due to the rain, which made it somewhat cooler, and Lita's mother wanting a new dressing on as it had come off overnight, we discussed looking over the old townsite of Kanowna, and the four of us started looking for the main street.

As old towns were laid out in a square and the hotel was always on the corner, we noticed just how big this town had been – it still had the train platform. We walked around the whole town then back to the shack and, would you believe it, Lita's mother came to a sudden stop and bent down and picked up a small amount of gold attached to some quartz. This sent Tom, Lita and I looking over every inch of ground our eyes could scan but to no avail. As much as we looked, the only real thing found by Tom and I were old ink bottles along and a silver tobacco tin. Then we heard Doug's car horn coming down the road, so we closed the shack and got into the car and followed Doug towards Ora Banda some ninety kilometres north of Kalgoorlie. We could see just how much dirt had been well turned, this as far as the eye could see, mounds and mounds of ill-fated diggings for the little yellow nugget.

We arrived at Ora Banda around mid-morning and Doug put his arm out the window for me to follow him through the scrub, through dry creek beds, up and over small saltbush then back in the creek again. This went on for about twenty minutes until he stopped, climbed out and waved us over. It was then I could see heaps of lace opal light, from green to blue and red, and some good samples of Chrysoprase.

Doug explained the various types of lace opal light to Tom, Lita and I while her mother began to collect the best samples of the various types of coloured stones. We spent some three hours looking and sorting then changing our minds and putting samples aside to come with us until it was agreed that we had well overloaded the car for the type of conditions we drove into this place. But we felt it was going to be worth it if all went okay on the way out.

We drove out of the saltbush and headed back to the shack for sunset and a long rest while looking over the quality of stones we'd collected. Some small talk followed on the best method of cutting and/or placing them in a special type of tumbler for polishing. All this Tom and I looked forward to.

Just before we went to bed, Tom mentioned that Doug might be going to the state battery as he'd been informed the previous day that his gold-bearing ore was being treated. He would let us know the following day. So, we bid each other goodnight and I left Tom with a full mind of the day's events and now looked forward to the next day.

Tom and I were of the same mind: we were both up and getting the fire sorted, then we both got buckets to fetch the water for the days cooking and washing. We both looked at each other and laughed as we knew deep down this was going to be a day well worth it if Doug was informed by the battery. For the rest of the morning, we all went for a long walk over the whole area of the townsite and, if one stood still and silent, you could hear the old mining town by the wind blowing through the deserted streets. Looking into mind's eye, I could almost feel and see the people gathering in small groups looking at each other's gold and hear the low voices as they huddled to keep their conversations secret and hide the size of the find, keeping a sharp eye open for the unwelcome onlookers. Then back to the real world as we tried to work over the town's major building site. We came across the longest railway platform I have ever seen, still there and looking as though it was expecting the next arrivals of the so-many wanting to strike it rich.

We walked further, towards a still-standing steel maintenance workshop for the locomotives and, at a further look, noticed that the machinery was still standing there as though the men had just walked out, the same way when the gold could no longer be found and the town's people left, leaving the hard-working miner still searching for the big find only to soon follow the rest back to Kalgoorlie or a new find which was always on everyone's mind and lips. It must have been really tough and heartbreaking to leave their loved ones home on the off-chance of finding the big nugget. Me? I was grateful for the information I had, and trying to understand it all had left me gobsmacked to say the least, at the extent of all the workings we have driven through over this past week.

Then mid-afternoon, Doug came over to inform us that his gold was the last on the list and should be treated around 4.30pm. He left with Tom and Lita's mother and I was to follow on later, which gave us both a break. Apart from that, we could both have a shower from a bucket and a complete refresh before we left for Kalgoorlie and the State Batteries. As we both had never seen a gold bar before, this was going to be the highlight of our trip to Kalgoorlie, which Lita and I have never forgotten.

When we arrived in Kalgoorlie, our destination was well signposted and it wasn't long before we were all together again, just in time as Doug came through the pouring room with a cold bar of gold and a broad smile. He walked up to us to show it off and let us hold it, at the same time telling us that it was worth around $3,500.00. As for the weight, I have forgotten but the memory of the gold bar has stayed with me.

After that, we departed for Doug's home where he spent some three hours talking to his old friends, Tom and Lita's mother, Kit. Lita and I went for a long walk around Boulder near Doug's home, staying in town and returning around 9pm when we left for the shack and bed. I well remember the chatter from us all, the main talk being the gold and the hard work that went into such a small amount – it seemed not worth it, yet once gold fever hits, that's your lot forever.

And so this holiday came to an end. It was our last night in the shack as the next day we would to leave for Perth – nice and early as I feared it was going to be a long, slow trip.

Mid 1968

Upon my return to Pearce, I was instructed to report to Education Section for reasons unknown to me. I arrived and was informed by the Education Officer that it had been requested by the Officer Commander that I was to sit an IQ test to help find a suitable mustering I could fit into. So arrangements were made for this test within the week and, upon its completion, I was informed I was suitable to be placed in the mustering of EDP [Electronic Data Processor] and I was advised to give it great consideration as this was a sound career move with endless opportunities ahead.

I knew this was the right move yet felt my educational background would fail me. Apart from that, I didn't feel I could sit in an office all day and would rather be outdoors. With all the thought I put into it, I nearly signed into the course then settled for ground support equipment, Air Movement Section. This meant I could do all my training at Pearce Base rather than be posted to the Eastern States. Leaving Lita behind in a flat by herself didn't appeal to Lita or me, and I kept her well informed of the situation due to the lack of funds as our rent was climbing out of control. From our first payment some six or seven months previous at $12.00 per week, it was now $17.00 per week, which really left us with very little to live on. I had even gone off the beer to make ends meet, as my service fortnightly pay was $55.00. This was going to improve when I changed musterings, but for now it was getting harder and each fortnight we both dreaded the rent man coming around as we never knew what the increase would be.

I was complaining about this to Andy and he mentioned that, after speaking to the Base Adjutant and showing him his rent book, he was going into the married quarters within the month. With this information, I was hot on the trail the next day and, by the end of the week, I was informed that I was to receive new quarters at Balga (corner of Wanneroo Road and Culloton Crescent) and was over the moon about it.

Andy's married quarters were also in Balga.

So it gave me great pleasure to tell the rent man to have a nice day as we were already 90% moved out before he mentioned what the rent was going to be for the next fortnight. Without much ado, we both got our last few bits and bobs and left for our new home at Balga. We both knew that things could only get better as from here it was forward only and the new mustering would bring a little more money into the house.

It wasn't long after that I was looking for some extra work.

There was a major construction company building married quarters at Pearce. I started to look around the project for something that I could make a trouble-free dollar, that is, nil equipment to buy. About the second week, while driving to the rubbish tip, I noticed how much building rubble was lying around on each building site. This gave me the idea that I could use the base tipper to remove it and dump it at the Base tip. So now the plot was set and all I had to do was ask the supervisor for the job and settle a one-fee for each block over the duration of the construction program. I was also interested in any small carpenter jobs.

The next morning, I was handed a sheet of paper with a phone number on it. I had no idea who it was for so I rang it during my morning tea break, only to find it was bloody Fred. Well, I couldn't believe it at first.

After a short discussion with him, he asked about jobs going around as he was paying rent much in the same place as I was and the amounts were almost equal. I mentioned that I was looking for work around building sites at Pearce and I was trying to figure out the cost of removing the rubble from contractors around the Balga building site near where I was living. We closed our conversation with arrangements to meet up at the weekend. This would be the first time Lita would meet Fred as he had only ever been a name and now that he was married, it seemed just fitting for both our wives to meet up.

I was hopeful of getting an idea within the week of the cost of rubbish removal. Lita was still working and travelling to Perth each day, which was a great help as we both knew that at long last all the extra work and money would allow us to buy our furniture as needed.

The first thing I had to do was to get the lawn in and growing, along with flower beds, but the ground was dry sand. Endless watering wouldn't make much difference to growing and keeping the lawn green, which seemed an endless task week after week. Then I thought of asking Andy to provide some ideas from Barracks Section as he was also involved in the garden upkeep of the Base. If he had anything being dumped that was useful, it would leave extra money as I was saving for our next trip to Ravensthorpe, about 500 kilometres southeast of Perth, to look over some disused gold and copper mines some twenty kilometres south on the Hopetoun Road.

The next day I drove over to the Balga building site and talked to the site supervisor to get the cost for rubbish removal. I was given a breakdown cost of the work so, armed with this, I headed off to Pearce for my daily duties. At the first opportunity, I went off to talk to the site supervisor and played my hand out. I was told by the Balga site supervisor that $20.00 per house was his rate, but I wanted $25.00 from this site as some of the yards were full of crap. Upon explaining this to him, he agreed, and so I once again looked over the building site and noticed that some large holes had been dug for lime mixing pits and, upon an even closer look, I felt that we could bury quite a lot of crap in them which would save loading the tipper and dumping time. I then left and returned to my section.

During that afternoon, Andy walked over from Barracks with the good news of cuttings and heaps of grass clippings so all I had to do was get the lot home. At the same time, Dad was posted back to Darwin and asked if I could help shift his furniture. Without any trouble, I made arrangements to drop all Andy's garden clippings and some gravel for my drive and headed home to Balga to drop them off. With that job done, I headed for Mum's to load up her furniture as required and stored it before heading back to Base, all this completed in one and a half hours.

When I arrived back at my Section, I was informed that I was going over to the refuelling depot for training reasons and it was here I met Trevor Schwartz. We got along great.

Apart from this, my weekends would be full working around the building site, making large heaps of rubble at each site and burying whatever we could in the used lime pits. I made arrangements for Andy to drive the tipper during his lunch break for $5.00, while Fred and I loaded as fast as we could. Then we walked back to Base while Andy dumped the load. We worked like this for the next month, and it was bloody hard work at times as we would be working over the weekends just to complete the project. I had to hand in our invoice each week and received our payment cheque the following week, which was hard at first but when it came through we were more than happy as both Fred and I had around $125.00 each and Andy had $50.00 for his time.

Over the following weeks, we kept this work up until all the yards were completed, then we all decided to give it a rest until more became available.

I was now on refuelling aircraft, usually around nighttime. This involved refuelling aircraft going through to Sydney from Vietnam and also night flying training once a week. This would make my daytime hours available to work around the house. We had inspections of the married quarters to ensure all was kept tidy and clean and I received a letter from my Commanding Officer that my yard required attention and had to be completed by the following inspection or I would be placed on a charge. I felt this was pretty hard going as everything I planted died; no matter how much I tried, I just couldn't get anything to grow. I asked Lita's Dad to come and see what could be done as he had just retired from being the gardener at Armadale High School. So, with all the help around, it appeared I needed a second course of action and two days before the inspection Andy brought two large loads of grass clippings and levelled them across the front yard and turned the sprinkler on. This gave me the idea of pots with plastic flowers placed around the garden and, after spending some $25.00, the job was completed. It looked a pretty sight from the road as the one thing I well knew was he never stopped to walk around – the driver would slow down enough to give him a good look then off they would go to the next home. With all in place, I left for the Base and hoped for the best. Two days later, a note from HQ was sent down to my section with a Well Done for the time and short notice given. I rang Andy at Barracks and told him about the note, and that I would get him a half dozen tinnies and invited him and his family around for a BBQ on the weekend.

All was now settling down to a normal routine with night shift and some early mornings. Although there was only five of us doing refuelling, we kept ourselves on the go all the time with little to no lunch breaks.

Over this time, Flight Lieutenant Hays was posted to 25 Squadron and had to do his continuation training on fixed wings or choppers. As Fred was Base crewman, it was like old times again, even when Flight Lieutenant Champion also arrived as an instructor for the trainee pilots. Fridays of each week after midday was the instructors' own time to go flying, and I would find myself with Dave Champion flying around. On one occasion, we flew across the 6WF station mast and did some split-arse turns over my house in Balga, where I could see Lita hanging washing out instead of laying down as she had mentioned she wasn't feeling too well. Then we flew back to Base for stand-down for the weekend.

January 1969

I continued doing my normal duties and, at times, I would go flying with Fred and Flight Lieutenant Max Hays around the Chittering Valley to do winching practice and some landing on rocky outcrops. Then it was back to Base and refuelling.

I was to report to the Base medical section for a follow-up blood test and stool sample, required of all members returned from Vietnam. These tests were carried out at Perth Hollywood Hospital.

On this occasion, I was the driver, with passengers Fred, Dave Champion, and Max Hays. On the way to Hollywood, Max asked me to drop into 25 Squadron as he hadn't had a chance to look over the place yet, and he was to take over at the end of the month. After a slow drive past, I headed off to Hollywood. We all arrived and were placed into screened areas where blood was taken. After this, we were given a small plastic bottle for the stool sample and directed to the dunnies to drop it in. Well, I just couldn't help myself again. I dropped this one the size of a scud missile and left it hanging out of the plastic bottle about 75mm with the cap sitting on top. It was still smoking hot and, as the proud owner, placed it on the tray while the others looked on. They just looked at me and started to laugh, and we all headed back to Pearce while a lot of small talk took place.

One thing that was clearly coming through was the continuation training over the following months, as I understood that all combat-experienced pilots could be called up for instructor duties at Canberra ACT, along with experienced crew members such as Fred and myself.

Apart from looking forward to the end of the month, it was now the weekend, and I was going up to Armadale to spend some time with Lita's family. Tom just couldn't wait to show me the tumbler he'd built using a small continuous electric motor and some pulleys geared down so it would revolve slowly. That was the one striking thing about Tom: he was very good with figures and maths and was also good when it came to small engineering works. He would improvise all the materials he found in his workshop. This used to amaze me and, over time, he gave me the confidence to work these figures out by using books to study the problem then putting it into practice. Sometimes he would say, 'it's as close as the pocket can provide', and from that I understood he wasn't going to buy anything and relied on all the bits and bobs lying about in wrapped grease rags just for this purpose. Whatever jig was needed, he would make it up first and prove it.

I arrived back to my duties and was instructed to report to stores for BOS, which was to remove old and unserviceable items like tools and small electrical goods and clothing along with documents. This was the second time I was placed for BOS, and it was always with an officer from the stores, a Sergeant and myself to ensure that all items were destroyed and burnt then buried. This was generally done over the day. I was to also help out with another on-Base rubbish removal. On this occasion, I had two civilians loading the tip truck. Although they were well into their 50th years, I knew them well and didn't mind when they had a beer with them, or not, as no one else wanted the job, and they were always there each day hard at it. We would make two or three runs to the tip and, as the day grew long, I noticed that Andy was driving the other tipper. I started to back up to the burning rubbish as I had always done. Then the civilians removed the tarp cover as they jumped down from the truck. I continued to reverse back while the tipper was rising, ready to release the load of paper as usual, when I felt this jolt and thought it had jumped out of gear. I was now stationary, but each time I tried to engage the gear, nothing happened. I started to see if I could get the load of burning paper off but to no avail.

Just at that moment, I noticed Andy's tipper coming down the road and called out for him to pull me out. At the same time, I found a coil of wire and pushed it over the front bumper while Andy was backing up to me, then I hooked it over his towing hitch, jumped into my truck and sounded the horn. He began to tow me out of the burning rubbish, but by now the back of my tipper was on fire. He couldn't see me but was given hand signs from the civilians to keep going. Some minutes later, I was still being towed around flat out by Andy. Then he came to a sudden stop. My truck slammed into the back of his tipper, sending it forward with a jolt. He put his foot down, thinking I was still on fire, then again stopped. Again, I slammed into his truck, but this time, I noticed the bonnet of my truck was getting smaller and smaller. While all this was going on, the two civilians were laughing their guts up as Andy and I couldn't understand what the hell was going on. When he decided to finally stop, he kept his foot hard down on the brakes until I, too, was stopped. We got out and I asked why he kept going. He said he thought I was still burning and wanted to continue racing around, but I explained that my motor was off and I had air-over-hydraulics and had no way of stopping, and I wasn't going to let go of the wheel. Then we noticed the extent of the damage done and burst into laughter. The front of the truck was stuffed so, after settling down, we headed back to Base using the same towing method until we reached the transport section where Dad was working. An old family friend, Warrant Officer Abercrombie, was Officer in Charge of Transport Maintenance. Without a problem, I reported that I had, under a difficult situation, saved service equipment while on fire, which resulted in some minor damage to the front bumper and fender. And that was the last I heard of the subject, though it took the skills of all the transport section to get it back serviceable. That was the last time I was to do BOS duties.

Andy was now very interested in looking around Chittering valley and the surrounding country beyond, so I began to make arrangements with the Taylors, our very old family friends. They always looked forward to having us up for the weekend shooting or fishing in the river. Now hat it was getting a little cooler, it would be the best time of the year to camp out.

November 1969

When I arrived home, I could hear Lita singing; she seemed excited.

"What's up?" I asked.

She looked at me and said, "Well, you're going to be a father. I am pregnant!"

"Boy, oh, boy! Me ... a daddy? Who knows about it? Have you told your family? ... When did you find out?"

"This morning."

"Well, let's go and tell the rest of the world!"

And with that, we went over to my Mum and Dad to give them the hot news that they were going to be grandparents. And after a quick drink, we were off to Armadale to let Lita's family know. They too were over the moon.

Early 1970

I arrived at my section on Monday morning and discovered that I was placed on night guard duties the coming Thursday. Although the beginning of the week was unadventurous, my whole world fell apart before the week was over.

On the evening I was rostered for guard duties, I contacted the Orderly Officer. To my surprise, it was Flight Lieutenant Max Hays, my old pilot and flying mate from Vietnam. I was also his support driver for the evening and it was my duty to be ready at any time, without notice, which made these nights very long. Most times, it was very quiet, then around midnight, I was contacted by the Base WOD and asked if I had seen the Orderly

Officer.

I said, "No, apart from letting him know I was his night driver."

This didn't seem to worry us as, at times when things were quiet, a small cat-nap was in order as long as three or four guards were standing around the gate entrance so it looked busy. When morning came, the WOD stood us down and I headed back to the transport section where I was informed that I was on rubbish removal for the morning as Andy hadn't arrived for work. I didn't mind doing this for him and drove down to pick up the civilians and got about driving them around as required. All the time, I was thinking of Lita and our baby and looking forward to it all. I was asked to dump a load and headed for the tip.

Upon backing up, I noticed a white Holden, which looked familiar, but I kept tipping the load out. After I'd finished and started to move off, I decided to take a closer look. I noticed the driver door was open, but no one was around. Then, as I drew closer, I noticed a body on the ground and recognised who it was. The car fitted the owner: it was my friend, Max Hays.

I told the civilians to remain quiet until I reported it to my Section Commander as this was serious. I just couldn't believe it. With all the ongoing plans we had for continuation training and the laughter from my dump in the plastic bottle, he was dead, and in such a place as the tip was very upsetting to me.

I headed to my section head without any delay as I knew he would treat him with complete dignity, regardless of suicide, as Max would not be entitled to a military funeral even if he happened to be a belated casualty from Vietnam. The flashback of him shooting up his pipe when it had blown out the window of our chopper did put a smile on my face.

I requested a closed-door discussion, which was never allowed without a Sergeant present, and without delay told him the full situation and who I believed it to be. With that, I asked for an hour to gather my thoughts as the more I thought about it, the more I just couldn't understand it. *Why? Why?!*

I had just settled down to my morning tea when two SP wankers bounded into the smoko room and started dancing around me. I just kept sipping my tea and refused to talk to them as this was my reason for not bringing it to their attention – they had just had their second taste of excitement over the past twelve months, first the communication line being ripped out, and now my mate's troubles, of which, if played down, he could have a military funeral.

I tried to explain that I was directly responsible to my Officer in Charge over anything that may happen …

"… or would you like me to entertain each of you with crap from all around the Base."

I knew it wasn't the right way but isn't that just me. I was on the whole, very pleased with the way it was kept to the minimum attention. So we moved on to play out our own chapters of life.

Though I had recognised it was Max Hays even though he had half his face missing and the shotgun lay beside him, I had tried to convince myself that it wasn't. Max brought many memories of Vietnam instantly back that I just kicked the shit out of the truck's tyres, trying to find some common answer as I believed we were losing a lot of returned Vietnam Vets through suicide. It was becoming more frequent as the federal election was coming up with Labor labelling us Vets as baby eaters and the like just to give themselves an edge to win, when in truth the edge was played out for the Vietnam Veteran. At most, no one gave a damn, as we were now breeding a gutless nation with boys standing up like men for the right to vote to give them the right to prevent them from helping a nation like Vietnam. This was confirmed by name-calling and a smear campaign to degrade those of us who did help, with tomatoes and eggs being tossed at us, but this was yet to come.

My mind would flashback to Vietnam and the bodies mutilated and ripped apart by mines and bullets as we tried to save them during dust offs, then returned to pick up the dead. All this bounced around my head, the thoughts unable to find a way out. I had looked up to Max for my personal strength, and I could feel his support without a word being said, but I just couldn't understand this.

Over the following week, I became quite stressed about it, then I was asked to report to the SP office for a chat!

As I introduced myself, all shit broke out as the Sergeant started with 'I should have reported the matter to them', all the while dancing around giving me the third degree.

"And then you named who the dead man is, and now the whole Base knows!"

I looked him in the eye and said, "After twelve months of active service, I do know who the fuck it is, and also the only one I told was my Section Commander, and I do believe you were informed at that time, so you should look amongst your own lot as it would give them a boost to tell their sad mates. And if this is what you brought me here for … to listen to your trivial bullshit … to make a statement to me …

"I knew the person, not only personally, but as my boss and friend, and if you have a problem with that, then you are all full of your own egotistical crap with a sad job …"

Before I could finish, he yelled, "Report back to your section!"

Max's sudden death had quite an impact on me, bringing back my nightmares. Although I was soon to be a father, this happiness helped to overshadow my Vietnam experience. My interest in gemstones also helped me to forget, most times, and the more I delved into the subject, the less time I had to dwell on it. On some occasions, I would drive up to Taylor's farm and wander over the cleared paddocks looking over various stones and placing them into a sample box, noting the grid co-ordinates for future reference, as one old-timer, Guss Picket, informed me that a large load of Kyanite was found across the area but never said where.

I was now well into planning my next trip but locally, and it wasn't going to suit Tom or Lita as I had made my mind up to walk from Toodyay to the Taylor's farm, some eighty kilometres as the crow flies. But walking up and down the hills would make it well into a hundred kilometres. This meant sleeping rough under the stars for four nights and four full days and carrying full packs of rations.

Trevor Schwartz, who had much the same sense of humour as me, and another mate, Errol Roberts, also a mate of Trevor's, wanted to come along. Although the going would be tough, both of them looked fit enough to walk the steady twenty-five to thirty kilometres per day so I decided they could come along. Over the next month, I studied the hills on the maps plotting a course to keep at a regular height through the valley, then cross the river three times and one creek, the Brockman Brook, the last section before Jumperkine Hill.

Although Tom would have loved to be with us, he did say that it was greater fun putting it all together and getting all the local knowledge as this Kyanite was mainly around Bindoon [old school]. My theory was the height cut through the Avon Valley could lead to sediments washing from the hills over the years which may have exposed it. I intended to remain at a single contour level, about mid to lower elevation of Jumperding Hill, Bald Hill, Smith Mill Hill, then Jumperkine Hill. This was going to be a long shot, but my intention was to find the possible source or, more to the point, see if it was around there.

Having a go, as was explained to me, was what fieldwork

was about, followed by good notes with backup data. So my plot was ready. Even though the weather didn't look good for it, we all took two days of our leave for this adventure. The last thing required was food, so I wrote a list of items to give Errol, from tinned beans, nine kippers, fifteen light-bite nuts, condensed milk, six sardines, twenty spaghetti, six to twelve tins of steak and kidney. While Errol was getting this from our Base kitchen, Trevor was to get all the lighting fuel [candles] and plenty of matches. As for me, I would carry the sample box and hammers, small shovel, two sets of the same maps with a good solid brass compass and above all this, some wet weather gear with bedding.

So now we waited for Friday to arrive. I was getting a bit concerned that our food hadn't been sorted and had to keep onto Errol about it. On Friday morning, both Trevor and I gave our kit bags to Errol for filling with the tins of food, and just in time as it was 'stand down'.

Trevor and I met up with Errol, and we walked over to his married quarters outside the Base and arrived at the same time as Lita – she was taking us across to Toodyay and would pick us up at Bill Taylor's farm four days later. Without any delay, we were off.

During the time going over, I noticed Errol was boozing from his tin and he asked if we could stop when we reached town to pick up supplies of booze. I really didn't mind as I felt like a drink too. Upon arriving, I decided to take a flagon of red wine while Trevor and Errol bought theirs.

We now had to make our way down a gravel track on the south side of the Avon River until we found an unused home left by the owner to rot away. Within minutes we found it. We bundled ourselves out of the car and let Lita go about an hour before sunset, which gave us time to settle down for the evening. We had brought a roast chicken from the pub for our evening meal. A candle was lit and beds were made ready then we sat around a small fire that Errol had got going and for the rest of the night we sat around talking about what we were looking for. I was not expecting to find it, but as long as we got a show, that would mean something to me and Lita's Dad.

The night seemed to drag on with Errol getting started on the booze as he thought the sun was on the way even though it was around 10pm. Trevor and I were slow to drink, trying to save it for the next day. About this time, it started to rain, which put a dampener on the night, so we went and layed over our kit and drank while talking about various people from the Base to the government and Vietnam. Then all was silent: I think I had talked them off to sleep.

It wasn't long before I was woken by thunder coming our way, and it was still raining, which wasn't in my game plan. But so be it. Soon we were all on our feet, packing up and getting wet weather gear on and, as planned, we left this camp at first light. The sky was still quite black with clouds but it was time to leave. I hoped it would clear up during the day.

Our first walk was up Kowalyou Katta, which was quite difficult as the ground was wet and slippery, but we kept going until I felt we were midway up. By now it was 1030am, and we had been walking for four and half hours. It was time to eat so I took my kit bag off and noticed only sardines. I asked Trevor to look for the tins of beans in his kit but he too only had sardines. At the same time, Errol was going through his kit, and that was full of sardines – we had about fifty tins and no can opener. *What a fucken mess!*

I looked over at Errol and just laughed, then said, "Wait here while I duck down to the store for a can opener," as I reached for my knife. And so began the saga of the sardines.

After two tins each, we set out again, but now, for the first time, I showed them a sample of what I was looking for. We emu-bobbed for the next hour on a bearing to our next location and recorded our position. Then we each opened another tin of sardines and used grass tree fronds to spear them into our mouths. After a long drink – we had plenty of water – we were off again, but it started to rain – it was just after midday. We had only covered nine to ten kilometres and had twelve more to do before nightfall. The rain grew heavier on each downpour but we kept all the important items dry under our armpits and on our chests. I could now see Jimperding Brook down in the valley, and we really needed to be at that location, so I told the others to get going towards it. I would be on the descent slope and be just behind them but they wanted to remain with me so we moved down, picking small samples up on the way. At around 5pm, we arrived at the spot, but it wasn't as I thought it would be – I had expected it to be much flatter – so we moved on until the Ranger's track was in sight then made camp in the long grass next to the track with some tree cover. The rain didn't stop enough for us to make a fire to boil water and dry out our feet and boots, but with all this, we were in good spirits. I got my wine flagon out and passed it around as we were half laid out and tired, but soon jumped up as more thunder and lightning was followed by more rain. We sat up looking at each other, seeming to be thinking the same thing, then we all reached for our tins of sardines. I passed the knife around and downed the lot with my fingers and followed it with a large drink of water. Then I went for my first dump in two days as I could feel the sardines backing up, and some of my farts were not very tasty so it was time to let loose.

I could see Trevor and Errol were looking for a nest to dump their goodies and the fun started as when we all wanted the toilet roll at the same time. Then off we went, downwind from our camp and, upon a very successful launching, we all headed off to the river for a clean-up even though it was still raining. But I felt much better afterwards, and so did the others.

Back at our campsite, we made up a shelter as best we could, facing windward. This was not in my game plan, even though I had kept an eye on the weather weeks before. But this was real now and we all had to make the best of it, because for me, I wasn't going to lose this chance as Tom and I had put a lot of time and effort into it. I was grateful for Trevor and Errol as it was always playing safe when this far from help. We were well sorted out when dusk arrived and began to get our heads down, though we were still talking about the next day. I had already explained that we would cross the river at this point as the river wasn't in flood, yet, but if the rain fell stronger over the next two days we wouldn't be crossing back at Bald Hill. But should it look okay, I wanted to stay with my original plan and recross the river at Brookman Brook.

During our nightly chat, Trevor asked me about this Kyanite and what it was used for. I wasn't sure about its use, but the area where the biggest loads were was some 120 kilometres north at Wannamal and just south of there at Mooliabeenee, and also in the middle of the Chittering Valley. The whole area was very much like Kanowna as the soil's age was Precambrian Complex of fine-grain Mica schist. As I had not long been back from Kalgoorlie, and had spent just over a week at Kanowna, my understanding was this was a matrix of quartz-muscovite. As a boy, I had noticed a lot of mica throughout the Chittering valley and also at Bindoon so I had decided to use my previous information and use it here. Even if I found a slip of a sample, it was a good start, and with that, I must have talked them off to sleep again as I wasn't asked any further questions.

I drifted in and out of sleep for most of the night, being disturbed by the continuous wind and rain and being concerned about the crossing of the river the next morning. I felt it was important as some twenty kilometres downriver was a farmer's equipment shed that would allow us to dry off and refresh ourselves and sleep out of this bloody rain.

It wasn't long after that we were all up and talking about the next move when the farting started, and we just couldn't stand each other's farts. Even when we opened two tins of sardines for breakfast, still farting, they just didn't stop. When I dropped one, Trevor started, followed by Errol, then me again.

Our first move was down to the river. It was just at knee height and running around fifteen kilometres, which should be quite safe, so with all our kit ready, I led the way across but walked slightly upstream to maintain the same footing under the same water rush. Trevor and Errol were right on my tail and, when I started farting, they had nowhere to go but to follow me. After some five minutes of walking across these low rapids, we reached dry land and sat down to remove our waterlogged boots and check all our gear again. We moved on, now walking on the north side of the Avon River, across from Jumperding Hill, then we started the big climb to the mid-elevation or thereabouts, with some fifteen kilometres left before sunset. We felt that we should move a little quicker as the ground and bush was more scattered, which was to our advantage.

I kept my nose to the ground looking for the mica, as did Trevor and Errol, and only when our pockets had a good handful of samples did we stop. I went over them with my eyeglass and saved the ones that looked okay. I wrote down the grid reference and location. Then we stopped at will, opened a can of sardines and moved on, each of us doing the emu-bob, then sorting out the possible good samples and noting the grid reference, all this while working, talking, and farting, to our heart's contents. What we did all notice was the distance between ourselves – it looked like 50 metres apart – yet I could still smell the both of them and didn't know if it was them or me, but I knew the wildlife around could smell us a mile off.

By mid-afternoon, we headed down towards the river and

the farmer's shed as we were very wet and rather tired. After three or four kilometres, we arrived at the shed, only to find it had two sides missing, but everything else was fine, so we began to settle in and have a dry night. This was now our third night and second full day of being wet and a little pissed off as now all our gear was wet through. Only the matches and the maps were dry. I did notice how quiet Trevor and Errol were while I was getting some bark from the dry side of trees and also blackboy stumps. Using the candle, Trevor and I managed to light a small fire and soon Errol was out fetching more wood. I found some roof sheeting and dragged it over for a windbreak as we were all getting ready for our sardine meal. It was with great showmanship that I tried to fart to the tune of *Waltzing Matilda* without follow-through, and this was going to be our 'bent but funny' entertainment for the evening. We all sat around the fire eating some four tins of sardines, and we agreed that something must have died in our bums as nothing could stink like this and still be alive. Then Errol decided to give us a tune, but after some failed attempts, he came to a sudden stop, just in case of the follow-through.

Being under shelter with fire and our gear getting dried lifted our spirits for the coming day. I wanted to cross the river at the base of Bald Hill about ten kilometres from this campsite, which meant we had a hard climb first thing in the morning, then about midday dropped straight down to the river near the Rangers tracks. As I was explaining this to them as we settled into our partly wet kit, but with less stress from the cold and without much ado, we were well asleep and only woken up with some thunder in the distance and light rain around us.

After a great breakfast of sardines and sardines, we headed up the north slope for about 500 metres. We could see our next destination and the river crossing. But the going was rocky and slow. Nevertheless, we got back into our routine of emu-bobbing as I kept a lookout for the downslope. Again, midday seemed to arrive quickly as we all reached for our lunch of sardines on top of sardines – bloody great as the farting started again followed by the need for a dump, so we all headed off in different directions and after it became much easier to find each other as we stunk like something that had been dead for weeks. The only thing that would come to play with us was fucken flies and it appeared they loved Trevor as he was the one yelling the loudest – I just put up with it – and Errol was getting the same way. The only time they left us was when it rained.

We started our descent towards the river at the base of Bald Hill and, around 1pm, arrived at the river. It looked a little faster at this point, and I put it down to the sudden drop in height and being at the narrow section. Without any hesitation, I started walking over to the south side, knowing they would soon follow me as it wasn't that rough but more dragging, which wasn't overly exhausting. Some two or three minutes later, when I did finally get to shore, I noticed they were just behind me. But I was now concerned that the river could be much more difficult at the Jumperkine Hill. This was some fifteen kilometres away and I had started to become worried. When we were all on dry land, we sat around and drained our boots and had a light snack of sardines then went back on the trail, but this time I decided to remain about fifty metres up the side of the hill as we could move much faster without forgetting what we came out here for. I could see we were all getting tired, but we needed to reach Cobbles Pool just east of Brockman Brook before nightfall. I mentioned this to Trevor and Errol, which seemed to give a little more effort towards our goal. Reaching into our kits, we got two tins of sardines out, downed the lot and headed off with our heads bent, looking and picking up anything that looked okay. I gave the samples the once-over, packed the interesting ones and jotted down our location and again repeated it all.

Around 4pm, we saw Brockman Brook and I knew we should leave straight away to cross the river, which took a short hour to reach. After giving it a long look over, we realised it was going to be much more difficult as the underlying boulders couldn't be seen. But I wasn't going to waste any time over this and we all started to cross over, holding onto each other for support. It was bloody hard going, but we made it and were in good shape. And that's all that really mattered.

It was now getting on to 5.30pm and we needed to dry our feet and get moving as the climb ahead was going to be the granddaddy of them all. I hadn't mentioned this before, but this was now the time, so while drying our feet, I quickly brought to their attention that the last five kilometres was through parrot bush, and at night through some of the roughest ground we had ever been through. We needed to be halfway up the Brookman Brook first as the crossing would be in the dark. So, we got our kit and left as fast as we could.

Just on dusk, we crossed Brookman Brook and again dried our feet, then climbed through our first fence and walked up the main slope of Moondyne Hill, completing it in the dark. With few cloud breaks allowing small amounts of stars to be seen, the plan was for Trevor and Errol to hold the map while Trevor set fire to it. I would take a compass bearing in the firelight. The most important thing was to hold each other's hand when the fire went out. The plot was started and a bearing was taken while the map burnt. We waited for our eyes to adjust then inch by inch headed up. On reaching the next fence, a barbed wire one, we climbed over then went again inch by inch moving through the bush. We all climbed over the next barbed wire fence then, in the still of the night, we could hear a power generator running in the distance. This was the Taylor's farm.

But the fun wasn't over yet as I was now getting my bearings to take the short way around to the airstrip through the parrot bush, so we held each other's hand as they followed me, getting slapped about by these prickle-leafed low trees. At times the dried leaves would bite into our wet weather gear, and it just didn't seem to end. It took a good full hour to emerge into the clearing and opening of the airstrip.

With a little moonlight coming now and again, we were able to walk free of the bush and down a well-used gravel track that I knew so well. Some thirty minutes later, we arrived at Eric's shed, wet to the bone, stinking of rotten fish and farting that bad that his dogs got upset. And all he could do was laugh his guts out while we tried to explain that I was to ring Lita up to take us home. This was eventually sorted, and we just sat around waiting and talking to Eric Taylor about our walk and the fantastic meals we'd had …

The farting started again as we opened some more tins of sardines for Lita and Dawn, Errol's wife.

Before long, Lita arrived, and we were off to Pearce, then back to Balga as Trevor was staying with Errol that night. For me, I just couldn't wait to have a good long hot shower and sleep in a dry bed without any lumps or ants, flies and mozzies.

The next day I was up early and ready to leave for work, feeling great as I headed for the Base. Before long, Trevor arrived and, when I asked him if he wanted a toasted sardine sandwich, he nearly dry-retched as he was still farting and stinking the office out. It was just as well we worked alone when refuelling as I don't think it would have been welcomed. During the day, we would see each in passing, getting on with the job at hand and come stand down, we left together. I mentioned that perhaps we should have a BBQ with our wives and get Errol and Dawn over. He agreed, and we left for home. By the time I arrived, I felt the previous four days had now caught up with me so I showered and sat back with Lita watching TV and promptly fell asleep.

I remember talking to Lita about the events of our long walk and the number of samples picked up, and it was going to keep her father quite busy for the next two months. Then I mentioned the sardines and that we'd had nothing else to eat as Errol was supposed to have sorted it out. I learnt then that the note I'd given him couldn't be read as all the pencil lettering was smeared – the only thing that could be read was ink, which said 'sardines', so that is why we ended up with fifty tins of the bloody things.

Dad was now working at the Base Fire section as an ongoing maintenance man from the Transport workshop. He would often have night duties when night flying was rostered and, like myself, would be refuelling as required. Generally, the flying was kept around the Base and known as 'circuit and bumps' for the trainee pilots night flying solo, as required. These nights were generally quiet, with flying over by 9pm and our equipment locked away for the night. One night, without warning, while parking up at tanker pool, a loud thud was heard but no sign of fire. I looked around and, at the same time, the Base crash horn burst into life, letting us know that one of our Vampire jets was down. So from the tanker pool, I made a quick call to Dad. He said there was no indication where it had gone down as it had only taken off two minutes earlier. I then asked him if he needed me as we both knew the whole bush area around these parts, and I could hear him talking to someone. Then he asked me to pick him up and head south along the Great Northern Highway.

Within minutes, we could see a small fire coming from the Walyunga National Park Road and, finding no one had yet arrived, I stood guard while Dad waited at the turnoff from the Northern Highway. He returned with fire trucks and a medical section doctor and nurse. Then Dad and I started looking around for the pilot, only to find his body still sitting in his set but without his arms, legs and head.

With it now being confirmed he was dead, two guards were placed on duty until the next morning, and I headed for home. Dad remained on Base as his duties were all night, and though I was by myself driving home, I felt that I should have remained too as I began once again getting flashbacks but in slow motion. I couldn't understand why I was having them. From where I sat driving, the trees in the night seemed to zip past ablur, but my mind drifted so slowly I could feel the pain of any movement I made, but my eyes were glued to the road ahead. Then I pulled into my driveway, which brought me back into the real world. Even though it was late, Lita was still up watching TV, waiting to get me something to eat and drink before bed as I would be up again at 6.30am and driving to Base by 7am.

She was always up with me, and breakfast was on the table so we could eat together. This was very special to me as at most I would have not eaten or brought some crap from the Base canteen. I often mentioned to my workmates that I had a wife who was far greater than I as she was always there with me, attending anything I needed even though she was six months pregnant and doing fine. But this was a new world to me and a daily learning curve. At times, I wasn't very focused on my situation as a soon-to-be father.

Over the next few weekends, Tom and I locked ourselves in his shed and slowly worked our way through the samples from Chittering valley. Nothing indicated the presence of Kyanite but I'd found some small samples of Mica and buck quartz, with some bauxite from Toodyay at the base of Kowalyou Katta North West. So the sample of Kyanite given to me by Mr Guss Picket was still a mystery at the lower Chittering valley.

Without much fuss, I kept five samples and dumped the rest and moved on to our next item, which was a trip south-east to Ravensthorpe, some 500 kilometres away, to look over the old goldmine workings and find some tin and copper crystals. Once again, Tom wasn't coming as we were doing it rough in the bush and would be on the move throughout the four days that was planned. Only Trevor was coming as I thought he just may have an interest or take it up as a hobby, like myself.

I decided to take one day off my leave and use one day from my guard duties and once this was sorted, and Trevor's leave, we were soon waiting for the following Thursday afternoon as we were going to drive straight from work and sleep on the side of the road as required.

This time the weather would be hot, which meant the nights could be very cold so we both packed extra gear. We didn't have to carry anything this time as the memories were still vivid from the last trip, and sardines were totally banned from our shopping list, not that we had one as we would be travelling back and forth between towns and only sleeping in the bush. So this trip would be luxurious.

I dropped Lita at her parents' home for the weekend and, without any fuss, Trevor and I left. We arrived around ten the next day and, after driving around Ravensthorpe, noticed plenty of workings from years back – it appeared that the town had grown from the centre of it all. We parked up and started walking around and reading some history boards, some for the development and downfalls from the mining to the farming. With all this, the pub was the local focal point as a building that in any Australian country town stood out amongst the rest, so it seemed only fitting we went for a visit and a chat with any locals. We ordered drinks, sat down and talked between ourselves while looking around at the men sitting at the bar. I outlined to Trevor the reason for being here and that it was quite relaxing from our first trip. As we began to look over our maps, a few of the men around the bar started asking us what we were looking for as they knew most of the area for miles around, so we let them know that we were looking for Wolframite, Azurite crystals, and

Malachite [or Auzumalachite crystals]. I noticed a person sitting with his elbows on the bar, sipping a middy and, for some reason, felt I knew him. As I tried to put a name to the face, he looked at me and said,

"Haven't we met, mate?"

Just as he spoke, it hit me like a ton of bricks. "Barry Pollard," I said, and we both stood up and, like long lost friends, gripped each other's hand. Questions about the past flew left and right, then he asked what I was doing in Ravensthorpe.

We pulled our stool up to Barry's and I explained that I was in the RAAF and that I'd taken up gemstones as a hobby to help me forget the Vietnam shit, and that it had been a lot better dealing with it, but I still had flashbacks, especially when the TV news kept jamming it down our throats every night. Apart from that, I was married and would soon be a father. He broke his news by saying that he'd divorced his wife at Katanning and his kids were living in Kalgoorlie. His eldest daughter was teaching at the Boulder School, and he was living at Hopetoun and had been working for the local Shire on and off doing maintenance; his kids came down every fortnight to see him.

With all that, we were now on our fourth beer, and this just had to stop. So I asked Barry where the best place was for camping out and was advised to go about ten kilometres south and take the track to Mount Desmond. Just off the main road, the shelter was good, so we departed the pub and headed south. Just as we got underway, Trevor hung out the door throwing his guts up and leaving his tri-colour droppings for the birds to feed on; he was like this until we reached the campsite.

Once out of the car, he gathered wood and stone surrounds for a small fire while I sorted the food out as we were both tired from drinking and now hungry. We slept for the rest of the afternoon and at 5pm rose and decided to drive down to Hopetoun, but changed our minds and headed back to

Ravensthorpe. Barry was still drinking and I started to feel a little sorry for him as I could well understand his past better than anyone else – we had both been there and done it. But that was then, and right now I felt I should take him back to our camp and give him a feed at least, as he'd been ever so good to me when I was having bad times with the Dutch prick.

I mentioned this to Trevor and he agreed, so when we sat down with him. I suggested he have a meal with us and could see in his eyes that he knew I was trying to offer him my support while around town. I mentioned that we would cook once we got back to camp but right now we needed some beer and milk for the morning. He said he was grateful and happy to have a meal with us; I then knew that he may not have many friends here, just like Katanning, where he always kept his quarter, and I couldn't see any change in him. So, after a couple of middies, we were off and again, Trevor hanging out the door throwing his guts up again.

At the campsite, Barry sat down and talked about our times in Katanning as Trevor and I started cooking our meal. After thirty minutes, we settled down to eating, and we could see Barry really needed this, and the offer was put forward to finish it all up. Upon eating his fill, we sat back and talked about the next day's adventure hunting and looking for samples. Then Barry said he knew a chap in Ravensthorpe who would be very happy to tell us where to look for the samples and show us over his workings just inside the town of Ravensthorpe. This was good news, then he mentioned that we could use his four-wheel-drive Toyota Landrover if he could drive my car around. This was a complete turn of events for us and opened up a whole new weekend of travelling around the bush as I didn't really like knocking our car about scrub-running so with all that good news, we settled down and had a few beers while the fire burnt out. Then it was on our backs looking at the stars.

We were all up at the same time and Trevor got the fire ready for breakfast while Barry gave me the drum about his vehicle and where all the tools were. Without a great deal of fuss, I got behind the wheel and drove it around to get the feel of it before getting all our gear stored in the back, then we all sat down to bacon and eggs, thanks to Trevor. Within the hour, Barry headed to Ravensthorpe in my car, Trevor and I following behind.

We arrived at a big hole in the ground, some twenty to thirty feet to the bottom, while Barry went off to find his friend. Trevor and I walked around the edge of this hole and I could see green and blue mounds hanging from the face of the hole. Then we noticed Barry and another chap walking our way, the man saying in a big German voice as he arrived, "G'day. I am Wolfgang," as he held out his hand.

"G'day. I'm David, and this is Trevor." And from that, he began to tell us about his find and the reason for the big hole. He showed me the Malachite crystals and said we could take as much as we liked, but the danger was we had to hang over the face of the big hole to retrieve them. I didn't find that much of a problem as we brought out the towing ropes and made a sling for me to sit in. We tied one end onto the tow-bar of the Landrover then drove forward while I walked down the face. After a few steps, I sat in the sling while Barry laughed at the stupid idea that was now working. As discussed, Trevor would drive forward for fifteen to twenty feet then stop while I picked to my heart's content. Then I noticed Trevor lying down, looking at me picking the best size and best quality to the best of my knowledge. I gave him the thumbs up and, within minutes, he was dragging me up and over the edge while I hung on till I arrived on flat ground with little damage done to myself or the crystals. I dusted myself down as Wolfgang came over.

"You are the best nutcase I have seen, or you are just very

keen to have these samples," he said as we walked over to his workshop. There, he handed me a weighty rock and said, "Here, you have earned this."

I looked at it. "What is it?" I asked.

"Wolframite [tungsten]."

I thanked him wholeheartedly as he explained it was a very good sample from this location but there just wasn't enough to open a large mine. He kept our attention as he walked us over to another hole that had blue crystals hanging out the side. I just had to get down there somehow. Then I noticed Wolfgang smiling, as if offering me the challenge to try and get down this hole. Trevor gave me the nudge and I nodded my approval. He went for the rope and with a few sound sheep-shank knots, I was down the hole. Trevor lowered me about ten feet while I grabbed the crystals on the way down then thumbed him to pull me up while still grabbing what I could.

On reaching the top, we were both pretty much stuffed but overjoyed with our fantastic samples. We started back to the four-wheel drive and packed them up to prevent damage and breakage.

Wolfgang offered us tea before we drove off towards town to pick up more stores as we were now going to head off towards the coast to Line Springs, then west towards Fortification Hill, then south to Waindaltop Pool over the next two days. Then we'd head into Hopetoun to change vehicles before heading for home in the late afternoon.

Though the trip through the scrub was uneventful, we did come across an old, rusted-out, very late model car, all still intact from the engine to the well-rotted tyres. What we couldn't understand was what was it doing out here, miles from anywhere and well off the beaten track. It was in a very pretty spot, which may have been an old campsite even though all indications of any habitation had long gone. But the old car had stood the test of time. We then left this spot but the memories still remain as I never put a closer on it by taking grid references and only remembered when we arrived at our destination for the evening. I could have kicked myself and now, with the next day coming up, we were both looking forward to a good feed and rest and getting home. All I wanted was on board, and I was over the moon with it.

When we arrived at Hopetoun, it wasn't hard to find Barry as there was only one pub and my car was outside it. Without much ado, I filled Barry's truck up with fuel and said goodbye as I wasn't sure when we would ever see each other again. Then we headed for home. After some five and a half solid hours driving, we arrived at Lita's family's home to a very warm welcome and the good news that our trip was well worth the run. But I was too tired to talk about all the events that had happened.

Trevor was shown his bed, and Lita and I also headed off as by now I could feel the full effect of the past four days, and it wasn't long before I was waking up to head off to Balga then Pearce and work. Trevor was very much as overtired as I, so we tried to get our heads down at work but the cat-naps only made matters worse, so we just hung in till stand-down.

I had left all the samples with Tom so he could sort out the very best and store them away while I would use the others to study and understand them and their structure. I knew it would be some time before I could get to that point, as I was still working through the basic facts at that time. But my mind wanted far more information – this thing was taking over, and rather than being a hobby which was the original intention, I knew I really should keep it that way. No matter how hard or easy it was to slip down and make plans for another trip, it would be unfair to Lita, especially so close to the birth – it didn't seem right.

The following weekend, my Uncle Don came around to see

me as he'd heard that I was away looking for gemstones, and he was very interested in finding out more. I explained how I got started and the reasons why, then began to go over some of the samples I had from our Kalgoorlie trip. Then I showed him the crystals [quartz] and I could see his excitement when the word 'gold' came into it.

He kept firing questions at me and I really had to slow him down. Being retired with plenty of time on his hands, he just couldn't wait for the next time I was going out in the field. But I explained I wouldn't be going out for some time due to Lita's condition and our situation regarding the birth. I just couldn't give him an answer when, and that seemed to put a stop to it. I mentioned that he was more than welcome around any time. I could explain what I do and my reason for doing it as it all comes together after the field trip. Still, a lot of reading and research was required long before we decided to take a field trip – we found that we could cover three or four types of stones with small amounts of gems attached but not of any commercial value. Still, it gave me greater satisfaction when it had been proved right.

July 5th 1970

Lita and I were doing our own thing around the house when she started getting labour pains. Upon satisfying herself that the time was right, we departed for the hospital and she was placed in the ward and made comfortable. I had to return to the house as we thought we may have left the stove on. I returned an hour and a half later, only to be told that we were blessed with a baby girl. All had gone well and both mother and child were fit, apart from the baby having jaundice, which the nursing staff kept an eye on. I was very pleased for Lita as she didn't have to go through a long labour, as I was informed this could give the child and the mother quite a lot of stress. So now it was over and we were starting on a new life with a child to take care of for the rest of our lives.

Over the past two weeks, we had looked over child names from a book Lita had picked up, and we had agreed on NICOLE, JOY [after her mother] DARCEY, then I contacted my family with the good news, and after three days, mother and child came home.

We never altered our lifestyle to suit the baby. We enjoyed our neighbours coming in and out throughout the day while we both carried on doing all the usual things around the house. The only thing that changed was keeping an ear out for any sound from Nicole, but, at most, she just had her nappy changed and was soon back to sleep. But Lita often dropped into her room to check that all was fine.

Two weeks later, we went up to Armadale to show off our new child to the rest of her family and her grandparents.

Tom and I would be together the following weekend sorting his findings, which I would do with him that weekend. Apart from all the rest, I mentioned to Tom that Uncle Don was also excited to go on a field trip as he would like some basic understanding of what to look for, even though I had explained to Uncle Don that it wasn't about long walks in the bush. Listening to me, Tom broke in and added that he should get out and join a Lapidary Club if he was just looking for gems. I agreed with Tom as most of our research involved crystals and understanding their association with minerals. It was very hard doing it ourselves without trying to explain our reasons to others, which must have sounded like double Dutch as there were too many tangents to the subject to give the general information. With the likes of Uncle Don, this could be very difficult, to say the least, so what Tom mentioned was the only way for him.

Trevor and I were still doing refuelling, and at times we had to train other drivers on the refuelling and de-fuelling procedures, along with keeping account of the amounts of fuel issued as we were accountable for all the Base fuel issued. We'd had a very good teacher, as one of the drivers had been in the tanker pool for six years and was removed to Base transport section to drive buses. On his first morning, he arrived at the fuel pumps and parked in a No Parking zone. I looked out and noticed it, and yelled out that he, of all people, should know better, but his excuse was that he was running late and needed to fill up quickly.

We only had a small fibro hut with two rooms, one used as an office and tea room while the other room stored oil and other flammable goods. Between the two rooms was a pigeon hole, used for signing for taken oil and fuel, so while this driver refused to move his bus, Trevor and I got hold of a ten-ton roller jack, pushed it well under the axle and lifted the bus just off the ground and headed back to the office. We sat next to the pigeon hole to watch the fun and it wasn't long before he came in and signed for the fuel then got onto his bus. He sat himself down and started it up, put it in reverse but it didn't move. He tried again, and still it didn't move. While this was going on, other personnel were in the oil room signing up the issued fuel and looking at the driver trying to reverse his bus. The driver then jammed the bus into gear with his foot flat to the floor and still nothing. At this time, I looked up and gave him a dumb look with my hands spread out. He then started jumping up and down while holding the steering wheel when the bloody bus fell off the jack and, with tyres burning rubber, came flat out towards the fibro hut and slammed into the oil room. This pushed the whole building out of shape and the front of the bus was stuffed and stuck in the building.

Trevor and I looked at each other. I said, "Look what the

stuff we have done!" and we both silently laughed our guts up. We couldn't look at each other for fear of laughing aloud as we couldn't admit to that – we had more important work to deal with, and our mornings were always busy without any skulduggery. Of course, the best reason was it could have been anyone on the issue list signing for the fuel and for that reason we got away with it. But I did ring Barracks section workshop to help make the damage look less while the bus was having the brakes tested. We never heard anything further about the matter, but the driver remained at Transport for quite some time while Trevor and I stayed at Tanker pool.

Mid November 1970

I arrived at work as usual, and headed off to the tanker pool and, as I arrived, the phone began to ring. The voice at the other end was my Section Commander asking me to report to his office ASAP, so I departed for his office. I couldn't think whether I'd stuffed up or not, so I just kept an open mind as to the nature of the call. Before long, I reached his office and was told to enter. With that, I walked in and saluted. I was then asked what posting I had applied for.

"Malaya, Darwin, or Townsville," I said.

"Well," he said, "you're off to Darwin. Report to HQ at the end of December."

Well! Well, that just made my day! I left his office and returned to my section to tell Trevor. I was off to Darwin and had to be there by the end of December. This left only four weeks to have everything removed and stored, so I began to get all the required information from Movements as to my obligations to travel by road rather than go by air. It was then explained that all our furniture would be stored, and furniture would be given to me rent-free in Darwin. With this in mind, I started hunting for some old lounges suites, dinner table and chairs, king size bed and mattress, cot with mattress and most of the items for Nicole, plus a washing machine, fridge, and garden tools. At stand down, I was off home very excited.

When I broke the news to Lita, she took it very well, and not a thing was brought up about her family. After all, she had married me as a serviceman and totally understood that postings were a part of our lives. But the good news about this was it was for two years at A-Grade rather than B-Grade. Being only six months without the wife, this could go on and on, and I had heard that had caused some major problems to marriages, so that evening we sat down at the table and I explained about the need to have some old crappy furniture and other household goods for storage so as not to pay rent for them. Then we decided to go up to Armadale and inform her parents of our pending move and ask if Lita could remain with them until I found accommodation. All that was okay by them, so I asked Tom if I could leave my tools and some equipment with him, which he could use as much as he needed. With that out of the way, we settled down to a meal and talked about the next two years and the type of place Darwin was. Obviously, they would miss Lita and Nicole as Tom was holding her and giving as much attention as he could. I couldn't stay any longer as I had a lot of things to sort out so we left not long after tea and arrived back at Balga and went straight to bed.

The next morning I was up early and sorting all my equipment to send up to Tom's, then left for work. I wasn't much good for my section as I spent more time getting wooden crates for storage then went off home at stand-down to load them up. I carried on with this for the remainder of the week, loading them onto a borrowed trailer and the next morning heading to Armadale to leave them there and return straight away to get the next load. On one trip, Lita was with me as I needed to clean each room out and leave only the minimum for packing to take to Darwin – Nicole's and Lita's. The rest of the items like the sewing machine and bedding was coming with me in the car as it had now been approved for me to drive to Darwin.

After all this was completed, I headed back to Armadale and had tea with Lita's family as her sisters had heard I was leaving for Darwin in two weeks and I was surrendering our married quarters within the week. All the furniture was going to Stores by the following week, and all that was needed was the crappy bits of lounge and dining table, beds, cots, washing machine, etc. Monday morning, Trevor and I got a flat-top truck from the base and loaded up the crappy bits, placed them all in my married quarters for inspection by Movements section that I was storing the items listed. Then I left for the base and my final clearance before setting off.

The last thing I had to attend to was getting the car fully serviced for the trip as most of the roads I'd be travelling were gravel, and some of them the worst driving conditions in the Australian outback. I attached a solid rack to the roof to carry our personal effects and extra fuel and tyres, while the back seat was also jammed full with gear. This left the front for sleeping, my cooking gear and a change of clothes.

Come the weekend, I said goodbye to my workmates and family, drove up to Armadale and spent the rest of the weekend with Lita. That evening we talked about the trip up and the roads I would be travelling on, and possible campsites ... also gemstones – my trip would take me through the opal fields of Coober Pedy. It would definitely be one of my highlights, about midway through the journey. The distance to Darwin from Perth was some 5,300 kilometres [3,350 miles]. This time of year was the wet season, which could delay the trip with flooded roads.

So my timing to travel wasn't going to be easy if that was the case.

I wouldn't let myself down because of the weather, but it wasn't far from my mind; I would deal with it when it happened.

Sunday night, I went to bed nice and early as I was leaving very early in the morning. When I woke, Lita rose with me and made a substantial breakfast. After forty-five minutes, I hugged Lita and Nicole, who was also awake, then left with, "I shall keep in touch as much as possible."

I drove until I reached Norseman, midday, about six hours and felt tired so I settled down to a flask of coffee and sandwich Lita had made, then took a short walk around the town. After checking all was okay with the car, I filled up with fuel and departed around 1.30pm, intending to sleep that night at the Balladonia Roadhouse. So for the next 200 kilometres, I sat back and relaxed and sang away to some tapes I had. About an hour later, I noticed the temperature gauge had risen to Hot. I didn't think too much about it until it started to rise higher, so I pulled well off the road and raised the hood to look things over. Steam was coming from a small black hose attached to the water pump, and a closer look revealed it had burst. As luck would have it, I had some reinforced hose on board that was about the same size, but couldn't do anything due to it being so hot, so I grabbed a tinny and sat around looking into the bush, and took myself for a long walk towards Fraser Range, returning about 4pm to fix the problem.

After five attempts, I managed to get one on when I heard a vehicle coming through the bush. Stuff me drunk, it flew out about ten metres from where I was parked, surprising me, as well as the driver. He came to a sudden stop, got out and asked if I was okay. I told him the problem and he offered to tow me to Balladonia. I wasn't sure about this as by now I had some four cans down my neck but I let him back up while I attached the rope. We were soon off down the road, and as there wasn't any traffic around, I began to wander a bit and I could see the driver laughing at me. When he put his hand out with a can attached so I just couldn't do anything but follow him wherever he went, sometimes in the gutter covering my car in crap and dust, other times driving in and out the white lines around bends. *What a fucken nutter!* But I just hung in.

After some of the most amusing driving, around 5.30pm, we arrived at Balladonia. I parked up then we went off for a drink of thanks. I offered him a meal but he was going through that night so I continued to fix the hose on and just before sunset tested it by driving some ten kilometres back the way I had come, then returned to Balladonia and camped for the night.

I was woken by trucks starting their engines and getting on the move and decided to leave with them as this was now the start of the great Nullarbor Plain, and I wasn't going to miss out getting the feel of it. I had been on a train looking out and wanting to explore this vast country some five years previous; now I had the chance to see it, and I was going to make the most of it.

I kept looking over the whole Nullarbor, stopping at garages along the way to fuel up, grabbing some ice before leaving for the next garage. By late morning, I was nearly at Madura with about 185 kilometres to go till the state border. I decided to head for Mundrabilla Roadhouse while I still felt fresh as it was only about 100 kilometres away. There, I had a meal and rested as I didn't want to overdo it – it had been two days of driving and my second night of sleeping rough so, by when I finished lunch, I cleaned out my car all the crap from I had filled up on then made up my nest for the night, then took a walk around this wild, windswept place.

The flies kept me waving as I strolled towards the coast and looked at all the relics from by-gone years as I walked in a large circle until I reached the car. I concluded that the gold mining at Kalgoorlie would have brought quite a rush from the east and, having nothing but a dusty uncleared track and little to no help, would leave one with nothing else to do but move on – it was such an unforgiving place to get stranded in. Even today, it would have the same impact as some of the vehicles travelling across were well past their used by dates and the drivers quite young.

For the rest of the evening, I looked up at the stars and drank a few tinnies then landed in my nest head-first for the slumber boss.

I woke well-rested and, after cooking a meal, cleaned up and headed for Eucla on the Western Australia/South Australia Border, some seventy kilometres away. By 7am, I had crossed from Sandgroper Country to the Crow-that-flies-backwards Country. I had driven some 1,273 kilometres in two full days, and I was now heading for Ceduna, some 510 kilometres further across the Nullarbor.

The condition of the road was as wild and unkempt as I'd been told, and I had to take a lot of care as the changing conditions gave no signs of bulldust holes that were as deep as the car nor the mallee roots hanging out from the graded dirt. It was not a time to sit back and relax. To top it all off, the wind grinding the ground lifted the dust and dumped it on my car.

For the rest of the day, I kept travelling, and at sunset, pulled over and settled down for some sleep, a cold tinnie helping to push me over into the land of noddies.

The next morning – if there was one – I was again woken by trucks and knew I had to get in front of them as I wouldn't be able to pass them with clouds of dust covering the road, or track. So, with haste, I got well past the first couple and kept going for Ceduna, still some 510 kilometres away. I arrived at sunset stuffed, but pleased that my car had run very well and without a problem. I was once again on hardtop road and soon found a campsite and pulled in for a long-awaited sleep.

After making breakfast, I studied the maps as I thought I could go across country from here rather than travel south to Port Agusta only to then drive north on the Stuart Highway.

I noticed a track that would take me across from Wirrulla and up to Lake Everard then onto Kingoonya, saving me some 550 kilometres in time and fuel, and it just may be that the road could be better – I just had to find the main turn off at Yantanabie which was about ninety kilometres away.

Before long, I was at the police station, which had a noticeboard for the likes of me: I gave the time and date of leaving and the time I expected to arrive at Kingooya and noted that I would be crossing Lake Everard. From that, I loaded extra fuel and supplies along with my support team then headed off on the beaten track.

This part of the country seemed much greener and had lots of trees and shady areas. After an hour of driving, I had to stop and open gates, drive through and close them again, leaving them the way I'd found them. The roads now began to show large rocks protruding out when climbing up small hills, which slowed me down but I wasn't in too much of a hurry. Around mid-afternoon, I made camp on a ridge, just for the view, as I was now looking down over Lake Everard. I cooked my tea and sat back with all sorts of things running through my mind, such as how Lita and Nicole were coping and hoping they were not overly worried about me, and how Tom was getting along with his granddaughter – I bet he was having all the fun that I couldn't have right now. Most of all, they were safe – that worry never crossed my mind. As for me, the view was great and my support team, the flies, were well on my case. Another day came to a close as I watched the sun hit the ground over Lake Everard.

I didn't get much sleep that night as I could hear the dingoes howling through most of the night and right next to my car. The racket was endless until I started the car and blew the horn for about five minutes, which helped shut them up until sunrise. At sunrise, I decided to start crossing the lake so headed off down on the main track until I was at the edge. Here, all the road signs disappeared into thin air so, with my map and brass compass, I took a bearing and, with my watch as a rough guide, headed off across.

After some thirty minutes travelling at 100 kilometres, I decided to stop and make a fire for breakfast. All was fine as there were no rocks or mallee roots, but halfway through cooking, I noticed the car was slightly leaning to the right. When I looked, thinking I might have a flat, I noticed the crust had broken and the car was sinking, so without delay, I jumped into the car and rocked it back and forth until it was free. Then I drove out of the mud hole and kept going to the far side, getting out at the Yerda Crossing only to look back and notice the smoke from my fire sending my breakfast skyward, an offering to the lake.

With that now behind me, I drove onto Yerda Junction and took the right-hand fork towards Kingoonya, arriving early midday. The local pub was open and I headed there to get news on the conditions ahead.

I was asked, "Where have you just come from?"

"Lake Everard," I said.

"Hell! Was it okay, mate?"

"Yes, mostly. I went through the lake to the crossing but stopped to cook my breakfast and nearly ended up staying as the car began to sink in the soft mud."

"Well, mate, you sure are lucky as nothing ever goes that way anymore."

With that, I booked my name on the Police board that I had arrived, and noted that 'all had gone okay, but the surface over

Lake Everard was crusty to mild mud'. Then I went back to the pub and got the news that the conditions up to Coober Pedy were extremely bad with bulldust holes the size of a house, and the weather wasn't helping as the wind hadn't stopped for the past two weeks.

"If you think the road up to Kingoonya was rough, well from here on to the Northern Territory border will rattle your balls off," I was told.

So, with that, I refuelled and headed off, intending to reach Coober Pedy, some 285 kilometres north by sunset. And it wasn't long before I was well and truly being rattled around. But I kept going at a fast but steady pace, the whole time taking in the view of the surrounding country and thinking about the early pioneers that found the opals, worked the diggings then moved on to the next find. What a life they'd had, and I wondered what sort of a person they were.

I kept going and arrived just before sunset. The only thing with lights on was the garage so I filled up with fuel and asked where the campsite was. He looked at me and pointed a complete circle. "Pick your spot, mate."

Then I asked for directions to the shops and was given the directions to town, which I just couldn't see until I was driving around. I then noticed that everything was underground. I found what I was looking for; bought supplies and a frying pan, and was given directions to a camping site, where I sorted myself out then went for a walk around the town by night. At every opportunity, I asked about looking around for some opals and found help from the locals. They showed me how to look, and told me what was around the town and that it was well dug over but finds were happening almost every day. I then mentioned that I was just passing through and was leaving the next morning.

They told me then about a place some three kilometres out of town that was signposted by the rail crossing – this was a good spot to look as no one owned it. So with that, I walked backed to camp and went to bed with all the events of the day running through my mind, and of course, Lita and Nicole. I would contact Lita when I reached Alice Springs in about two days' time.

The following day, I was up early and somewhat excited to get out of town to the rail line to try my luck. On arriving, I was soon out and about looking, keeping in mind what I was told the previous night. For the next two hours, I did the big emu-bob and found opal in shells, also on a long crab claw that looked full of opal. Taking all my samples, of which was plenty, I packed them away then headed off for Welbourn Hill about 200 kilometres up the Stuart Highway. After filling up with fuel, I carried on until it was nearly dusk and arrived at Agnes Creek. A short time later, I was well gone for the night as the only thing that woke me was the road trains heading south. This was a good time for me to leave and, after an hour, I crossed the border into the Northern Territory. At long last, a sealed road, which was a very welcomed sound underneath the car.

Now the country was becoming greener, and I was in need of a shower and shave at the next major watering hole, which was Kulgera. I also decided to rest up for some time as the dust was well into my system. I was spitting red dust and muck; it was in my eyes, ears and all over my body. Apart from that, it was right through the car, grinding on everything I touched from my water bottle to my dunny paper – it was time I gave myself a good scraping and put some order back into my sleeping quarters.

Around 1030am, I arrived in Kulgera and rolled up to the pub. After getting my room sorted out, I cleaned out the dust from the car, which was a major job, then got all my gear straightened out then went off for my shower. With all this sorted and feeling like a new man, I headed downstairs for a beer and a meal.

While looking through my books, I noticed that moonstones were had been found just outside of Victory Downs, about forty kilometres south-west of Kulgera, and also at Kulgera Station. Then a sign on the bar wall read that a BBQ for Christmas was being held at the Victory Downs Station that evening, and I thought about going over there. I was the only one in the pub, which gave me time to catch up on reading about the next major gem and mineral site, but for now I kept telling myself to leave for Victory Downs. Then a young fella came in, ordered a drink and started talking to me. He and the barman seemed to know each other, and he could see that I was half reading and half thinking when he mentioned the BBQ. He asked if the barman was going, but he wasn't, then looked over at me. He was told that I was staying the night.

"Do you want to go, mate? It could be a fun night."

I walked over to the bar, holding out my hand. "I am David, and I would love to join you."

"What are you reading?"

I told him I was interested in gemstones and that I understood Moonstones had been found at Victory Downs. He said he knew where they *could* be found but they were not good quality, which didn't matter that much to me, so we had another beer and, around 2.30pm, walked towards my car. He said it would be better if we went in his long-base four-wheel-drive, and I agreed as I wasn't feeling too much like driving.

About twenty miles along the way, a small tribe of Aboriginals were walking in the middle of the road, waving for us to stop.

I said to this young fella, "They could be needing something so we'd better check it out."

All they wanted was a lift to Victory Downs for the Christmas BBQ, so I nodded for them to jump in the back after the young fella said it was okay. We arrived at the station a little dusty and dry, let the Aboriginals out of the vehicle where a big tribe was gathering, then drove off down to the main part of the complex. As we got out, we were asked by the local police officer where we had just come from. After some small talk, we both paid for the BBQ pack and sorted our beer, then sat back and watched the locals having fun. The young fella was now cooking the snags when the police officer came over to me and asked me to remove the Aboriginals we had brought into camp. I looked at him and asked why.

"They are creating trouble with the other mob as they don't belong to this tribe. You brought them here so you can take them back where you found them."

This seemed out of order, so I replied back, "That's your problem, mate, not mine. As you represent law and order, go get stuffed."

He looked me straight in the eye and slammed his hand on the table. "Out here, I am the law, and what I say goes, so get them bastards out now!" And with that, I jumped up and asked him, "How far would you like me to take them down the track, sir?"

At the same time the young fella arrived back with our BBQ snags and was given the drum about the Aboriginals and that it was up to us to get rid of them, so with some talking, and bribing with six tinnies which I placed in the back, we soon had them jumping back in the vehicle. We both jumped in and drove like hell for around forty minutes, then it was time to get them out. We had a plan to stage a breakdown, so I started to pull out the Stop button, letting the vehicle splutter until it stopped. We both climbed out and jumped up and down that the truck's fuel line was cracked and told them to all get out. They did and, as the two women wandered towards a tree, I got the young fella to hold onto the tailgate and at the same time got the young

Aboriginal to hold a large tin under the exhaust pipe to catch any fuel that came out, then I got into the vehicle, noting the young fella hanging onto the tailgate. Just then the older aboriginal started to open the passenger door, so I lent over and grabbed the handle and slammed it shut and locked it. Immediately, I fired the vehicle up, dropped the clutch and started speeding off. At the same time, this old Aboriginal had started running alongside the vehicle. I looked out the back to see the eyes of the young fella, who was hanging on for life, then flashed back to the old Aboriginal was now well on the hop. I looked at my speedo and just couldn't believe it – he was running at twenty miles an hour and I was still picking up speed. I still couldn't believe it when he almost got to twenty-five, then he was gone in a cloud of dust. My mouth was well opened as I couldn't believe anyone could run that fast. *What a guy!* I thought.

Then I pulled over to let the young fella in and started driving in a large circle and at the same time mentioned to him about the old Aboriginal running alongside. He'd noticed it as well, so this was something we both laughed about as the last thing I remember was the size of his eyes just before he left, or should I say, disappeared.

We arrived back at Victory Downs and were soon back talking to the police officer and filling him in on the staged events. I fetched a can of beer and went back to finish talking to him about the runner when this boondy [rock] came flashing between us and slammed into the beer hall. It was followed by more, but this time we both headed for cover. After some large rocks finished breaking the fibro side of the building, the police officer noticed it was the same bunch of Aboriginals that we'd driven out of the station. I looked up and couldn't believe it – he was right – they were all standing in front of him telling him about our adventure. That's when I noticed the old Aboriginal holding his pants up, and the younger one holding a bleeding head. They were taken to the first-aid post and sorted out while the police officer explained the other side of the events.

"The first thing is the young Aboriginal got hit by the underneath of the vehicle and cut his head open when you drove off. The older Aboriginal had his belt caught in the bloody door and that is why he was keeping pace with you. It eventually snapped, sending him to the ground, cutting both his legs and feet."

We both looked at each other, laughing at the complete circle of events. And so we settled in and gave Father Christmas a big welcome. It ended as a good night with me buying beer for the small tribe I'd had to take out of the station, and we both got into the vehicle and fell asleep within minutes.

The next morning we were up with some of the locals who were still drinking and having a BBQ breakfast, so we joined in for our fill and left about an hour later. As the young fella was driving across to the gem field, he mentioned that he was off to Ayers Rock the following day and would I like to join him. Of course, I said yes, then we arrived at the location of the moonstones and before long I was doing my emu-bob collecting samples. After two hours, we both headed back to Kulgera where I stored my findings. We just happened to drop into the pub and settled into a few beers and a talk about the next day's trip to Ayers Rock. Apparently, he was taking a vehicle to the Aboriginal tribe for their use and was returning the same day. I was to be picked up at Erldunda at six in the morning. As it was some 75 kilometres up the track, I was going to leave this pub at 4pm to get settled down and, as I had not long eaten a sound meal, I was fresh and ready and looking forward to tomorrow's adventure, even though it was going to be a long day. Ayers Rock is 246 kilometres west, on a typical dry and dusty outback track that was well-graded and allowed drivers to sit at a speed around 110 kph, sending dust clouds billowing up for miles. But that was the way things were out here, the young fella explained.

I was woken the next morning by a tapping on my door window, the young fella giving me a hand sign to leave now. I dressed quickly and was out within minutes. The sunrise was well worth getting up for as the colours that danced from rise to rise were shades of puce then full purple, then around another bend more colours in various shades until full sunrise arrived. Apart from that, the trip out was uneventful and, after nearly three and half hours, with The Rock well in sight, we arrived. We were expected and the vehicle was handed over to the ranger. An older one was filled up with fuel and checked over and, once that was completed, we had lunch and I headed off for a quick look around. Then up onto the huge monolith standing out in this wildness as a monument to nature's fury or design. Or is it a monitor, keeping us under observation while maintaining the local tribes with the disciplines and duties to respect this site that can only be regarded as a very special place for them, as it is was for me? I could almost hear the past of all the tribes dancing, their chants echoing from the surrounds from the base of this huge sacred site.

It was a pity I couldn't stay on for another day. Even though I had a fantastic time, we just had to leave and the return trip wasn't a patch on the morning one. It wasn't long before we were back in Erldunda and I got our meal cooking and the cold beer was running nice and easy for the rest of the night. As everything happens, the day must come to a close as the young fella was going on his way south and first thing in the morning I was hitting the road for Alice Springs, about 200 kilometres north up the track. As I was about one day out of my schedule, I needed to get some road surface behind me over the next two days.

I was well up and ready before the sun began to settle across the vast open plain, bringing with it the flies and heat. Then about mid-morning, I arrived at Alice Springs and drove slow enough for a quick look after crossing the Todd River. I filled up with fuel for the next stop, which was going to be Tea Tree Well. I reached there by mid-afternoon and refuelled to go onto Barrow Creek and get my head down as that was around 500 kilometres for the day's drive. After doing my meal, I had a little evening light left to read up about the road ahead.

The next day, I was going to stop at Devils Marbles for breakfast and climb all over them before heading off to Daly Waters, about 600 kilometres up. This would then have me in Darwin around late afternoon. So that evening, I had a pub meal and got my head down and before long was up and fresh ready to go. This day would be a non-stop trip to Darwin, seeing Mum and Dad and giving Lita a long-awaited phone call.

December 22nd 1970

I headed off around 5am and it was evident that I was well in the tropics, having crossed over just outside of Alice Springs, about 1,000 kilometres south. I could now feel the humidity and sweat dripped from me as I kept drinking water. Before long, I reached Katherine, stopping only to fill up with fuel and fill the icebox with tinnies, then it was back on the road north with only 340 kilometres left to travel and some nine hours of daylight left. With the good condition of the road, along with little rain to flood them, I could well get there by midday.

By that time, I was incredibly tired and a little bum sore when I arrived at the main entrance of the Base. Getting directions to Mum and Dad's married quarters, I arrived at their house at 12.30pm on the 22nd December 1970, with a very welcomed cold can and a warm, long chat about all the events over the past few days. I also talked about Lita and Nicole and the need to contact them that evening.

Apart from that, I sorted my quarters and room, then headed straight for the canteen to make that most important call to Lita and let her know I had arrived.

"It won't be long before you'll be up here with me," I told her at the end of the call.

Then I headed back to be with Mum and Dad, and Peter and Wendy, for small talk and relating the events of my trip through the red centre. As always, Dad had overly worried about the problems before I started, so I told him about the minor breakdowns – like the bypass water pipe bursting and the time and effort it took to repair it. He had to look under the bonnet to confirm that it was okay, while I told him it hadn't been a major problem to start with. I followed on with the frypan I'd left at Lake Everard due to the surface being too soft for my car and told him how I recovered myself from it.

"Well, it all must have worked as I wouldn't be here talking to you about it now," I said.

Then our conversation moved onto Darwin and the rainy season, and how lucky it was that I hadn't been stranded by the flooding across the Stuart Highway from as far down as Katherine to Adelaide River. Then I stopped talking about my trip and told them about Nicole and how Lita was coping being with her family, which brought Mum to pass on the general information that would help them both. I could try getting rental accommodation from the Greek families who owned them and, with that information, asked her for directions so I could follow it up the next day.

Come midnight, I had to get to bed as it had been a long and trying, tiring trip, and I was now happy to be here and put closure to it. Tomorrow, a new one begins.

I rose feeling completely drained and covered in sweat, and now noticed the control of the wet season – the humidity was the same as the temperature, and a little hotter than Vietnam and so typical of tropical wet weather. In the Northern Territory, two seasons come in one year – the Dry season, for about nine months with an all-round temperature of 25 to 30 degrees Celsius – this followed by the *knockcumdown* winds, which is followed by the Wet season just before Christmas – tropical rainfalls along with lightning and thunder, and in some cases, cyclones just to keep you on your toes. During these times, half of Darwin leaves to have Christmas south with family.

So I showered and headed for breakfast, soon noticing how big it was on drinks and other fluids with plenty to select from. The morning meal was also plentiful and with all that now resting over my belt, I headed off to HQ to report for duty, then reported to my section commander, Sergeant Pritchard. After making myself known to him, I headed back to Mum and Dad's as there wasn't anything happening at the section, and my orders were to stand down until Christmas was over. I was to report in the new year, so the rest of the week was my own.

I spent the rest of the day being shown around Darwin and the possible renting area, which was close to the B. It looked quite clean and tidy. This was important for Lita and Nicole, and even though it was only short term, I wanted it that way as well as I am very fussy about my standards of living, and presentation was very much a part of my life. This I was going to insist on with Lita regarding Nicole and I would be there to help as much as I could.

January 1971

I was offered rental accommodation on 18 January, and arrangements were made the same day to fly me to Perth to pick Lita and Nicole. That afternoon, I arrived at Perth Airport and was so pleased to see them both. They looked so well and I was so eager to cuddle them I couldn't let go for a couple of minutes. Then I noticed Lita's mum and dad standing there. After a short conversation, we left for Armadale, me doing all the talking about the events over the past month, along with the type of accommodation we would be staying at until married quarters became available.

It wasn't long before we arrived at their home and packed the rest of Lita and Nicole's things as we were flying out at 10am the next morning.

Then we had some time for the three of us. Nicole looked very pretty and was full of smiles and giggles and I hoped the flight up to Darwin wouldn't affect her too much. I did mention to Lita that she would have pressure in her ears so we might have to hold her for comfort as the flight we were on stopped at almost every town on the way up. It would be best if she was well awake. Apart from that, this was also the first time Lita was to fly so I began to build her confidence up.

Before the night was over and all goodbyes were said to the family, it was time for bed.

Soon enough, we were both up sorting Nicole out then getting ourselves ready. By 8.30am, we were off to the airport and, without much ado, left Lita's mum and dad and boarded the plane. We were given the front row seat as it had a cradle that dropped down for Nicole as I had asked for the position from air movements. It was great as other passengers had to hold onto their babies. Then we were off and I could feel Lita becoming a little tense so held her hand and explained that the banging sounds were quite normal and the pressure would build up and that she should blow hard holding her nose. Then it was Nicole's turn, so I picked her up and gently held her and gave her a bottle to suck on, which gave only short term relief, then we all sat back for the duration of the trip. Lita had the window seat, which kept her occupied looking out over the vast country we lived in.

For the next five hours, we were up and down until we reached Darwin. We were both happy to be on the ground again as Nicole was becoming a little upset as she couldn't get her proper sleep.

Mum and Dad were there to meet us, more so waiting to get their first look and cuddle of Nicole. It was great to see them all as this was now another closure and a new one about to start. I was still a newcomer to Darwin and I wasn't going to miss out on anything that was going. But for now, we had a light lunch at Mum's then headed off to our rented accommodation to get Nicole settled in, and unpack and store everything away. It was now that I noticed Lita feeling the full power of the heat.

February 19th 1971

We were a little disappointed with our rental as there was very little hot water and what we did have smelt like swamp water. I asked the housing section what the waiting time for married quarters accommodation was and was told about one month and that we should give our notice now. With that, I explained the situation to Lita and also that Mum didn't mind us using her house to wash in. On the 19th of February, we began the task of getting our personal effects across to the married quarters but, upon a second look, I found the place uncleaned and in such a shitty mess so I complained to the housing officer. The previous tenant's wife was having a shower when we arrived and should have vacated that morning, so we drove over to Mum's house just around the corner and stayed there until it was sorted out. By 2pm, I was given the okay to move in, and upon opening the door, we were both knocked back by this stinking smell that left me running around to open all the windows.

I straight away drove to the housing officer and asked him to inspect the house, so he came around; took a lot of notes as both Lita and I were thoroughly upset about the condition she had left it in. He asked me to sign his visit sheet and asked that I send him an account of the work and cleaning needed to get the house in a habitable, clean, and tidy state. Not only was the house a shit pit, but the whole yard had grass over two metres high. I had no option but to accept this situation and set about getting all the cleaning material from Barracks. We dropped Nicole off with Mum, and Lita and I spent the rest of the day and evening cleaning up – from cat crap to cobwebs hanging down from the ceiling fans a good metre long. Then I noticed a tea-chest sitting on the rear veranda and, without a problem, opened it and found the previous tenant's personnel effects inside. I decided to finish loading it with all the shit, cat crap and cobwebs, along with dirty washing rags and kitty litter, and whatever else I could get into it. Just on sunset, we both started to clean the kitchen out, and the wall started to be covered with cockroaches. This was the last straw as I now had to bomb the place for the night. Upon doing it, we spent the night around Mum and Dad's with me sleeping downstairs, which was fine by me.

The next morning, we went around to finish cleaning as the furniture – which matched the furniture we had in storage in Perth – was arriving that afternoon. So our hands were now full of cleaning, and me having all the fun loading all the remaining crap and all the dead cockroaches into the tea chest. By late morning, I resealed the box and wrote 'Unwanted crap – send down to owner' across the lid. Then I sent a small account down to the Housing Officer. Soon after, I was sent a small cheque, which the old tenants would be charged for. The furniture arrived and was installed, then I headed off to pick Lita and

Nicole up, returning to the house for a new start.

I would leave for work around 7.30am. It was a short walk to my section, so I would come home for dinner and, with plenty of daylight left, I set about cleaning the yard up – it was like a jungle. After my domestic duties, my neighbour came over to introduce himself and his wife.

"G'day, I'm Bill, and this is my wife, Fay."

He was in Transport section, and I mentioned I was too, then our talk was about the condition of the house. Bill mentioned that he was a cook at the airman's mess, and Fay was employed as the lazy fat cow, as he would often introduce her. We arranged to get together for a drink the following night.

It was fantastic that Mum and Dad were just up the road as Lita and Nicole would call in so Mum could have some quality time with her granddaughter, as they had missed out due to being in Darwin when she was born. I could see how proud they were and couldn't wait to have unlimited visitation time once we were settled into our own place.

The next evening we went over to Bill and Fay next door for a chat and a beer, and while talking to Bill, he informed me that he would like to build a BBQ. We began to talk more about it and I felt it would be great to build it on the boundary fence line. He agreed with that, so over the next couple of weeks, we gave ourselves a project to get the materials. I was to get all the concrete blocks, and Bill would get the metal hot plate and grills. Slowly over the weeks, we collected all we needed and began to construct our BBQ a little at a time jointly through the week.

The weekend I kept aside for Lita and Nicole as we wanted to explore Darwin and its many treasures, from its beautiful beaches and pre-war relics, but the most remarkable thing was Darwin. It had an easy way of life, and there just didn't seem to be a rush to do anything, yet 75% were government employed. The local traders were very dependent upon the Army, Air Force and Navy. There was no fresh milk, or TV, even though the population was 15,000. But the main event for social gathering and entertainment was going to the race track, where the winner was decided out of view from the spectators while the race was in progress. The jockeys would hold up behind the tree line where the deal was struck then off to the finish line they'd go. This would entertain Dad as from here, the atmosphere would get better if the jockeys disagreed and the fighting started, over which could end up with two winners or the race being run again.

Apart from the races, which I had no time for, we at most would travel from beach to beach, and it was brought to my attention about the hidden dangers on the beach and in the water. Sea-wasps were out in force, and though they looked like jellyfish, they could kill a child in seconds. Then, if that wasn't enough to deal with, rockfish would also be stranded in rock pools after the tide went out. If these were stood on, a grown man could be killed. I, at times, became very paranoid about these hidden dangers and tried not to overreact, but in the end, it was better to stay away from the beach during the wet season, and so we began to use the Base swimming pool, which gave us more fun as Dad and Mum would join us.

Mid March 1971

By now, we had our home looking neat and clean. At this time, I was asked by my section commander Sgt Pritchard to build a smoko room, storeroom, and sleeping quarters for nightshift. My task was set, but getting material was a far greater problem as other sections were also adding on various storage rooms. I did not give up.

I also noticed this painter going like the clappers painting the eaves of the transport maintenance workshop, so I asked him for a job. He was delighted about it, and I said I would be there after stand-down at 4.30pm. So for the next week and weekend, I too was going like the clappers painting.

Upon finishing, I was paid in full as agreed, $8.00 per hour, and well worth it as Lita and I put it aside for a new car. I was still waiting for the materials to start my project, then noticed that materials had been delivered for the main roof repairs of transport, so I slipped off to Barracks to find out who it belonged to. They couldn't give me an answer so that weekend, Dick, another member of the transport section, gave me a hand to start building with these materials.

All walls were completed but required standing and the sheeting off for Monday morning. Just after roll call, the whole section gave a hand to stand the frames and fix them together then the sheeting was added to the external walls. While this was happening, other members painted the external walls. By mid-morning, the project was 99% completed and waiting for the electrical work. But for now, the first stage was over.

The whole project was completed on the following Monday morning, and, at the same time, contractors arrived to start on the roof. For some reason, there seemed a shortage of material, and Cpl Hill, who was in charge of the new equipment store, was asked if anyone had removed timber that was delivered the previous fortnight. Of course, he had no idea, and I wasn't asked where I'd got the material.

We now had some clean and tidy restrooms, which made a big difference to all of us. Three or four weeks later, the Base Commanding Officer did his monthly inspection. When he noticed the work we'd completed, I was informed by my section commander, Sgt Pritchard, that I was given two weeks leave for work done out of hours. I was over the moon about this and couldn't wait to plan a camping trip to go gemstones hunting. At this time, I was asked if I was interested in buying a Mini Moke from a service member who'd been posted south. He wanted $500.00 cash ASAP.

Upon looking over it, I made him an offer for two hundred less than he was asking as I didn't have much of a mechanical mind. He was leaving now, which placed him in the position that he had to accept my offer. So I paid him $300.00 and drove over to Dad's. He felt that I had a good deal apart from the paintwork, which looked like it was painted with a large, very well-used yard broom. At this time, I met an old friend of Dad's – Phil Corne – from his first posting to Darwin. They both loved the bush and, at times, went duck shooting and hunting wild pigs. About two weeks later, Robbie, Dad, Phil and I, with Phil driving the Moke, spent an overnight hunting trip near Batchelor, some 100 kilometres south. Phil knew the area and the type of wildlife to be expected. He explained that wild pigs had no respect for anyone or anything, and they could be a threat to us, especially if they had their young piglets with them.

Not long after leaving the main track and driving through grass some two metres high, Phil swerved to the right, which sent my wallet and ammo flying out, along with my hat. He then jumped out and headed off towards the thick jungle growth while Dad, Robbie and I began to load our weapons. I had a double-barrel shotgun about 700mm long; Dad had a high powered rifle, while Rob had a .22 standard automatic. But Phil had a Colt 45 with a 275mm barrel that sounded like my shotgun.

Without any warning, we could hear Phil blasting away. Then this bloody big pig came racing through the long grass, heading straight for the three of us, leaving no clear sight of Phil's location. This meant I couldn't get a shot off. By this time, the big pig had Dad in his sights. It gave out a loud snort and bolted directly for Dad. Rob and I just couldn't see where the hell Phil was when, without any warning, Phil ran behind it and dropped it dead with one shot from his Colt revolver.

Dad looked over at Phil with a long and relaxed, "Thanks, mate."

We all took a good long look at the size of this beast and measured the length of his tusks before Phil removed them. Then we laid them over an ant nest and headed back through the high grass, where I soon found my wallet and some of the ammo. We returned to the water hole to set up camp.,

First, we had to throw a rope over a tree but found that a problem so I climbed up. As I stood on this branch, my head became tangled in a green tree ant nest, and I found myself rocking and rolling, trying to get myself free from it while holding onto both the rope and the bloody branch. The ants now ran down inside my tee-shirt, leaving me nothing else to do but jump into the water hole. All I could hear coming from Dad, Rob, and Phil was laughter while I was tried to retain my balance and get out of the ant nest. But once I dropped into the water, I couldn't stay under long enough to remove them so I jumped up to the surface, trying to pull them out from my hair as much as I could. Then I ducked back under until all ants were off me, and typically, the others still laughed at my predicament.

We eventually settled down for the night around a small fire and lay looking at the clear sky and the sharp quality of the stars through the Milky Way. The sounds of the bush at night when there is no wind is quite heart pumping as Vietnam wasn't as quiet and the smells were without the strong perfume that seemed to hang in your nostril. Then came the stink of the flying bats as they bombed the canopy cover, and all the silanes and movements were changing to the dawn chatter.

At dawn, I looked over the flat country and noticed some twenty wallabies around eighty metres away, so placing myself on one elbow and poking the others to take notice, I was going to shoot them from my position with the .22 automatic. I could hear the bullet slam into the target, which didn't seem to disturb the others. By this time, we were all picking one out and, from our position, had three clean kills. We stopped shooting as this mob of roos couldn't see or smell us, I think due to the flying fox crap over the canopy.

The rest of the morning was spent cutting and cleaning our game for the BBQ and we return to Darwin that evening.

I found Phil very good company as he wasn't outside his station in life but more a man that loved the outback and the way the indigenous people lived and hunted. Phil also had a full-blood native girl and a daughter by him, Treisa. As our friendship grew, he asked me to help change his shed into a small home for his family. I got my next-door neighbour, Bill, to give me a hand and some three weeks later, we completed a very basic accommodation unit. But during the time we were helping him get it all together, he was asking me about the gemstones and how to look for them and identify them, so on some occasions, I would bring along a sample stone and explain what it was and its origins, followed by the location where it was picked up from. This opened the doors for me also as he showed his girlfriend, who knew what it was but only from the missions around Alice Springs on which she had grown up. Over the next two weeks, I showed Phil all the rocks I had of any quality and said that I was going to the Bureau of Mineral Resources for maps and general information regarding gemstones etc. I left Phil a small book on field studies for gemstones.

Over the following weeks, I gathered as much information as I could on two locations – Fergusson River and Pine Creek – including all the explanatory notes compiled in 1967. I felt I had the latest information available to me, then requested maps from the Base flight deck and started to compile a list of points that could have some interesting questions to be unravelled as the Military maps gave a far better coverage and with good contours of heights and the dotted locations of buildings, which was so important for any unknown eventuality. As for the Geology maps, they were very basic, with no grid reference point to work from. The one thing I did find from these Geology maps was the word 'Falls' was shown in the Daly River, which passed through Rock Candy Range. I found this a little odd, to say the least, as nothing was mentioned on the Military maps. Apart from that, I was trying to get my two weeks Leave from my section commander, but each time I put in a Leave form, I was refused on the grounds that the section was low on staff. After some six times of requesting Leave and being refused, I confronted my Base Adjutant and handed him all the refused forms and asked for his assistance as I was trying to travel down the Daly River before the wet season. He was aware that I had been granted the Leave and rang my section Commander and requested a completed form be sent to his office within the hour. Boy, I knew he wouldn't like what I'd done, but at the same time, he just always seemed cranky over some matter or rather somebody else.

I left the Adjutant's office and headed for the flight deck with my maps and the locations we would be camping at, where we would mark a large X on the ground with a can of silver paint when we arrived at each location, preferably before nightfall. Then I headed off to stores and equipment to sign for our Punt boat and a 1hp seagull outboard motor. I was also provided with two telescopic aluminium oars, which we were asked to test out, a minor first aid kit, and a couple of smoke bombs. Then I returned to sign for my leave for the coming weekend and returned to my section Commander to let him know I wasn't going to ignore him.

I walked into his office and mentioned it was the only way as I had done the work for the section, and this trip down the Daly River wasn't going to be postponed due to the amount of work that had been done to get it all together, from the location and using the river as a road, then getting all the documents and information, then the time it should take to float down the river as we were only taking one gallon of fuel with us for the hundred or thereabout miles, and maintaining a trail of information should we fail to return.

With all the above, it was the best time to make such a trip as the river was, to our understanding from the local Police Station at the Daly River mission, running around five kilometres per hour. Dad had to take us down to Claravale, an abandoned farm some fifty miles southwest of Cullen Siding, twenty miles south of Pine Creek. Now all was in order, leaving only some food items and cooking utensils. With Phil dropping around each evening to go over the type of country we were going to walk around, I felt our best location was to remain close to running water or old creek beds as most of this area had been worked over for gold, tin and copper. But the thing I was most interested in was Tourmaline, which had been noted, and I believed that no work had been undertaken to find out what was there apart from the gold and tin and, of late, uranium at Rum Jungle. However, our main objective was to find and note the location of all the material found using my style of map reading and the grid reference to prevent anyone else from using it.

Mid June 1971

So all was now complete and Lita and Nicole were well settled and, with nothing to overly worry about, we loaded up Phil's VW ute with all the gear we were taking. We settled down at home with a can of beer with Dad and Lita as Phil was staying over that night so we could leave around 8.30am.

During the evening, Dad recalled his adventures when out with Phil. He always found some humour in the things that went wrong or were not planned, and as the night went on, our banter soon came to a close.

We were up at dawn to a typical tropical June morning with clear skies, the temperature around 27C. Arriving at Pine Creek some 155 miles south, we stopped for our last beer, then left for Claravale Homestead on a gravel track for the last fifty miles. We arrived at the Daly River just after midday and noticed the river was running faster than estimated. We measured the flow and rounded it out that we would arrive about two days early, then got our gear loaded and waved Dad off. Then we left the Claravale Homestead for the long haul north-west.

We placed ourselves in the centre of the river using the telescopic aluminium oars and let nature drift us down while I began to plot our course and our first night stop some twenty kilometres away at Laurie Billabong, which was between the Daly River and no name ridge. But my first stop was Bradshaw Creek, about an hour's drifting. When we arrived, I found the banks too difficult to climb so we passed on for the next best landing and walked back. I found nothing but mud and gravel, although I did take a sample from the wash where the creek and the Daly met. Then we returned to the punt and set off for the last leg for the day, arriving around 5.30pm to get our camp set up. Phil headed out to catch our meal for the night while I was out collecting dung and firewood. Just around sunset, we both settled down under our canopy with a barbecued barramundi when the whole jungle came to life.

Listening, Phil told me what type of bird it was, and this was kept up for most of the early evening. Then he explained that he had spent some time living with the Aboriginals and during the day they would do dotted paintings to let other tribes know what tucker was around. From this, I could well visualise how these people passed on from generation to generation through song and dance but more so through their paintings, and though Phil was still talking, I must have slipped off to sleep as the next thing I was woken up by birds squawking. The air was full of sounds that I had never heard before, to the point we both couldn't hear ourselves talk, but laughed as we got about packing up for the next leg to Banyan Farm [Abandoned] and stopping at Jinduckin Creek. We were also stopping to look over the area where the rapids were shown on the map.

So once again, we drifted down the Daly. Phil now looked for other tucker while I began to take some photos and kept an eye on my compass. When the river changed its course to the southwest we needed to head for the bank and check what danger these rapids were going to be and whether we needed to carry the punt and our gear around them.

But for now, our first stop was Stay Creek, about five kilometres up, as this creek ran down to the Daly from a rocky outcrop that I was very interested in looking over. Once we arrived, we covered up for the walk up the creek until we reached the crossing, picking up and looking over various stones and only noting and packing those of interest. We carried on until we reached the crossing, where I explained to Phil that some of the samples had banded Agate which was very interesting as the further we walked up the creek, the less the Agate appeared. I believed that the walk back would confirm this and, as the time was now against us, we headed back to the punt, picking samples here and there only. Once in the boat, we headed off for the rapids using the outboard motor for about 2km and, upon the river changing course, we looked for a suitable place to land. When the river twisted to the north, we pulled onto a sandy beach and walked on the north bank. It was quite clear that the rapids were minor in length but flowing fast with little waves, which we both agreed we could manage okay as long as we could keep ourselves from slamming onto the hidden boulders.

So we strapped our gear down and unhooked the outboard

motor then headed for the rapids using the telescopic aluminium oars to push ourselves away from the rocks. We looked at each other, my thumb up to Phil for good luck, as we started to gain speed. When the first boulder was hit, followed by another, we both began to use the oars to push ourselves from them. But my oar buckled in two, leaving a short stump to push with. Then the same thing happened to Phil's. Our speed doubled from the first point of entering and we both just laid flat down and let nature take us to the end. I could see the trees hanging low and scraping across the gunnel, passing just over my head which was being wiped by the branches. I had no idea how Phil was going as I was flat out in the front. Then, just as fast at it had begun, it was over, the punt starting to spin in small circles and slowing down to a smooth sound. We both raised our heads and looked at each other and noticed we were okay, but the aluminium oars were completely stuffed so we slowly moved to the bank and dried ourselves by laying on the rocks and laughing at the event that was a ride of a lifetime. It was a good thing that Phil covered all the guns and ammo as they were dry and ready to use.

After a short break, we were back in the slightly damaged punt and heading down to Jinduckin Creek, and arriving there around 2pm, then once again we were on foot on the north bank picking up samples over a 2km walk then back to the punt and onto our camp for the night at Banyan Farm.

Looking over our samples, it became clear that quarts crystal was the prominent denominator. I brought to Phil's attention that we could have time at the next stop to get some samples, and he agreed, but first we needed to get our tucker. With that, I hung a line over the back while Phil was ready with my shotgun. It wasn't long before he downed a duck and I hooked a Barramundi, so we cleaned them and used the outboard motor for the last two kilometres to our next campsite, where Phil started a fire while I placed our X marker. The tucker sorted, we walked off south to Banyan Waterhole, about 500m from our camp, still picking up samples and storing them. Then we went back to camp with a large amount of dung as the mozzies were getting worse as the evening went on. This camp was a sandy beach with no stones, so I dug a hole and lit a fire, placed the cow dung in it so it would blow it across us, as this helped to stop the mozzies. We dined on duck and fish then sat back to talk about adventures of the day and hope that all from now on should be less traumatic but much more rewarding as we had noticed a big change in the Geological Formation from when we started until today. Even though it was good news for me, Phil was also getting the same idea about it, yet there was more to go over.

With the event of a full day, I was settled near Phil in my sleeping roll when I found the smell of the dung overpowering and decided to move my kit alongside the dung fire, and it wasn't long I was being tapped on the foot by Phil

"Good morning," he said, "hop up and come here.

As I did, he pointed to the ground, saying, "You lucky bastard, Dave."

As I looked down, I noticed the track from a crocodile that had slipped past me about a metre away during the night and there were no return tracks. Phil mentioned that it could be a female and she would have eaten before coming to her nest. I wasn't worried too much about it so Phil asked me to lay down over its tracks with my arms stretched out. Upon doing so, he said it was around 3.6 metres as my arms could just reach its claws. That was disturbing news and, to cap it off, he mentioned she would be passing here within the hour for the morning feed. With that, I was packed up and we were in the punt floating down the river again. I did ask Phil for a little more understanding and best way to handle a situation such as the one we'd just had, and his comments were "Get out quick," and that's about the best way to deal with it.

So we were well on the way to Oolloo Homestead and to stop over at Ban Ban lagoon. While we slowly drifted down, we talked about the complete difference in the countryside from alluvium, soil, sand and ferruginous gravel, as our Geological map had shown and from this, which could provide us with much easy digging should we need to. But for now, we both sat back and let the running water carry us down, only checking our position each hour while looking over every stone we had and trying to collate the hard information in front of us when we heard gunshots in the distance, which wasn't much to worry about in itself as hunters and prey walked out here together. But the river seemed endless and with wildlife all around it wasn't hard to understand that, with all this fresh water about, one could quite easy melt into this solitude and quietness.

I thought that when looking at the pleasure this was giving Phil. As for me, it was something I knew I would never forget.

Although we had time to relax and ponder our thoughts, we still had to retain our survival needs and, as we passed Jool Chung Creek, we stopped and looked over the area but found nothing as it wasn't a major flowing creek, so we once again settled back and, with a fishing line out for our evening meal, then about 4pm we arrived at Oolloo Homestead and Ban Ban Lagoon, which was just up a small creek from the Daly River. We arrived, made our camp in this very pretty spot surrounded by warm water, lush grass, relatively dry, and as we pulled the punt onto this spot, we noticed a small roo nearby that was going to be our meal for the night. As I shot it, the bloody thing moved, leaving it wounded and me having to go into the water and finish it off. Phil started yelling at me to get a move on as I had brought some small crocs into the water and, looking back, I could see the eyes just out of the surface. Keeping my cool, I started dragging the roo back to the bank while still cutting the hindquarters off. Then Phil let loose a couple of rounds, sending the crocs to the bottom of the creek and me now hot-footing it across the top of the water like God but throwing the meat high onto the bank as Phil let loose more rounds.

Most days, we would swim in the nuddy and, on this occasion, I was in the nuddy, apart from a bayonet, my belt and scabbard. But I was soon on dry land well-winded, with Phil rocking with laughter at the sight of it all and me stinking of blood and guts, which I washed off at the lagoon as Phil started the fire to cook our evening meal.

For Phil to skin the roo, we hung the meat between two very close trees, and cooked it with a burnt coating of flesh to prevent the flies from blowing it. Phil then rolled up the hide into a pillow and we started to get our campsite sorted but this time with loaded guns at the ready. I pulled our canopy over a low tree, pinned the back to the ground and placed rocks over it, then let the front hang loose. With the smoke coming into the canopy, we settled back like a pair of bush hillbillies eating our roo.

Then just after sunset, we were bombed again by flying foxes, and their crap could be heard slamming onto the canopy cover. Nothing we did helped our situation … until Phil let go both barrels of my shotgun through the canopy, leaving a hole big enough to pass through.

For a split second, all was quiet, then they started again. Once more, he let loose two barrels and made another hole. Again, silence. Then once more it was on, but this time we were being bombed by crap. I just stood up and pulled the canopy from the tree and we both slept under it. After some time, all was quiet. The next morning revealed the damage and without much ado we packed up our gear and left this very pretty spot and were once again on the Daly River.

Our next stop was where the Douglas River met the Daly River. We started up the outboard motor as this spot was going to be worth a good looking over and we needed to get there to allow us that time. We planned to arrive around 9am. Plenty of good landing spots as sand was well washed down from the open plains and dumped into this area would reveal the bigger picture and save our time. When we pulled the punt onto high ground, I could see that some stones were banded Agate. I called to Phil, then noticed quartz, so we began to collect what we could. I noticed Phil taking care to collect samples worth keeping. As I looked harder, I noticed some quartz with slight green and some with blue and also red, and the very first thing that went through my mind was Topaz or Zircon, forgetting Tourmaline was on my list. For some reason, it never entered my mind. But more overwhelming was the amount lying about. Although the quality wasn't very good, at least we found the wash and would be going home with something of worth. We stayed there till mid-afternoon then drifted off to Belbowi Billabong and the road that led to Tipperary at the Beeboom Crossing, which was just over halfway.

All was well with us, and around midday, we reached the crossing and decided to look along the south bank. Walking west, we found nothing at all for a full kilometre so headed back to the crossing and walked east on the north bank but still found nothing except small Agate scattered around. So we headed to the crossing and set up camp for the fifth night and a long rest after the flying fox drama. Though we were near Tipperary settlement, we didn't feel as though anyone else was within a hundred miles of us, and with the number of things we'd done – and still had plenty to do – made Phil and I very conscious of each other's welfare. This I found an easy bond as deep down I felt Phil may have been an only or, more so, a lonely child. I never asked him, and I never found out; he just seemed very content with the way his life was and wasn't materialistic – apart from the important things that mattered the most, which was his wife and daughter.

I could say the same for myself. I knew I had something inside me to strive ahead, and my mind was always trying to learn more even though I wasn't given the grounding and, more to the point, was used and abused – I still have no respect for those who made decisions that wouldn't allow me the very basic rules of learning the three R's. But now, I had a family, and I would not let them down because of my history. From now I was making decisions for them as well.

It always seemed that when the quiet times arrived, and with living in the manner we were, the mind moved through many subjects. Both laying there talking over some past or the events of the next day seemed to put a steady closer to the day.

We were up early and feeling fresh for the next leg – stopping at Moon Boon Creek for the day and night and just before the falls and Rock Candy Range. This area around the Daly seemed unsettled. As we passed through the black soil plains, we noticed the range ahead but, at times, couldn't stop if we wanted to. We just allowed ourselves to keep drifting down. On this day, we had the remainder of the roo meat hooked onto a line over the back of the punt, and around midday, I was taking some more photos of Phil while sitting at the rear of Phil standing on the front of the punt holding up a duck he had shot. I felt this almighty pull backwards at such a fast speed that nearly sent Phil into the river. At the same time, water came over the back end of the punt. I tried to let the line go but to no avail; I even found it hard to move. Then, without warning, it stopped. We both grabbed our guns and waited, as we knew this was a big crocodile and it was hungry. As we waited, I pulled in the 8mm nylon cord and, to our disbelief, found it cleanly cut so, without any lost time, I started the outboard motor and gave it all it had for some three to four kilometres down the river to the start of the Rock Candy Range, some 1,000 metres to Moon Boon

Creek, where I drove the punt straight onto the dry land. We had both found this episode quite disturbing and felt we should head up to high ground for the night. And that is what we did, leaving the punt well up before setting off. We walked for about two hundred metres up the side of the range and had a good view of the river below and the white water over three locations. Although this wasn't planned, it wasn't a bad idea as the view was

fantastic, and the way through could be plotted. So the rest of our day was spent prospecting around this area just south-west of our night camping spot. I placed an X as our location on this ridge and we remained there for the day and the sixth night, not finding anything but the views.

The next morning arrived without any drama, and after eating the duck that Phil had shot, we were back on the river, loaded and ready for the rapids. Once we settled down, nature took over and we lay flat on the bottom while feeling the boulders grinding at the hull. Again, wash came over; we passed under trees with branches slapping my face but hung on until the spinning started and we knew that the first one was over. We passed Fish River then through the gap of the Rock Candy Range, which was over 5 kilometres long.

There was no turning back now as the ride of our life was about to unfold. Again I put my thumb up to Phil for good luck and hung on tight for fifteen minutes or so, finding at times we were going backwards, then sideways, then another spin around and a loud bang of aluminium hitting the boulders and the grinding under the punt. Then all was over and quiet.

Without delay, we headed for the banks to look over the punt for any major damage, then decided to travel onto Austral Creek for the final night out as the river was much calmer. As we arrived at the creek, we noticed a punt jammed against some rocks and started to look around and yell out for anyone who might be there. But to no avail. So we hooked it up and started to fire some rounds off every five minutes but still no answer.

So we pulled up to make camp as planned. From here on was about three hours using the outboard motor the next morning. Though Austral Creek was small, it did have some very nice samples of Agate and Topaz and, with the events of the day, we decided this was the finish point, so we both went down to the river and caught two Barramundi and had our last night talking about what the future would bring and the times we'd had and also some spooky bits. But we were here now, and we could smell the end of the trail and a long rest on this, the seventh, night and without any event.

We were up washed and ready to leave at sunrise, and so ended this dangerous place.

I was going to look forward to doing it all over again but by land, during the dry period and, camp at one spot only. But for now, it was time to say goodbye.

About midday, we arrived at the Daly River Mission with a greeting from the local Police inquiring about our trip and asking if we had any crocodile hides. He could see there wasn't any. We informed him of the punt we had found jammed under a tree and left it with him for the owner. Then we contacted Dad to pick us up. He arrived around 3.30pm, then we loaded up and left for Darwin, Dad asking all about the trip and did we find anything worth the trouble of going. Even with all his questions, we both, for some reason, fell asleep and were woken at the main gates of the RAAF Base and home to my loving wife, Lita, and Nicole. It was a good thing that I'd found time to sleep as she was full of questions about our trip.

Our entire trip was too much for me to explain, apart from the highlights, but I did mention that I would love to do it again soon and tried to stay awake for the rest of the day – I had one more day's leave and I wasn't moving from the house.

After sleeping in a soft clean bed, I was woken by Lita with a cup of tea and soon started to tell her some of the ordeals we had endured and how hard life must have been for the people that chose to live in such wilderness miles from anything. But I did assure her it was great to be back, and I had been thinking that I should try and get some extra work outside of my Service hours. She never said anything as it wasn't in her nature to stop me from working and trying to get ahead as the Service pay was crap, and after hearing what the civilian workers were being paid, did make me a little hungry for the extra cash.

Though I had plenty on my mind while I was away with Phil, I also had this matter on my mind but never mentioned it. So the next day was once again upon us and I was given a lift from Bill, my next-door neighbour, and he began to fill me in with the past week's situation on the Base, and the trouble with the Federal Government and money borrowed from overseas which brought some tight moments for ourselves.

Upon arriving at my section, my Sergeant explained that all transport was being put into mothballs until further notice. This was the start of discontentment within the ranks and file and left me with no doubt that I was getting extra work.

I began my job by jacking up the vehicles that were sent down and removing the wheels for storage. Then I covered each vehicle with a light sheet. I was, for most of the time, scratching my balls and penis but never thought anything about why until I dropped my pants and saw what looked like a couple of large blood warts hanging from my penis. I got hold of our section medical box and, finding the surgical spirits, rubbed a small amount over the blood warts. Didn't that make me start dancing around with my pants down to my knees!

I headed for the wash bay and hosed myself down but knew I needed medical help so, without delay, I headed straight to the Base Medical Section. I was sent straight in to see the doctor who knew me from Pearce Base. When asked what my trouble was, I dropped my pants and showed him the blood warts. He immediately said I had kangaroo ticks and they were infected; he sent me straight into Darwin Hospital for emergency surgery.

Within the hour, the operation was finished, and I was in the recovery ward. I opened my eyes and felt a heavy weight holding me down. I started to remove it when one of the nursing staff came over to see if I was okay. When she asked what the problem was, my thoughts came back as to why I was there. So I looked at her and said I was doing a stock check, which brought us all to laughter. I was then sent off to a ward and about an hour later Lita was at my side with Mum and Nicole

I explained my reason for being there and Mum mentioned that Dad had removed three ticks from the back of Phil's neck as he had blood running over his sheets. I was asked how I ended up with them on my penis, which must have been when I was cutting the hindquarters from a roo while in the nuddy. Phil had used the hide as a pillow, and this was the only thing I could put it down to. I remained in Darwin Hospital for two days then was sent to Base Medical wards for further recovery as Dr Scott explained that I was very lucky to have got this seen to, as the type of tick I had would have sent my penis gangrene. I would be staying in the Base ward for two weeks with treatment twice daily, so I thanked him for that and was grateful for that gruesome reminder never to skin a roo again.

My stay in the Base hospital was very boring with no one to talk to but the staff in the morning and the afternoon and at mealtimes. There wasn't any TV and the radio didn't provide any points of interest. I wasn't allowed out of bed, apart from the basic toilet needs; I wasn't allowed any books that may have content to cause an erection or excitement but I was offered crosswords and newspapers and books on my interest, which was Geology. Lita and Nicole came once a day in the afternoon and for only a short time, by order of Dr Scott, and it was during these visits that she brought sweets and biscuits. I couldn't hold Nicole or have anything on the bed as I had a cage over my lower body which helped air to flow around the stitches, of which I had five or six, but it was always something I looked forward to.

On my second week, I was able to move around the ward for short periods. Looking along the passageway, I noticed a full-sized skeleton standing on a support frame, so I placed it in the bed opposite me, crossed its legs while in a sitting position, gave it a newspaper to read and stuck a thermometer in its mouth. Then I got back to bed and waited for the doctor to arrive as he had done every morning over the past week. When he did arrive, he asked how I was.

"A lot better than he is, sir," I said.

He walked over and checked the skeleton's wrist for a pulse then read the thermometer. Looking over at me, he said, 'He has lost a lot of weight." Apart from that, he requested I call the staff if he tried to get out of bed. Then he came over and started to talk about a problem with some of the service members he was treating with a type of tablet that was making them lose their sex drive. He wanted me to start taking them during the week as a trial, as I wasn't allowed to have sex. And though he couldn't understand the reason for the loss of sex drive, I agreed to help him with his trials and received the first tablet that morning. As for Mr Bones, I was to keep an eye on him.

That afternoon Lita arrived, with a laugh as she noticed my roommate. She asked who my mate was and how long he had been in here and what his problem was. I explained something had frightened him out of his skin and he was here for the rest. Then I told her about the tablets which caused the loss of sex drive and that I could be home by the end of the week.

And so, by the end of the week, I was allowed to go home and given another two weeks' sick leave, which didn't impress my section commander. As for me, I was getting a little restless on my first day, though Mum, Dad, Peter and Wendy came round for a visit and, just after they left, Phil came over followed by Bill next door. So it appeared I was well thought about or more so the laughter of it all. Then we were by ourselves and I could once again hold Nicole and play with her on the floor, which was much cooler than the lounge. During my time with her, I began thinking about my next trip away.

When Phil came over, I mentioned doing an overnight trip down to Edith River Falls and his eyes just lit up with delight. This was one of his special places and, once I had healed up, we would be gone.

About a week later, with the issue of my lost foreskin behind me, I looked forward to spending an overnight trip with Phil travelling around the eastern side of the Stuart Highway, alongside the Fergusson River then around to Edith Falls, then back to the Stuart Highway. But Lita asked about taking them both out also, and she was right, so I made arrangements with Mum and Dad to drive down to the Daly River Mission – but first, Phil and I were going on this trip as he was going to Groote Eylandt in the Gulf of Carpentaria on a contract cooking for the mining staff as this was Phil's profession. So this was going to be the last chance for quite some time, and I was hoping she would understand – I trusted Phil's ability out there and he knew the area very well.

That seemed to satisfy her, but I knew I couldn't let them down no matter what might happen – I was taking them to the Daly River Mission and Dad was going to show us the hot springs before heading on to Adelaide River.

So with my sick leave and the weekend in sight, Phil and I left on Saturday morning. He loaded up his VW the night before with plenty of fruit, water and loaded guns on board, along with two jerry cans of fuel. Then we started talking about what lay ahead. I was more interested in the country with its unfound wealth and my limited ability in Geology. But what I felt I knew had driven me onto another tangent on the same subject, and while much of the information I received at most was confusing to read, the man who lived in the area had the knowledge and understanding – it had started from the very basic person and was handed down. From this, I knew we could shortcut the pre-planning and just go have a look and ask those who lived there.

Before long, we turned off the Stuart Highway and headed up the south side of the Fergusson River. Around 2pm, we stopped at an old Aboriginal site. He explained how he'd found it then showed me some stone spearheads, being very careful not to disturb too much of the area when he picked up various objects. He handed them to me and I couldn't believe what I was holding and the time it must have taken these Aboriginals to chip away at the rocks. Phil placed them back as he'd found them, then we walked up a small rise and, as we looked over this site, it became quite clear that it had been used for many, many, many, years by the number of tracks leading in all directions. These tracks were now covered with undergrowth which was slowly taking over. But it was still very clear as everything for the basic survival was around – water, fish, roos, emus and of course the river and its banks which drew all kinds of wildlife to it.

We walked back to his VW and left the site undisturbed, and I have no idea of its location as I did not note it down. And that was the way Phil wanted it to remain. We spent the rest of the day heading for the Edith Falls and, close to late afternoon, we arrived. What a sight for sore eyes! While Phil sorted out the camp, I went off up the mountain doing my emu-bob, picking up and putting down all matter of stones, starting at the base and walking towards to top of the falls and a short walk over the top and then returned, arriving back at camp just before sunset. I had plenty of samples to look over on the return trip in the morning. As the night took over this spot, it brought along a large amount of wildlife on foot and flying. This seemed like a major spot as the night calls never stopped. When one mob did stop, another started, and with a bright full moon, it wasn't difficult to understand why it attracted such an abundance of wildlife.

We were both up nice and early, a little tired but soon ready to head back to Darwin and the real world. During the trip, I began to look over and break the stones I had to throw away the rubbish. I kept the ones of interest for a later time to look and ID them. I soon found myself drifting off to sleep and Phil tapping me to stay awake as he also felt tired. So I began to sing my guts out while he had a country and western tape playing and this was on for the next two hours of the trip home. On arriving, he left to say Hi to Dad as he was heading off to pack up for the Monday flight to Groote Eylandt. And that was the last time we went out bush together. I was always sent a message from him via Dad and Mum, but right now it was family time and the need to stay home with my family and friends was a high priority. It was great to just sit back with Bill and Fay next door with the BBQ going. We spent the last few hours joking about and talking about the trips and places we had been to as Bill and I had something in common – and that was we had both been to Vietnam. Neither of us could get over all of it. And with the public still calling us baby-eaters to make us feel like low life didn't help.

From this and the fact that he was also looking for extra work, I knew we could do it together. Although we had different skills, we both had worked in the building industry so we began to look around the Darwin area. This helped to keep our minds on matters other than Vietnam. The fact that TV had not yet reached Darwin was also a great benefit as the news was full of crap reporting and something we never missed.

Bill and I, although both in the transport section, never had contact during the day as my section was at the other end of the Base, but come stand-down he would give me a lift or I would give him one back home. Then we would take the ladies out while we went fishing until the sandflies started.

So this was our well-settled life and I looked forward to it. But this was going to change as Bill mentioned that a job at the Eleven-mile peg had called for tenders. He asked if I knew how to handle it. I'd had a small amount of experience when with the Department of Works so come lunchtime the next day we both headed off to the Works Department and requested a tender form. That afternoon at stand down, we left for the Eleven-mile peg, and I couldn't believe what I was reading: this was the same work I was doing at Pearce before I joined up with the RAAF. I read it over again and again, then when we arrived at the location, I explained to Bill how it worked and what was the wire-mat for. But the contract was for the 1.5m high fence with standard gate, all in timber and open pickets, but the one single thing was not to break any wire underground. I explained that it was like a spider web over 50 metres in diameter and should we cut one, its whole purpose was lost and they would know if that was the case. So we headed back to Darwin, stopped at the hardware store and got a price per metre of the various sized material required, then headed back home for the night's BBQ. While the girls were chattering away, Bill and I sat down and I explained it all in more detail. He understood reasonably quickly, then we discussed the tender, the cost of materials first, e.g. working out the materials in metres, divided into lengths suitable for two or three spans then multiplying by the cost for timber etc., etc., etc., for the remainder of the materials. Then came our labour, and we had to be very fair with each other on this matter; then overheads and insurance. By the end of the night, we had most of the work completed apart from not having any tools and equipment nor the vehicles to transport it all down to the Eleven-mile peg.

We left each other with the thoughts on how to put it all together and make it work, and it wasn't until I arrived at my section that we could get it signed out and no money involved. I contacted Bill and passed on my thoughts and he agreed that was the answer. But now for the transport! I was thinking of Dad but only thinking, and as the day passed, it hit me like a ton of bricks: transport was being sent south to Tindal RAAF Base as it was also being placed under mothballs. They were leaving without any load. It could be a long shot and the driver needed to be hungry enough to drop it off. It was a gamble, and I had never gambled at anything

Upon arriving home that afternoon, I contacted Bill and put it to him. He mentioned a name that I knew and so began the ploy as our plot came together. I learnt that the third person was also interested in working, and this Bill explained that evening around the BBQ. So we then decided to have a small chat with the third person, Leo, and the next day we headed off to the dry mess and put our cards on the table. My question was why he wanted the work and why was he so keen to be a part of this project. His answer was he needed the money and wanted to get involved with this type of work; he was already engaged in a cleaning job that was crap work and crap money, and he felt this could give him the break he needed. So that was all we wanted to hear.

We set off back to our section for the rest of the day then all headed for Bill's place to go over all the matters of materials and labour, along with transport and hand tools. It was time to submit our Tender, but first I was going to ask about payment: how do the draws get worked out? Was money held back, and when would the last payment be made? These were the final matters I was concerned about and needed the answers to. I explained that I would go to see the department the following day at lunch break. And that left only one more issue ... and that was to sit back and have a tinnie with them all and we would talk the following evening.

At lunch break the next day I put the questions forward and was interrupted with the answer that the material was being supplied by the department and only labour was involved. Payment was upon completion of the project. This was good news to me as we were also covered by insurance. I received a second tender form and headed back to Base with the good news and the new forms, which could be signed that day for consideration by Monday.

That evening, I told Bill and Leo that I was putting in the tender at $1,200,00 for the labour and overheads. This they felt was far too much, but I stuck with my gut that it was the right figure. The only thing we could lose was the job, and from that it was agreed. We signed the tender and sealed it up, and Bill handed it in the next morning.

From here on, it was waiting time. I was becoming very busy at the section with more vehicles being mothballed which was putting the drivers and the maintenance section out of work. At times, we would pull something apart just to put it back together again, and it wasn't much different right across the Base. There was also a lot of discontentment now and some members did not sign up for further service. To top it all off, we still had guard duties and they seemed to come around quite quickly as the roster wasn't done very fair.

I well remember that serviceman who'd sold me his Mini Moke, then unbeknown to me, had done a bunk [AWL], his ticket was paid by me according to the Base SP, and I was given a right talking to. Upon him being returned to Darwin, I was placed on duty while he was in the cells. He noticed me straight away. I asked him what his caper was, and he said he wanted out of the RAAF and this was his ticket. But for now, we had to keep an eye on him. The usual thing was for prisoners to get the brass cleaned up and, during the early evening, when he finished he wanted to keep working so the WO in charge of guard duties – Abercrombie from Pearce Base – and I were to ensure we'd keep an eye on him. After all, what could he do locked in his cell? Given he was keen to work, I brought out the white plastic paint for him to paint the webbing and also the ceiling of his cell, then I went for a meal in the guardhouse. As the night grew cool, I decided to check on how the prisoner was going and stood there, mouth flopped open and dribbling while trying not to laugh. The silly fucker was standing with paint all over him, and the wall behind him. In fact, he had painted the whole cell, from the light globe to the floor, bedding and bed, and the cell bars. He stood in the corner saying, 'Can't see me, can't see me.' This brought all the night shift in to the lockup for the funniest thing I have ever seen anyone do to themselves. It took some time to stop laughing over this matter but each time anyone went in to help get it sorted, you just laughed till it hurt, and had to leave without doing a thing as he was still standing there saying to anyone that entered, "Can't see me, can't see me, can't see me.'

By this time, the WO arrived and was taken into the lockup. He too came out laughing his guts up, and I wasn't able to talk to him without laughing. For that matter, no one could do anything for about an hour. Eventually, a hose was used to clean up the mess and the prisoner was sent over to the Army Barracks. I, however, was dragged over the coals for not keeping an eye on him and was given a second night duty. I ended up sleeping in the refreshed cell after my shift as I was rostered very late through the night. To cap it off, Lita wasn't too pleased as we had plans made for that night.

About two weeks later, Bill received a letter from the Works Department that we'd won the contract and work would commence once we signed the paperwork. So arrangements were made for the three of us to go in during lunch break and commit ourselves to a nice little number. The name for the banking account was D B L Fencing Contractors, and all we were waiting for was the material to arrive on-site by the following week. In the meantime, I started to get the mini moke ready for work and, with all the trades on the Base looking for extra cash jobs, it wasn't long before it had a bull bar and a trailer hitch with toolboxes on each side of the wheels and a 500mm X 60mm pipe attached to the front for a 50mm lighting pole. The yellow paint remained the same, and I was now looking for a trailer, but the cost was outside my budget and I just couldn't afford one.

Each evening after work, Bill and I would be out the back cooking meat for the girls while I was looking after Nicole and giving her some quality time. She really enjoyed it as I quite often got down to her level and chased her around like a dog. This to me was less of a mess than owning one them as I just didn't have time for a shit machine while in the RAAF. Then Bill would join in the fun and by the time the meat was cooked and we were seated, she was ready for bed which Lita would do. Then we'd spend the next hour or so sitting around talking of the places we would like to see while in The Top End. Deep down, though, I knew I wasn't going to have much time once I started work.

August 1971

At the beginning of this month, we decided to pass on our car and buy a new one – a Toyoto Crown for $3,500.00 – as the other one was costing too much to maintain. This was our best way out for Lita and Nicole, as I would often get worried about her not having the chance to go to town. Now Dad would be able to teach her to drive.

Each evening, he was around and they would go out to the back of the Base for an hour and then drive back home. I was so happy for her when she got her driving licence; now it was up to her to gain more of the independence I wanted for her, like the other girls around the Base that would visit her. It was great times. She could slip off to the pool or Mum and Dad's and not depend upon me after work now I was starting a second that I couldn't see myself not keeping on with. So now that all was in order and the materials were on-site, the next day the three of us prepared for the morrow's action.

Driving out in my Moke the next day, the three of us started digging out post holes and kept this up till sunset and the sandflies started attacking us. Then we departed the site tired, dusty and dry. After dropping Leo off, Bill and I got home to a long cold beer and, of course, the BBQ was well on the way as we talked over any problems that could be improved upon. Bill mentioned lighting and fly spray. Apart from that, we finished our meal then bid them good night and went to bed and some time with Lita. But it wasn't long before I was up again and back at work, feeling great and looking forward to the project that night with Leo and Bill. Come stand down, we were soon back at the site and digging holes. It was a good thing that the ground wasn't too hard though, at times, a crowbar was needed. Once the sandflies attacked, we had to leave and I mentioned to Leo about getting some flyspray from stores but explained that it was not a requirement for transport. That evening, Dad was at home when I arrived to see how Lita was getting with her driving when I mentioned to him about sandflies. He told me about cloudy ammonia, which we got hold of for the next day, along with a small generator and light. And didn't that make a big difference to the work output – except for one thing: the ladies complained about the time we arrived home as we'd stayed till after sundown.

Having the evening meal late wasn't on by the wives so we went back to normal times, except for the weekends, which was normal working hours. This was okay up to a point, as I felt it was dragging out. When Bill mentioned it as well, I again looked at what was going to be suitable for all of us and, upon a short discussion, it was decided to include a fourth person. This I put to Dad and he accepted. And so a team was formed, one for digging, one for standing posts, and Dad and I bolting the rails to the post. As the digging was finished, the pickets were nailed on. So this was now coming to a close on Day Nine, and we were all looking forward to a little time with our families.

Bill and I set about getting our account in order to submit for payment and, upon working out each of our hours, rewarded us with $357.33 each for four days in total, and Dad for his two days $128.00. Without any extra work to add to the account, it was submitted the following day. One week later, the cheque was in the bank, and we began looking forward to our next project. But this time, we were looking for something a little more involved, and around Darwin rather than travelling the distance as the time to and from amounted to some four hours on the road in travelling. This time could be far better spent on a project around the Darwin area itself.

It was great spending some time with Lita and Nicole over that week and getting my yard in order as I was to learn how quickly grass grew in the tropics. I had to keep the place in a total state of inspection at all times.

At this time, Bill and I restructured our ideas to introduce the sub-contractors method of employment, such as a single item of work being carried out for a set fee. We both felt this would not only give us a lot more time at home, which our wives approved of, and gave Bill and me a lot more confidence, but it didn't help with our drinking habits. At times I felt I was neglecting Lita and Nicole while drinking with my mates, even though she was there with me. I was always pissed by the end of the day, and for that she would confront me to ease up. I knew she was well within her rights to show a little anger and would lay off for a while. Apart from that, Bill and I would have our little chat over the fence each evening, of course, while having a tinnie or two.

Christmas 1971

Although I was still in the Airforce, my mind and heart were centred on our contracts. Mostly, it would come to mind when I was on night duties; it wasn't the duties that were the problem but I did feel that Lita was becoming restless with me as the only real time I didn't drink was while I was on duty. Now that Christmas was coming fast, it didn't help and probably deep down she was getting homesick for her family. These thoughts haunted me during my night duties, and I felt I wasn't putting her first, even though I would arrive home from work each afternoon quite happy – of course, I hadn't been drinking, and I held these moments as very special as my time with Nicole would always remain with me, mainly due to me not remembering anything about how my father or mother held me. There was just nothing, nothing but a dark hole, not an ounce of light to give me some guidance. So I responded to Nicole in the best way I felt a father should, and also my wife. I suppose somehow I did lean on Lita's ways as a safe platform to play upon, and it seemed we both gained strength from each other. Only when Nicole was bedded down would I open a tinnie and follow the norm by sitting back relaxing.

Two weeks before Christmas, I was asked to be Father Christmas, the reason being I was the only one on the Base trained and experienced to hang out of a chopper at 500 feet above the ground. I felt that I should involve Lita with this as it meant once again I wasn't going to be with her and Nicole for the arrival of Santa. On bringing it to her attention, she had no problem with it because Nicole wouldn't remember it as she was two years old, but we would have the photos to show her.

So come the big day, in the middle of a typical tropical wet season, I dressed up as Santa and set off to fly firstly across to the aboriginal mission to drop hundreds of lollies across the playground – it is something that I shall never forget, seeing them dropping out of the trees like monkeys and racing across to the playground to grab handfuls of lollies. We left as quickly as we'd arrived as they had never expected this event. Then we flew across to Darwin town, doing a lolly drop before my arrival at the Base. It seemed that all of Darwin was waving at me as we flew at low level across the crowd below, dropping the remainder of the lollies then coming to land with a greeting as one would do. I looked out for Lita and Nicole, only to frighten the shit out of her when I tried to give her a hug. So it was a great day well remembered.

Febuary 1972

For some reason, Bill was becoming disgruntled with me. I felt that his wife had maybe got to him about the time we were on-site rather than being with her, even though she could have been with Lita next door. But we decided to part and, upon settling our accounts, he pulled out of the contracts, leaving it all to me, which brought some hard times trying to keep up with it all.

I therefore decided to make one of our workers the foreman. As he lived next to Bill, which might cause him some stress, I put the question to Bill. He had no problem dealing with it as he had now been posted to Queensland and was leaving in three months. So with this good news, I confronted Steven and put the offer to him, and his wife, for him to act as my foreman on-site with a set pay rate. They were very happy with it all, and we decided to get together the following evening to go over the work at hand and the oncoming contracts.

That evening I explained to Lita that this was our last year in Darwin. It would be to our advantage if I remained working as we were making good money and could she put up with me carrying on with the projects. I also mentioned that Steven and his wife Margaret were coming over the following night. Lita already knew Margaret as a neighbour and seemed to get along fine as she never mentioned otherwise to me.

So the following evening, I explained to Steven and Margaret all about using sub-contractors, and his role was to make sure all the materials were on-site and placed in the work location required each day after work as that is when the fun starts. I would be getting the following day's material sorted out and also be on-site to help the workers out, as would be expected of him as well.

Steven and I got along really well and so did the girls. Overall, things were looking up – Steven and I were drinking less while on the job but had a couple of tinnies when we finished, which we always kept to 2100hrs, which was good enough for all of us.

On one occasion, the girls decided to give us a surprise by arriving on-site with a table and chairs, a complete dinner set and roast chicken with all the vegies, followed by a bottle of wine. This confirmed they were both very happy with our situation.

I did notice some small changes in Lita while she was with Margaret, or perhaps they had found something in common and the grounds to build a good friendship. I also noticed that Margaret could see the difference in Steven as it appeared they were sometimes nagging about some crap. As for me, Lita never said anything, apart from my having a couple of tinnies with my mates. I could understand this, so I asked them why the fancy dinner on-site. The answer was they both had never seen us for a Sunday meal so felt they should bring it down to us, which brought laughter to the rest of the men on site. In turn, their wives did the same thing the following weekend, setting a good relationship with all our workers. And of that, I was very pleased.

Though Steven and I still arrived home after having a couple of beers, it didn't upset the women like it used to as we were working hard from 7.30am till 2100hrs, so a couple of beers after working was okay.

By now, I had very little interest in my service life. I didn't really apply myself to my daily duties, just performed the basic requirements within my section and tried to avoid any extra duties. I began to spread myself really thin between the two and kept looking for more work. Then this chance came to me from a company called North Cement, a large company with its base in America. I contacted them, and a meeting was arranged for the following night. I explained to Hutch, the company Manager and Contracts Manager, that I was in the Service and so were all my employees. All the work carried out was during stand down hours and weekends. He did ask me about cost and material supplies and I informed him that I was labour only and it was up to them to supply all the materials. Upon that, we set a fee for man-hours and I was informed the material would be placed on-site at Berramar, just south of Darwin. Hutch then mentioned they had just purchased the property in question with a large shed on it. He needed to get the contents removed so we made arrangements to have a look over the site and at the contents in the shed as he had not been inside to see what was there to be removed.

As arranged, I was at the Berramar site and took a good long look over the area where the proposed six-foot fence was to be erected while waiting for Hutch to arrive. When he arrived with his boss, the shed was opened and, to his surprise, it was half-filled with Sorghum seeds [about the size of poppy seeds]. At first, he couldn't believe the amount of it stored there. And how do you shovel it up, as it was like dried beach sand? I noticed his concern and put my views forward as I thought I had a way to do the job and would let him know the following day. He accepted that and, upon looking over the site, I mentioned that all the post holes would be dug out the following night as I understood the materials would be arriving the day after.

Then we left for the office of North Cement and, after some small talk, I left for the site where Steven was working and brought him up to date with this new client, then headed for home to be with Lita and Nicole, bringing her up to date with our new project.

The next day I arrived at my section and asked Leo and Bill if they wanted some work driving a tipper from 1800hrs till 2100hrs, and they agreed. I then contacted Hutch and advised we could remove the sorghum that evening. He made arrangements at the receiving end, a storage shed some two miles away in which we could tip and run at the same time. So that evening, I got hold of the front-end loader and headed off via the back gate to Berramar and started loading up the two tippers. It was easy, very light work and we kept this up until it was 99% complete, as the remainder was scattered across the concrete floor, which we left. It was now after 2100hrs, and we all returned to Base via the back gate and then on home resting by 2200hrs with a job well done.

The following day I was informed that all the materials were now on-site and the hole boring was completed by our private contractor, which doubled our workload as he had spent all day on the job. This was great for us as it gave the impression we belonged to a large firm, and as this just wasn't the case. Then the Boring contractor informed me that the supervisor for Orlet Homes wanted me to contact him regarding fencing around a new housing development. Which I did, and like-wise gave him a price per metre run. I returned to the Barramar project while still daylight, arriving there as Steven was setting up the lighting and the generator. I hooked up the hired cement mixer to the back of Dad's trailer, which was full of sand and blue metal [stone] at which time our two workers arrived and the fun started once again. Steven drove the Moke over the holes and one of the labourers placed the 2.400mm steel post into it while the other labourer and I mixed the concrete and placed it into each hole under the light attached to the front of the trailer. After an hour, we all took turns driving as it was hard going for most of the time. Upon all this, we would have a tinnie. It took two nights to complete the posts and, on the third night, we ran the wire and strained all the strands to the braced corner posts, getting ready for the chainwire the following evening.

The next day I was informed that Maureen and John were coming up to visit Mum and Dad and I was asked if I had any work for John to do. When they arrived, I put him to work fixing the chainwire to the strained wire and posts. He was grateful for this rice bowl and was a fantastic worker. And so, before they left, Darwin the four of us went out for a meal, and our first taste of a Bombay Alaska – it just seemed like yesterday when they'd arrived and now they were off back to Perth, and me back to the same thing night after night.

I learnt from Lita that friends of her Dad and Mum were coming to Darwin for a two week holiday and they had asked if there was anything we needed. I asked Lita to see if they could bring our TV up that was in storage. From the next letter, we expected them to arrive by boat by the end of the month and I made plans to have two weeks leave and spend every minute with Lita and the Wrights [the egg man from Armadale 1960]. When they arrived with our TV, Len couldn't quite understand why I so much wanted the TV as Darwin didn't have a service for its use. But I explained it was to become a reality within the year. Then I explained that I had taken two weeks off so we could head down the track and camp over some of the greatest spots in the North, which we did and gratefully all enjoyed it to the full.

Before long, we were saying our goodbyes and I noticed it was getting harder each time Lita saw her friends depart.

During that year, TV was introduced, but on the big night the power suppliers decided to go on strike. Typical, so with all this in the air, the TV channel went ahead using their backup generators. I carried our TV downstairs and plugged it in and soon our neighbours brought their deck chairs over with a few tinnies and spent the rest of the night watching the opening and the events of the new Channel, which brought Darwin into the 21st century.

Our holidays with the Wrights was great; it allowed Lita and I to spend some quality time out camping. Our first night was at Howard Springs, some 30 miles south of Darwin, and our first chance for Lita to sit back and talk about her family, who I knew she was missing a lot. Questions flew around about Armadale and the changes it was going through, which Len was not too happy about. But, in the long run, it had to grow up like most of the outer districts. Perth was small and well spread out, and Len felt that Armadale was missing the growth boom by providing State Housing Development, which is what he didn't want.

Lita did miss home though at times she was very happy with Margaret and Bill's wife, Fay, for company, and I could see her coming out of her shell and giving her a chance to notice the other service members' wives how they handled their situation rather than think she was all alone.

August 1972

By now I was well known throughout the Base as an employer of labourers and not a day went by that I didn't have someone asking me for work. It seemed like one big project, with Steven and me running around from job to job. We had no contact until the end of the night when we would go over things while having a few beers, before the next arvo when it all started once again.

October 1972

I was notified by North-Cement Manager Hutch that a position for a trouble-shooter for the company's big investments throughout the Northern Territory, and my wages would be $30,000.00 a year and, I would be on call at all hours. This was a big pill for me to swallow and I really needed time to give it some good thought. The one thing I knew was they were impressed with the way I got it all sorted and completed within the contract time and cost. Over the following month, I couldn't get it out of my mind and how to put it to Lita, as the ground was quite thin as it was without putting any extra crap on the heap. But it had to be mentioned and, though I was very busy over that month, I felt that it was time for me to let Lita know, as an idea came to mind for me to apply for an extra term in Darwin. It was with this that I confronted Lita.

But Lita said we had done out time in Darwin and it was time to think of the whole family unit. I knew she was right and didn't take the job, stating to Hutch that staying in Darwin would affect my marriage as my wife wasn't happy with our current situation. That is how we left it and over the next three months I slowly did less and less work. By the time I received my posting to Melbourne, I wasn't happy about that either, so I began to hand all the work over to Steven without any money changing hands. For my last thanks to all my workers, I invited all those who had earned $200.00 and up, to a send-off BBQ at our married quarters just before leaving for Perth.

So for the next ten weeks, we began to get ourselves sorted for my posting to Tottenham Stores Depot, Melbourne. It was also at this time that Lita mentioned that Nicole seemed to have a turn in one of her eyes. We took her to the Base medical section and had Dr Scott take a look to give us some direction should that be the case. I had never really noticed it until Lita mentioned it and it appeared when she was tired. Dr Scott mentioned that it could be a lazy eye or an overpowering muscle in the other, but nothing major at this stage of her life.

November 1972

I was now ordered to report to Tottenham, Victoria, by the 23 January 1973 and began to get the final bits sorted out and our car ready for the long haul south. Just as we were nearly ready, Lita informed me that she was about six weeks pregnant and felt really great for it. During this time, we made arrangements for our final bash – the biggest BBQ with around 100 people coming and going over three nights and two full days. I had the Base cooks make the total meal – roast pig and side dressings, all at a very nice rate.

On that Friday afternoon, the large bell sounded and the fun began with some 25 to 30 people attending that night. Some just lay out on the lawn until sunrise. Then the breakfast mob arrived, the night-shifters, Saturday morning getting me out of bed and having beer with my cornflakes followed by several large cups of coffee. Then it was on again with the dinner mob, and some from the previous night turned up still hungover.

Then the music started, with our neighbours joining in with friends from all around Darwin. To think all this was before 11am. Lita got Nicole sorted out and was soon joining us and looking really great for it. When the dinner arrived, the BBQ was also up and running. I mentioned to Steven that I was heading up for a nap and it was up to him to keep it under control and I quietly slipped off to sleep at around 1300hrs. I was up around 1700hrs and once again ready to party, giving Steven time to get his head down while Lita, Margaret and Fay helped with cleaning up as the first trailer was full of empty tinnies. I was moving around half pissed but enjoying it after two years of solid work and these guys here had made it work for me. I knew I should have made the decision to stay put as the hard work was done and the rewards were just coming in, but it was too late now and I accepted my actions for my small family.

Everything was going fine with everyone returning for the second nights' feast and the second keg, along with another twelve boxes of Emu lager, the gentlemen's drink in the North – the commoners would bring Vic lager, but we still let them join us. So the second night was well on the way and about 2200hrs the service police arrived to make sure all was well and no one was out of control. We all stood tightly locked together, making sure we remained standing, but slowly rocking to and fro to the James Last music. They left, and we never could figure out how many of them turned up as we think they looked all the same right down to their stripes. I said four; some said six, but we agreed during another tinnie as we still stood hanging onto each other. By then, Steven had returned and was the only one standing by himself. We asked what his secret was and could he hurry up and help us stand up. Around 1am, the mob started to fall over and within the hour we all fell flat on our back, sleeping. I don't remember the sun rising that day but bodies lying all over the place. I learnt we had twenty in the huddle but we never found out who was the first to drop. Yeah, that was some night.

I remember getting into the bath and hearing my name called for roll call, and once again, it was on. With all the energy I could muster, I shaved, dragged on some clean clothes and helped the girls out for the final day/night.

By this time, we were feeling the worst for wear, then around midday, the next mob started arriving and the BBQ was ready with Steven and me standing waiting to cook, both of us on coffee for the rest of the day. As the crowd grew to around 30, we all began to get into the swing with some rock and roll, followed by James Last. Then around sunset, we all finished the food and the last of the grog and wine. Whiskey was then brought out for the final hours and once again we were holding each other up. This time we managed twenty-five hanging onto each other and grabbing hold of anyone that might fall over. This was truly the last man standing, but with a couple of women in the huddle, and some dirty fucker farting just added to the greatest night I'd had for some time, one that brings a great deal of pleasure and laughter for me.

It was nearly 2230hrs when we once again started to fall into a big heap and just lay there until sunrise. What a fucken party and a fantastic send off!

So that morning, I went to work, leaving the mess for the women to look after. At midday, I went home for lunch to be told that my large whiskey bottle was missing. I had a feeling who had taken it, and at stand down, Steven, a sober Bill, and I headed off to the caravan park.

I arrived at this caravan site in the middle of Darwin and, upon finding his unit, just kicked the door in to find him asleep in his underpants and my JW next to his bunk. I grabbed the bottle and felt like doing something as a reminder that I called, but I had never hit a drunk, and in his case, he was well out of it to wake up. So looking around, I found some eggs and flour and tipped the lot over him while he lay there. Of course, this drew the others to join in, so not only was he covered in broken eggs and flour, they tipped his cooking oil, Weetbix, and a jar of honey over him. Then we all left, leaving the door open for the night beasties (insects).

We arrived back at the barbecue and continued partying, and, once again, the sun rose on bodies lying all over the place. Like the previous day, I headed for a kip, and again around 3pm, I was at it in full swing while Lita and Nicole went over to Mum and Dad's for the day. As this was going to be the last day, I just wanted to see the end of it.

Again the guests arrived, and once more, it was on for the night. I stayed sober, up to a point, feeling rooted and tired, but I was not going to surrender, so we carried on.

During the night, Lita and I were called up for a special thanks from all the friends and workers we'd met while in Darwin. I must say that was the first time I felt truly great inside as I stood and thanked them all for their words. Deep down, I knew I would never see any of them again, but at least they would remember me and their stay in Darwin.

I was now getting rid of all the equipment Stephen didn't require and decided to sell him the Moke, but he asked me to get rid of all the gelignite that was rolling around the floor, *and* the caps in the glove tray. I explained they were safe as long as he kept the caps away from the gelignite. But he insisted I get rid of it anyway, so we headed into the bush to explode the bloody lot. Once I found a safe place, I tied the twenty sticks to this tree and placed all the caps on top and, with a five-minute fuse, lit it and headed for cover. The loud bang was heard in Darwin some two miles away, and this brought my Darwin adventures to a close.

Although I had spent only two years in Darwin, the place always stuck in my mind as the last frontier of Australia, its many multi-culture races giving it an air of being laid back, and yet there didn't seem to be any racial discrimination as we all worked alongside each other. It was nothing for a white man to live among the Aboriginals and be very much settled to their way of life. Our friend Phil Coyne had even fathered a child with a native girl from the Santa Teresa Mission, forty-three miles southeast of Alice Springs.

During the times Phil and I were together, he would often tell me stories about these missions and what happened to the native girls once they reached sixteen years old when they became a cost factor and a burden to their system. So, after their education up to high school was completed, they were shown the gate and the road to the nearest town. It's these young girls (and boys) that have now become the fringe dwelling Aboriginals in Darwin.

It's a sad fact that once they arrived in Darwin, they didn't have anyone to turn to for help. But the biggest problem they were confronted with was acceptance by their own race – the Aboriginal has separate tribes and no two tribes really get along. Therefore a young girl is taken from her parents by the mission for the welfare of the child, (or in my opinion to support their bullshit and impose their ideas on them for the grace of God), that child is just not welcome back into the tribal camp and, in fact, is very much chased away.

This had been going on since the mission arrived in the Northern Territory, so it's no wonder they become social outcasts. And the Aboriginal drinking rights brought them a great deal more problems.

Phil and I talked a lot about this problem, and although he never knew my background, I could relate to the Aboriginal situation first-hand. In Phil's case, it was a bitter subject, one that didn't have a solution at that time. Now, twenty years later, it would appear that much has been done for the Aboriginal and their way of life that most tribes are now setting about finding their own children. As I sit here writing, the thought of the situation is exactly the same as the orphans brought out from England by the Catholics, and that records were not kept of parents – or if they were, they were now not available or just plain lost in the system. Apart from that, I have heard that most have been reunited with their tribal families.

Phil's native girlfriend, Paula, was on all accounts a confused person, very well-spoken and educated with beautiful writing. Her manners were well above most white girls her age. Phil tried to show her his full support by providing accommodation and a home life for her, but these he found quite difficult to do owing to the fact that it was not socially accepted by her native friends. He even had me build this pig-sty set well into the Darwin jungle into a home for her, and it looked like it started to work as one day she arrived to do the internal painting. But it wasn't long before she was off on walkabout with her friends.

On some occasions, Phil would take me out fishing, Aboriginal style, and of course, he would have a native with him. On one trip, he was going to show me how to catch 'muddies' – mud crabs – found in the mango swamps just outside Darwin. Once we arrived this Aboriginal with spear in hand started to prod the ground around him, then Phil started doing the same. After several minutes, and with a lot of excitement from the Aboriginal, the sound of the spear hitting this object was like a hammer striking wood. Then he bent over and drove his hands into the mud up to his elbows and pulled this bloody big mud-crab out by the back, with its snappers facing away from him.

Phil looked at me and said, "Well, Dave, that's the art of knowing how to catch them."

Then it was Phil's turn. The sound was right but when he drove his hands into the mud and pulled the crab out, its snappers were facing him, which brought quite a lot of excitement to Phil's face and he sent the bloody thing air-borne in my direction. When it landed near me, it stood high on its back legs and started to snap at me and all the while I was trying to get my legs unstuck from the mud. I was down to my buttocks and found it quite difficult to move slowly, let alone fast.

After that, it was my turn, but all I could find was empty stubbies, and no matter how much I tried, I failed, but it was a real eye-opener in the way the Aboriginal has lived and is still living in his natural environment.

As for Phil, I believe he is now chief cook on Groote Eylandt in the Gulf of Carpentaria but he still keeps in touch with Mum and Dad and, of course, they always pass on my regards to him.

December 1972

We were now getting ready to leave Darwin, and I intended to depart before the real wet season started. Dad and Mum were to leave two days later with Tom and Jan, who were in Darwin for a holiday. So on the 15th, we departed for Tennant Creek about 600 miles south of Darwin with a stopover at Mataranka to experience the thermal springs before pushing onto Tennant Creek.

I was towing a trailer, so we were self-contained to camp out wherever possible, but on this trip, I only carried two jerry cans of fuel rather than the five as I previously had when driving to Darwin, as I believed there was plenty of fuel stops across to Queensland. Arriving at Tennant Creek, I filled the car for the long leg east, and though it was around 6pm, I decided to drive most of the night as that was the coolest time, giving Lita and Nicole a better trip.

We were about twenty miles out from Tennant Creek when

the bloody car started to splutter, sporadically at first but becoming noticeable at low speeds. I felt it more important to keep the car going no matter what and drove all night with the car spluttering its way along the Barkly Highway. Boy, was I pleased when dawn arrived. My average speed was around 25 miles per hour, and of course, the only thing I could think of was that could cause this problem was fuel. Therefore I wanted to keep moving in the hope it would clear itself. As luck would have it, we noticed a house set well back off the road and when I reached there, it was the local Police Station.

Just outside Avon Downs, I pulled the car up to a big shady tree and started to go over the fuel lines, and my fears were right, all the filters were full of red dust, which must have been in the underground tanks at Tennant Creek. As I was being filled up there, a tanker was filling the ground tanks. But what to do now was the problem.

Then a policeman came up to me and asked if all was okay. Once I explained the situation, he offered an open hand to help.

He was soon joined by his wife, who invited Lita in for a cupper. While the women were away, this young copper (about my age) said not to worry about the fuel in the tank. If I wanted to empty the lot out, he could take me over to Avon Homestead for some. So I set about cleaning the lines and washing the tank out. When done, he took me to the homestead where I bought fuel from the manager, then refitted the tank and, without much trouble, the car started.

I didn't know what to offer the policeman and his wife for their kindness; the only thing I could think of was to give them all the fresh fruit we had. And would you believe it, he told me they hadn't seen fresh fruit for over twelve months and he was ever so grateful for it, but in my mind, I would have had to get rid of it that day as the Queensland border was around 100 miles away and no fruit can be taken across the border for quarantine reasons.

We departed the Police Station that afternoon, but I couldn't help thinking, what a place! There was nothing to see in all directions but spinifex and saltbush, but I believe they were happy with their isolation, yet it wouldn't do me for an extended period of time.

We arrived in Camoolweal just inside the Queensland border and decided to check on the condition of the road to Mount Isa. The only place that would have this information was the Police Station, so I made my way to the traffic office. But when I entered, I was told to put a shirt on before I could discuss my affairs. I couldn't believe it: this was the outback and this pelican pumper was telling me to cover up? His attitude was way out of line, and I stood there looking at him, stuck for words.

Then I turned around and walked out, only to stand on his bloody dog's tail, which sent it off howling down the street. When I got back to the car, Lita asked me what the trouble was. I just looked at her and started to laugh, saying, "You won't believe it, but the Pelican Pumper in there won't let me know the road conditions ahead because I haven't got a bloody shirt on!"

So, dumbfounded, I drove off towards Mount Isa.

"What's a Pelican Pumper, David?" Lita asked.

"Just a bastard that fornicates with wildlife," I replied. Still, it beat the shit out of me that I had to have a shirt on when a sheila could get away with a singlet (vest).

So now I was on my way, not knowing what lay ahead of me. I was always one to take extra precautions in the outback, but upon looking further at the map, it wasn't far to Mount Isa and we would be there by late afternoon. But instead of staying in town, we decided to look for a good camping spot for the night.

The next morning, we drove onto Winton down the

northwest highway, refuelled and rested, then headed off for Toowoomba, where I was going to spend a day with my old mate Errol Roberts from Pearce. We arrived around sunset, quite stuffed from our trip as we had now spent three nights on the road. I was looking for a long rest, but that was not to be as, when Errol heard I was coming, he had already made plans for us. So my first night saw me legless, to say the least, while the girls were at it hammer and tongs.

We stayed with Errol and Dawn for two full days and during that time he showed us the sights of Toowoomba. While in Queensland, I wanted to get out in the bush to show Nicole a koala bear and just before sunset, we found this young one by itself, not too high up a tree. With little effort, I managed to climb up and get hold of it, and, before coming back to the ground, I gave it a good cuddle. It hung on for grim death. Once I was down from the tree, Nicole's eyes lit up like spotlights; she was so amused at how soft and gentle it was to hold. She showed no fear in animals and loved Australian wildlife, and at any opportunity, I would show her the beauty that was around her. But as all things are, it had to be put back where I found it and she accepted that they lived in trees and we lived in houses.

It was now the evening of the 21st, which didn't leave me much time to get over to Western Australia, as I had promised Lita I would have her home for Christmas Dinner, and I couldn't break that. So that afternoon, we left Errol and Dawn for Perth, but it wasn't long before I was looking for a camping spot. I must have covered about two hundred miles before resting that night and it seemed like hours had slipped by when I awoke. I felt really fresh and eager to get going

This day I was to travel through NSW and part of South Australia, only stopping for fuel and a couple of hours sleep in Broken Hill. On the morning of the 24th, I was passing through Port Augusta and heading across the Nullarbor plains and not stopping other than for fuel. On the morning of the 25th, I pulled over for two hours sleep at Coolgardie, and around 6am left for the last leg to Perth.

Although it was Christmas morning, I felt like and looked like shit, but we arrived at Armadale right on midday, just as Lita's Mum and Dad were sitting down for Christmas dinner. Although they were happy to see us, I couldn't wait to find a bed, and it was around midnight when I awoke. They were still at it with other members of her family there, so after an hour, I found myself in bed again.

Over the next couple of weeks, I had to repair the trailer as the axle had suffered the rough roads of the Nullarbor plain then gave the car a good going over before I departed for Melbourne. As my family were scattered all over the place, I spent a dry night come the new year, and I don't remember drinking a great deal the whole time I stayed with Lita's family.

I contacted Maureen regarding their trip over to NSW as John was posted to Richmond but, like myself, came over to see his family living at Collie, south of Armadale. From that, we decided to leave on the same morning together, as I was going by myself and we could swap drivers along the way.

January 1973

We departed Perth on the morning of the 31st with the intention of seeing each other at Coolgardie, but somewhere along the way, we lost each other, so that evening, I slept out in the bush, and the next morning headed for Cocklebiddy. Around midday, I stopped the car and pulled out the deck chair and, with my JW in hand, sat back to celebrate Australia day in the vast open area of the Nullabor. It drew some attention from passing traffic but I didn't give a shit – I was staying put and having the time of my life waiting for Maureen and John.

About 3pm, who should stop but John, and one look at me told him I was not in a fit state to drive, but he had picked up this pommy bloke who was going to Melbourne and thought I would like the company. I said to him, 'As long as you keep the ice flowing and the JW over it, not a problem to get you there.' So with Maureen now driving my car until I became sober to take over, we moved onto Ivy Tanks, and after a quick meal, set off for the night run across the roughest road in Australia – the unsealed section of the Nullabor that I had been over three weeks earlier.

This young pommy bloke asked me how long it would take to reach Melbourne and I replied, "About three days, mate!"

Then he pulled this map out that showed Australia the size of England, and said, "But it shouldn't take long, as it looks around 500 miles on this map."

I looked over at him and started to laugh. "You'd better sit back and enjoy it, mate, because it's going to take three days at the minimum."

He just couldn't believe how big this place was. Then I started to wonder about Wales and its size, and started to question him on his travels and whether he'd been to Wales. He started to tell me it was nothing like this and that you could cross it in a couple of hours! He had been to Cardiff on one occasion but didn't think much of it.

His reason for coming to Australia was his girlfriend was now living here in Melbourne; they were going to get married once he settled in. But what surprised me was that he had travelled over land that long way to get here and he certainly had plenty to tell me about his trip. Of course, this helped pass the time away over the next day.

I arrived in Melbourne around 7pm and we parted company in town, but my problems were just about to start as this was the first time I had driven around Melbourne. I was totally confused as to where I was or if I even knew the road rules, but what made it more difficult was the rain – it just never let up enough for me to see the street signs. As I arrived on a Sunday night, there was no shops, garages or hotels open for me to make enquiries on how to find Tottenham, so I slowly drove around while drinking my JW. Then I noticed a light ahead and made my way to it, only to find the car was swamped to the door windows, and the bloody thing had stalled in it. Shit, what the fucken hell have I dropped into? And so, getting out of the car, I could see I was under a via-duct which was flooded. Bloody great, I thought! And the trailer was well and truly covered with water.

Everything in the car was wet – my camera was totally submerged – my shotgun and ammo – books – maps – my clothes, including my uniform, shoes, hat, and overalls. When I opened the boot, my toolbox and my cases were full of water. I just couldn't believe it! How the bloody hell did I get into this mess? And there just didn't appear to be any water on the ground yet it just dropped away as I entered the via-duct. It was only when I stood back to look that I noticed how flat and misleading it was, but now I had to get the car out and get me dry.

With the help of two other people who were caught in the same mess, we managed to push the car out and get it started. Then, as luck would have it, I found my flying suit on the back window ledge high and dry. Once I got that on, I started to warm up and, to help this process, I started on my JW again.

I was given directions on how to find Tottenham from my two helpers, and so started my journey again but was soon lost and just kept driving around. The whole time the rain never stopped and, in fact, grew worse. It must have been early morning as the traffic was gone and I felt rather pissed off with Melbourne on my first night. By now, I was becoming a little drunk, and the last thing I can remember of that night was stopping at these red lights and being woken with a chap tapping the window asking me if I was okay.

"Yeah," I said, snapping out of my sleep. Shit, I thought, I must have fallen asleep at the lights! So, with the motor still running, I gave him a wave and drove off to find the nearest garage and before long I was on the road to Tottenham.

On reaching the Base, I contacted my section commander and filled him in on my situation and that I was going to be late for duty, but his reaction was for me to report to him there and then. And so, with only my flying suit on, I did, and the next minute I was marched up to the Base adjutant where I was to explain again my situation, all the time thinking 'what the fucken hell is this shit all about! And who the bloody hell does this prick think he is, sitting there like lord mucker thumboo.

I was starting to show my anger at all this bullshit and asked what was the reason for me being there, then he blurted out: "What are you doing with a flying suit on? And where did you get it from?"

I just looked at him, leant forward and said, "I have not long returned from flying duties in Vietnam, and if you get my records out you'll find the fucken answers there. And with no disrespect, I don't like being talked down to!"

Well, he looked at me and told me to not be so insubordinate; otherwise, I would be on a charge! And with that, I was told to leave and get my uniform on and report back to him in the pm hours. Needless to say, I left but with a lot of anger in me. Turning my attention to my section commander, I asked him if he treated all his posted members the same. He never answered me, which I thought, 'I too can play the same game.' But more so what was on my mind was what the hell had I come to? What sort of a shithole was this? It just seemed that everyone here had an attitude problem.

I was fortunate enough to have my uniform drycleaned by 2pm and had dried my shoes and hat out. I made my way down to HQ, and once again fronted the adjutant. His attitude had changed towards me, but mine hadn't changed towards him even though he said we started on the wrong foot and for me to disregard our first meeting. Then I was told to report to my section. I departed his office feeling no better about it, and when I arrived at my section, things were just the same there. So, *Welcome to Tottenham, Dave*! I thought, *what a shit pit*.

A week passed before anyone started to talk to me. Apart from doing my day duties and keeping to myself, I was not going to let these bunch of pricks pull me down to their level, and so I treated them as they treated me. I was given all the shit jobs to do and carried them out without any complaints. In fact, I would put more effort into it to let them know that I wasn't bothered by doing shit work.

I put my name down on the married quarters' list as I now wanted to get Lita and Nicole over with me, but as the weeks drew on, I was going backwards all the time, never getting on to the frozen six near the top, but just under it, so I remained living on Base with all the single men and subjected to the rosters from guard duties to hut-slut with the only place to entertain myself being the wet mess.

Mum and Dad were now living at Laverton, about six miles away, and I would often go over to see them, but I just couldn't settle down and found myself soon back at the wet mess drinking and playing pool and all the time not one of the other members from my section would associate with me. It just appeared that I wasn't liked enough or they felt threatened to be with me, so I decided to associate with the Base drunks and let them all get on with their own lives.

April 1973

It was now coming up for the Easter long weekend. I decided, along with Blue (my drinking mate) and one of his friends, to take off for a short tour of Victoria's southeast, just to get away from the Base. So we left Friday after work and headed for Philip Island about 100 miles south. The first place we stopped was San Remo pub, and though we had to set up camp, we just carried on drinking till dark and, half cut, left for the Island. We found a well-isolated spot and started to erect the tent, but we were too far gone, so our first night was spent sleeping over it in a drunken state.

The next morning was heavy going for us: the sun was hot and our throats dry but, given our state, we slowly rose and started to organise our camp for the next two days. After I cooked us a big meal, it was time to have a look around the island.

That afternoon when we returned to camp, we found another tent set up in our location, which didn't bother us until I started playing my James Last music. Within five minutes, these blokes around our age came over complaining about the shit that was in the air. I looked over at them and told them to piss off and find somewhere else to camp if they didn't like it. Besides, it wasn't even loud.

Then one of them started giving me a mouthful so I put my finger up, telling him to get stuffed. With that, he walked over, asking me who the hell I thought I was.

I replied: "The bloke with the music, shit head."

Then he put his head down and started running towards me with a lot of anger on his face. By the time he got to me, Blue had tripped him up, sending him to the ground. This brought the other two over to get amongst us.

With that, I yelled out, "Fuck you lot!" and started to punch and slap the three bastards around. The biggest bastard left with a bleeding nose while Blue and his mate were standing their ground, punching the shit out of one chap that just wouldn't go down. So I turned him around and landed a king hit to his check, and that sent him to the ground, upon which we helped them pack up and told them to fuck right off out of our sight.

We all felt rooted after tha,t so we decided to head for the pub, and of course, we spent the rest of the day playing pool and drinking. We were about to leave when two big policemen came into the bar and asked where we were camping. After telling them, they asked whether we had been involved in a fight.

"Yes," I said. Then he asked what happened and I told them one of them started to lash out at me and Blue tripped him up, sending him to the ground. Then his mates hoed in, which left us no choice but to defend ourselves.

"Okay," the copper said. "But one of them has a broken jaw and is laying complaints, and if it's true what you have said you have nothing to worry about."

Then I said, "He could have broken it hitting the ground, as he hit it pretty hard."

"Well," the copper said, "don't leave the island until you come and see us first."

I said, "That's fine by me," and with that, we all left before I was over the limit.

So that evening we went to Cowes then at sunset headed off for the Penguin Parade for which Philip Island was famous. Although I was happy enough to be away from the Base, I really wasn't enjoying myself., Lita and Nicole were on my mind, and now I had the Police to contend with. But, all in all, I joined in with my mates anything that they wanted to do. We soon found ourselves back at camp, having a few tinnies and making an early night of it.

Blue was the first up the next day, bashing up breakie and boiling the billy. After we downed that lot and got the camp sorted, we left for the pub again as Blue wanted a game of pool. So once more we were at San Remo drinking and having a good time, when these fishermen also wanted to play pool, but the rules of the table were set by coins laid out in turn. We had about $5.00 worth out, so we just played on. Then one of the fisherman asked how much longer we were going to be and, in fairness, I was happy to let him and his friends have the table. But Blue had other ideas, and said:

"If you pot this ball, the table's yours, but if you miss it, you can kiss my arse," and with that, set the ball up and stood at the end of the table telling this bloke to have a go.

They weren't sure at first at what Blue was up to, me included, but when this bloke walked up to the table and with great care lined the cue up and with greater concentration took his shot and missed, well this started Blue off. He jumped onto the table, undid his belt and, in a flash, had his arse out telling this bloke to kiss it.

I looked over to where they were all standing, some six or seven of them, big buggers with it, but Blue was still at it.

"Come on, ya bastards. Kiss me arse."

Looking more than angry, the mob started to walk towards us, and I don't mind saying I was a bit concerned about the situation.

I looked across at my mate and told him to prepare himself for a quick exit while I got Blue out. But by now these fishermen were at the table, moving slowly. I looked up at Blue, jumped up and grabbed him by the shirt and, with all the strength I could muster, landed the biggest king hit to his jaw and brought him crashing to the floor, his pants still around his ankles. With this, the fisherman stopped dead, and one of them said to me, "Is he your mate?"

"Yes," I said. "But better him on the floor than me. After all, it's Blue that started the trouble and me that finished it. And remember, if he's my mate, what the hell would I do with you bunch?" So we dragged Blue out of the pub, past the fisherman and headed back to camp.

The next morning only two of us were up; Blue was still sleeping and around 10.30am I started to worry about him. He was snorting and having trouble breathing, then I noticed blood over his sleeping bag and decided to wake him up. When he did, he showed great pain to his face and nose and said he didn't feel so good and what the fuck had hit him. I told him I did it as he was being an arsehole at the pub, and when he started to get his memory back he started to laugh, which started the bleeding. So I got him some ice and let him lay there until he felt better.

That day we remained in camp, and while Blue was suffering in silence, his mate and I decided to leave the next morning early. Then the question of the Police came up, and then, while in two minds, the idea of telling them that Blue had got a broken nose in the fight may well help our cause. So that evening, we all went down to the coppers and Blue lodged his complaint about his nose, putting the shoe on the other foot. But we decided to leave it at that and said we would take him to the Base hospital at Laverton. We left the Police thinking how lucky we were and, the next morning, we left for home with Blue not feeling the best for his Easter weekend.

We dropped Blue off at the Base medical section, saying that someone hit him in a pub miles away from where we were. He remained in hospital overnight, and the next while at work, his mate came over to tell me Blue had a broken jaw, broken nose, and a fractured cheekbone.

"Shit-a-brick!" I said, "this could be big trouble if the truth came out."

"Well," his mate said, "Blue understands that, and as far as he is concerned, it wasn't you, but the doctor has asked the service police to look into it."

I was never questioned over the matter, and when I saw Blue again, I wasn't sure of his reactions towards me, but he threw his arms up, saying, 'G'day, Dave. How the fuck ya going, ya old bastard'. And so, from that, I knew all was okay with him. It wasn't long before we were all at the wet mess talking about the weekend but not how Blue got his HEAD JOB.

During the next few weeks, I saw a slight change in my section as new members were coming in and the old ones were posted out, but there seemed to be a very tight ring amongst a certain few. It was that few that seemed to have the will over everyone else. I still couldn't figure them out and even though we were sometimes on the same jobs, very little was said to me. They just seemed quite frightened and, at times, disturbed when in my presence. All this crap had me lost for words.

One morning I was asked to step into the section commander's office, WO Wacksel, (or commonly known as the Weasel). He told me to pack a kit as I was going on a recruiting run through La Trobe Valley for two weeks. So the next morning, an officer from the recruiting Section in Melbourne and I set out for a preliminary run. We stopped in all the best places overnight and each day would call into high schools to make an appointment for the following month.

Each town we stayed in would find us at the Returned Servicemen's League where all our entertainment was found and the booze was cheap. On the last weekend, we went up to Bombala in NSW for a game on the pokies, and as this was the first time I had played them, I could see how easy it was to become addicted to them. But in my case, I found it quite boring after an hour or so and gave it up as a dead loss in time and money – I didn't like to hand over for nothing, but it did help pass the time away and gave me the chance to really see how the other half live.

On our way back to Base, I asked the officer for my travelling expense money. He just looked at me and said, "We'll have to wait until we return, Dave, as I have put the lot on the horses, and lost most of it!"

"You mean to tell me that you've spent my money!" I said.

"Sorry, Dave, but I usually get it back on the second trip!"

Well, what could I say? I just wished he'd told me before I spent most of mine on the bloody pokies, but I knew one thing for sure: the next time we were going out that I would be looking after the cash, and fuck what he said about that.

Two weeks later, we were on the road again but this time we had an extra person, Margaret, a WRAAF driver from my section, who helped me retain the travel expense until the end of each week, apart from the officer – I would give him his for the horses in the hope he would win some of my money back. The first-weekend stopover was at Morwell, and it was here that we took ourselves to the R.S.L Club and made our way to the pool tables when this member yelled out that no ladies were permitted within the pool area. I looked over and asked him why not and he blurted out the club rules. To avoid creating a problem, Margaret left the Club for the local pub while this officer and I played pool. Not long after, this member came up and asked if we would be interested in a game. I just looked at him and said, 'no thanks, mate. If you can't play with another serving member, then sorry, you can't play with us'. He had nothing to say to me regarding that comment so the officer and I finished our game and left for the bar where the night's event was about to start.

We had arrived on the night of the annual oyster race and it wasn't long before I was talked into having a go on behalf of the Airforce, so I paid my fee of $5 and sat down to a feed. First came a half dozen naturals, then a half dozen cooked. This was followed by a glass of beer, then I started.

"One dozen here," and down they went. Then another dozen cooked, then another. After some seven dozen, I was looking for a beer, but at the same time not wanting to leave it too long between bites, and so I got stuck into it again and right on twelve dozen I started to slow down, and asked only for six cooked ones then six naturals. I washed the lot down with the last of my beer. Then I quietly left the club as the official winner of the year and a record of 13 dozen being eaten.

When I got outside, I could feel the ocean pulling me, my guts swaying too and fro, then the sound of the surf was in my ears. Again the ocean started pulling me towards it, even though I was some fifty miles away I could hear the pounding surf. My guts swayed left to right, but with all this going on I never threw up, but slowly made my way back to the motel and went to bed. The following day I wasn't allowed within 100 feet of Margaret or the officer, and it must have taken two full days before I stopped farting. My poor arse was sore after that ordeal.

We returned to Base, and I decided to check up on my points for a married quarters, and found that I was once again back down the list. I became very angry over this method of selection as it was totally unfair, so I asked for a parade to the Base padre. Once I got there, I explained my situation regarding Lita being pregnant and the time she had left, and should I not get her to Melbourne soon, she wouldn't be able to fly over from Perth. I left it with him to see what he could do for me.

A week later, I contacted him again, and he hadn't done anything about it, so I decided to ask for a parade in front of the Base C.O. Again I explained the situation and his comments were that of the Padre, which left me no alternative but to look for private accommodation near the Base – more so near where Mum lived. So my next weeks were filled with looking around, and through one of the transport members, I acquired this old timber house in New Port. It was old and damp, without any heating or furniture, apart from a fridge, so my next move was to contact Lita and inform her what I'd done and explained that it was only for a short period and I was in the middle of organising her ticket to fly over.

My luck was not with me during these times, as I drew the money out of my bank on a Monday and decided to wait until I got a trip out to Tullamarine airport, but come Thursday, the money had been stolen from my room. In fact, I had just got in and undressed for my shower, leaving my overalls on the floor with my wallet in them. On my return from the showers, I noticed my clothes had been moved around the place, but I never thought of my wallet. The next morning, it wasn't in my overalls where I knew I'd left it. I looked everywhere for it but to no avail, and the more I looked, the wilder I became. Finally, I reported the theft to the Service Police Section. Apart from telling them it was missing, I knew they couldn't do much about it. But just before I left, this Service Policeman wanted to look at my bank book and that really got my back up. But it did confirm I had it on me and that I had withdrawn the amount I'd said.

Having lost the money, I became very suspicious of everyone, and the one person I did have my eyes on was a John Cranney, a real pisshead who had tried to befriend me through drink. He was always broke and borrowing money from me, but after the night it was stolen, he started to distance himself from me, which gave me a reason to watch the bastard.

During this time, I tried to get some of our personal effects held in storage for the house. Once again, that proved difficult as it was still in Perth so I borrowed bits and pieces to tied us over. I now had to draw more money out of the bank, but this time I went down and paid the airfare the same day and contacted Lita, expecting her to fly the following Friday, to be in Melbourne on the Saturday. Come Saturday, Mum, Dad and I picked Lita up and brought her back to Dad's place where we stayed the night.

I couldn't believe how much Nicole had grown and how pretty she looked, her hair and smile just like her mother's. Lita wasn't so good in her confinement and only had a month left. She was feeling all the pain that pregnancy brings but all the time retained a sense of humour. We were all pleased to be united again after some five months apart. Then the next day I showed her the house, which really didn't appeal to her, but I assured her it was only for a short period. Then it was down to the hospital to get booked in and then back home to get settled in.

That night Lita just couldn't get to sleep due to the coldness of the place. No matter what holes I blocked up, the draught would still be there. But there were other things disturbing her, and that was the strange noises throughout the house, followed by this smell now and again.

The next day I went to work and said all should be okay and that she should just do the best she could with the one room. When I returned home that night, she had moved the bedding into the kitchen and just said it was the warmest room in the house, so I sealed up the gaps of the other rooms and started to settle down. But once again, the noise started, again followed by this smell. I could see she wasn't happy about living here. Then she asked me if anyone had died in the place. I couldn't answer that, but I did ask why, and she said she could feel someone around the room all the time, passing her. I told her she was over-reacting and that it was probably the draught, but she wasn't having that.

The next thing, our radio crashed to the floor, the fridge it was standing on not even running. Then we both felt the cold around us even though the door to the kitchen and all the other doors and windows were closed. While this was happening, the fireside in the room showed no sign of the flame flickering. I knew then that we must have a ghost or something camping with us. To hide my concern, I tried to find humour in our situation, telling myself there had to be a logical explanation for these things to happen. But no matter how I thought about it, the fireside convinced me that the bloody place was haunted and it was upsetting Lita and Nicole, and I would have to try harder the next day for a married quarters.

We lived like this for two weeks, then on the Thursday of the third week, I was offered a married quarters at Laverton, just around the corner from Dad and Mum's. Without any hesitation, I took the place without checking it out, but knowing where it was sold me. So that weekend we were on the move, and even though I had paid a month's rent for the house we all were only too pleased to be out of it.

Our furniture arrived the following week and we were settled in at long last, then two weeks later, Lita was having labour pains so I rushed her to Altona Hospital where she was confronted by this bloody old matron who told me to get out of the hospital. I couldn't believe it. Lita was in pain, and she worried about me. Then Lita told her the baby was coming and she did nothing about it. So once again Lita told her and upon her checking she could see she was right. Then she started to panic to get the doctor in, but it was too late as the birth was already over. So, on the night of the 20th of July 1973, Michelle Anne was born, and I felt really pleased that all was okay with Lita. As for me, I was a father for the second time and, like I was when Nicole was born, I had to tell the world.

It was now that I started to realise that a transport driver's wage was not enough to maintain the four of us and our bills, so I offered to go on any trips to Sydney that were available. The competition between the other drivers however was high and so I just had to battle on. By now, we were even using our savings to live on, and I could see hard times ahead unless I did something about it. It was also about this time that the others within my section started opening up to me. This seemed to help the fact that I was not alone in disliking the place and the 'Weasel', but it sure made things a little happier all round.

I became very good friends with Leo Backus, a Dutchman with a better than average attitude, and it wasn't long before we found some common ground in rocks, so on weekends we would head off with my family for the bush to look for gold or whatever else was around and at the same time sightsee our new surrounds.

That year came to a close without much excitement, although by now we had made some new friends. Most of them went on leave to other states for Christmas, and so our first time here was spent with Mum and Dad.

February 1974

The Vietnam war was now hitting the headlines which brought great stress and torment to those of us who had been fighting there, but more so from people within the Airforce and stationed at Tottenham, as I found out one day when I arrived at Base., I was given a mouthful from a pisshead corporal in the wet mess. At first I ignored him, but he just kept up his abuse, referring to me as a baby eater and a warmongering bastard. I looked over at him and asked him if he was talking to me and if so to wash his mouth out first. Then he started again but this time I got hold of his collar and asked him if he knew what he was talking about. Like all arse holes, he didn't and when I let go, he started again, but this time I was going to floor the prick. But Leo came up and said it would be better if I left because they were all of the same mind. So I left rather than be put on a charge for hitting a corporal.

This issue was not confined to the Base as a few nights later, while in my uniform, I was given the same treatment by the civvies who worked on the Base and once again I was asked to leave.

Before I started on them, I couldn't help thinking what a bunch of bastards the newspaper reporters were, stirring up trouble within the Forces, but more so the Richard-craniums (dickheads) that believed it. Even worse was the protests being held in Melbourne and other states. It was not in my opinion to express the feeling regarding Vietnam, a popular political front, but to create havoc for those looking for political ground to view their points to the masses at the expense of the returned veterans, and being one of them did give me concern.

As I was a Transport driver, I was required to be in uniform while carrying out my duties, and as I was a returned serviceman, I had to wear my ribbons and half wing, but these symbols were soon recognised by that public that I was a participant in the killing of babies and raping their mothers while disembowelling the men, or that is what they believed. Of course, I would end up having to duck for cover as the eggs and tomatoes landed around me, followed by the abuse. It even got to the point I wouldn't wear my uniform once I was off the Base, and although I had returned from Vietnam some six and a half years previous, I couldn't understand the need for the public to attack a serviceman like myself who had gone to active duties as a peace-keeping force, which I was led to believe. Now after so long, this war was becoming a very sore point for all the families that were about to have their sons conscripted into it.

But like all politicians, they need to find common ground with the masses. The opposition party of that time used the Vietnam conflict on two fronts, and the first one, I believe, was to stop the troops being sent, as it was a no-win situation, and the conscription to stop, but the second one was that the troops were just killing anyone they suspected of being VC, and of course, there was the ignorant public expressing their views by abusing us in a very hostile manner, when there was no substance to any of it, other than using it as a tool to win the minds and hearts of the public for their political gains to win the coming elections.

It was now that I started to hit the beer pretty hard, and not a day went by that I didn't have a drink of some sort. And there wasn't a shortage of drinking partners as most of us within my section were well browned off with the place, and the changing policies within the Air Force didn't help matters. Our wages were shit for the time we put into our duties and, because of these conditions, the discharge rate was becoming quite high, and the number of members getting out, put greater pressure on ourselves.

It was now also time for me to do a lot of thinking about re-signing for another three years, and though I was given some two months to consider this, a new policy by the Airforce helped make my mind up, as I was to be given a $1,000.00 bonus, (more a bribe) should I re-sign. And so, on the 25th July, I signed on for another three years even though I was becoming discontented with my career as there just wasn't any advancement within the transport mustering.

I arrived at the Base the day after I signed on for three years and was confronted by Leo and Charlie. Within half an hour, while on duty, we took ourselves to the Base canteen and brought a bottle of Vodka, took it into the billard room and started to down it. Once that was finished, it was my turn to buy, and again we drank it, then it was Leo's shout, followed by Charlie's. By now I could hardly speak, let alone stand, and once I was told to fetch the next bottle, I got down on all fours like a dog and made my way to the canteen. But I was confronted by a pair of bloody big boots that belonged to a service policeman I knew. He asked me what the hell I was up to, and I just looked up at him and barked like a dog, then I started to bite his ankles. He told me to piss off, and with that, I walked off, still on all fours, into the canteen and, grabbing hold of the counter, just asked for the last bottle of Vodka and fell backwards to the floor. Then I did a runner to the billiard room, where we started to down it, but we only got halfway into it when we saw the Service police coming. We just managed to hide the bottle and get hold of a broom and made out we were cleaning the place when he entered. He asked who was driving the tipper outside and Leo said he was; then he was asked to shift it, but he was a little concerned about Leo's condition.

Then I said, "Not to worry, mate. We're leaving once we put the rubbish in the bin," and that seemed to satisfy him. So, after he left, we followed him out, and although nothing was said between ourselves, we drove the trucks around the rear of the hangars and finished the bottle.

By now I was in no condition to drive and decided to somehow get the truck into the transport hangar and leave the Base for home. Leo and I managed to park the truck and I went looking for dad to drive me home but he was unable to, so I left the Base but have no idea how I got home.

I woke up and found the room in half-darkness and noticed the time of 7 o'clock.

"Shit!" I said to Lita! "I'm going to be late for work!" and with that, I put my uniform on and headed off for the Base. As I was driving there, I noticed other members from my section heading the opposite way – in my half-drunken state realised that it was only nighttime and not morning. *You bloody dickhead*, I kept saying to myself.

So I returned home and told Lita that I wasn't required at

work that night, but she just laughed and said she knew I thought it was morning but thought it best to let me find out my way. It was then I started to realise that I had a drinking problem and not just a small one. It was something I would have to talk to the Base Doctor about.

The next morning, Leo, Charlie, and I were called into the section commander's office to explain our whereabouts the previous day. Once inside and the door closed, the Weasel started by saying he knew exactly what went on but wanted to know what brought it on. While he was saying this, I then knew that he knew nothing but was looking for a reason to have us charged, and so I said: "Well, speaking for me, I do have a problem, and with no disrespect, that problem is you. For a start, you don't know what happened yesterday; otherwise, you wouldn't be asking now, but my main problem is the attitude of this section and how the trips are always given to those members who suck up to you. Because I choose not to bow down to that level, I am overlooked all the time."

Well, that sat him right back in his chair, sending him red in the face and looking for words. I started again by saying that Leo and Charlie were helping me as I was ready to pack up and leave even though I'd only just re-signed on the previous day. "But apart from that," I said, continuing, "you have not been fair to me since the first day I arrived here. You have given me every shit job there was to do and I completed them without a complaint, but you and others in this section have been trying to ostracise me for reasons I don't know and believe me, it is quite noticeable to the other members in the section!" With that, I shut up, thinking he just may go back to his first question.

Then he stood up and, looking at Leo and Charlie, said, "Is this true?" and the both of them nodded and said, "Yes, sir."

He said, "I understood you three were on the booze," and they just looked at him, astonished.

"Good God, sir! Do you really think we would do that?"

With that, they were asked to leave, then I was asked a few more questions about my gripes and, although I mentioned that I had worked some fifteen days of leave up, he always knocked them back when I needed to take one day's leave off.

He said, "I wasn't aware of that; I guess things need to change. Is that okay?"

"Yes, sir. And I'm sure you won't have this happening from me again." And with that, I was told to go.

When I got outside the office, Leo called me over and thanked me for getting them off the hook and how I changed the position from the three of us to me.

"That's okay, Leo," I said. "He's such a wanker that he even forgot what we were in there for." So the two of us got about our day's work.

About a month after that event, I was called into the office and told to pack a kit as a Tony D'arcy and I had to drive up to Sydney the following day. I loaded up for Sydney that afternoon with boxes for Regents Park stores, and the next morning we left. It wasn't long before we reached our overnight stop. During this time, I told Tony that my trailer brakes didn't feel as though they were working. This was confirmed the following day as we headed through the hills. I was unable to apply the foot brake in case the vehicle jackknifed on me, so we decided to have Tony stay in front and, using his brake light, I could change gears before arriving at the crest of the hill. But on one occasion, I was unable to do this and headed down the hill at such a pace the vehicle's wind pressure was making willy-willies. By now, I was doing around 90 miles an hour and hanging on for grim death. By the time the truck reached the next crest, I had noticed Tony had stopped to wait for me, and when I did finally come to a standstill, he was in fits of laughter due to the expression on my face. I was thankful, however, that it was a straight stretch of road without any traffic on as I came down it in the middle so the truck and I would have a better ride during the rest of that day. The following morning arrived at Regents Park, where I put the truck and trailer in for brake repairs.

On our trip home, Tony and I had a more open discussion about ourselves, our section and our workmates. He mentioned how some of the members avoided me because I was an A.S.I.O member – (Australian Security & Intelligence Organisation). At first, I just looked at him, then said, "What?"

He said again that I belonged to ASIO!

"Bull shit!" I said. "What a lot of crap! Is that what they think back at the section?"

Tony nodded yes!

"And when did all this start? And who the fuck started it?"

"Well," he said, "from what I understand, the word was around before you arrived and we were warned not to say too much to you. In fact, it would be better to distance ourselves from you when you arrived."

"Well fuck my dog's arse!" What else could I say? I looked at Tony shaking my head. "I might be a lot of things, mate, but the one thing I'm not is a spy for the Australian government!" But no matter what I said, it wouldn't make much difference, as it would be quite natural for me to dismiss it as crap, but I did ask him to recall who told him personally, but he couldn't remember or possibly didn't want to, but I now knew why I was being ostracised.

I did a lot of thinking for the remainder of that trip, and once I returned to Base, I started to look for the maintenance sheets for the trailer to see who had carried out the last inspection. As I suspected, no signature was on them, so I headed off to my section commander's office. Once there, I opened up with, "Good morning, sir. You would have heard about the trailer brakes failing. Well, since I have been back, I have done some detective work myself ...."

When I said that, the Weasel looked at me with his mouth open and was going to say something, but I just said, "Hang on, sir! You won't have much trouble marry the trailer to a driver over the last twelve months, and just maybe you can bring it to the attention of the other drivers the importance of these inspections because *this* fella was in a life-threatening situation that I'm so wild about that I am going to write a complaint to the transport officer to make him aware."

"You don't have to go that far, Dave," he said, "just leave it with me and thanks for bringing it to my attention first!"

"Yes, you're probably quite right," I said, "and after all, it wouldn't look too good, especially with my honorary signature at the bottom!"

He looked at me dumbly at first then asked, "What honorary signature?"

"You know, sir, the one that everyone else knows about ... L.A.C. Darcey (ASIO)."

When I said that, he started to shake and grabbed the back of his chair. I could see how uneasy he had become, and he slowly made his way to sit down and looked at me again with his mouth open, but with nothing coming out.

Then I started to level with him. "Look, sir, it's like this: I have never been involved with ASIO, but there appears to be someone in this section that has passed the word around and, by doing so, has made my time here so far shit-house. I don't give a rat's arse about the truth, but I do when the bullshit is being spread about regarding me!"

He soon snapped out of his coma and, still looking at me, said, "Well, I for one did hear but I chose to ignore it but I'm not responsible for the others. As to where it started from, I have no idea."

I then returned to our original discussion of the trailer and the lack of pre-inspections signatures, then I left his office feeling a whole lot better for settling the score with ASIO, and bringing to his attention that his 'arse lickers' weren't doing their job. Maybe things might now change for the better.

Over the next three months, I never went to the wet mess so my drinking habits were kept to drinking over the weekend. I would arrive home and, apart from doing little things around the house each night, I would get my books out on geology and make plans for my next holidays to go bush with my family, but these were hard times to save money or find the extra cash which kept putting it further and further out of my reach. I became quite frustrated as the months just dragged on, and over time, I was losing interest in my hobby.

At work, we were informed the Weasel was discharging himself and our new section commander, WO Belamey, whom I hadn't heard of, was taking over. When he finally did, a complete change to the roster for trips away was drawn up to allow each one of us the chance to earn some extra cash – we were paid $25.00 per day extra for being on the road. This roster did upset the 'arse licks', as they now found themselves doing the shit work around the Base.

September 1974

I was now being sent up to Sydney regularly, and after three trips away, over a period, our bank balance was starting to regrow, to the point I decided to take Lita home for Christmas, which was only some six weeks off. I needed at least a month's leave as I intended to drive over to Western Australia, so whenever possible, I would do extra duties just to build up my leave and help me stay away from the booze.

December 1974

Lita and I managed to save up $900.00 for our trip and I had some 28 days leave built up, so on the 19th, we left Melbourne for Perth. Apart from the heat, our trip was trouble-free. This was Lita's second time across the Nullabor and, as always, she read a book and fell asleep. As for me, I wouldn't stop apart from fuel, while Nicole and Michelle played and slept.

We arrived at her Dad's place and was given the usual welcome. While they got at it again, I was soon in bed and out like a light. That Christmas, although quiet and spent with George and his wife (Lita's brother from Geraldton) and their children, was broken by the news that a cyclone named Tracy had hit Darwin around 1.00am Christmas day with wide spread damage reported. By day's end, reports of the total devastation and loss of life put a real damper on our Christmas dinner, memories of all the friends we'd made up there who were now suffering from the after-effects of the cyclone sinking in. I wondered how they were spending their Christmas dinner.

During the time we spent with Lita's family, I contacted some of mine and, although they were pleased to hear from me, and they did ask me to come over to see them, I didn't feel like driving the ten miles and mentioned it would be better if they could make the effort. But no one did, which I was rather annoyed over as I felt that I had just driven 2,000 kilometres and they couldn't find the time to drive the ten miles to Armadale. It made me think that I really meant nothing to them. So once our holidays were over, I was soon back on the road to Melbourne.

March 1975

Although our neighbours kept to themselves, we did have a fireman from Point Cook make himself known to me but he generally kept to himself. Sometime later, he told Lita that his wife wasn't well and was in hospital; he asked Lita to look after the kids while he went to see her. Of course, she didn't mind, but over a period of time we would see this woman in the yard on some occasions. Then one afternoon, I was working in the front garden when I heard a voice ask me if there were any fairies on the roof. Although I heard her the first time, I asked her what she'd said, and again she'd asked if there were any fairies on my roof.

Well, I looked at her and as it was the first time she spoke to me – I didn't really know her – so just said, "Well I haven't seen any today, but the little buggers were all over my roof yesterday, but then it could be just a little too hot for them today. But if I see any I'll let you know."

With that, I started to walk away, trying not to laugh. When I got inside, I let it all out; I just couldn't help myself. I laughed that much that my ribs hurt, and the tears ran down my face, and all the time Lita was trying to find out what was so funny. When I told her, she too joined in, but we both kept looking at each other and started all over again, then when we finally stopped, she told me that she was 'the wife' and she had a mental problem. Well, that started the pair of us off again, until we could laugh no more.

About a month after that, new neighbours moved in on the other side and introduced themselves. I learnt that he knew a Jeff Milne, the son of David Milne, who Aunty Pat married (Butch's mother). We decided the three of us should go for a Sunday drink. As I had been off the booze for some time, it wouldn't take long before I'd be pissed, but I was looking forward to seeing Jeff as it must have been eight years since I'd set eyes on him, and since then he'd gotten married. His wife was with him in Laverton.

So the following Sunday, we took off for the wet mess at Tottenham and started to drink, but then I soon realised what sort of pisshead I had living next door. His name was Bob. Well, I knew Jeff could drink, but Bob was a real piss artist of the first order. We were there only for about three hours, but in that time, we finished some 36 glasses of booze, and the prick went crook when I said I'd had enough. Then Jeff said he didn't want to go and before I knew it, he was throwing a punch at me. *Shit! I might be half pissed but this is stupid!* Grabbing Jeff and leading him to the exit, I told Bob to come along as I was going home before things got any worse. Once outside, Jeff started to swing another punch and I ducked that. I didn't want to hit him because Bob was being a real arse hole.

We got home and had a bloody good laugh and went our separate ways, but the following weekend Bob was all for it again. I wasn't going, but instead, he said we could play pool in his house, so Jeff and I went over and couldn't believe it when we entered the front room: this bloke had a full-sized billiard table in it. After he set the balls up, he would stand all over the furniture to have his shot. Well, I couldn't do that no matter what, and Jeff was also of the same mind, so we left. When we got inside our place, we just cracked up over it. Jeff decided to go home, but arrangements were made for a piss up the following weekend.

During the week, I was sent off to Sydney, and upon my return, I was invited by Bob to come out for a drink. I really didn't feel like going, but the next day was a Sunday. Jeff arrived and Bob noticed his car in my drive and again asked us to go to the wet mess. As much as I didn't feel in the mood, I told Lita I wouldn't be long, and the three of us left for Tottenham. Before long, we were all at it hammers and tongs, but this time Bob was really in the mood for the booze, and he was out to break our last record.

Three hours later, we had now drunk 38 glasses and I found I just couldn't handle any more. But I finally drank it down and then Jeff started to take a swing at me, with Bob egging him on. I got hold of Jeff and once again headed for the exit, telling Bob to stop his shit-stirring. When we finally all got outside, Bob started again on Jeff, and this time Jeff landed a clean punch to my face. I looked at Bob and said, "For everyone I cop, mate, that's one I'll land on you." So I turned around and planted two good punches to Jeff's face and walked over to Bob, but he could see I was quite serious with my intentions, and like the wimp he was, he just said for us to all to cool it. With that, we all headed for home, Jeff looking the worst for wear, while Bob wasn't sure about me. When we did get home, Jeff's wife looked at him and asked what had happened and, Bob being the Broadmouth, blurted out that I just hit him. That sent her in a shitty with me and, looking at Lita, I said, "There's more to it than that, and as far as I am concerned, you're the one that started this shit, Bob."

With that, I started to walk up to him but he jumped his fence and headed for his house like a real wimping rat, and Jeff and his wife left without a word. The next thing Bob's wife was calling Lita to the fence asking what was going on and she just said that we were a little drunk and Dave had hit Jeff.

Then she said, "I don't want Dave to keep asking Bob for a Sunday drink."

Well, that got Lita's back up as she bloody well knew that it wasn't me that was always asking to go. Then she said that it was Bob that was pestering Dave and Jeff to go and not to blame me when her husband even started telling Jeff to fight Dave. So the two of them left with no more to say, and Bob never came over to see me, and I wasn't overly worried about that, apart from the woman thinking what a pair of pissheads we were.

Nicole was now under an eye specialist as it was suspected she may have a weak muscle in one eye, which would indicate a lazy eye, or the possibility of an overpowering muscle that could show the same results. At least we now knew that it was taken care of and the expense was not going to be a problem.

After some months of treatment that she was to wear glasses and upon bringing her home after the fitment and paying $80.00 for them, the fireman's kids from next door just ripped them off her face and, without any hesitation, rubbed the special plastic lens es on the concrete path. It happened so fast that neither Lita nor I could do anything about it, apart from not having them over again. To make matters worse, the fireman said we shouldn't put glasses on kids so young, but I just told him to go fuck his fist and not bother us again.

October 1975

Although I was away quite often, I would look forward to my leave with my family. During these times, Lita never ever complained to me, and I would often think of Darwin and the times she must have had a cause, but while she was here things just seemed to suit her.

Her mother and father were now making plans to come over to see her before the end of the year, so I decided to take some time off for the lot of us to go camping around the Gippsland area as Lita had not been down there yet. When they arrived and settled in for the first week, I took two weeks Leave and we departed for Philip Island. On arrival, we set up the tent, and at sunset all headed off to the fairy penguin parade. The kids really enjoyed it and so did Lita and her parents. e spent some five days travelling in and around the south of Victoria

It was now that I was starting looking for another method of making income, and as I wanted to put my carpenter skills to work again. I set up the carport into a workshop and began to make furniture, first for ourselves then the neighbours. This expanded to making kitchen units and free-standing units. Although I was in demand, the only reason was because I was cheap and the work was good. I remained quite busy, which kept me well off the booze and away from the pissheads of the Base.

That Christmas was very quiet for us that year. Lita's parents had left some two months earlier, and there just didn't seem to be anyone around as Mum and Dad had gone back to Perth as Dad was now thinking of retiring out of the service. So Lita, I and the kids would go further afield and spend the day looking around at other locations and towns.

January 1976

I started work after the Christmas break and began to think that I should do something to improve myself as this job I was doing was a dead loss to me. While I was in the section, this new member who had posted in started to talk to me about going to the education section and doing a service English course. I asked him what was required to get a pass to enter, and on the same day, I enrolled to study each Wednesday afternoon. For the next two months I found it really hard as I was totally confused as to what was expected from me. Upon handing in my first assignment, I was asked to see the instructor after class.

I didn't quite know what to expect but went in with an open mind to find out. Straight off, he asked me if I'd had much schooling so I sat back and gave him my life history, stating that

I was now more than anxious to learn, especially English. I also explained that my writing wasn't the best as I had never been shown, and the only way I had taught myself was by capitals, and all the reading I had picked up was from the newspapers. I also told him that I wasn't stupid, that I had never felt backward, but that I'd always hidden these weaknesses. I had never had anyone to help me, and when I told him that I had only been to school for four and a half years and wasn't shown much in that time he offered to help. So from there, I was given the basic kids' books to learn from.

As it was now affecting my normal working duties, I was unable to see him each Wednesday, but instead I was to post my work to him. This was fine until one day I was stopped at the main gate and had my bag checked out for contraband. They asked my reason for bringing a briefcase to work. When I told this service policeman that I was doing a course, he asked me if I had permission to carry it in that area.

I looked at him and just said No, and that I had no idea I would need it.

Then he said, "Sorry, mate, but you'll have to leave it here until stand down hours," and with that, he took it off me and left me dumbfounded. When I reached my section, I was told to make my complaint to my section commander and he told me to write an application out and he would strongly recommend it to the base CO.

Two days later, his answer came back: he refused my request on the grounds that it wasn't required for the normal course of my duties. Well, this fired me right up. There was no way I could carry these books under my arm, and so my section commander just said for me to wait outside the compound and he'd send a vehicle up to get me each day, as they didn't inspect the vehicles.

"Okay!" I said, and so from that day on, I was driven the last few hundred yards to work.

Meanwhile, Rick Cleary, the new member posted to our section and the one that was also doing his English course, had the same trouble, so before long the pair of us were travelling to work, and as he just lived around the corner from me in Laverton, this saved both of us petrol by taking turns.

Before long, I was on the road to Sydney again, and because of these trips, I was unable to keep up with my school work. But each day after work, Rick and I would get a bottle of booze each and finish off before arriving home. On one of these occasions, I parked the car in my usual place and while Rick was getting the beer, this silly young prick in a jacked-up car slammed into the side of my car. Though he paid for the damage, it was the start of a string of accidents over that month.

My second one happened while coming home from fitting a kitchen unit into a friend's house – I was involved in a fourteen car pile-up. The cause was a drunk driver running off the narrow road leaving his rear end blocking a lane. He just couldn't be seen. My car had the rear end caved in, which was repaired. But the following morning I was put on this petty cash run around Melbourne, and around mid-day, I was looking for a shop when the next thing I knew, this bloody car was sitting on my bonnet. *Fuck, where the hell did that come from!* I couldn't believe it. I was doing around five miles an hour and not a vehicle in sight, then this bloody car landed on my bonnet.

I got out to see if the driver was okay, and just as he was getting out, this Army officer came up to me and said," "The other driver came straight through the intersection airborne and landed on top of you." Of course, this was great news for me and I made my accident report out at the Base and was left alone for the rest of the day.

The following week I had a job driving a flat top into the rail station and soon settled back while driving through Footscray. Without any warning, this VW in front suddenly stopped, leaving me no room to pull up. *Shit, this is big trouble*, so before the dust settled, I was out of the cab and looking fucken wild. I threw my hat on the seat and started to walk over to the VW. When the driver noticed me, he just drove off. I looked at first, thinking what the hell are you up to, and then I started to wave him down. In fact, I yelled, "Come back here! Come back here!" Then the penny dropped, and as I was still yelling, I began to say, "See you later. Keep going. Don't stop."

While this was going on, an old chap came over and said, "I don't think he's overly worried about it, but he did come from around the corner and stopped in your lane while you were looking the other way."

So I contacted my section and explained the situation to them and was told to go and look for him as he had probably gone around the corner and died on me. Well, I was in no hurry to find out so I just made my way back to Base and filled another report out. But this time, the service police were brought into it, and no matter how much they wanted to know, I kept saying I didn't see much, and by the time I got out, he was already on the move. I couldn't even tell them the make of the car. With that information, they just had to let it go. As the damage to the truck amounted to a bent licence plate meant the accident report was torn up.

March 1976

Our Commanding Officer was posted out and replaced, and at times I was rostered to drive him to Melbourne or the airport. Even if I returned to Base without him on board, I was always given a salute, as most of the guards were young servicemen not long coming off training. The reason they would salute me was because I had ribbons and a half wing. As I never had my hat on while driving, they couldn't tell the difference until one day I picked up the CO and, upon arriving at the base, the guard looked at me and waved me on as he was now used to seeing me. But the service policy was to salute the CO in and out of the Base, so I pulled the vehicle up to bring to their attention that I had the CO with me. But again he waved me through, and so not to cause any embarrassment, I drove off,

I dropped the CO off at HQ and made my way to the transport section and, just as I arrived, my section commander called me over. "Look, Dave!" he said, "the CO has just got off the phone and has asked me to provide another driver and someone without ribbons etc." He then asked me what had happened. I told him it wasn't unusual for the guards to salute me rather than the CO because of my Vietnam ribbons and that he must have noticed that the CO didn't have a ribbon to his uniform. I believed that was where the problem was, but what could I do about that? John, looking at me, said, "Well, if that's what he wants, I have no other alternative but to take you off the roster."

I was now getting right pissed off with the Airforce and the system. I just couldn't get myself into anything without some bastard trying to make waves for me. Not only was I now grounded from driving the CO, I was put back on the mule train driving around the stores on Base – not that I minded that so much, but the paperwork involved must have been designed by a disturbed mind; it was nothing for any of the drivers to sign their signatures to some 100 items, just to take it less than 25 yards into another warehouse.

I will never forget the day I came back from a medical appointment in Melbourne, where it was discovered that I had skin cancer on my nose. After having it removed, I was told I would have to have treatment and check-ups for the rest of my life. This news upset me quite a bit and though I was now back on Base driving the mule train, my mind wasn't on the job. When I started to drive away with the seven bomb trollies loaded with stocks, a CAT TRAP fell off, and I didn't hear it.

It was brought to my attention by the warehouse Flight Sergeant and, after I removed it from under the trolley, the Flight Sergeant said not to worry about it, just return it to the main stores. So once they unloaded the trollies, I did exactly that, and left for my section to stand down for the day.

The next morning I arrived to find John asking me what had happened yesterday regarding the cat trap, and I told him as I really had nothing to hide. Then he told me that the warehouse officer was placing me on a charge for destroying public property. I looked at John and started to laugh, saying, "Who the fucking hell brought that on? I just don't believe this shit! Perhaps we should go and see this dickhead and sort it out with him."

So the two of us headed off for his office, and once I got inside, I knew it was going to be hopeless. This officer was the one I ran into at Pearce, wanting to know why I didn't have my hat on.

John tried in every respect to have him drop the charge, but this little twit wasn't having it, so I ended up in front of the Base CO. Though I had photos to prove the method of loading, he looked at me and said it was conjured up by me. I even had the bloody Flight Sergeant backing me, and half the base drivers came as witnesses, but this prick, along with the twit from the stores, wasn't having it. I was guilty and nothing was going to change that. At the end of the trial, I asked for a Court Marshal as that was my divine right. You could have heard a pin drop when I made that statement. I was marched out and sometime later marched back in, and given the sentence of five days CB, (Confined to Barracks). On top of that, I had to pay for the replacement of the bloody CAT TRAP.

But the pain of it all was I couldn't have a Court Marshal because the amount of money involved wasn't sufficient, so I asked for a parade in private, and that was granted. Once the others left, the CO asked me what I wanted. I started by saying that I had never been on a Base like this where everyone I had worked for had shown such a high rate of discontentment that morale was so low it was non-existent, and this was brought on by the way the place was run. I, for one, could now understand why the Airforce was losing so many experienced people and they were being replaced by people who thought they were God. From the very first day I had arrived, I'd had nothing but trouble, and as far as I was concerned, I had no more interest in a service career after this day.

It did nothing for my case, but I really didn't think it would.

I asked for a parade in front of John. There I let him know that it was nothing but a Kangaroo Court, but if I was put back on mule train, I'd be doing it by the book. He agreed that if that's what I wanted, I could have it, as I explained to him I had five days CB, and that should be enough to create a lot of problems for the warehouse officer.

So the following day, John called a parade for all the transport drivers and told them that, over the next week, everything going into or out of the main warehouse was to be double-checked by a specialist driver, and if there wasn't any available, then wait. So the first day, nothing got moved out of the warehouse at all, and when the word got to the warehouse officer, he was down to John's office flapping his arms and giving him shit. I believe John told him that the drivers were working by the book and there was nothing he could do to change that so he'd just have to put up with the inconvenience.

The next day, I was called down to check a load on one of the trucks, and as soon as I looked at it, I told the driver it was no good. The lot had to be taken off and reloaded. During that happening, I was called over to another warehouse and did the same thing, so that day, no stocks were moved. By now, the message had reached the CO, and again John was confronted about the rechecks before moving vehicles. And again, nothing could alter the Base rules.

By now, all the drivers were involved in it, and no matter where you went around the Base, trucks were being loaded or unloaded, but on this day, and after twice reloading, it was time to move. But instead of that, I put the vehicle in as U.S. (unserviceable). When I was asked what it was, I told the stores people that the interior light wasn't working. Well, this brought the truth home that I wasn't going to fucked about by the warehouse officer. He soon came down to find out what was up, and having the drivers' handbook with me, I just opened it up and pointed out that any vehicle that is U.S. should not be moved until a fitter checked it out, and when I told him that the interior light wasn't working, he hit the roof. But I stood my ground hard. As he left, a fitter arrived and replaced the bulb and so, after three days, I moved the truck to the next warehouse some 25 yards away and stopped. Without delay, it was unloaded within minutes, then I returned to the main warehouse to start all over again.

When I arrived back at the transport section, John told me they were going to train up some stores people to handle all the Base stocks and remove the responsibility from ourselves to them. He had such a big smile on his face it could be seen 25 yards away. By the end of the week, the move was made and at this point, I knew that if I put one foot wrong, I would be on another charge. I explained this to John – whether I was on Base or not, I could be in the section all day and some bastard would report me being somewhere else or see me doing things other than my normal duties, which we both proved right.

As I wasn't being sent to Sydney now, Rick Cleary and I

decided to do some moonlighting at a foundry. Although the work was shitty and the money poor, it was handy at the end of each week, but after some four weeks working every night till 11pm, I was asked to become a foreman. I accepted on one condition: that should any of the equipment be faulty then our output would be down for that night. So on the sixth week, Rick and I started to grind these units down to place a large steel ring onto the rest of the grinder. As quick as a flash, the grinder caught my glove and dragged it and my hand still in it between the grind wheel and the rest plate. The first thing I realised was the steel wheel fell onto my foot, followed by the pain.

Shit! I couldn't believe it! I removed my glove to find one of my fingers hanging by the skin and the others bleeding. I called Rick over and asked him to run me to the hospital as I had just cut my hand. Getting into his car, I looked around for a bottle of booze and downed it in the belief it would help the pain. Once I was in the hospital and showed them my hand, I was attended to straight away by an Asian doctor. He looked at my finger and just wanted to remove it.

I started to yell, "You're not going to pickle my fucken mate."

But he kept saying that there was nothing that could be done because of the damage. Again I sat up on the operation table telling him to get dog-knotted. He was not having the bloody thing.

He could see I was serious about saving it, so he told the sister to fill me up with painkillers and let me go till the next morning. I have no idea how many painkillers I had, but I do know I was as high as a kite and loving every minute of it.

When I got home, Lita wasn't pleased about the injuries but couldn't help laughing at me being so high. After my bath, I slipped into a coma until the next morning. Boy, was I suffering for it. The pain by now was too much and I just had to get to hospital to sort this bloody mess out. Though I knew that I'd be in the shit for moonlighting without permission, I found myself bending the truth by saying I had an accident at home while using my bandsaw. I told Rick this and for him to let the others know what my intentions were. So for the next two months, I was to work in the transport section and be at the hospital each week for skin grafts. Though there was plenty of pain with it, at least I still had my finger.

While stuck in the transport section, Leo and I set about doing our smoko room up. We built new tables and chairs, and I repaired the kitchen. Although this did keep us busy, it also gave us time for badminton which we both enjoyed and played each lunchtime. Even though I only had one good hand and Leo a bad heart, we were able to amuse ourselves.

Leo and I had played badminton since we were at Tottenham, and it was now that the rest of the drivers were taking an interest in playing. Of course, there were quite a few great players amongst us, but the rules always brought arguments and the main person to start was Rick. For some reason, he just wanted to be right, and rather than argue about the point, we let it go. Then one day, I decided to write to Lita's sister Jan for the rules on the game as she was a member of the Western Australia Badminton State Team. Two weeks later, the rules arrived.

On the following Saturday, Leo, Rick and Rick's wife came around for a drink. After an hour or so, I brought up the subject of badminton and that I now had the rules of the game. Before I had finished my sentence, he grabbed my collar and began to punch me in the face. Well, totally surprised and dumbfounded, I fell back into my chair. I was just about to get up when I noticed the girls staring at him in shock, but more so Leo was now grabbing my arms to prevent me from taking a swing at him.

The next thing, Rick was asking me outside, and before I knew it, Leo was pulling me out. I now started to ask him what the bloody hell he was proving. Then he started: "Come on, have a go."

By the time I had walked over to him, one of Lita's friends, Fay Cramp, came over to me and said not to fight the silly bugger. She stood close to me and I could see Rick's fist coming down. I brushed it aside, but he did again, and again I brushed it off. Then I asked Fay to step aside

While I was looking at her, Rick landed a king hit that sent me to the ground. The next thing I remember was Leo picking me up and looking to see if I was okay. My lip was bleeding so I went and checked it out and decided to go to Laverton Medical section for repairs. On the way out of my house, I looked over at Rick and told him not to be there when I got back. I ended up with three stitches to the mouth.

On the way home, I asked Leo what had I said to bring that all on, and he just said 'Badminton', and that Rick was just an arse hole.

"Well, Leo," I said, "he too can get dog-knotted from now on, but as for you … why didn't you let me hit the bastard? Twice you stopped me, then when Fay stepped in the bastard landed one."

The next day I noticed Rick talking about me and so, not to show him that it was over, I walked over to him, saying,

"You may have landed one now, but when you're half pissed and being held back, it'll be my turn to party, so don't think you're any sort of a hero because there were others around when it happened." And from that, he shut his mouth, and not a thing was ever mentioned about it. He was never to play Badminton with Leo or me again, and in fact, the other drivers soon got pissed off with his childlike manner.

Lita and I soon became very friendly with Rick Cramp and his wife Fay, who lived in Broadmeadow some eight miles away. This meant we saw a lot less of the people around me, yet Rick had not long joined the Airforce, and Tottenham was his first posting. It really didn't impress anything upon wanting to remain in the service, but we did spend a lot of happy times together.

October 1976

I was once again back on the road to Sydney and it was a good feeling to have the extra cash and leave. Though I didn't like being away from my family, I did enjoy getting away from the Base. The trip to Sydney would take five days turnaround if all went okay, but being on the road gave me plenty of time to think about my situation, and once again, I was feeling the need to learn. While I had not been able to keep up the previous study, I felt there must be something else I could handle. My mind often drifted back to Darwin and the business I had developed out of nothing, and no matter what I thought would generate an income, there always seemed to be something that would hold it back.

I had always felt quite confident in myself in trying anything new that was put in front of me, and regarded a challenge as the basis of learning more about my own ability and proving that having a go was the only way to master any problem. Hence why I enjoyed Geology so much. It didn't matter if my problem solving came out wrong, and as much as I felt it was right, the thing about it no one around me knew any different. But when I did find the right answer, I would be over the moon with it. I guess this was how things were for me, but I knew I had the persistence to keep trying no matter what until that problem was solved.

I also felt common sense was a big factor, and though we all have different levels of common sense, I never put mine above anyone else's, yet I was always confronted by those within my section who knew it all, and I never challenged them. Likewise, they never challenged me over my geology, but it did provide me with some entertainment when these know-it-alls started to tell you the way things were caused or made.

I then stopped giving my explanation on various subjects, this due to at times being referred to as a know-it-all. I began to then sit back and listen, but more so observe, and this is where I could see more clearly that they were very good with words but their facts on whatever subject they were talking about weren't quite correct. The one thing that really did come across was the way they used the technical words to explain themselves.

It just appeared to me that I was surrounded by people who knew a little about a lot, or a lot about a little! On one occasion, I asked the driver, "Why don't you take a job in the field that your interests lay in," and his reply was, "No, Dave. I love driving and I can't see me doing anything else!"

I began to wonder about this and thought maybe he just wasn't confident or, like myself, not educated enough and that brought the truth home about myself. *The lack of education, that's why I'm a bloody transport driver.* I felt that I was no different to the rest of them, as one thing I knew was, if I had the chance again I wouldn't be here sitting behind a wheel between Melbourne and Sydney.

Although I had no one to talk to about my thoughts, or more so I didn't want to talk about them, I was beginning to wonder whether I should do something else along the lines of my other abilities. Keeping an open mind over this matter, I put together my strong points: first was Carpentry, then the Building trades, like Bricklaying, painting, plastering, then Driving, and last was Geology. I really didn't have much apart from these points, but the last thing was *ME*. Could I do it? Again that stubbornness and determination all came to one thing – being ignorant enough to have a go, and that just the typical question or statement often put in front of me. Although I was 31 years old now, I knew I hadn't achieved a great deal or, in fact, provided a sound future for my family. I could stay as a transport driver in the Airforce – at least I had a secure job but no advancement. Then there was ME again: how did I feel about it? I wasn't over the moon with what I was doing now. Then what about the kids? – with me being moved around from Base to Base wouldn't help their education. No matter how I put it to myself, I couldn't find an answer.

I returned from this trip only to be sent back to Sydney but this time in convoy with Tony D'arcy again, and though it was a five-day turnaround, we arrived back at Tottenham around 6pm. Usually, the duty driver would take us home from the Base, but this night Rick Cleary was the driver, and upon locating him, we found that he was a little drunk. Tony wouldn't go with him so he contacted his wife to pick him up and, when she arrived, asked me to go with him but I declined the offer as I knew Rick just had to get out of the wet mess and this would give him that opportunity.

Tony left, and Rick got the Kombi van allocated for the night. I loaded my kit into it and started to strap myself into the seat when Rick drove off like a madman possessed, straight through the main gate without stopping and around onto the main drag. Then down went his foot to the floor. I looked over to him and said, "You don't have to prove your driving skills to me, Rick, so don't you think you should slow down."

But that just made him worse. As he came up to the Sunshine overpass, the bridge divides into two, like a Y fork, which he only just missed. I started to yell at him to stop the fucken car, and that I wanted out, but that fell on deaf ears. Without stopping for oncoming traffic, which I was hoping he would as I intended to jump out, he swung the van around in front of them, causing them to take evasive action, and, as he rounded the corner, he mounted the footpath and drove onto the nature strip.

"Fuck ya, Rick!" I said. "You're off your rocker, mate, and I think the best thing is for you to stop and let me drive."

He just said, "Get rooted, Dave. I'm okay, don't you think I can handle it?"

"No," I said, but I also knew that I had prepared myself for the worst. I got hold of the seat belt and tightened it around me, lifted my feet onto the seat, and hung on for life while this wanker proved to me that he was a wonderful driver.

By now, he was doing 73 miles per hour, and I was thankful that was all the vehicle could do. It wasn't long before the next corner arrived and again he drove around it at such a high speed that both lanes were used, sending traffic in all directions. Then his foot went back down to the floor and once again he was off. This time I never said anything to him. We got around two miles down this road when we became airborne over a large drainage hump, and when the vehicle landed, he was steering from side to side, trying to keep it on the road. Just as he managed to get it under control, we hit the second drainage hump and again we were airborne.

I looked over at Rick and said, "Can you handle it now, mate?

He said nothing, and all I could hear was the motor screaming its guts out and what seemed to be a lifetime in the air. When we finally came to earth, he was once again rocking from side to side, but this time it was far worse. He just couldn't bring it under control. The next thing the vehicle started to head off the road, straight for a power pole, and without looking at Rick, I told him, "It's no good, you're going to hit the fucken thing!"

By now I was beginning to shit myself as he must have slipped into a coma. Then I yelled at him: "Roll the fucken thing;

just roll the fucker!" With that, he grabbed the wheel and, with one good pull to the right, sent the vehicle slamming into the power pole, hitting it right on my side door, and sending the vehicle end for end three times. All during this, my eyes were open, and what a sight! It looked like I had gone through two nights and three days as it was sunset then dark.

While this was happening, the windscreen popped out and, in slow motion, it followed the rolling vehicle. It came to rest in the mud along with the front of the vehicle, sending glass and stagnant water all over us. When we finally stopped, I looked over at Rick and said, "Are you okay?"

He looked at me and said, "No. I'm in fucken big trouble now."

I replied, "Well, don't worry about that. Are you hurt?"

He said, "No. Only my dignity."

Well, I thought myself quite lucky. My left shoulder had come out of the seat belt when we were rolling over, and my door was gone, in fact, my side of the vehicle was opened up like a sardine can.

We were soon out of the wreck and I realised that I wasn't so good. My head was spinning, and my eyesight was a little blurred. Rick was just walking around kicking the shit out of the wreck, knowing that big trouble lay ahead for him. As neither of us had drawn blood, we both thanked God for that. Then Rick started to ask me how to get rid of the piss in his guts and I said, "Just shove one finger in your mouth and one up your arse, and if that doesn't work, swap the bastards around." At first, I thought he was going to do it, but I did add. "Perhaps you should try drinking the stagnant water around here," so he got down on all fours and did just that.

Then the public came to see if we were hurt and, though we were fine, we knew it would have to be reported to Base.

Without us noticing, a police captain came up and asked us

what had happened and I just said a blowout in the front and we ran off the road. Rick looked up at me and continued by saying, "Yeah, no worries, mate. The RAAF is sending a vehicle out to tow it out!" and with that the police captain left. Then I got into a car and went to Laverton medical section where I was diagnosed with a slight concussion and had to remain in hospital overnight. When Lita came to see me she wasn't pleased, as she hadn't liked Rick since his last hat trick.

The next morning I reported to John, my section commander, and I knew he was busting to find out what had happened. As for the others, I could well imagine what they were saying about it. When I got into his office, there were two service policemen waiting for me. Without any hesitation, they started by saying they knew Cleary had been drinking, but they wanted to know how the accident happened, and I told them the truth. It was no good covering up or hiding any information from them, but I did tell them that I never saw him drinking, and that was the truth. But I could smell it on him. Once they left, I told John that Rick was nothing but an animal: he wouldn't stop and was totally ignorant of his responsibility, not only to me but to his duty for that night.

I told him that neither Tony nor I had any drink during the time we were on the road. I hadn't seen Tony that morning but John confirmed it as he had asked Tony earlier when he'd arrived at work. I still wasn't feeling that good and asked him for leave – it was approved for the next day.

The reason I wanted this leave was that I had been asked to build some wardrobes for a friend of one of the drivers who I had just done a kitchen unit for and, after telling him I'd do it, I was sent back to Sydney with Tony. So this was the only chance I had. While making it over that week, a transport driver from Laverton who'd I built a double bunk unit for noticed my car outside this person's house and realised I was working there.

Instead of knocking on the door, he just came in, walking on his hands. As he passed the kitchen, the lady of the house screamed as all she could see was a pair of legs going past. Well, upon hearing her screaming, I came out of the bedroom and found Max on his hands.

I stood there looking, then broke into a laugh, saying to him, "What the hell are ya up to, mate!"

After getting to his feet, he blurted out that I should come down to the wet mess for a beer and, as I was thinking of knocking off, I agreed. So the pair of us left for the wet mess, but once I got there, I just didn't feel like drinking. It was one of those muggy days and working in that house had left me feeling drained.

After two or three beers, an old friend of Dad's that had known me since I was a young boy at Pearce came in. Though Max and Ralph were drivers at Laverton, we drivers from Tottenham would never see each other, but seeing Ralph there started me talking about the family. Before long, I was getting quite pissed and in need of a leak, so I took myself to the dunny and found I couldn't undo my fly, so I undid my belt and pulled my jeans down to allow me to do my trick.

I must have been halfway into it when Max walked in and, looking at me, just laughed. He moved to the back of me and pulled my jeans down to my ankles and, as I was about to turn around to tell him to piss off, I slipped over and landed on my side with full force, with my head in the urinal. The wind was knocked out of me, and I lay there for about a minute. I could feel urine running up my nose but I just couldn't move; in fact, I couldn't talk. I rolled my eyes over to him and said that I didn't feel so good, but by now he was laughing that much he didn't hear me. Then just after he finished himself, he realised I wasn't moving and got down and asked if I was okay. By now I'd had enough of the piss running up my nose and with all the strengh

I could muster, I said, "No! I have hurt myself inside."

Max raced out to get help and it wasn't long before he arrived back with Ralph. Between the two of them, they got me to my feet and, once I was up, I did feel a little better. But I was pissed off with Max, and the fact I was drunk with it. So we made our way back to the bar, downed two more and, during that time, I realised I couldn't walk straight. So Max and Ralph took me home. Max didn't want to confront Lita with me like this so they went around to Dad's place and he drove me home. Upon arriving, Lita just opened the door and told Dad to chuck me on the bed. By now I was totally out to it, but Dad and Ralph left after telling Lita that I would wake up with sore ribs and ankles.

The next morning I sat up in bed and the pain in my side brought the memories of the previous day back to me. "Shit, I said, "I don't feel so good in the chest, Lita. I don't think I can even get myself dressed for work."

Although she never said much to me, I could feel the air was shitty!.

She helped me get some clothes on and I took myself down to Laverton medical section where it was discovered I had broken two ribs and fractured two others, so once more I had to face John and explain my problem. This time I'd be off for about six weeks, but it did give him a bloody good laugh when I told him how it had happened.

During this time I decided to take Lita home to Perth for Christmas, as I had promised her that whenever possible and we could afford it, we'd go. I had to stay on Base though until my ribs had healed, and I was once again hanging around the section cleaning out vehicles and washing them down.

I applied for three weeks leave for Christmas and in due course we were off to Perth. While driving across, I mentioned to Lita that I had to make my mind up over the next couple of months as I was due to resign for another three years, but I really felt that I'd had enough of this crap. While in Perth, I was going to see how much work was around in the building industry.

She said, "Well, that's up to you, Dave," and I reiterated that I felt strongly about getting out of the service as it was just a dead-end job for me without any chance of advancement.

Christmas 1976

While our time was going to be short in Perth, I wanted see as many people as possible for a future job within the building trades. So most days, I travelled around looking and meeting various people and, wherever possible, I would ring them up. But Christmas this year was a little disappointing as I hadn't remembered that all builders had closed down. I still managed to contact quite a lot though, and I felt more and more confident as the days passed. I made up my mind and I told Lita to keep it to herself at this stage, but I intended to get out of the Airforce.

February 1977

Not long after I returned, I was to drive the Autocar, a large tank rescue vehicle used for transporting goods and other vehicles, and a young fitter up to Queensland to deliver their new fire tanker. Apart from the trailer brakes, our trip went fine, but as we were reloaded with another fire truck to go to Regents Park auctions, we decided to take the coast road down.

The purpose for taking this young fitter was to train him up for driving on the roads and, once we were out of any towns, I would let him take over driving. One evening just before sunset, I told him he should now be looking for a truck bay, and with that, I saw this big flash from the passenger seat and asked him if he saw it too. He looked out the rear vision mirror and said it looked like we were on fire.

I told him to look for a safe place to stop but he was unable to come across one, so I told him to pull over as much as he could because the fire was now totally visible from the cab. When we came to a standstill, I grabbed the little fire extinguisher but all it did was spit out a short bust and stop. So I raced around to the front of the Autocar and took off one of the big fire extinguishers and held that to the seat of the fire, but it was no good. Then the fitter got hold of the last extinguisher and applied that, but again it ran out before the fire was out.

We looked at each other, and I said, "This ain't gonna look good in the papers, mate – one RAAF truck burnt while carrying a fire tender." On saying that, we both thought *what a pair of dickheads*.

Without saying anything, Jerry, the fitter, grabbed the keys to open the side panels to get another extinguisher out but when the door was opened, all of them had been cut through with an axe.

"Shit, mate," I said, "this is now bloody serious," and by the time we opened all the panels up, we found only a small unit, and with that we were able to see what the problem was: our main axle drive had snapped off at the hub and, with the wheel still attached, had come out of its housing, enough to let the oil out onto the brake drum. Each time the brakes were applied would induce the heat, and as we were now travelling down a hill, Jerry would have used his brakes quite heavily, but what to do with it? By now we had a big mob hanging around looking on.

When the metal was cool enough, we began to jack both the trailer and the load, and though the jack was for 15 tons, I knew that we were going to be at it all night.

At first, we dug under the sump and placed the jack there,

then with some timber, blocked it up. Removing the jack, we repeated the exercise until the hub was off the ground, then I got a chain and started to tie the hub up but found I needed to jack it even further up.

Once we were satisfied that all should be high enough, I once again started to chain it up. While this was going on, the crowd got bigger but at least some of them had a torch, which was a big help. But now that I felt confident, I kept tieing the chain up. Making my last knot, I put my hand through the centre and grabbed hold of the other end and just got my hand out when the trailer slipped off the jack, snapping the loop of the chain and leaving me in a state of shock. It just missed by millimetres. I felt really lucky and thankful that I wasn't caught in the loop of the chain as it would have taken my hand clean off at the wrist. But I couldn't stand around thinking about it and got right back to work.

Jerry and I pulled the wheel out with the axle still attached. Looking down the road, I said, "Well, mate, we may as well let the bastard go and wherever it stops is where we will camp for a couple of days." Once we let it go, we finished up sorting the truck out and was back on the road but at such a slow speed that left a string of cars behind us that took an hour to pass when we finally came to rest in a quiet little hollow.

The next day we were up checking the vehicle for damage and getting a message back to Base for the parts. We were about twelve miles from Grafton on the Pacific Highway, and once that list was sent by phone, we made our way back to camp. I started to worry about how long we would be there, and just on nightfall, I walked over the road to where the only house was for miles. We knocked on the door and made ourselves known, and after that, these young people allowed us to use their shower and toilets.

We were now stuck there. On the fourth day, a car pulled

up and the driver asked us if we needed anything, and I said we could do with a ride into Grafton to find out how things were going for parts. He took us in and brought us back, then asked us how was our grub was holding out. I knew how much we had but was more concerned as to how long we would be stuck there. To answer his question, I said, "Well, we could do with a feed," and with that he took us up the road about a mile and into this banana plantation. After all the introductions, his wife cooked up a meal. We stayed there and tried to offer ourselves for work but he was just happy to see us right.

The next morning I heard the sound of glass and getting up out of the cab, I saw a milkman and asked him to drop a bottle a day off and paid for a week supply right then. With that, we settled in. That afternoon I got the newspaper delivered, then Monday, the chap organised some bread and that was full circle for home deliveries.

The rain had started on the evening we broke down, and it hadn't stopped, and although it wasn't heavy, it was just a bloody pain being wet each time we went out to stretch our legs or Jerry to check the vehicle.

It also gave me the shits when I had to cook in it as there wasn't any dry ground around, but more so the timber in the area was too wet to build a fire to at least dry our clothes.

Jerry wasn't a bad sort of a young fella; he seemed to accept our situation as a natural part of our work and never complained about a thing. This made our time together far easier because I had enough worries without the thought of being stuck with a bloody whinger. I guessed his attitude was because of his Asian descent as they had more tolerance towards situations, but it was a pleasure for me not only because of these reasons but also his company was great.

Each morning while Jerry repaired bits on the vehicle, I would start our day off by switching on the siren to let our neighbours know we were up and at it, then bash our breakie together. And still the bloody rain came down, but, on this particular morning, large pools of water had congregated around this little hollow we were in. Jerry felt the need to jack the axle up to prevent water from getting into the sump. With that done, I mentioned to him that I was going to the RSL for a couple of beers and did he want to join me. *Well, stupid question, Dave!* So we cleaned up and departed for the RSL.

We arrived at the door and I asked the chap there if we could use the facilities of the club for the afternoon, and he just looked at me and said, "Yes, mate, you'll be okay, but that monkey with you can't come in!"

At first, I wasn't sure what he'd said, and looked at him with my mouth open, then I said, "What was that you said?"

He said, "You're fine to come in, but you'll have to send that monkey with you back to the plantation!"

Well, that fired me up. "Who the fucken hell do you think you're talking to, mate! This bloke is a serving member just like myself and is also entitled to use these facilities."

I looked at Jerry and before saying more, but Jerry walked up to the doorman and said, "I might be a monkey to you, mate, but what zoo did they find you in, you fucken gorilla," and at the same time put his RAAF ID on the counter. He kept talking: "Anyway, this monkey has a name and I would like to use your facilities," and with that started to walk into the main lounge. *Well*, I thought, *good for you*, and followed him in, but we could feel the atmosphere was so thick you could cut it. Nevertheless, we stood our ground and got our beer even though the barman showed signs of great stress.

I felt for Jerry over this as it wasn't that long back that I was the centre of attention over the Vietnam protest, and yet this seemed to be the norm in this part of the country and the first time I had ever witnessed it. It all came down to the fact that the

Asians were moving into the banana industries and taking over some of the local plantations, so here we have a bunch of single-minded idiots idolizing the thoughts of others and complaining to each other like the typical bar-room politician that this lucky country is no more because of the Asians, yet if they got off there arse for five minutes they just may be able to see that the only people outside working in the rain were the Asians.

We stayed there for that Wednesday afternoon happy hour and kept a high profile around the pool table, and each time Jerry went up for booze, I'd give him a wink to let him know that I was one hundred per cent behind him. I wasn't going to let this bunch of pricks slice our afternoon up because of their preconceived opinions.

On sunset, we decided to leave for camp, and on the way out I told the doorman that we'd be back the next day.

We arrived back to find the whole area under water and had to make our way through it to get to the vehicle, but the main concern was the sump. So during that evening, while working in water halfway up our legs, we began to jack the sump as far as we could until we ran out of blocks and just prayed the rain would ease up enough to let the ground water run off.

Although the next morning it had, I told Jerry I was going to contact Base and let them know our situation and that our food and money were critical. Upon my return, Jerry was talking to the person who'd provided us with a meal two days previous, and he was there to see if we could come up again for tea. Well that was great, I thought, as the pair of us had been wet for the full day and needed somewhere to dry our gear, and so we left with him.

Our situation was like this for the following week. Then on Wednesday, totally out of the blue, our part arrived, and Jerry and I got about replacing and getting underway. Leaving that hollow in ankle-deep water after three weeks and being on the road again was the greatest feeling. We never had time to think about the friends we'd made but I'm sure they understood how anxious we were after being there for so long.

We arrived at Regents Park and unloaded the fire truck, then I got my kit and started to head for the showers, as we both looked like wild men from the bush – we hadn't had a shave for two weeks and our hair was a total mess, along with the fact that I was in civvies while driving as my overalls were still wet. I hadn't got far, however, when I came across my old section commander from Darwin, and as we'd never got along while I was up there, I didn't think much would have changed now. I was right. He took one look at me and said, "What the hell do you think you are up to LAC Darcey!" and before I had time to explain, he started on me, saying what a shower of shit I looked like, what a disgusting mess, and where the hell have you been dressed like that?

Without thinking, I just said, "Get knotted, sir," and before I could finish, he said, "Right! I'm placing you on a charge," then the prick told me to go and disinfect myself and report back to his office in uniform!

I then told him he better get his facts right before doing that and said to him, You'd better ring Tottenham and talk to John." But he wasn't having that, and so I thought, *Well fuck you, mate!* and without waiting around, located Jerry and told him to get his gear into the truck as we were leaving right then, and on the way out I told him what had happened.

When I got to Tottenham, I went straight to John's office and told him the full story. Upon seeing the pair of us, he started to laugh as we hadn't even had a wash before we left Sydney some two days previous, but this time we were well on the nose and looking completely rooted for our ordeal. But he did fix it so I wasn't charged.

I was given a week's leave for that breakdown, and during

that time explained to Lita that I was more than anxious now than ever to get out, and so I started to organise my tools and equipment. I brought a few electrical tools from the profits of my cabinets and left them packed, ready to go over to Perth, and slowly got about my business in acquiring as much stock as I could to give me a good start once I was out. Though I still had some four months to go, I wasn't letting anything pass my way.

I arrived at work to be confronted by John saying that I was to take the Autocar up to Wagga-Wagga, and I was to train another driver, so the following day I was off with Bill, who had been at Tottenham for about three years and had been trying to get onto the heavy vehicles.

Although our trip to Wagga Wagga was without trouble, I was given a backload to RAAF Base, Sale, in Victora. To shorten our trip, I decided to go over the mountains along the logging tracks. I had never been that way before so I pulled into the local Police station to ask, but it was closed, and as I had already started the trip, we kept going.

Not long after leaving Tallangatta, it started to rain. This was okay until we reached Mitta Mitta when the sealed road stopped and the dirt started. With the rain, it had turned into a mud bath, and I began to wonder whether I should turn around but there just wasn't any place to do that for the size of the vehicle, so I kept going. I explained to Bill it would be better if I drove as I wasn't sure about the conditions up ahead and he felt the same way about it.

Before long, the track went to a single lane and the truck tyres were well into the muddy and slippery track of the logging trucks, and I could feel that Bill wasn't sure about this road. I could see how concerned he became when the truck started to slip sideways, but I assured him that all was fine and explained that, in situations like this, he should watch my actions. After an hour of this, he felt quite confident that he was in good hands.

We were now starting to descend the mountain and, though the truck was screaming as I kept it in low gear, the weight of our load kept pushing it on. To avoid applying the cab brakes, I would turn the wheel into the bank and hit the trailer brakes, which helped retain the speed and keep the vehicle in the ruts. We reached the bottom, but the road did such a hairpin turn onto a timber bridge I was unable to move the vehicle around it.

I stopped the truck and took a good long look at the bridge and the angle I needed to get around it. Then Bill picked up a rock and dropped it over the sideless bridge to hear how deep it was – we never heard it hit anything.

I told him not to worry about that as the main thing was to get the vehicle over it, not in it, and for the next hour in the bloody rain, we worked our guts out to build a makeshift ramp to get the rear wheels of the trailer over and onto the bridge. After satisfying ourselves that there wasn't anything else we could do but have go, I climbed into the cab, thinking, *This is bloody dangerous – one wrong move and the trailer with its load could end up in the river.* I only had one chance, and it had to be the right one.

With Bill standing on the bridge while I made one last attempt to reverse to adjust the front wheels to get the maximum turn, I changed into forward and started to mount the bridge while Bill gave me some guidance. Then with the greatest of ease, I drove the front tyre upon the bridge gunnel and with half the tyre hanging over the edge while keeping my eyes on Bill's directions, gunned the motor, giving it all it could take. When changing gears to get more speed out of it, I noticed Bill jumping around, waving like mad, then he bolted for the other side, as I kept on moving. Then I heard the rear tyres of the trailer scraping along the gunnel, this followed by a bump as they mounted the gunnel. In turn, the front tyre descended back onto the bridge proper, then it was my turn to give this vehicle all it had to offer.

By now I could see Bill with his mouth open and pointing to his head, meaning I was a complete nut-case.

Then, with luck, good guidance and God's help, I was over, only to find what Bill had been jumping up and down about. When we got to the other side of the bridge, he noticed a sign reading: Maximum weight: TEN TON. My first thoughts were: *Shit, we must be twenty-ton all up*, then I said to Bill, "Well, mate, someone up there must be looking after me."

And he replied, "No, Dave. No bastard would be that stupid!" But he did also say that he wouldn't want to be on the road with anyone else now, as he'd learnt one hell of a lot over the last week that he couldn't get in six years on Base. He told me that John had told him that he'd get a lot of experience on the road with me, and after that night, he felt really confident to do anything.

Bill drove the rest of the way, and all he could talk about on his return to Base was the night we were stuck trying to cross this bridge. From then on I couldn't get rid of him, although he wasn't too bad to get along with; he just wanted to hang around me all the time.

As for me, I could feel this discontent amongst the other drivers as I was being sent away far more often. They had started distancing themselves from me, which made me now feel as though I was an arse-lick. But, as they didn't know I was being discharged soon and I wanted all the extra cash I could get, that was fine by me as I knew it would only be spent on the booze. Therefore, their attitude towards me was their problem, and if they wanted to ignore me, then stuff them all.

Before long, I was on the road again with Bill, but this time we were going to Sydney Regents Park, but this time I let Bill do all the driving, his first stop Gundagai for fuel.

Then we were off to Goulburn. On arriving, we headed for

the RSL club, and it was here that Bill began to do his trick. I had never seen a bloke chat up the girls like him, and though he was good for a laugh, he was after something more serious. He was soon was talking to this young girl around twenty-four years old, slightly plump and average but that didn't seem to worry him. As long as the girl was friendly, he kept on talking to her.

Eventually, he came over to me with her and sat down, saying he was going for a meal and would I be here or with the vehicle later. I told him I'd make a bed on top of the load and not to worry about me. Then just as I was about to finish what I was saying, this bloke came up to the table and started to talk to the girl. They seemed to know each other pretty well. The next thing was we were invited over to their place for a meal. I looked at Bill and said, "That's up to you, mate," and with that, we all left, but not before we picked up a case of booze.

We arrived at their house and started drinking and generally talking about the Airforce. About three hours later, this bloke asked me where our truck was parked, and of course, I answered him, "At the Police station. Why's that?"

"Well, I was thinking that you may as well stay here tonight, but I'm not driving to the cop-shop to get your sleeping gear."

"Look," I said, "drop me off at the pub, while I walk around and get it, and while I'm out, I'll grab some more booze," knowing that is what he wanted anyway. So we left Bill and this bloke's girlfriend singing and dancing around.

After grabbing our sleeping bags and having a couple of beers, we headed back to his house, only to find Bill in the bath and half-drunk with this bloke's girlfriend washing his back. As we stood there, Bill started to wash his hair then, without any idea of what he was doing, reached up to the shelf and took down what looked like a bottle of shampoo. This bloke's girlfriend started to yell at him not to use it, but Bill wouldn't let it go; he hung onto it and rolled around the bath while we just stood back and pissed ourselves laughing, then again she tried to get the bottle off him. Again it was on, with water splashing over the edge of the bath and covering her with it.

"Stuff ya then!" she said. "Use it if you want to," and walked out with us.

Ten minutes later, Bill came out of the bathroom with a towel around him and a sober, not too happy look. Again we pissed ourselves laughing at the sight of him. At first, I couldn't believe it: he just stood there looking at me with this dumb expression, trying to find the words. Finally, when he did snap out of it, in a half whimpering voice, he said, "Look at me. Look at me. I've changed colour … what the fuck happened?"

I didn't know exactly what was going on, but this bloke's girlfriend said that he just washed in the dye she used for wool. Well, that cracked me right up; I just couldn't stop. In fact, apart from Bill, we were all in fits of laughter while Bill tried to figure out the best way to get it off.

Around two o'clock in the morning, and after some six or seven baths later, Bill was looking more normal, but the BLUE DYE was still over his legs and feet. He came up to me and said, "Dave, you won't say anything about this, mate."

"Shit, Bill, how could I explain it, apart from saying that you're cold, and that's going to be a little hard as it's now summer. But don't worry, I won't say a thing."

So the night ended with us departing from Sydney around 8.30 the next morning, with the idea of seeing them on our return trip, but we never did, which was probably a good thing.

We arrived back at Base on time and each went our own way, but I couldn't help noticing the way the other drivers still ignored me so the following day I asked Leo to see me at the wet mess for a beer. Once there, it wasn't long before the subject of me came up.

"You've changed a bit, Dave," Leo said. "It seems that you

don't want to have much to do with your mates."

I shook my head. "It appears that they have an attitude problem with me, and you know what, Leo, I couldn't give a shit right now, as every time I come back from a trip, they distance themselves further. Apart from that, I haven't been in trouble of any sort while I've been away, and if that doesn't tell you something about me, then you must be just as blind as they are."

He looked at me. "What the hell do you mean by that?" he asked.

"Look, Leo," I said, "I figure that if I'm around, they have someone to talk about, and you know what that ends up as for me, so while I'm out of sight, I'm also out of mind."

"Yeah," he said, "but now you've been called an arse lick, Dave, and I know you're not, but it's just that you don't say much or, in fact, do anything at all but ignore us."

I looked at Leo and knew I could fully trust him. "Leo, you don't know yet – I haven't told anyone my plans – but I've decided to discharge myself come July, and I'm trying to keep out of trouble and save, as well as make some extra cash."

"Shit, Dave, you're really getting out?"

"Yeah," I said. "I've had all the shit I can handle from here. Apart from a few blokes on this Base, I just can't stand the rest, and if anyone knows, you do. You've seen it all happen, from the shit I put up, which hasn't made it easy for me. But the decision to get out was easier than the one to stay."

I left Leo that night asking him to keep our conversation to himself, and arrived home to find the kids playing as usual and Lita getting the tea. I soon mentioned to her my conversation with Leo and the general attitude of the drivers and that I was now more than ever ready to get out of the service and settle into civvie street.

During that week Lita and I talked often about the future

that lay ahead, and the one thing that was brought up was where we were going to live. I told her that I would be happy if she made that decision as I had no objections.

I was also gearing my mind up as to what type of house we should get, as I was entitled to a war service home loan, so from that night I started designing various house plans. This brought Lita and I into some arguments at times, as she was always one to worry about the money end of things. I was a dreamer and looked forward to being better off, while Lita was more than happy to have the basics. I always felt, though, that if we did get a loan and build our house, I might as well design what I felt would be big enough for us all.

The most important thing on my mind was the kids' future and being settled in one place long enough for them to have a sound schooling without any interruptions or upheavals that wouldn't allow them that one basic right. As a person who never had the ground rules taught, I felt the real need to make sure that didn't happen to them. Also, while living in the married quarters, I noticed how the other kids behaved and how aggressive they were – and it wasn't only the boys doing it – the girls were just as bad.

At first, I thought it just might be me getting older, but while we were in Darwin, Lita and I could see the difference in the kids there after just arriving from Perth. Then, with Lita spending some five months in Perth, I could see a greater change in the way the kids just had no discipline. I had stopped on one occasion to chastise a group for kicking the shit out of these shop shutters and was given such a mouthful of abuse I was left wondering what sort of parents they had. But it did help make my mind up that I didn't want my kids to become a party to that sort of lifestyle.

I wouldn't say that I was the world's best father or husband in any respect, but I only had ourselves to think about and put to use what I missed out on, even though Lita would often say I was wrong. We began to argue over issues that were in the best interest of the kids, yet all the time Lita set the ground rules, so at times I felt a little hurt. It soon passed, but I did find I was getting less and less involved, and that was my choice because I somehow felt Lita was right and my facts were based upon her upbringing, which I liked, apart from being too overprotective to allow them the normal tumbles in a day's play.

Nicole and Michelle would always want to help me bang nails or tacks in while I was making furniture, and though they could see Dad standing there banging away, they just had to join in. Each time I said no meant nothing to them, so I would weaken and end up giving them a small hammer each and a tin of tacks, but after hitting their fingers not once but twice, they would end up crying, and all the time going mad at me as they just wanted to do the same as me, and that was to hit the tack in with one knock of the hammer, so after many tries, and a lot of crying, they only ended up with sore and blue fingers.

Although Nicole was now six and Michelle three, their different personalities could be seen. Nicole was attending school just over the road and had settled in quite well; she would come home each day with her drawings and show great pride in her achievements on paper. She just loved talking and drawing and when she joined the two together I could pick up this tenderness and innocence she captured on paper. Although I wasn't there all the time to see them, I would make the effort in my spare time to ask her what she had drawn.

Michelle, or Tiger, as I sometimes called her, all she did was roar and eat, but it was noticeable she was jealous of Nicole. If Nicole was reading or showing me her drawing, she would want to join in. I didn't mind, except that she would push Nicole aside for me to give her attention. Nicole wouldn't say much, and me, trying to be the father to them both, never realised what was happening. I guess these rules stuck for a while but were soon brought to my attention when Lita said to me one day that I didn't seem to have much to do with Nicole these days, and I was paying more attention to Michelle, but in my mind I felt the best thing to do was give Michelle some attention first, and after that I could pay more attention to Nicole without Michelle pushing her way in, as she usually did

"Well, Dave," Lita said, "you're wrong. You should give them the same time together."

"Alright," I answered, and so after that I would try and give them the time together, but the fighting and crying ended up giving me the screaming shits. I tried to explain to Lita that I just prefer to talk to them quietly, but she could see for herself how things turned out. And when I came home from work, it was the last bloody thing I needed.

April 1977

With Easter now just around the corner, I thought I'd have a go at selling some eggs and hot cross buns on the Base, so during Easter week and just before the break, I drove to Laverton, Point Cook, and around Tottenham, taking orders from some 150 members. Then, while doing my duties, I made a slight detour to the Red Tulip factory and paid nearly $365.00 for eggs, then headed off to the bakers in Footscray for the hot cross buns.

Although I was running from Base to Base, I decided to start from Point Cook and, after filling the orders, made this sign reading 'HOT CROSS BUNS for sale' and hung it on the vehicle, then I left for Laverton and once again filled my orders. But I was having trouble selling the buns, so my last chance was at Tottenham. Upon arriving, I set out as fast as I could and kept on the move all the time to make sure I wasn't sprung at my caper. While I managed to get rid of all the eggs, the bloody buns were hard to sell. However, I just managed to quit them, apart from two dozen. I left these in the smoko room for the drivers, which was just as well as the word got back to John. When he came into the smoko room and found all of us eating them, he asked me where I'd got them from.

"Footscray bakers," I said. "Why's that, John?"

"Well," he said, "I got the message that you were selling eggs and hot cross buns."

"Yeah," I said, "I was only giving a few blokes some buns they asked me to pick up, and the rest I paid for and brought here, as you can see."

Nothing more was said about that, but when I arrived home I counted up my cash, and the results were $575.00 less $365.00, which gave me a clear profit of $210.00 for the day's work. I called Lita over, telling her what I had done and the extra cash we had, and that I was now going to use it to buy some more tools. So that weekend I spent the whole $210.00 on electrical tools and left them in their boxes for shipping to Perth.

During the next two months, we geared ourselves up for packing. I was still finishing some furniture off so had very little time to help Lita, but as our main concern was how long it would be before we got a house and what we should take ourselves and what had to go for storage, this left us with the problem of where we were going to stay. Then Lita thought that her Mum and Dad would let us stay there for a while, which made her choice much easier as to what went to storage. As for me, I packed all my tools up and left them in the shed to take with us.

At the end of May, I was sent up to Sydney for the last time. It was a wet trip up, the rain never stopping, and about halfway back, while stopping at a roadside cafe, I heard that parts of

Laverton were flooded. For some reason, I had this strange feeling that I was amongst those flooded so bolted from that cafe and drove like a bat out of hell.

I arrived home around 4.00pm to find Lita up to her knees trying to lift the furniture up that was for one of my clients – it was too late for that, I thought –let's have a look at the tools.

Upon opening the shed door, I could see all my electrical equipment was underwater. It just broke me up to see that mess. I had spent two years saving and two years making furniture to buy these tools for my future work, and now they were rooted.

Lita put her hand on my back and said, "Great neighbours we've got, Dave. They were looking out the window, watching me lifting and struggling to get the stuff out of the water."

When I looked over, I could see them standing there and got pretty wild with them. I yelled and abused the shit out of them, but knew that it was no good to carry on like that, and though everything in the shed was covered, I took it all into the house and started to pull them all down and dry them with the hairdryer in the off-chance that I might be able to save something.

The next day I contacted my insurance company about the matter and was told that they couldn't pay up on rising water, and because no panels were broken, I had no claim, yet I was covered for storm damage. But the bastards never paid on that technicality, so it only left one thing for me to do and that was to dry out what I could and send the rest down for checking. After a week or so at a cost to me, I repacked it all but this time stored it high off the shed floor as the rain hadn't stopped long enough to empty the drains.

To me, this was like the welcome I had received on arriving, and now I was going, it seemed to me the Melbourne weather was trying to say goodbye.

Then when I arrived at work one morning, I was given another application for discharge, my section commander saying to me that my previous one wasn't filled in correctly – it was something to do with my future employment and that what I'd put down on the application was unknown to them.

I looked at John and began to laugh, and he asked me what was so funny.

"Well, John," I said, "when I filled the last one in, and it asked me what my future employment was, I wrote down that I was going to be a 'Tram Seat Sniffer'."

"Shit, Dave! You didn't tell them that."

"Yep," I said, still laughing over it.

"Well," he said, "you'd better get it sorted out this morning as you haven't much time left."

So I filled it in as 'unknown at this point in time'.

The following week I received my posting to Pearce for discharge and so began to make the final arrangements to leave. While getting myself cleared from each section on the Base, I noticed a change towards me. It was as if I was a traitor to the system; I wasn't made to feel that I had filled my contract and wanted to move on and better myself. The further I went into it, the worse it became for me. Then with only two days left, I was instructed by the Transport Officer to buy a new hat and shoes, and though I told him I was being discharged, he said it didn't make any difference, and as he was the last person to sign my clearance sheet, I knew he had me by the short and curlies. I was pretty wild about having to buy these items and could find no one to help me around this situation. So, upon meeting his request, he signed my sheet.

Before I left his office, I told him that it was people like him that was turning members with years of experience away from the service, and that the time I had served under him had been the worst in my career and that I was now really pleased that I wouldn't have to put up with his shit anymore.

He looked at me and pointed to the door without saying a word, and I didn't say anything else to him just in case he put me on a charge. But hell, I wanted to say plenty.

Although I was now ready to leave Tottenham, I still had three days left before departing for Perth. During that time, I wasn't given much time by the other drivers. Some of my old friends did take the time to see me, and I invited them to have a final drink with me, for old time's sake. I was also starting to question whether I had made the right decision to get out of the service, and was becoming a little confused. Maybe I just needed a change or a posting out of Tottenham, but now that the ball was rolling I decided to give myself the chance, knowing damn well I could re-enlist should I change my mind.

The evening of my last day was spent in the wet mess having a quiet drink with my old mates, and without much ado, I departed for home. Lita was now sorting out the final bits for me to pack in the car and the kids and our dog Marty were ready. At midday of the following day, we left after saying goodbye to Nicole and Lita's friends.

I had no plans for stopping overnight anywhere as I intended to just keep driving until I needed a rest but, when it was dark enough for night driving, my headlights just did not seem strong enough to see clearly and after an hour or so, fog suddenly appeared and made matters worse. But I kept going, but soon found myself on the wrong side of the road and a bloody semitrailer coming straight for me. I grabbed the wheel and pulled it hard to the left while the semitrailer pulled to the right, just missing me. *Shit*, I thought, *I haven't ever experienced this type of driving before.* Somewhat shaken from my ordeal, I got out of the car and realised that my lights weren't working, and was more than pleased that we were okay. So now I knew the problem, I drove to the nearest garage where we camped for the night and made arrangements for the part the next morning.

I never did get the part from that garage as I needed as much road behind me as possible as I only allowed four days to travel across to Perth and I felt sure I could pick up a headlight in Adelaide. But this was not so, so I kept driving while I had plenty of daylight. I found the part in Port Augusta and fitted it while Lita and the kids had a meal. Then after an hour, we left for the big night drive.

It wasn't long before the kids were asleep, Marty included, while Lita stayed awake and made hot drinks for us both. Around 2.30am, I pulled over for a quick rest while it was cool and was soon in the land of nod.

We were woken by these arse holes driving around our car, blowing their horn and acting like the real dick heads. So to avoid any trouble, I got my shotgun from under the seat and hung the barrel out of the window just to let them know that I was ready to party. When the dust settled and they noticed the shotgun, they left in the same manner as they'd arrived – bloody quick. I was now well awake and, with the events that had just taken place I couldn't see me sleeping at all, so I drove on until we reached Eucla at about 5.00am.

I refuelled the car and rested for about half an hour, and while looking down the road thinking it was going to be a real scorcher of a day as the sun was just breaking the horizon, I felt that I'd better get going. The main problem on my mind though was the bloody roos that usually moved around at first light, so I asked Lita to keep an eye open just in case I missed seeing one and had to brake heavily.

Not long after leaving Eucla, we began to notice the roos on the edge of the road and so I dropped my speed to around 25 to 35 miles per hour. While staying alert, I noticed headlights in the rear vision mirror coming at a fast rate of knots and no sooner had I mentioned it to Lita that this vehicle passed me.

"Shit," I said, "that's one silly bugger looking for trouble." He must have been doing around 100mph as I felt our car move from his wind.

Then Lita said, "Well, at least he'll frighten the roos out of our way."

"Yeah," I said. "That's if he doesn't get clobbered first. Look how far up the road he is," and just as I said that I noticed his brake lights and blue smoke from his rear end.

I looked at Lita and said, "God knows what we'll find when we get to him."

A good three minutes later, we arrived. No one was outside the car, but it was stopped in the middle of the road so I drove past it and reversed up to him and got out and started to pull out my towing chain. Looking over, I could see the blood and guts of the roo he'd hit and the damage to the car. When the driver got out, I could see that the blood and guts were not only on the outside – his wife was covered in it from head to toe. Luckily, they were not hurt, but the car was a mess with half the radiator spitting steam from it. The headlight and fender and half the bonnet was gone. I told them they were lucky to have their lives – his wife wouldn't get out of the car but sat there in total shock.

I told this bloke that I would tow him to Mundrabilla about forty miles down the track, and once we arrived, I told him that he could expect a long wait there as parts for his car would be hard to get. So we left him and his wife with their troubles and headed off for Cocklebiddy where we fed the kid and ourselves and I gave myself a good hour's rest before we left for Norseman and onto Coolgardie. We arrived there at around 7.30 pm, and while I was refuelling the car I heard this loud noise coming down the road. *Bloody hell!* It was that pelican I had towed that morning coming down the road like a mad man. Well, he pulled up and asked me what the road ahead was like and I told him that the next 130 miles were the worst for roos on this road and, though the garage owner said the same thing, it didn't make any difference as, when he filled up, he left at high speed. We drove on to Southern Cross that night but I never saw them again.

We spent that night at Southern Cross and departed for Perth at first light, arriving in Armadale, where Lita's parents showed great interest in the kids. Me? I climbed into bed and stayed there until the following morning when I put my uniform on for the last time and headed off for Pearce to have my final discharge papers signed. By 10am, I was given a handshake and told I was now a civilian without any thanks for the last twelve years I had given to the Air Force.

I guess I felt a little hurt and somewhat confused as I walked out of the Base that day. I really didn't quite know what to expect or what was expected of me. I felt alone and without anyone. This feeling of emptiness stayed with me until I reached Armadale. To ease the feeling, I took myself down to the Tudor Rose and had a bloody good drink on myself, and there became very pissed off and disgruntled inside. Though I had made the decision to get out, and I was now out, the way I was treated I was so happy that I hadn't given them twenty years of service. But now I was on my own, I had some serious thinking to do over the next couple of weeks.

Part Eight

Work and Family

25 July 1977

Over the following days, I worked from sun-up till sunset. By the ninth day, I informed the site supervisor that the work was completed and was given another house to fix out. This one was a lot smaller, and by Sunday, that was also completed. On Monday, the site supervisor mentioned that I'd better pick up my money, so I arrived at the office and was handed a cheque for $920.00. I first looked at the cheque then thought he had made a mistake, and when I told him that I thought he'd overpaid me, he said that it was correct. Well, I was over the moon: what a lump I'd got, so I was off down to the bank and straight home to Lita.

I felt good that day. Although I wasn't happy living with her parents, at least my work was coming together for me. And the time in planning our future looked better from that point.

The next day I decided to contact Defence Homes to make an application for a war service loan, and over the next week I was in and out of various building sites fixing doors and kitchen units. Then I was contacted by Fini Homes again to start on a new home in Armadale.

When I arrived there, I asked the site supervisor about a corner block that was being cleared, and he told me that they would be building on that one next week. I asked him for the plans as I might be interested, and being the sort of bloke he was, he gave me all the information he had, and from that, I explained to Lita that we just might be able to afford it.

The following day I started to fix this house out and by Friday it was nearly completed. Deciding that I should get a steel cover made for the trailer, that afternoon I drove over to see my long lost mate, Barry (Butch). I found his address in an industrial estate and he was really pleased to see me. We talked for hours about what we'd been up to over the past twelve years, and before long we were down the pub drinking over the lost times. Butch was now running his own sheet metal business, called Superior Steel Manufacturers. That gave me a laugh as the size of his workshop was not bigger than a garage, but I liked his style.

Once we got down to business in what I needed, I left the trailer with him for a week with the intentions of picking it up the following Friday – the reasons made for that date was so we could get on the booze again.

I decided to return to work for the rest of the day, which was a good thing as I met Tony, the owner of Fini Homes. He told me that he could work out a deal for me if I brought that block, and while I listened to him I felt quite confident that it could work. So I started the wheels in motion with the Defence Service homes, stating my intentions, and tried to organise a loan from the bank over the phone but was told that I had to go down and see them.

That afternoon, Lita and I, armed with my banking books, headed off to the bank I had been saving with since I was fifteen years old, and the account I opened at that time was a Home Saving account so I felt quite confident that we had no problems.

At the bank, we asked for the Loans manager and once he arrived, we made ourselves known to him and the reason we were there. But after explaining to him, he told me that I couldn't have a loan because they weren't giving loans out for at least another month. So I asked him for a withdrawal form and started to fill it to take all our money out, and though he said to hold on and not be too hasty about it, I said, "No loan, mate, then you can't have my cash," and I handed him the withdrawal form, and said, "Put the lot in a bag."

Once that was done, we left for the next bank in the street, and, waltzing up to the counter, I placed my bag of money in front of the Loans manager there and asked him about a loan.

But the answer was the same as before, so we walked out of there and into the next bank, only to have the same thing happen. But this time, we had only one bank left.

We walked up to the counter and this time I asked for the manager, and after explaining to him that I was getting a War Service Home Loan and that I really needed a bridging loan, his answer was 'Yes,' so i told him he had better look after our cash and I'd be back to sort out the details the next day. Upon giving him the details the next day, I notified Fini Homes that I would be buying that block with a new home.

The following Tuesday, I was asked to start on my house and I wanted this to be one of the best jobs I had done, not to say that all my previous ones were bad but because this was our first home, I wanted it perfect in every respect. I worked alongside the roofing carpenter for the first stage and after a couple of weeks I installed our kitchen and did the final fixing of all the skirting and doors. The feeling I had was so great that I wanted to celebrate it and so, knowing that Lita wouldn't have a drink, and for me to take booze back to the house was a no-no, I left to see Butch and how he was situated.

Not long after I arrived, he shut up shop and we both headed for the pub, and even though it was only around 2pm, we gave it heaps till around 4pm. But as Butch was running short of cash, we decided to leave, intending this time to arrive at his place sober. Well, it wasn't long after leaving the pub that I thought I had a flat tyre so I pulled over and just as I did, a police car pulled up in front of us. Before I started to say anything, he asked me to move it.

"Okay, officer," I said, "but I thought I may have a flat tyre," and started to walk to the rear of the trailer, only to find all was okay. The Police officer was now yelling at me to move it, so I got back into the car and, just as I started to settle in, they both came up, opened my door and told me to get out as I was drunk.

A short blow in the bag confirmed that I wasn't, but it did give me a fright, as I felt they were gunning for me, so I looked at Butch and said, "Well, old mate, I don't know about you but this fella is in need after that," so we headed off for Midland where I parked the car outside the pub and got stuck into a few glasses of beer.

When we were finished and ready to leave, on the way out I decided to go to the dunny, only found myself in the bloody Women's as some bastard had taken the sign off. I never noticed this until I was on my way out when I was told that it was. I felt a right proper dickhead and Butch just stood there laughing about it.

My troubles started when I was walking to my car. Butch said, "Look the bloody coppers are at the car," and with that I knew that I couldn't drive away. Just then this bloke from Coles pointed to us while calling the police and, as I didn't quite know what we had done, I followed Butch in leaving the area. As soon as we got around the corner, we began to run. We went up this short lane and over a brick wall behind the Town Hall, then over another brick wall where my car was, but the Police were waiting, and we were nabbed and lumbered into the paddy wagon, the pair of us asking what was this was about. Much to my surprise, I was charged with drunk driving and Butch with disorderly conduct. At 5.30pm, we were both behind bars.

We decided during conversation that we'd both better stay away from each other for a while until things cooled down. When I did finally get to sleep, it was with a lot of thoughts of what to do the next day. I didn't worry so much about the drunk driving charge, but more so that way Lita just left me there, and the fact that I wasn't going to be received with a welcome only added to my mental torment, but I did feel strongly about leaving Armadale for a while as I knew I was upsetting her family. Where to go was the question. I needed work and if Butch would come with me as he said, no telling what would happen. The one thing that I knew was we both had to stay off the booze, no matter what.

The next morning saw us both in Midland Court, and though Butch had his charge dropped, I had to pay $350.00 fine. Upon being released, we drove around to Butch's place and picked up some equipment and placed it in the trailer, then I drove up to Armadale and left the car in the drive. As Lita came out of the house, I told her I was off. "Don't know where … don't really care," and with that, Butch and I headed back to his place to do some serious thinking.

Around 5.30pm, Sandra came home from work and when she saw Butch and I together she started on him. Butch, like me, was non-violent to women and just took it in his stride, but when Sandra told him to piss off and not come back, he looked to me and said, "Well, let's go," and after he packed some clothes, we left in his van. Only we didn't know where to go, so we stopped at the first pub and sorted things out. The one thing we needed was tools and they were at Armadale so the decision was made to get my car.

We arrived in Armadale during the night at about 11pm. When I tried to get the car, Marty started to bark which brought Lita's father outside, so I decided to leave it till the following morning. We slept in the van and woke up cold and hungry. Then around 9.00am, I walked into the yard and told Lita's father that I was taking my car and, though I could see the pair of them were upset, I said I'd give Lita a ring later, then I left before Lita returned home from taking Nicole to school.

Butch left his van at a friend's house and, around 10am, we headed south with no particular place to go. We bought some clothes at Pinjarra as the ones I was wearing were stuffed, and so the pair of us left looking clean but feeling dirty. From there, we headed for Albany to try and find work, Butch doing all the driving. We took things easy until we reached Wagin where we camped in the local cemetery as we felt it was the quietest place in town.

The next day we reached Albany and started looking over the local building sites; there were only a few so it did take long, then we headed down to the beachfront and the Star Hotel. After some time just sitting there contemplating our next move, the publican started to talk to us, and the subject of building came up. He said he couldn't find a builder to handle a small job for him, which made my ears prick up. I told him that we could more than likely do the job, so he asked me if I would look at the job as it was next door on the pub grounds. I was out that door in a flash, whispering to Butch to leave the talking to me. He said he intended to, as this was outside his line of work. Well, it wasn't long before he arrived with the keys to show us around this disused building with a single room on the second level. He said that he had just won a contract to accommodate twelve fishermen from a fleet that was arriving next month, and what he needed was to divide the big room into nine small units.

"Well," I said, "that's not a problem. I'll work out a price for you with labour only, and you pay for the materials and our tucker and accommodation," and so he left Butch and me up there to sort out the price.

As soon as he left I told Butch that this could be ours if the price was right, and by that I meant labour only. There was about two weeks' work and if we charged him $75.00 per day it'd be a good price owing to his situation, but we would have to put a lot of hours in. I reckoned about ten hours per day to finish it in two weeks. We put in the price and got the job, left him with a list of materials we would need and headed for Two People Bay to pack up our stuff and left the place as we found it. Then it was back to Albany and the Star Hotel, where we settled in for the night.

At this point, I mentioned to Butch that we had to stay off the booze until the job was completed. He said, "Yeah, that's fine by me, but after two weeks, you'll be the one needing a beer."

I told him that I was going to save as much money as possible from this job and if I could leave here with $900.00, I'd be going okay.

Butch looked at me thinking it out for himself. "Sure, we could do it, Dave," he said.

"Well, I'm going to give it my best and I'll be fucken wild if you get on the piss while I'm up here working, okay!"

Butch said, "Let's do it!" And so the ground rules were set.

We worked hard over the first week, only stopping for meals and sleeping, but on Sunday afternoon, we took half a day off as the work was going along real fine and on Monday morning were well into it, pleasing the landlord with the results – he would often come over just to see how we were progressing, and upon each visit, he could see the difference which brought a smile to his face. This was going to be our last week there and, the end being in sight just spurred us on.

The next night I received a call from Lita wanting to know what the hell we were up to, and when I finished talking to her, she told me that the house was ready to move into and when could I be home to sort things out. Well, this was the best news I'd heard all week, and I told her that I would be at Mum Darcey's place and that I wasn't going to Armadale, but I would stay at a motel for the night. We said our goodbyes and I headed off to the bar where Butch was drinking orange juice.

"Butch," I said, "let's have a beer, old mate."

He looked at me and said, "I knew you would weaken," and before I could say anything else he ordered two glasses, then in the same mouthful asked what had brought this on. So I told him what Lita had said and that we were on our way back next

Friday.

"Good," he said. "I need to see Sandra and sort things out as well." So, after a few more beers, we both left as we wanted to get out as soon as possible.

Come Friday, I told the landlord to have the cash ready as agreed and straightaway he wrote a cash cheque out for $2,100.00. I passed it to Butch and told him to go to the bank and cash it while I finished off the last few bits. He gave me this strange look and then left, and about ten minutes later, he returned. I noticed his eyes were on everyone, and I asked him, "What the fuck's up with you, Butch?"

When we got inside, he pulled out the cash and said, "I've never seen so much money in one heap."

We arrived back in Perth around 3.00pm on Friday and arrangements were made from Mum's place that Lita would meet me there. She turned up at 5.30.

It was now two weeks before Christmas and I had a hell of a lot to do.

Christmas 1977

We moved into our new home two days before Christmas and, though the place was finished inside, the yard was a mess. So for the next few weeks, Lita's father and I started on the lawns and gardens, and as Lita's father was a retired gardener, it gave him an opportunity to apply these skills, of which I had very little. The big advantage was that he had been planning the style of garden Lita and I liked.

It may not have been the biggest house in the street, but at least my repayments were the best at $75.00 per month, and Lita wouldn't have to work to help with the repayments, like a big percentage of first homeowners – unless something happened to me that changed our situation.

Our furniture had been in storage for the past six months. Some of it was okay, but the damage done to my equipment and household items got my back up with the Service. While we were covered by insurance provided by the Air Force, we felt let down, as the choice of removalist was not the best but I had no grounds to complain as I was now in civvie street and therefore of no concern to them. Over the next few months, we did get some repairs carried out and what we had lost was compensated by cheque, but Lita would have much sooner had her things as the money couldn't replace them.

Nicole and Michelle were now settled into their rooms, and Lita and I were in the final stage of school enrolments. Everything just seemed to be working for us and I would at times sit back and think what the last six months had brought our way. Yeah, I may have been in debt and work was something I had to find. Once I did, the rewards were good both from the achievements and the independence point of view, so I couldn't understand why most ex-servicemen found it difficult to resettle into civvie street. I do remember that I joined the service as a young single man of nineteen, and I suppose this may have been why I felt it much easier as I was now married and had two children and of course I was thirty-two years old, which could be why I didn't find it hard.

I now felt quite cocky when it came to working; I felt I could handle any amount of it that came my way. More to the point, if I was looking for it, I knew one thing for sure, and that was I had to sell myself, not only with confidence but with an attitude that I had to make people believe and trust in me. I had found that only those aggressive enough were the ones in work. I would buy equipment to suit each project that came up, and once I got into it, there didn't seem to be anything stopping me.

My first priority was to support my family, and the only way

I knew how to do that was work, and during the times I was doing small jobs around Armadale I knew it would last forever. I began to think back to the time I was in Albany with Butch and the money we both earned there, which led me to keep an eye on the ads in the newspaper Wanted pages.

January 1978

I contacted Butch about going to the northwest for work, and during our conversation, he mentioned the name of two building companies, so we decided to both go into Perth the following day and see what was offering for tenders.

The next morning we met and, once inside, we got hold of the right person and put our case forward. Shortly after that, I was offered maintenance and repair work on an hourly rate and the list was endless of the jobs that required attention. So without much ado, we departed with the name of our contact at a place called Karratha, 1,500 kilometres from Perth. For tax reasons, we decided to form a company, and while we were thinking about this, I thought I would drive over to see Mum and Dad just outside of Perth.

When we arrived, we were greeted with open arms, like always, and it wasn't long before I told them we were going north for a couple of months as there was plenty of work for the both of us. Though Mum never said much, Dad looked rather surprised and, with the previous events still fresh on everyone's minds, he came out with the fact that each time Butch and I were together, it was like putting Nitro and Glycerine together as we were too much alike, and a bloody danger to ourselves.

Butch and I left about an hour later and started to laugh at what Dad said. It was then I said, "Well stuff it, Butch! Let's register it as our company name," and back to Perth we went to fix it up. After about two hours, we were officially known as Nitro and Glycerine, Building Contractors. It was then back to see Dad and thank him for the idea. We all had a good laugh over it.

Then we left for Armadale to see Lita and bring her and the kids back to see Sandra for a visit. Getting into planning, Butch felt we should leave two days later to arrive up there on the Friday afternoon. I had no reason not to agree, so the rest of the night we spent swimming and drinking with our wives and explained to them that it would be worth our while as the money was the same as we'd earned in Albany.

The following day saw the pair of us repairing, cleaning and fixing the tools and car as, apart from the twelve-hour-long non-stop drive, we both wanted enough equipment so no work slipped past because of the lack of gear.

While Butch sorted his tools out, I found some day-glow tape and stencilled the name 'Nitro' and 'Glycerine' onto the back of the trailer, which raised eyebrows when we drove around to the local garage for fuel and oil – the one thing we did notice was no-one went near our car, and we felt this was a good sign that things were safe within.

The following evening around 4pm we left as it was much cooler to drive at night than during the day. This was my first time by road above Geraldton, and apart from the red, flat-top mountains it was as barren as the Nullarbor plain.

We arrived in Karratha around 2.30pm, located the area supervisor, who showed us the single men's camp. From there, we unloaded our gear and took a long cool shower then had a feed at the mess and headed to the wet mess for a couple of lagers. There we met three other men who were working for the same company – Syd, his son, and another chap. Syd was around 55 years old and looked quite pissed off with the place. His son didn't say much, nor did the other chap, but Syd brought to our attention that the foreman-cum-supervisor was a bit of a wanker and was forever pissed; perhaps we would get more joy from him than he did. The rest of the night we spent talking about the work ahead, and when I asked Syd where he lived, he said about three miles from Armadale at a place called Byford.

On our way back to the sleeping quarters, I mentioned to Butch that everyone looked pissed off with the place and some of them were quite a miserable bunch, but he said that it was because they'd been there too long and it wasn't much of a life without a sheila.

The next morning we were given a list of things to do and from that first day I could see the supervisor wasn't well organised as, when we arrived at the first site, no materials were on the job, though he was quite sure everything was there, so this meant we had to go back to camp and find bits of timber to start. Around 11am we finally got our first nails in. I didn't like being stuffed around, but Butch just took it in his stride, and that was the way things were like up North.

I remember that first day and how hot it was working – it was enough to fry the brains – but most annoying thing was our tools were, at times, too hot to handle. I also noticed that the harder I went, the more I sweated and this would make the handle of my hammer slip around, so I knew that speed wasn't helping. Remaining cool meant less problems, but by the end of the day, I was drained of all my energy and was really looking forward to the fart-sack: the minimum hours worked up North was ten per day so a full night sleep was going to be the answer.

Butch and I worked like this all week and by the weekend decided to take the day off to rest and sightsee our new surroundings. Afterwards, we ended up at the wet mess for the rest of the day. It was still quite clear that the rest of the mob there were just plain miserable, so I said to Butch that we should perhaps give them a laugh. So we slipped off at sunset, got hold of two sheets of newspaper and placed it between the cheeks of our arse. Then we lit them and started to run around the boozer, fanning our pure white glowing bums while this piece of paper was burning. Well, this brought out the change in them; they were laughing like nothing I'd heard before. Butch couldn't hold his faggot any longer and let it go while I stood on top of a table in the nude, fanning my arse and feeling the heat. Then Butch came in saying, "You think that's funny? Well sort this out," and with that, he turned on a fire hose, putting the faggot out and knocking me off the table, then he turned the hose onto the drinkers, and that brought the house down.

We had a lot of fun that night and became the centre of attention every time we walked into the boozer over the next week.

Syd was, by now, thinking about leaving as he had already been there for some eight weeks and had other work around Perth that was now ready for him to start. This gave Butch and me the job of finishing off and undertaking what Syd couldn't finish, so over the next two weeks we were flat out working sun-up till sunset to make the extra cash, and each night back at camp we only had a couple of beers before calling it a day.

We had now been away from home for four weeks and were feeling pretty tired and somewhat sick of working the hours we were, so we took the weekend off. We found out there was a local dance on the Saturday night, so we dolled ourselves up for the dance, both of us ready for a few laughs. But when we got there, it was like a morgue with people sitting around tables and no one dancing. Butch caught a table with three sheila's and a bloke and thought he would ask one for a dance. As I began to walk over, Butch waltzed right up to the table, dropped to one knee, put his hand out and asked one of the sheilas for a dance.

When he was refused, he looked at them and said, "Well, what the fuck did ya come here for?" and got to his feet, and so did the bloke who was with them. I thought the shit was going to hit the fan, but Butch and I walked away, only to find out later that night that they were the local Police and their wives.

We left not long after, thinking that with the driving ahead, we had better not look drunk or, in fact, be drinking, and of course, we arrived back to camp and spent the rest of the weekend washing and sorting our gear out. I could feel Butch becoming restless and I suppose I wasn't much different in some ways. So the following day after work we headed off for a spot of fishing and spent the evening on the beach until late.

As luck would have it, rain kept us indoors the next day and as we were in town decided to hit the boozer for a game of pool and a few black and tans, (stout). After some eight hours drinking, we were still sober and decided to drive back to camp. As we passed the drive-in-movies, Butch blew the car horn and I looked at him and said, "That will draw the police for sure."

No sooner had I said it than the blue light was behind us. While we both felt okay, we weren't sure how we'd do with the breathalyser. I looked at Butch and asked, "Are you going to stop?"

He said, "Stuff 'em, Dave. We'll have a laugh – watch this."

At the entrance to the camp, Butch slowed the vehicle down and pulled up outside the wet mess, just to give the others there a laugh. I looked around at the police walking over to the car, then Butch drove off, which sent the police running back to their car. The wheels spun as he left, covering everything in red dust. Then Butch came to a sudden stop, and the police had to slam their brakes on hard. By the time they got out, we were standing there asking them, "Is everything was okay, officer?"

They walked up to Butch, saying, "Smart-arse! Here, blow this bag up."

I wasn't involved so stood there looking at these police officer s telling Butch to blow the fucken thing up.

Butch told them to shove it up their arse, but this last time I said to Butch, "Blow it, mate, before you get in the shit."

"Okay," he said.

By now, the police were watching every move Butch made; he started to blow up the bag, and it grew bigger and bigger, then this police officer said, "That's enough, mate!" but Butch kept on blowing and blowing. Then the officer again said to stop.

Butch said, "Make up your mind! Do you want me to blow it up or not?"

By now, it was the size of rockmelon. Then the police officer grabbed the bag off him and, looking at it, threw it on the ground and stood on it.

"The next time I come across the pair of you, I'll can you," and with that, they left amidst the laughter from the blokes at the boozer.

We were now thinking about going home. We had been away for six weeks and felt we needed to get out before we got into extra trouble, so we organised our departure for the end of the week, leaving late on Friday evening. That day we got our money and a pile of food and hit the road for Perth.

After four hours behind the wheel, I took over from Butch, stopping only for fuel and drink; we arrived home around 10am and boy was I happy to get into a hot shower and bed. After the weekend, Lita filled me in on all the latest news and family gossip, and I noticed how much the kids were growing. We spent the rest of the week taking things easy for a change.

Although I worked around Armadale for a few weeks, I just couldn't find enough to keep me in full-time work, so I got hold of Butch and we decided to head north again, but this time to Port Hedland. So the following Monday, we went back to the contractors we'd previously worked for and found they had six timber-framed homes to erect. I gave them a price the next week and by the end of the month, we were once again getting ready for the trip up north. One piece of equipment we needed was a radial arm saw, so arrangements were made through the supplier to have one ready two weeks later, which meant we would have to return to Perth to collect it.

April 1978

Butch picked me up around 4pm and we once again were heading north. On the way up, Butch mentioned Uncle Ted was in Port Hedland and perhaps we could stop over with him until we sorted things out. I thought it a good idea as we didn't quite know what to expect once we arrived. Butch drove his vehicle up this time and it was an added advantage as I could get some sleep while he drove the first 400 miles. As we wanted to get there without delay, this meant going flat-out and only stopping for fuel.

It rained quite heavily during the night with large areas flooded. Just before Nanutarra Roadhouse, we came across a car broken down. The driver was under it, so we stopped to see if he was okay. Once he climbed out from under the car, we could see he had petrol burns from trying to block the hole in the fuel tank for the past six hours to no avail. He looked a mess so we got the first aid box to fix the burns and then started to fix the hole with Araldite and a bandage, but it was hard going as first. Butch got under for about five minutes, then I took a turn, and after each time, we would strip off to our underpants and wash in the pools of water on the roadside.

After about an hour of this, we finally fixed the problem and gave him some petrol to make sure he would reach the next roadhouse to the south, which was about 70 kilometres down the track, then Butch and I departed and before long we arrived at the Fortescue River. Without any further delay, we drove across as we felt that the night storm would soon be raising the water level and leaving us stuck there.

It was a stinking hot, muggy morning so we held up at Whim Creek for a counter lunch, played pool and other games then headed off for Hedland again. We arrived at around 2.30pm, and found Uncle Ted sitting on a barstool at the Last Stop tavern. We hadn't seen him for some twelve years so we downed a few lagers before he showed us his caravan and said we could stay as long as the job went, but we needed to pay him for rent and tucker and that was soon settled. Then it was off to locate the site and find some capable workers.

We arrived on the site to find the supervisor there, and upon making ourselves known to him, he explained that the materials were on the way up from Perth but the flooding had delayed the trucks getting through. The flooding was expected to subside in two days so this left us with a problem of timing our trip back to Perth for the radial arm saw. We decided to call it a day and, though I wanted to settle down for a good night sleep, Butch and Uncle Ted wanted to hit the piss. To not disappoint them and in case we came across a carpenter that could handle framework, I went along.

We left the tavern bloody late and pissed as farts and without any meal, so my first night in the van was broken with Uncle Ted snoring his guts out and Butch farting near his face in the hope he would stop. But the only thing I could see happening was Uncle Ted's face becoming pebble-dashed from Butch farting at close range.

That morning we awoke with Uncle Ted coughing and heaving his guts out, then silence, which was broken by the top of a beer can being opened for his breakfast. I just lay there thinking about the day's work and also what lay ahead if we stayed with Uncle Ted. Though I kept my thoughts to myself, I told the pair of them that we needed to get to the site and organise ourselves around our work.

During that morning, I asked Uncle Ted if he would look after the internal fixing while Butch looked after the external cladding and I took on the roofing. With that sorted, we were now in desperate need of carpenters. Uncle Ted knew some tradesmen and left the site, saying he'd see us at the camp for dinner. It was then I asked Butch whether Uncle Ted's was the best place for us to stay, as I was becoming concerned we would end up on the piss each night. Butch said not to worry; Uncle Ted was okay, but that didn't help or answer my question. We had the contract, not Uncle Ted, but I felt that he just may make things harder for us because of his set ways.

I decided to give him the benefit of the doubt, but I was going to make sure I stayed off the piss as that seemed to be where all our troubles always started, and one extra piss-pot wouldn't make life easy for the other person.

That week went quick after the timber arrived, and we were well into it, and by the end of the second week Butch and I headed back to Perth for the radial arm saw. We left on the Friday afternoon to be in Perth Saturday morning, so this meant no loss of time while driving down. As things went well for us, we arrived in Armadale at about 7am. Butch left me home for an hour or so, then I said goodbye to Lita and once more we were off. After we picked the equipment, we and headed flat out again for Port Hedland. We arrived midday on Sunday, only to find Uncle Ted pissed out of his head and nothing being done the previous day.

I never said anything to Butch but my look was enough to let him know I wasn't happy about the situation, so we unloaded and went back to the caravan where I cooked our evening meal. Though the air was light, I felt I was the one creating a bad atmosphere, but I wouldn't say what was on my mind as this was Uncle Ted's way of living and the fact that we were in is van didn't help much, but where to find accommodation was a problem. That evening we all ended up going to bed quite early and the next morning awoke with Uncle Ted coughing and heaving his guts up.

In the following weeks, we worked from sun-up till sunset, at times feeling the heat which would quite often bring us to a standstill, but we never gave up. Once we had the frames standing on the first house, it was up to Butch to clad the outside while I put the roof up. Uncle Ted found a fixing carpenter and a framing carpenter at the Last Stop Tavern and set them to work, the framing carpenter helping me with the roof.

One chap arrived with a bag over his shoulder, which I thought a bit odd for a carpenter but, as I had a problem getting men to do the work, I had to finally accept anyone with the brawn to handle the job. But with this chap, it was different.

I told him to start cutting the four by twos and after an hour I could hear this squeaking noise and decided to investigate, only to find him using a tenon saw with about six teeth in it.

"Shit, is that the only saw you have, mate?" I said to him.

He answered, "Yes, it's a bloody beauty for this work," and looking at him, I said, "That's no good for what I require, mate, so pack a bag and piss off," and with that he went looking for Uncle Ted, but I also put a stop to that and helped him off the site by picking his bag up and throwing it onto the road.

Our situation hadn't changed back at the caravan with the drink, and I was now getting quite pissed off with the type of worker Uncle Ted kept picking up from the Last Stop Tavern; I decided to talk it over with him right there and then. But good tradesmen were hard to find, he explained, and we had no other choice but to use what was left even though they were half pissed most of the time. I really had nowhere else to look and it was about now that I was becoming deeply concerned about the contract and our finishing date.

By now Butch was getting a little pissed off with me complaining about the work or the lack of it being done, and it wasn't long before the shit hit the fan. I started arguing over the piss and the lack of food and the general way we were living and, from my outburst and showing my complete discontent all round, things changed – not much at first, but Uncle Ted and Butch realised that beer wasn't a real substitute for food and the times working had to change if we were to complete the project on schedule. So after another discussion, we all decided to take one and a half days off for relaxing.

So the following weekend, we all went fishing down at the Port Hedland docks, and though we only caught a half dozen small ones, it was great to have a different meal on our return to the van. Apart from that, we all enjoyed our weekend break.

Over the next three weeks, things hadn't changed much and the project was by now well behind, so the supervisor asked me how I was going to get it complete on time and would I mind if I just completed the first two homes. I told him to leave it with me and that I would get back to him the next day with my answer. I discussed the problem with Butch and we both felt it would be for the best, and so the next morning I surrendered the remaining six homes. By mid-afternoon, the bloody supervisor had a full team of framing carpenters on site. Butch and I got pretty wild over this and confronted him about where he found them as he knew I was desperate for carpenters. But it was no good arguing about it now as they had already started the job. Then Uncle Ted said it looked like a backhand job had been done on us, and I believed him on that score. So there was nothing else to do but get on with our own job and get out of the place quick.

Handing over part of the contract gave us a little more time to complete the two homes we were building, so we retained our weekends off and took ourselves fishing or down to the local

Walkabout Tavern for the session.

On one of these occasions, Butch and I started to play up again, as Uncle Ted told me to relax a little more and stop worrying over the work situation. That's when I got on the piss to get myself out of my mood.

It gets quite hot in the north, and we would sometimes take a long dinner break and start again in the cool. However, one Friday, about three weeks before we finished the homes, we left the site early and headed for the Walkabout Tavern. Just on sunset, we decided to go for a swim in the guest pool, so we dropped our shorts and in we went in the nude and had a great time for about ten minutes when the landlord came and told us to get out. After a little while and some words later, we slipped on our shorts and headed back for the bar to Uncle Te, feeling much cooler for our ordeal. We settled down for a couple of more lagers, but around ten o'clock, we started again.

We dropped our shorts again and dived in the pool, then we climbed out and threw a wooden table in the pool. Running around the pool, we jumped on top of the table as if it was a surfboard. This provided us with a lot of laughs, so I threw another one into the pool so we had one each. By now Uncle Ted had settled down to watch us, and a guest at the motel was also outside but that didn't worry Butch or me; we just kept it. In went more poolside furniture until they were all in the pool, then the next minute, the landlord was yelling at us to get out. But we wouldn't. Within five minutes, Uncle Ted came over and said the Police were on the way, and I believed him. Scrambling out, I grabbed my shorts, made it to the fence and sat down to watch Butch still carrying on using the furniture as a surfboard. Then I heard voices above me and knew the Police had arrived. They were talking among themselves and I heard one say, "Where's the other one?" Then one of them looked down and saw me sitting beneath them. "Alright, mate, get up here, right now."

I knew my number was up even though nothing too bad was done, but once I got around the fence, this bloody copper grabbed my arms and handcuffed me from behind. While this was going on, Butch was watching them. The other copper by now was walking around the pool telling Butch to get out, but not Butch. He kept saying, "You want me out, then come in and try, wanker." Again he was told to get out, and each time Butch swam near the edge of the pool, the copper would try and grab him but he would dive under. The copper was getting quite shitty and his mate, who was still holding me, asked if I could get him out before Butch got himself into more trouble.

We walked up to the pool and I persuaded Butch to get out, which he did. He was soon handcuffed and dragged to the paddy wagon. On our way there, we both noticed Uncle Ted lying flat out on his car bonnet as if he was asleep.

When we reached the paddy wagon, the copper holding Butch told him to get into the back. Butch said no, so the pair lifted him up and tried to throw him in, but Butch placed both his feet on either side of the door, yelling at them. They just dropped him to the ground, leaving him winded and in some pain. I looked at one of them and told him to leave him alone and the next thing I copped a bloody big fist in my gut. Butch by now was back on his feet and still refusing to get into the paddy wagon. They started with one fist to the face, then another to the gut and between the two of them delivered about six good blows. All I could do but was watch as by now the landlord was holding onto me.

By now Butch was winded so the two coppers picked him up and threw him in the wagon, then I was also thrown in on top of him. We both looked a mess – our shirts were ripped and we felt quite sore and battered as we lay on the floor of the paddy wagon.

On our way to South Hedland lockup, about twelve miles away, we noticed that the padlock on the cage door was off and, muttering between ourselves, decided that on the next turn off we'd jump out and make a run for it as we felt Uncle Ted would be following in the van. But the driver didn't slow down enough for the big break out as each time he rounded a corner, it was at high speed. Perhaps this was for the best, as no telling what sort of trouble we would have been in.

The next day we were both in court and fined for being $50 each for disorderly conduct and given a month to pay. Uncle Ted picked us up and we started work as if it just was part of a night's entertainment. As the day dragged on, I became more convinced that Dad was right about Butch and myself and looked back over the past few months with Butch and the trouble I'd been in. I decided that, once this contract was finished, we would part ways, and within the month and after paying my fine, I told Butch I wanted out and could he take me home. Somehow he too felt that it was for the best as I was once again complaining about our living conditions, so we loaded up all our gear and headed back to Perth about mid-afternoon.

Although Butch and I were the best of mates, we both talked about our situations, and this would be the best thing for us, but not to say we wouldn't stop having the odd beer now and again. We talked a lot on the way down to Perth on that trip, and it was only when we reached the outskirts of Carnarvon that we noticed a police car passing us.

Butch said, "He's going to turn around and pull us over," and sure enough, we noticed his headlights coming towards us. Butch said, "Stuff him, Dave," and as his luck would have it, he noticed a dirt track and switched his lights off while the police car was about a mile behind us. He continued down this track at a high rate of knots until it came to a small shed with some other buildings around the place. Parking up, we started to settle down, deciding we might as well spend the night there.

About ten minutes later, sure enough, we noticed this police car arriving. He drove around looking for us, though we hadn't done anything wrong. I couldn't understand why the hell we were hiding, but as Butch explained, when we left Port Hedland the Police there would have rung the Police in Carnarvon to keep a look out for us as we could be drink driving. Even though we hadn't had a drop, Butch felt that it was better to give them the run-around and try to avoid them as they just might find something wrong with the car. Well, this left me quite stunned to think what sort of a bloody mess I'd found myself getting into again, and during that night, I knew that once I was back in Perth and out of all of it, the happier I'd be.

We left Carnarvon early the next morning and arrived in Perth about mid-morning, stopping first at Butch's place before driving onto Armadale, where all my gear was unloaded. Then, without much ado, Butch departed, saying he wasn't sure where he was going but, if I needed him, to ring his mother up at Fremantle. And with that, he was gone.

I filled Lita in with all the events that occurred while we were in Port Hedland and, though we had finished our contract, we never made a great deal of money. What we had made we would have to hang onto, apart from our normal weekly outgoings.

March 1978

Although it was great to be home, finding work locally was rather a problem, and I only gained small jobs here and there. One day, on our shopping day in Armadale, I heard my name being called and, to my surprise, there was my old mate Syd who I'd met in Karratha. During our conversation, we filled each other in on the work situation and the lack of it, then he told me he was waiting to hear from a mining company at Agnew that was taking on maintenance carpenters and asked if I would be interested in going.

I thought about it, and as much as I didn't want to, I just said, "Yes", thinking that most likely it was just hot wind.

About a week later, Syd arrived at my door saying that we'd both got the job at Agnew. Our trip up was paid for and the money was quite good with everything thrown in – tucker and bed – the only thing was we had to leave in two days and the work we were doing was 71 feet above ground level. The length of time away was one month, so I decided to get ready and said that we'd take the ute Lita's father had just given us.

Our destination was Leinster, about 26 kilometres from Agnew, and the full trip was some 963 kilometres, so Syd and I left around 4.30am as, once again, we wanted as much road behind us before we felt the heat. This trip was to take me to Kalgoorlie, then north to Leonora towards the outback of the Great Victoria Desert, and as the trip was without trouble I felt a little happier as the day drew on. We arrived at Leinster at around 5.30pm and soon found the single men's quarters and, of course, the mess hall. Then we both got a good night sleep, thinking about the coming day's work.

We were both up early and quite eager to start but, when we arrived at the office, no one was around, so we decided to find out for ourselves just what was going on. We soon located the manager's house, and though he didn't like being disturbed, I told him I didn't either but I was here to get the job location and the materials. With a sober grunt, he made his way down to the mining site and explained what was needed.

We stood outside this bloody big building around 80 feet high that had an open eaves line. Our job was to somehow climb up and fix steel sheeting to the eaves. Syd just looked at me and said that he hadn't been told about this, then he turned to the manager and said, "How the fuck do you think we are going to get up there for a start. And the second thing is we expect the money to change if you want us to do it!"

I stood back looking at him, then asked, "Who the hell said that it could be done from a ladder? It's going to take three men about seven weeks to complete the job under safe conditions."

By now, he must have seen that Syd and I weren't too happy about being dragged up all this way to find that some wanker hadn't passed on the full details of the job. We all headed back to the office to discuss what, if, and how we could do the job. We realised at this time that the manager himself was nothing but the local plumber who had just taken on the maintenance contracts for the mining company, so both Syd and I asked him for extra cash, or he could pay for the third man, but instead, he settled to pay for seven to eight weeks work and if we were finished before that he would still pay for that period of time.

So our first day was spent looking over the building and deciding how best to tackle the situation. We both agreed that hanging a gantry down from the overhanging steel supports and using a pully to hoist the sheets up was the only way to complete it.

So the next day, we arranged to have the gantry built while we sorted out the ropes and safety equipment we needed as this was a very dangerous job – the one thing I did know was that, once up there and the body sweat mixed with the dust, it would turn into mud and make things more difficult to hang onto. By the end of the day the first gantry frame was made and we put it through the test to make sure it fitted and it was light enough for one person to hook it on. After satisfying ourselves it would be okay, the other three were completed.

The following day saw the pair of us up and down the face of this building and by the time it was dark we had only installed two sheets, so this meant, with 90 sheets to install, the project was around forty-five days or just over six weeks. We seemed to spend more time putting the gantry up than installing the eaves lining, and at the end of the day, with there being no booze, we headed straight for the fart sack once tea was downed. We both worked like this for the next five weeks and decided to have a weekend off – Syd wanted to play golf, while I was looking forward to the rest.

That Friday, I rang Lita, as usual, to let her know how things were. However, upon her answering the phone, she said, "Well, you'll be pleased to know I'm pregnant!"

I asked her to repeat it and all she said was, "You heard me."

Well, I was really delighted over it, but Lita, I think, wasn't too keen, so after saying goodbye to her, I armed myself with a beer and told Syd my good news.

Saturday I spent doing my washing and resting, and come Sunday a couple of the other men working there asked me to come along to Sandstone for the session, some 120 miles away. Five of us left together around 11am, with about four dozen tinnies.

What a trip! We were full as farts by the time we got there and just in time before the doors closed. We all managed to down a couple then were thrown out, along with another four dozen tinnies for the trip back. We had a great day, and to top it off, we all went native for a while chasing these bloody big bungarras (lizards) – not that any of us were sober enough to catch one. But it did provide us with a good laugh before we returned to camp.

Syd and I finished the eaves during the sixth week and was given another small job to do, but I wanted out and so did Syd, but the manager was becoming a little funny over the money.

We were now into the second days' work repairing this building when I told Syd I was going to confront the manager the next morning about our money and that we wouldn't work until we received our wages. Sure enough, the next morning we were at the office waiting for him, and at around 10.30 he showed up full of himself, but I wasn't budging. I told him to get our wages ready before midday or I would let all his workers know that he was broke. With that, he became quite hostile towards me, but again I said that this was the fifth time we'd had to come for our money and this time we wanted it, not later but right now. Reluctantly, he pulled his cheque book out and finally paid us with a cash cheque, which we sorted out at his bank, then we went back to the office to let him know that we were leaving after lunch. Then Syd gave him and his wife a good talking to about running people around, which got them pretty wound up. Though I was now outside the office, I could hear the rivets popping in the roofing sheets.

Syd and I had already packed our gear up and, within the hour, we were on the road back to Perth, with Syd feeling quite proud for getting his anger out. I did find him quite straight when it came to money matters, and like myself, I didn't like being stuffed around and I guess that's *why* I felt this pair were just as likely to pull a fast one on us. However, we arrived back in Perth early the next morning

As tired as I was, we headed off to see Mum and Dad once the kids were home from school, and after breaking the good news, they were delighted. Then Dad asked me about Butch and his whereabouts, and as I hadn't seen him for the past eight weeks, I had no idea. So not long after arriving, I decided to head for home as I hadn't seen a good bed for some time and I was looking forward to that.

Work now became quite a problem on the local front, though I was doing small jobs from time to time, so I decided to head to Coolgardie and look for myself. Within that week, a bricklayer and I headed off, and though it was not far from Perth, we arrived there midday.

I found my old friend Doug Cable and explained to him that I was looking for any building work. He told me to see a friend of his, so that evening I met the chap. When I told him what we were looking for, he was delighted. So on my first day, we found a little job for the next day. Doug put us up for the night. After we completed that job, he asked me to look at the local Catholic Church as the barge board had suffered some storm damage. When we arrived, there just wasn't anything there, then he told me the job had been on his books for three years as he couldn't get anyone to do it. I told him that, even though I hadn't done it before myself, the fact that one side was still there would provide me a pattern.

The next three days saw us setting out the barge board, and, as the church apex was around 40 feet above the ground, our job was quite tricky, but by counting the bricks up from the footings and measuring the width, I was able to establish the roof pitch. From this point, we started to build up the barge board until it was completed. While this was going on, I advertised via the local radio station that we were available for any maintenance work within the Coolgardie area, and had plenty of response from it. One major job that came our way was out at Salmon Gums, about 300 kilometres south, so at the end of the week, I went to check it out, only to find it was the local hotel and motel. Apparently, the liquor licence board had paid them a visit and left them a work order that had to be completed within three months.

The order left with them was quite large and, though it mainly dealt with the kitchen area, the owners also decided to change the bar area around in the lounge. This meant quite a lot of work and time in working out a price for the job. So for the rest of the weekend measurements and drawings, along with photos, were put together. By late Sunday evening, we both departed for Perth and arrived in the early hours of the morning.

During that week while driving back from Lita's parents house, I noticed a small development of home units being built just around the corner and stopped to check it out. I wrote down the builder's name and phone number from the site noticeboard and looked around to see what stage some of the units were at. When going past the site office, I looked in and found no one there but, with my cheek, decided to use the phone to ring the builder.

"G'day," I said, "Can I speak to a Mr B. Dowling?"

The voice at the other end said, "That's me."

"Okay. This is David Darcey. I'm ringing you from your Armadale site office. I'm wondering if you need a fixing carpenter for this job."

Well," Bill said, "if you want to give me a price, I'll be down there in the morning."

"That's fine. I should be able to have it by 9.30am if that's okay ..." and so, after saying goodbye, I set about costing the job for second fixing in one unit and arrived back at home just before sunset to tell Lita about the events of the day.

I was up early the next day getting quotes for the pending Salmon Gums Hotel project, and at 9.30am, I drove around to meet Bill Dowling. Within a few minutes, we were well into the cost and, though he accepted my price for the fixing out, I wanted to know how and when I was paid.

When he said, "After the completion of each unit," my eyes lit up with delight, as the usual way was weekly, so by now I was more than eager to start, especially as the material was on site. For the rest of the week and the weekend, I was flat out working, and by midday Monday, I had finished the first unit. I contacted him straight away and was told to push on to the second unit. By that afternoon, I was well into that and had it completed by Friday. It was important to me to work long hours when the work was available as I needed a constant cash flow, but I also knew this building company just might be able to provide me with the break I was looking for – a continuous supply of work.

May 1978

Bill and I hit it off pretty good and before long I admitted that I would be more than keen to remain working with his company, and apart from pricing the Salmon Gums Hotel job, which I wasn't sure if I would get or not, I was available to undertake any amount offered. So I remained working on the units till the end of the month – I had finally got the job at Salmon Gums – so with all my work completed, I contacted Bill to let him know that I was going away for two weeks and he should get the other units ready. The main thing was to give him the confidence that I would be there, as I said.

Arrangements were made to leave on the Saturday for Salmon Gums with the bricklayer that was previously with me as he knew what he had to do. But this time we took his son along as well. While driving to Salmon Gums, my thoughts were on that job and the planning, which was to start on the call of the last orders that night as I had already ordered the concrete for the floor. I just hoped that all would run smoothly once we arrived.

We arrived around 9.00pm and unloaded while I was talking to the landlord on the timing and how important it was to have access at 11pm. Once that time arrived, we were at it with sledgehammers and crowbars, ripping and tearing out the unwanted crap and all the time, I was yelling and pushing the other chap and his son to put their backs into it. Around 4.30am, the lounge floor was ready for the concrete placing, which left us a couple of hours sleep.

The next morning I was up at 6.30, and the bricklayer and I

started on the kitchen, ripping out the old and setting things up for his day's work as the bricks were also arriving that morning. Around 8.30am, that too was ready, just as the concrete and bricks arrived. While he started on his project, his son and I laid the concrete. Though he wasn't very strong, nor in fact had worked like this before, I could see he was becoming quite weak, but with the help of his father he kept at it.

That afternoon while the bricklayer and his son were building the new wash house, I started on the new septic tanks and leach drains. After having the local back-hoer dig the drains out, two were ready to install. We now had to wait for the concrete sections to arrive.

Late that first afternoon, we all installed the new bar and, with the landlord's help, the pipes for the beer were also installed. By around 8.30pm, the lounge, apart from the new carpet, was completed, but by now I was more than ready for bed even though the bricklayer was still at it.

The following morning, the section for the leach drain and septic tank arrived, and by mid-afternoon, it was finished, along with the brickwork to the washhouse, which only left the kitchen to start ripping out the next day.

The project was well on scheduled time but I never gave up pushing the bricklayer and his son for the rest of the week. Finally, when Saturday arrived, the only job left was some wall-tiling around the cookers and wash areas, so we decided to take Sunday off and have a look around Esperance, mainly to relax on the beach with a few tinnies, which went down a treat as we hadn't been drinking from the day we arrived.

The following Tuesday saw the whole project complete. Before we departed, I was handed my money and paid the bricklayer and his son the amount agreed on. Then we set off for Perth later that afternoon, arriving in the early hours of Wednesday.

I rested for the remainder of that week, dwelling on work and that perhaps I should look around for more of the same type as the money I made was about $1,000 per week, while fixing the units out only brought home $400 to $450.00 a week, and for that I was relying on a steady flow of work. I formed the idea that I just might be able to start a small company myself within a few months.

The following Monday, I rang Bill and told him I was on-site and once again well into fixing, and around midday he arrived. While talking to me, he asked if I could look after the site on a day to day basis, and as I didn't see any disadvantage to doing it, I said yes, so apart from being the last to leave, I also had to take care of making sure that all the units and the site office were locked.

I worked like this for about two months. Then Bill asked me to give him a price for twenty-seven home units in Fremantle. As I hadn't any other work at that stage, I was delighted to comply, so over the next few days, I found myself at the Fremantle site doing measurements and costings.

The major problem at the Fremantle site was the lack of any supervision from the foreman, and if anyone on site required him they had to look for him at the local hotel, which I had to do on several occasions. This wasn't at all correct for a man in that position, however, that's how things were. Apart from that, the other chaps working for Bill were great, and the young apprentice to Bill – Rosco as he was known – became quite friendly towards me and showed me over the site and the plans in the office.

Bill knew of the situation at the site and also didn't like it, but explained that he was in the middle of moving him on but couldn't find a replacement. As he was discussing this problem, I handed him the quote for the job and, though he glanced at it, he really showed no interest so I guessed he must have had the foreman on his mind. I eventually left for home with no definite answer as to whether I had the job.

Apart from some minor fixing at the Armadale site over the next two days I never saw Bill, but Rosco arrived saying Bill sent him over to help me out. As I hadn't had much to do myself, I found this rather odd but we managed to find little things to occupy ourselves. Then Bill arrived. He came straight up to me and asked whether I would like the foreman's job at Fremantle. Well, this came as quite a shock to me as, while I felt confident in my work, running a full site was something I hadn't any experience in whatsoever. I well remember answering him with, "Can you give me a couple of days to think it over?" And we left it at that.

When I told Lita about the position, she was delighted for me, but I still wasn't sure. I knew I could do the job as long as I had some backup from Bill and felt a bit more confident, so I decided to have a go – I really had nothing to lose – so the following day I rang Bill and gave him a Yes, and he was delighted to hear it. So arrangements were made to meet him on site the next day to sort things out with the existing foreman.

We arrived at Fremantle and Bill handed me the site diary and ran over various points with me, but at this time, no one knew that I was the new site foreman. It became quite clear there was a complete lack of checking any of the finished work, and this became quite apparent when Bill's mood changed to anger. Then, in a fit of rage, he decided to locate the foreman to explain that he was giving him his holidays, and once we got down to the hotel and found him, he was told to remove his gear off-site within the hour. We left for the site again, where everyone was informed of the change, and to my surprise, everyone else was pleased with it.

September 1978

The first thing I wanted to settle with Bill was a wage, and to my surprise, he made me an offer that was quite favourable: I would keep all the fixing contract and receive $250.00 a week from the company. This would bring my wages to around $700.00 when the fixing started in a month's time. Now that was settled, I, with Rosco as my off-sider, started cleaning up the mess left by my predecessor.

That first week Bill was on site every day explaining as much as possible and each day was something different. What I was learning was of far greater interest to me in the way a building site was organised, and once Bill left, I felt much more confident and any doubt was now gone.

My first task was to draw up a bar-chart for the whole site up until completion and, though this kept me quite occupied for the full week, it proved the biggest asset and was totally appreciated by the tradesmen. It was also soon learned that I never moved an inch once I made a decision over site running; this, I felt, kept the trades following behind each other rather than them picking the best first that would pay them bigger money and leave me waiting for them to return when they wanted. I was soon wise to that, and told them that if they didn't arrive back on site on the day written down on the bar-chart, then don't bother coming the next day as I would have someone else doing their work. When I fired one team that was stuffing me around, the others realised I meant what I'd said.

Rosco was a bloody good asset: he kept me informed of equipment and stocks that were short and when things were needed, and it was him that rang and made the order with me signing as they arrived. So for the next twelve weeks, we were all so well organised that five of the units were finished. The current rate of work meant that five units a week were completed and being handed over to a delighted Bill. But now it was Christmas, and for four weeks the building industry just stopped. This would slow up my project so, with Rosco's help, we ordered all the items required for the trades to work over Christmas.

During that first week back, I had the labourers booked in to clean down the brickwork and it became quite apparent that one of the labourers was a little simple, to the point of not understanding the bar-chart. On one particular morning, the bricklayers arrived to complete some flower boxes at one end of the three-storey units, and after they received their instruction from me, were well into it. Then I told this simple labourer to clean the bricks at the opposite end of the same building, but on the third-floor window sills. On top of this, it was a Wednesday morning which was quite busy as I received the workers' accounts and, after making sure they were in order and the work had been completed, I would ring through to the main office for settlement of their accounts by the Friday. During this work, the bricklayer returned to the office looking quite upset, and was somewhat covered in red spots. Angrily, he told me that I'd better get that bloody brick cleaner shifted as he was dropping Hydrochloric Acid over him! I could see by the red spots and also the anger that he wasn't impressed, so I told him to tell the simple labourer to go to the other end of the same building, and with that he left.

Ten minutes later, the same bricklayer returned but this time he was wild and had a look that meant trouble.

"Dave," he said, "you either shift that stupid labourer or I'll bury the mad fucker!"

While he was saying this, I couldn't help notice more red spots over him and to top it off, his singlet (vest) was by now full of holes. So I said to him, "Tell him that I want him at the office," and again he left, still bloody wild.

I was quite busy on the phone to Head Office when the labourer came finally in. My mind was on the events for accounts and settlements before Friday, and I just looked over to him and said, "Empty your bucket and wait for me in the smoko room."

He left. But two minutes later, he came in and asked me for a siphoning hose. Without thinking, I just waved my arm and pointed to my ute. "Look in the back ... should be one there," I said.

Then the voice on the other end of the phone said, "Sounds like your hands are full this morning, Dave."

Just then my hair stood up on end, and my mouth fell open, and for a split second I was silence. Then I realised that something wasn't right with that stupid labourer. I dropped the phone and bolted for the door. Looking across the way, I could see the stupid prick getting ready to siphon the acid from his bucket to the main container. Well, my heart did a flip, and I was over there in a flash and sunk my boots hard into the side of the bucket, sending the acid over the ground while at the same time pushing the labourer to one side.

I looked at him and said, "I think it's time I gave you your holidays. With that, he well understood what I meant, and said,

"You can't fire me."

But I replied, "I'm not firing you, just giving you a long rest, and me with it." Then I went back to the phone and told Bill to send his wages down that morning as I'd had enough – he was a danger not only to himself but to all the others on site.

January 1979

Though I was kept quite busy at work, my homefront was now gearing up for the new arrival of our third child. Lita was suffering from bad bouts of coughing midway through her confinement, and though this did concern me, there just wasn't anything that could be done for it. Nicole and Michelle were becoming very excited and somewhat rowdy at the thought of our new baby. And so, on January 16, we were blessed with a boy and both agreed on the name 'Adam' (first son) Horton (Lita's maiden name) Darcey.

I was there and helped bring him into the world, so this was a very personal moment for me as I wasn't there when Nicole was born and, with Michelle, the sister wouldn't allow it. So I was over the moon, and it felt like the full circle. Being a part of the birth allowed me the chance of responsibility, not only at birth but for the rest of my natural life.

Things in general were looking pretty good for us now, as I had a steady income and plenty of work ahead, so I decided to carpet the whole house out in the same month. And I also decided to register a business name. By the middle of February, it became official – I was the principal proprietor of TOWN AND COUNTRY BUILDING CONTRACTORS, and from here I started to take on little projects to feel my way into the other side of contracts and to be seen doing them.

Although Bill became concerned at first, I explained to him that I wasn't leaving his company, merely trying to expand on my ideas. I said I could even sub-contract my time out to his company, which would leave himself clear of any tax and insurance for myself. Within a short period of time, this was how we went, though I had to keep a very close eye on everything I was doing, which increased my paperwork, but the main point was, it worked for the pair of us overall.

The Fremantle project was closing fast and so my time on the job wasn't required as often, so each Saturday midday the boys would down-tools and head off to the local Railway Hotel for the jazz session where we would join in the fun. We would all have a great time till about four in the afternoon and then it was back home, where once again it became apparent that I was drinking too much as Lita would often have her say, but I would have a shower and head for bed to sleep it off.

May 1979

Bill arrived at the site and asked me whether I would like to supervise another project but this time down at Mandurah. Of course, I jumped at the chance and arrangements were made for a site visit before the end of the month. When that time came, I found out it was for twenty-seven home units on the coastal front, about one mile outside of Mandurah, at a place called Halls Head.

Being a very hilly site, it was going to propose a few small problems for me, but I knew that, with Bill's backing, I could overcome any doubt or difficulties once the job was started. At this given point in time, nothing was done, which would give me an advantage as I could study the plans from day one.

I was now stretching myself quite thin, as I was still doing small jobs at the Arrnadale site as the clients moved into their units, and I was running back to Fremantle to check that the units were finished before handover. My time running between sites was starting to give me the screaming shits, as I wasn't paid while on the road, so I had to either up my price or arrange my time for each site so I wasn't backtracking on myself.

Before long, I was back and forth to Mandurah full-time and, as the distance from Armadale was around forty miles, I decided to look for cheap accommodation now that the first trades were arriving on the site. I booked a room at the Peninsula Hotel for bed only, which proved quite cheap as the cost of running back home each night was around $5.00. Staying in Mandurah for five days was $10 less than travelling and also allowed me to be on-site early.

Although I was employed as a sub-contract supervisor, I needed other work to occupy some of my spare time, rather than spending it all on-site, but after two months, I hadn't found anything local, and found my wages were somewhat lower since taking this project on. But I kept at it until one day I hadn't received my brick orders. This was quite odd so I contacted the brick firm and asked when I could have the delivery. To my surprise, I was informed that they would arrive when the Head Office paid last month's account, so I contacted Bill to find out what was happening. He told me to put the bricklayers on hold until we cleared up the backlog and cleared the accounts from Fremantle.

As I still had around four thousand bricks on site, I just couldn't lay the bricklayers off until Head Office sorted out their problems, so I decided to inform Max, the lead Subby, and though he wasn't happy about it, he kept a small team on-site for the remainder of the week, but come Friday when Bill should have arrived with the cheques for the previous week's work, he became bloody wild when he didn't turn up as usual. I contacted Bill and told him of the situation and that I was left with no other alternative than to let the bricklayers go but that I had kept them on in the hope that he may have settled his troubles. He then asked me if I could give them some money, and though I was now also worrying about my payment, I said I would think about it and try and clear it from Armadale to the Mandurah bank.

Shit, I thought, *this is not what I really expected*. Now that I had formed a friendship with Max and his team, I was stuck with telling them that no money was available and also keeping them on for another week when I knew something was up proposed more trouble. From this decision I'd made, I told Max that I could give him some money to help tie him over. The next day I cleared $500 after telling Bill that I needed it back as a personal cheque as soon as possible. This helped Max and kept the peace for the following week, but when we hadn't heard what was going on, I became quite anxious as now I was due for one month's pay plus the $500 outstanding.

We both decided to confront Bill, and the following morning we were at the main office to get answers. We were given various 'hold on until we straighten it out' statements, we both found that it was now at an end for the short term and left with the same impression – that we were in for a fight to get the outstanding amounts.

My first move was to forget my loyalties to Bill as I had found him quite straight with me and the fact that it was him alone who had given me the break I'd been looking for. So that afternoon, I rang Bill saying that, apart from the lack of money to myself, was there anything I could do. He did ask me if I could keep an eye on the Mandurah project and keep himself informed as to my whereabouts should the situation change with them.

I now informed Lita of the change in our circumstances and the money that was passed over to Max would leave us a little short until I found other work. The rest of that week I spent running around putting a price on anything local just to keep my running cost down.

Christmas wasn't far off, which also started to worry me as once again the building industries just closed down, so I knew I had to take whatever was offered. Minor maintenance work around Armadale helped keep us going, then over the next few weeks I decided to see about getting our home extended as Lita and I had often felt that should a reason come up we should perhaps do it – our reason was young Adam would soon be needing a room – so I went back to the Defence Service Homes to see what was available under our contract with them. To our surprise, I was entitled to a further $10,000.

I soon started drawing up the plans, which I had been

getting plenty of experience with. Once the design was approved and myself listed as the builder, we were given the money to go ahead with it. This gave me the chance to not only put the addition on but I closed in the carport and turned that into my office, which provided me a place to work from. Each child having their own room delighted them, although it was great to have the extra area, it did increase our repayment to $145.00 per month, which I didn't mind as, while I was doing the job, I was also being paid for it, and with the remainder of the materials I erected the front verandah, so thing were now making Lita a little happier.

Just after I finished our extensions, I won a sub-contract job at a new adventure park being built right on the entrance to Armadale. This was called Pioneer Village and, once again, I'd taken work on that I'd never done before. This time though my brother-in-law had the experience and explained how to do it, so over the next three months and two weeks through Christmas, I was hell-bent on getting on with it. I worked the best part of twelve hours a day, by myself at first, so the supervisor on the job asked me to try and find some young carpenters, so I placed an advertisement in the paper and received two local responses. They were around 18 to 19 years old and had worked for the Department of Works as apprentices, but their problem was they always arrived to work stiff and sore, taking their time in the course of their duties, and this was a worry to me. At the end of the day, they would run off the site like bats out of hell. I asked one of them one day what was the trouble in the morning, and his answer was, he was playing football the night before and felt stiff and sore. I looked at him and said, "Well, mate, I bet your wages will look just as stiff if you come to work for me like that again! This isn't a place of rest."

He looked at me, thinking hard, but I again told him, "I pay your wages and I do expect something in return for what you receive." I did get a response, but it was short-lived. One morning I wasn't at work early, and arrived to find them sitting around. Straight off I told them to pack up their tools, as I didn't need to carry any more dead weight, and with that, and a mouthful of shit, they left. By mid-afternoon, I contacted Rosco at Fremantle, who was only too eager to get over and help me out. Not long after that, my old workmates were on-site, and for once the project was moving; in fact, we completed my section within the month, and I was now eager to win the contract to nail some 30,000 shingles on the same building.

I was soon notified that my price was accepted for the shingles. While that was going, I also won the contract for the balustrading to the two-storey motel being built on the same land, so this left my hand full up until the shingles were just about finished. I was then asked to do a small job for the owner who was staying at the Narrogin Inn, also on the same land. And soon after, that too was completed. When I handed him my account, the supervisor informed me that money was hard to get out of him, so I gave him the usual week then decided to confront him in his office, where I asked him when I could expect a cheque from him. He was a little shitty with me, but I made it quite clear that I expected it the following week as I had workers wages to pay.

The following week I hadn't received my money and, with wages to pay, I cleared that through my bank. On Friday, I walked into his office with my hammer in one hand demanding my money or I'd start fucking his joint up. He could see I wasn't mucking around this time, but again he was putting me off. When I walked up to his desk and started to tap it with the hammer, he told me to come back in the morning. Reluctantly, I left, but I also knew that I was starting to get my back up over it. So I walked downstairs to the lounge and stood there for a good minute when the bar-maid, who knew me, asked whether

I would like a drink as I looked pretty wild about something. I said nothing to her other than yes to the drink, and after receiving it, I took my first mouthful when he came downstairs. He looked at me first then at the bar-maid, and said to her, "You know not to serve a customer dressed like that in working clothes!"

Well, that fixed it for me. I pulled my hammer out and slammed it on the counter, and yelled at the top of my voice for all to hear: "While you owe me $700, fuck-wit, I'll drink anywhere in your pub I like, and if you want me out, then pay for the work I've done.":

He started to look red in the face, but at the same time turned to the bar-maid and said, "Just give him another drink," and asked me to sit down and cool off. But I found that pretty hard to do. With the way things were, I figured I owed the bank money for the first time, and my repayments were due, along with the fact that Lita would be expecting her housekeeping. Halfway through my second drink, he came into the bar and handed me a cheque for the full amount, but that didn't change the way I really felt, so I told him I was staying for a while and, with that, I got quite merry before going home.

My projects at the village were completed and, as my luck would have it, I was offered a job at the Kalamunda RSL Club, through a friend of the family. I gave my price for that job and was given the go-ahead, which I started after completing some minor work I was doing around Armadale.

May 1980

By now, I had a good list of names of workers that could undertake small contracts I offered. Once I started the Kalamunda toilet block, I was soon on the phone to them, and soon after that, I had the limestone footings in and the slab down. The next thing was the leach drain and for this I used the local back-hoe digger, as he understood the soil conditions in that location, I knew I wouldn't have any increase in price.

I arrived on-site, and we both discussed where the drain had to run and the depth, then I left for another small extension I was about to start at Medina. But my old problem started again of spreading myself too thin, so I placed an ad in the paper for a labourer and ended up with Rex, a big lad of six feet and built like a real brick dunny. He was a real nice guy. I started him on the Medina site and soon saw his worth. I paid like good workers who could think things out without me having to hold their bloody hands.

The next morning I received a phone call via Lita that something was up with the drain at Kalamunda, so this gave me the chance to take Rex to look at his next job. On arriving, I could see that the digger opeator wasn't too happy, and it wasn't long before I understood why, as he lifted up a Tele-com cable that had been cut in two.

"Shit, this is big, big trouble," I said, and then looking further, I could see why. Looking at the digger operator, I said, "You must have used two sticks of jelly to fracture this ground!" and though he never said much, the thing was the trouble it was going to bring. Looking around, I noticed the sign for cable location and, knowing that it would have to run back to the road, went over to the boundary to find the other peg. When I did find it, it wasn't in line where the cable was; in fact, it was around thirty feet away, so I told the digger operator that I'd contact Telecom and mention that we just blew up their cable.

Some five minutes later, this chap arrived not too happy at first. Then another car arrived, then another. *Fuck, what have we here*. Then the questions flew. I told them that the pegs were incorrect and that we had checked first, but it didn't seem to matter. As far as they were concerned, we blew up the line and we had to pay for it.

"Piss off," I said. "You placed the markers, and we followed your rules," and with great pain and charm, I started to win them over that nothing had been done out of order. "Your markers are in the wrong position!" And with that, they gave instructions for a temporary line to be laid.

I wasn't too happy with the digger operator over that, as this was the first time I had used him. I just wanted him in and out that day, but with the previous events, I was now into my second day and the rain had just started making things worse.

Just as I was about to leave, this chap came flying around the corner from a restaurant on the same land with a meat cleaver in his hand, yelling at the lot of us for busting the phone line. He was going to sue the lot of us for the loss of trade. I looked over at him and said, "Piss off, you stupid bastard. Don't blame us for the way your business is going," but he kept on dancing around with this meat cleaver until the digger operator walked up to this tin box and pulled out a stick of jelly with a fuse attached. Upon lighting it, he threw it over at him, which sent him flying for cover and calling us a bunch of dick-heads as it landed near him. Well, this brought the whole lot of us into fits of laughter; in fact, my ribs were so sore from the events that took place I couldn't work.

I remained on-site but the chap with the meat cleaver never showed up again. I have often thought of this bloke and the surprise look in his eyes when that lit jelly came his way. There wasn't a detonater in the jelly and the silly bugger never hung around to find out if it was alive or not; he just bolted for cover and could be still there for all I know.

About this time, I decided to contact my old mate, Butch, as I couldn't get hold of a roof plumber for the toilet block. I rang him at Fremantle, where he lived with his mother, and she put Butch on the phone. After putting my request to him, he became somewhat stand-offish, and I asked him whether he wanted the job or not. He said that his mother felt that we had better not work together as we always ended up getting in the shit, and though I was desperate to have my job sorted out, I couldn't believe that he was being told by his mother to keep away from me as I was trouble. We said our goodbyes, but it left me feeling quite annoyed that Aunty Pat blamed me for Butch and his behaviour. I was left with doing the job myself, stewing over the thought of me being responsible for Butch's situation, whatever it was at that time.

Rex was now proving himself a top man on the job. When the time came to start the Medina extension brickwork, I arrived on-site the morning the bricklayer was about to start. But his problem was the sand wasn't dumped in the correct place, leaving little to no room to gain access onto the site. I decided to get it shifted, so rang the local bobcat driver. To my surprise, it was my old childhood mate, Max Broad, from Bullsbrook. Straight off, he said, "Darce, bloody hell. How the fuck ya going?"

I wasn't sure at first who I was talking to, but when the penny dropped, my hair stood up. "Swallow me bloody knob! That's you, Max," I said, and it wasn't long before we were into a full conversation about our past exploits. Eventually, arrangements were made for him to come down that morning to shift the sand for me.

When he arrived, we just stood there looking at each other, then I started by saying, "I wondered how you'd been getting along from time to time. Must be a good fourteen years since I last saw ya, mate, and apart from which ya haven't changed much."

"Well," Max said, "I was working with the old man on the farm, but we kept arguing a little and I wanted out, so I left, and

Jeff took over. Apart from that, I'm married now with two kids, and living just outside Rockingham for the past couple of years and loving it. But the last thing I heard about you was over the radio when you were in Vietnam, and sometimes our mums meet up and pass over a bit of information. But it's good to see ya after so long, Dave, but right now, let's get this sand shifted and I'll buy a couple of beers for lunch."

So while Max started on the sand heap, Rex and I removed brick rubble for the ease of working around the extension. Then we heard this loud thud! Looking over to where Max was working his bobcat, I saw a head of water about thirty feet high, and looking at Max, I could see that he wasn't too pleased with his situation as, apart from ripping out the water main to the house, he was being covered in water which by now had stalled his machine, leaving him completely saturated and somewhat annoyed, but more so over the serious trouble he'd be in for breaking the minister's water main.

The problem now was what to do!

The first thing I did was get the bobcat out and for Max to get it going. On doing this, I told him to leave things up to me and that I would see him at the pub later. Then I told Rex and the bricklayer to leave the site, so Rex left with Max and the bricklayer and also went down to the pub. After they left, I cleaned up around the sand heap and let the water do the rest as if it hadn't been disturbed. After checking that all was fine, I rang the local Water Board and told them that some silly bugger had dropped a load of sand on top of their meter and water was gushing out pretty fast and that I thought they better take a look at it. After that, I left the site for the pub where the others were waiting for me. Upon arriving, I told them what I had said regarding the broken meter.

"Shit, Dave," Max said, "do ya think they'll fix it without cost?"

"Yeah," I said. "You see, Max, I said I never ordered the sand. The client did that, and as far as I'm concerned, it was put in the wrong place anyway. With a bit of luck, we won't hear a thing about it." Though Max was rather grateful for fixing it for him, I still wasn't sure if I would end up with the bill.

As it was now too late to restart any job, we all stayed at the pub for the rest of the afternoon. It was great talking to Max about old times and the things we got up to. I well remember him asking me about Bindoon and the last six months there, as Max was also sent to Bindoon by his parents to learn about farming, and though I hadn't mentioned this earlier, it was that we never saw much of each other during those times. Yet he well understood the floggings and the hardship we'd had, but I never mentioned any of this to Max before this. I suppose it was because we became quite isolated in our thoughts and kept to ourselves most of the time.

Max asked me if I would like to meet his wife after leaving the pub, and I agreed. Later that afternoon, I met her, only to find out that she knew quite a lot about me – told to her by Max. I didn't mind this so much, but I wasn't sure just how much she knew. Bindoon Boys Town soon came into our conversation and though I didn't want to talk about any of it, I could feel the hair on the back of my neck starting to stand on end. My breath caught for a few seconds before I started to change the topic in the hope of fobbing the subject off. I asked her about her own family and how she enjoyed living at Rockingham, and the subject of Bindoon never came up again. I think she knew that I didn't want to talk about it.

After an hour or so, I left Max and his wife and headed home and told Max not to worry too much about the water meter and that I'd see him the next morning on-site.

*****

David in later years.

Editor's Note

This is the last of David's writing that was submitted, until his final entries where the search for his family became a reality. We felt that David had a story to tell regardless of the abruptness of the ending. His story shows that the trauma of his early years when in the care of Christian ogranisations never left him.

Part Nine

Finding Mum

3rd October 1987

I shall never forget that evening. I had arrived back from Sydney where I'd been for the Welcome Home Parade of Vietnam Veterans. Mum Darcey and I sat down and discussed the possibility of obtaining my file from the Catholic Migration Centre and perhaps making contact with my Welsh family.

I had often felt torn between my loyalties towards my adoptive family and the longing to find my natural mother, as this family had supported me through good times and bad and had showered me with a family love I had never known. How to put this longing to find *my* family to my adoptive parents was something I could never come to terms with.

My mind would constantly drift back to Wales and those early but clouded memories of someone waving me goodbye, which always gave me hope that I had some family there.

I was overjoyed when Mum brought up this offer of help. I can only conclude that her feelings must have been emotionally high as she too had recently had the opportunity of meeting her long-lost relatives. My brother Tommy explained to me that it was indeed an emotionally charged event that he was certainly proud to have been a part of it.

With this on my mind, my thoughts drifted back to Sydney, and the Welcome Home Parade, which was belated by some twenty years. I had stayed with a friend of the family, Nora. After knowing her for so many years, it was only now that she had poured out her emotions to me regarding her child, whom she had adopted out at birth.

It saddened me to think that when a young, single woman got pregnant, her parents would push her to be rid of the embarrassment, irrespective of the long term mental anguish of the mother who wanted to know and see the child.

We had discussed this subject for a good few hours, and it

was then that I decided to tell Mum of my longing to find my natural mother. Nora agreed and said not to delay the search for my family any longer.

I had, for many years during my married life, found it difficult to openly impart my inner thoughts and feelings of finding family, but especially could not speak of the abuse and cruelties of an orphan's life. I felt it better to leave these things unsaid as my wife had always looked upon me for strength and support. Following my conversation with Mum and her showing her eagerness in helping to trace family, I slowly began to also be open to Lita of my longing to find family.

Lita had been brought up in a sheltered environment and was subjected to rigid rules, but was never without the care and love of her family. I explained to her some of my inner emotions regarding her family's association with each other, and that I had never really had these deep feelings of family connections, which often made me feel the odd one out. This seemed the right time to investigate the whereabouts of my family.

I explained to Lita that Mum was really seeking my permission to make inquiries regarding the information held in my file, which Mum knew was being withheld at the Catholic Child Migration Centre (CCMC) in Perth. This lifted a big barrier for me, which I had felt confronted with for so many years. I was overjoyed at Mum wanting to take this course of action and naturally had no objection to her doing so.

Some five months after this discussion with Mum, I received a phone call at work.

"Son, this is Mum. I just thought I'd let you know that I have located your file, but they won't release it to me. You are the only person who can pick it up at the Catholic Child Migration Centre anytime tomorrow."

Armed with this information, I notified Lita and told her I was heading to Perth right then to collect it. I left my office like a bat out of hell, with no explanation to my superiors except throwing my arms up in the air and informing them that I would see them tomorrow as a matter of urgency had arisen.

Travelling to Perth seemed to take forever, with all the thoughts running through my mind about what secrets of my past would be exposed.

Arriving at the Catholic Child Migration Centre, I explained what I had come for, and without any barriers, I was given my file to read, but I was informed that I shouldn't get upset at information about myself as it was collective thoughts and opinions of me as a child.

I quickly browsed through some of the first pages but couldn't retain any information – my mind was too full of mixed emotions. The main thing I could think of was to get the file to Mum, so we could go through it together.

The Catholic Child Migration Centre informed me that other relevant information regarding me could be picked up from the Child Welfare Department in Perth, so I headed straight there.

Upon arriving, I was amazed at the compassion shown by the personnel of this department and their unwavering efforts to obtain 90% of the information in a matter of an hour. The Government of Western Australia had just passed an Act through Parliament stating that all information held at the Welfare Department regarding 'orphans' should be released.

I was not aware of this.

The passing of this Act also helped in obtaining further information from the Catholic Child Migration Centre. Not long before that, I had read in the press about a man who had broken into the CCMC to obtain his file. I believe this case brought to the Government's attention the desperation of the orphan migrants to know about their past.

Once this information was handed to me, my heart became

full. I started to flick through the file and noticed the first page was a letter dated 1956 from Mum requesting the Department to allow her to care for me over the weekends. It saddened me to think that it had taken some thirty-odd years to eventually see documents relating to my past whilst under the care of the Welfare Department.

Satisfied that I had sufficient information to begin searching for my family, I thanked all those concerned and, with an emotional goodbye, they wished me success, followed by the offer of more assistance and counselling if needed.

I travelled across to Mum and Dad's house, some six miles in the inner suburbs of Perth. I arrived unexpected but as always warmly welcomed. I didn't have to explain the purpose of my visit, as one look at my face said it all. I handed the file to Mum and told her the events of the day. Then Mum, Dad and I began to read the contents.

We sat around the table with open minds.

On the first page, we were confronted with a shipping document with my original name in heavy print: **Winston Franklyn Derek Lyne.** We looked at this with amusement, and I had to confess I was truly grateful for my name change! We had known my given name for some time, and it was often said that with a name like that, it would not be difficult to jolt memories back in Wales.

My mind started to drift back to those early days of my childhood and my recall of a woman sitting in a green field crying, and, although I was only seven years old at the time, that memory has never faded. I had put my arms around her and she had offered me a bar of teddy bear chocolate. I don't know the time-lapse between that and my next recollection of being waved goodbye through a train window. There were two people, one most definitely a woman, and the other a mist of confusion. Although I had no tears in my eyes, I could clearly see the woman was filled with sadness. I had no idea where this train journey was taking the other children and me, but being so young, there was certainly no fear in my mind.

I have for many years recalled these precious memories, especially when depressed or moody. I have never told anyone about them; I guess I felt keeping them to myself was the only escape out of my depressive moods. I certainly found them quite comforting in my childhood and early teenage years.

The reason for my being placed in an orphanage had never been known to me. My records showed that I was admitted on the 20th April, 1946, into Nazareth House, Swansea, Wales, aged eight months, the reason stated being: 'This child's mother was unable to look after him as she had to go out to work daily.'

I remained at Nazareth House until the 20th of August, 1952, aged seven years and one day.

27th October 1989

It's 6.00 am on a typically warm Australian October morning. I'd usually be up by now and organising my work for the day when suddenly the bedside phone burst into life, bringing my mind back to the reality of the outside world. With a sudden jerk and a bit of annoyance on my part, I reluctantly picked up the handpiece and answered the call with a sobering grunt.

A voice burst into my eardrums with a bright "G'day, Darce. Does the name Winston mean anything to you?"

I lay there silent for a moment, stuck for words. My mind became totally clouded and stagnant when again the voice over the phone jolted me back to reality.

It is seldom that I have ever been unable to compose myself to any early morning phone calls, but I knew this particular call was going to put to rest that nagging unanswered question that had affected the normal running of my day-to-day life, a life that began some forty-four long years ago in South Wales.

I burst out with a "Yes!! Winston was the name given to me by my natural mother."

The voice on the end of the phone identified himself as John Lewis, a Rotarian friend of mine. I felt this overwhelming wave of mixed emotions envelope my clear thinking. I could only think to ask John how he'd learnt this information. My wife placed her hand on my back as she sat up in bed, and said, "I bet it's about your mother in England."

I could only acknowledge her with an emotional nod as I tried to pull my mind into the reality of what was happening. Lita continued the conversation with John with great excitement as I was now delirious with excitement and making no sense in what

I was saying. But I had to satisfy myself by knowing how John had acquired this information.

Then came the biggest breakthrough in my life: John said briefly that, apparently, two women in South Wales had been trying to contact me via Mike Russell. I couldn't believe my ears. My blood pressure raced out of control, along with my emotions.

John explained to Lita that Mike was not at his home address in Cervantes, but that his house cleaner had taken the call from Wales knowing Mike was in Perth. She'd decided to contact John, hoping he would know Mike's whereabouts due to his close association with John. John was also aware of my early life and felt strongly that this call was regarding me. So, when the caller from South Wales asked to speak to Winston, John knew it was about me. Not wanting to miss out on gaining the contact, he passed on my office phone number for them to contact me that afternoon.

Three months earlier, during our Rotarian meeting, I was asked to give an introductory speech, during which John became aware of my personal status as an 'orphan'. After the meeting, he confronted me with an offering of help. Mike Russell, a friend of John's, was also an 'orphan' cared for in his childhood by the Christian Brothers at Castledare and Clontarf orphanages. Mike Russell was about my age and had recently had success in finding his long-lost Welsh family. It was with mixed feelings that arrangements were made for Mike and me to meet up. This would be the second time I had met one of the boys sent out to Australia as an 'orphan' since childhood.

Three weeks after John's offer of help, Mike and I were finally introduced. He had travelled the 186 kilometres from Cervantes to Perth to meet me. I did not recognise him in any way, but many associated memories of our childhood rushed back to me, even those I had forgotten or chose never to discuss

– especially the mental and physical abuse we had at times suffered at the different orphanages we were sent to.

Mike explained how, for many unsuccessful years, his plight to find his family was abruptly stopped and told me any information could only come from the Catholic Migration Centre in Perth. I had often wondered what could be gained by holding back this information. When Mike expanded on his thoughts, I became aware of the most shameful misuse of 'orphan' labour for the monetary gains of the Catholics.

I spent some time with Mike that night, and it saddened me to think that not only the two of us but also hundreds of other children were the victims of this kind of abuse. And even now, as men and women, we were still being penalised through no fault of our own. I did, however, feel very fortunate at being adopted into a most loving family who had given me the greatest support and the time to heal all my childhood sadness.

I suggested to Mike that perhaps the Daily News might take an interest in the story. I believed this could help those men and women who had or were still trying to get the Catholic barriers down, and also give them hope and to not give up their searches for family.

I am a strong believer that I was never an 'orphan' but more so an embarrassment to the British 'Welfare system' and placed under the care of the Catholic organisation to be sent far away to another country.

I handed my file to Mike and we progressed through each page, pausing on any titbit of information. Then Mike offered his assistance in tracing my family and explained that he might be able to ask his family in Wales to help with newspaper ads. With this, I felt confident of being successful.

What happened next ...

Written by Suzette Darcey

Mike Russell from Cervantes placed an ad in a South Wales paper that was noticed by David's stepsisters. They had found a birth certificate sometime earlier and had been trying to trace Winston, their lost stepbrother, from their end, not knowing his name had been changed by the Catholic institution.

This was a turning point that changed David's life.

Letters and phone calls followed, going to and fro, trying to establish roots. David eventually raised the funds to fly to the UK to meet his long-lost mother, Joyce, and, on 20th July, 1990, he flew to meet them all at Heathrow.

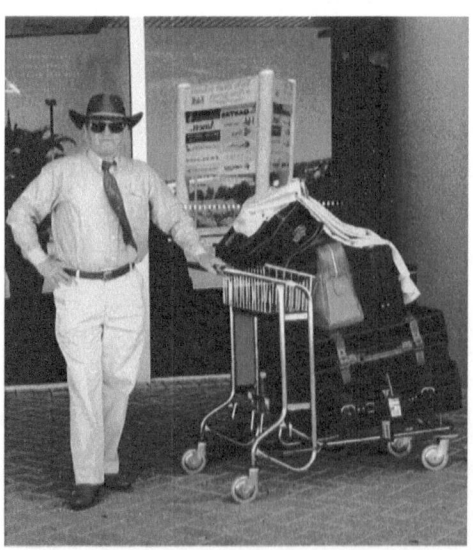

David at Perth Airport heading for Heathrow

David with his birth mother, Joyce

It was a very emotional time as all the family turned up to welcome David, making up for all the lost years.

David spent almost six weeks getting to know his stepbrother Phil and his two stepsisters and mum. The one sister, Carol, was so ecstatic to find him that she came back to Australia with him – her Mum paid for her ticket.

On David's return – he was only home about a week – things were not the best, so he and Carol moved out of the family home and rented a house for about six months. Then his birth mother in the UK had a kidney removed and was given only a few years to live. So David wound up his business and returned to Wales to be with her for her remaining years. He and his stepsister found a flat near his mother so he could visit each day. He worked at the markets with his brother and settled into a life in Wales.

David in Wales

I came across a letter David wrote when I was going through his things – he now has Alzheimers and is in a nursing home. The letter was about our first meeting. It is uncanny as we both seem so in tune with each other.

"I entered the hall with an uneasy feeling - yes, it was the night of 18th October, just what I'd expected - people dancing with self-confidence, embraced with bodies swaying to the Foxtrot - or was it the Quickstep? Just as I thought once again, my confidence to dance with such grace was holding me back, though I wanted this fear to pass. I felt that I had to calm down and settle my mind, so laughing I couldn't be seen I slipped into the shadows and held back while entertaining my thoughts to the music.

I'd, for a good 4 years, hadn't allowed myself the chance of a social life and when the chance became available, I became rather standoffish. This did worry me as I was now on my own. Though I showed plenty of confidence on the outside but knew the fear was well within as I hadn't been dancing for some 25 years. I remember well the good times but not the steps, so what was my fear? - the mixing - the dancing or the sheer blind nonsense of me not thinking it through clearly.

"You're a bit stupid, Bastard Darce." *It's more the embarrassing situation of not knowing how to dance yet you're a dip-stick; now calm down and enjoy it and do something for yourself.*

My old mate Bill had for some five weeks tried to take, in fact, drag me along, but I wouldn't go. I felt I wasn't able to meet the woman of my dreams: it was only a dance hall.

That evening I was at a loose end again when

Bill came over and told me to get ready and that I was going with him. I just felt I was ready for it, I remember under the shower I felt a magnetic pull to go with him. My sixth sense was also telling me to go and this special feeling of joy and mixed emotion was pushing me harder and harder. In the past, I knew something ahead was happening but just what could only come from going out and seeing.

"*Well, Darce, what do you think?*" *Bill said.*

I snapped myself out of my coma and quickly realised my feelings were crumbling around me. What was this strange happening? Then, just as I looked over Bill's shoulder, I could see her sitting down, and for some reason I couldn't explain, I knew that I had to dance with her. But too late ... someone else got in before me, yet I couldn't keep my eyes off her. Bill had left the table and found a dancing partner while I just sat there and watched her gliding with such grace and confidence, her hair, the way it hung, her hips in time with her feet. Good God, I just couldn't stop my eyes staying fixed on her and, for just a flickering moment, I thought her eyes were upon me. I started to blush and realised I was staring. But I just couldn't help it.

The dance finished, and still I held my breath; my pulse was high and racing. Was this true? Was this the night! Not my luck!! Such a beautiful, graceful woman. Is she alone? I asked myself.

"*Come on, Darce. You won't know unless you ask,*" *Bill blurted out.*

So trying to get the courage was my next move and, once again, I thought our eyes met but this time I saw a smile. Was this for me? I just had to meet her, and without giving another thought to what the dance was, I glided up to her table, explained I wasn't very good at dancing, however, if she was game would she like to dance with me!

I looked into her beautiful brown eyes and mentioned I felt like a bit of a dipstick as I hadn't danced for some time. I was now holding her in my arms but trembling inside. I felt really great and the longer we smiled and talked I had the feeling of Jericho collapsing around me. Gone. The barrier was gone. I found I could look at her and hold nothing back. Then the music stopped and I held her hand back to her seat, I found I was a magnet, unable to separate, yet needing to release her. Then the dancing started again and this time we became embroiled with laughing, and neither of us could concentrate on the footwork."

I'm sure there was more he wrote, but that was all I found. My recollection is so similar,

It was 18th October,1994, when I was at a dance at the Newport Athletic Club with my girlfriends when I first met David.

I saw this guy in the corner of the room; his eyes were like sparkling diamonds – they were dancing at me, his glare so intense. Later, he came towards me so I got up and walked to the edge of the dance floor. He said, "I would love to dance with you, but I don't know how to do it!" and with a big breath, he added, "I just want to put my arms around you and give you a cuddle."

Well, I was bowled over. Never had I heard a line like that before. We danced and danced. He was so different from anyone I'd met before. We talked and talked, he was so interesting.

On driving my girlfriend's home that night, one of them said from the back of the car, "You seemed to be getting along very well ... who was he?"

I relayed that his name was David Darcey. They laughed.

I relayed that I had a date with him the following evening after my granddaughter's seventh birthday party.

My mind was in overdrive as what had just happened meeting him. The thought came into my mind that he was different from anyone I had ever met and this guy was going to change my life!

And the rest of David's story is in my book.

About the Author

David Darcey, born Winston Franklyn Derek Lyne in Wales in 1945, was placed in an orphanage at eight months old, then shipped out to Australia at the age of seven to commence his life in Castledare, Clontarf and Bindoon Boys Town. Eventually adopted into a loving family, he constantly struggled with the lack of education provided to him by the Christian Brothers, yet went on to become a hardworking businessman and a family man before starting the search for his biological mother. David's initial cruel upbringing in the Christian Brothers orphanages gave this truly rough diamond the will to survive and succeed when all the odds were against him.

www.ingramcontent.com/pod-product-compliance
Lightning Source LLC
Chambersburg PA
CBHW021137080526
44588CB00008B/92